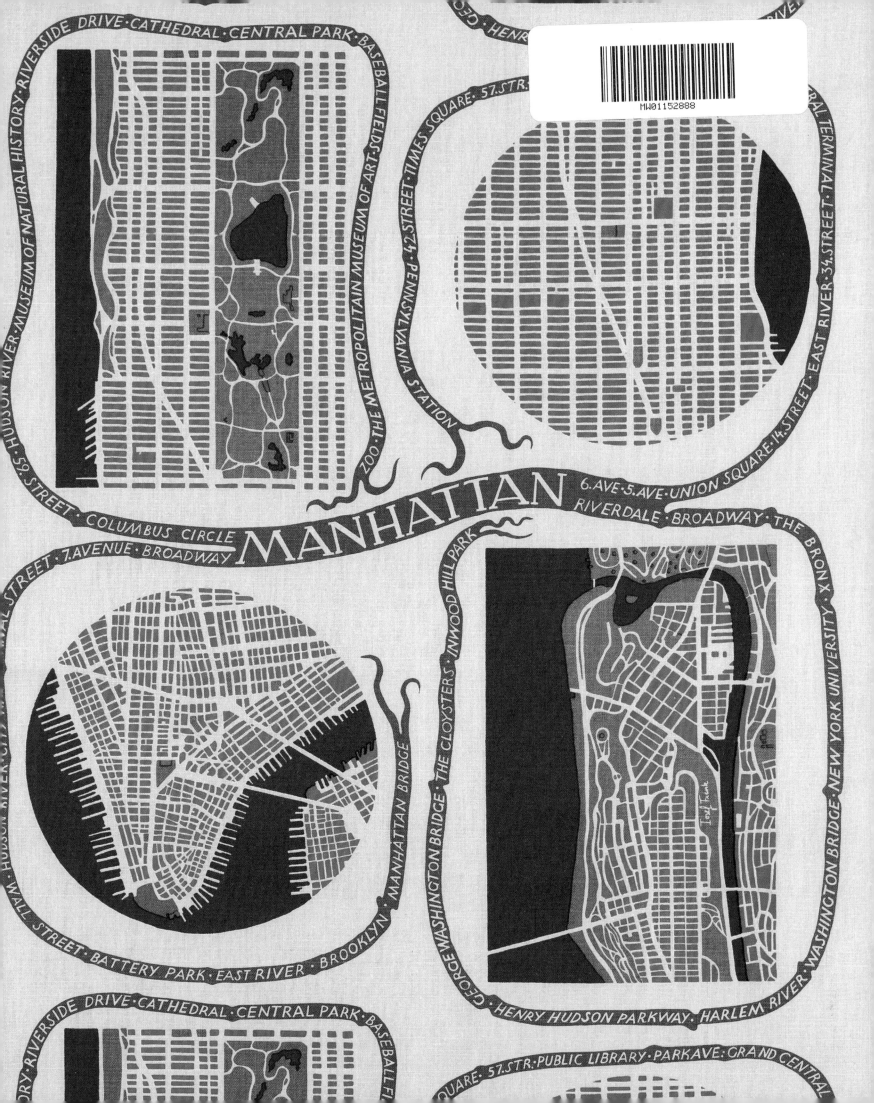

MANHATTAN

DENMARK   FINLAND   ICELAND   NORWAY   SWEDEN

BOBBYE TIGERMAN
AND MONICA OBNISKI

With contributions by
GLENN ADAMSON
ARNDÍS S. ÁRNADÓTTIR
CHARLOTTE ASHBY
GRAHAM C. BOETTCHER
DANIELLE CHARLAP
LESLIE S. EDWARDS
KJETIL FALLAN
DIANA JOCELYN GREENWOLD
DENISE HAGSTRÖMER
HELENA KÅBERG
ALEXANDRA LANGE
CARA MCCARTY
MONICA PENICK
HANNAH PIVO
ROSANNE SOMERSON
ERICA WARREN

SCANDINAVIAN DESIGN

AND

THE UNITED STATES

1890–1980

Los Angeles County Museum of Art
Milwaukee Art Museum

DelMonico Books • Prestel
Munich • London • New York

DIRECTORS' FOREWORD

Scandinavian Design and the United States, 1890–1980 offers an alternative narrative to the canonical history of modern American design, which has largely been understood as a story about Central European immigrants who became towering figures in our country's design legacy. This exhibition presents a new international dimension to this history by considering the many Scandinavian designers who immigrated to the United States, the Americans who studied or worked in the Nordic countries, the campaigns to market Scandinavian design to American consumers, and the key figures who championed sustainable and accessible design practice.

At the Los Angeles County Museum of Art (LACMA), this exhibition follows in a series of meticulously researched shows about the intricate networks of modern design, beginning with *California Design, 1930–1965: "Living in a Modern Way"* (co-curated by Bobbye Tigerman) and followed by *Found in Translation: Design in California and Mexico, 1915–1985.* At the Milwaukee Art Museum (MAM), this project aligns with the museum's core objectives to advance new scholarship, engage with contemporary issues, and connect to our communities, in particular those of Scandinavian heritage throughout the upper Midwest.

We commend Bobbye Tigerman, Marilyn B. and Calvin B. Gross Curator of Decorative Arts and Design at LACMA, and Monica Obniski, Demmer Curator of 20th- and 21st-Century Design at MAM, for their dedication in bringing together an extraordinary group of objects to tell this seemingly familiar yet largely unexamined story. We are also deeply grateful to the Terra Foundation for American Art for recognizing the importance of this scholarship and supporting this groundbreaking exhibition. Many individuals have supported this exhibition since its inception in 2014, and MAM would like to extend its sincere thanks to Melinda Scott Krei and Ken Krei and their son Andrew and his wife, Margaret, for their commitment to education. It is a great privilege to honor the memory of Melinda with this exhibition.

We are honored to partner with the Nationalmuseum, Sweden's museum of art and design, and the Nasjonalmuseet in Norway, and pleased that they are participating in the exhibition tour. Finally, to the institutions and individuals who have generously lent their works to this exhibition, we extend our sincere thanks.

MICHAEL GOVAN
CEO and Wallis Annenberg Director
Los Angeles County Museum of Art

MARCELLE POLEDNIK
Donna and Donald Baumgartner Director
Milwaukee Art Museum

INTRODUCTION

BOBBYE TIGERMAN AND MONICA OBNISKI

In the early 1950s, *House Beautiful* editor Elizabeth Gordon spotted the *Röd Krokus* (Red Crocus) hanging by Swedish designer Ann-Mari Forsberg in the newly published book *Contemporary Swedish Design* (p. 12). She found contact information for its producer, the Märta Måås-Fjetterström studio, at the back of the book and ordered one for herself. Gordon used the hanging several times in her professional capacity, illustrating it in articles in her wide-circulation magazine and including it in exhibitions that she organized. In 1964 she donated *Red Crocus*, along with her extensive textile collection, to the Cooper Union Museum (now the Cooper Hewitt, Smithsonian Design Museum). The catalogue documenting Gordon's gift, *The Wonders of Thread*, featured *Red Crocus* on the cover, extending its reach yet further.[1]

This anecdote about the public life of a single wall hanging demonstrates one way that Scandinavian design proliferated in the United States and underscores the important role of publications in those efforts. The lavish *Contemporary Swedish Design* book, published in Stockholm in 1951 and distributed by New York publishers, was intended "to give readers abroad and in Sweden a cross-section of contemporary Swedish design as it is expressed in things for the home."[2] If Gordon exemplifies its intended audience, the book was wildly successful in bringing Swedish design to broader American consciousness, and Gordon's use of *Red Crocus* in print and exhibition contributed to the American fascination with Scandinavian design.

Scandinavian Design and the United States demonstrates how Nordic approaches to modern design and Nordic objects themselves made an indelible impact on American design culture and material life from the late nineteenth century through the early 1980s. It also considers the United States' influence on Scandinavian design. The catalogue traces how Scandinavian design became an integral part of what we now think of as "American design" by examining immigrant Scandinavian designers who settled in the United States, Americans who studied or taught in the Nordic countries, the use of design as a diplomatic tool, the ambitious campaigns to market and export Scandinavian design, and the emergence of sustainable and accessible design movements. While Scandinavian design has traditionally been associated with comfort, organic form, and the use of natural materials, recent scholarship has sought to debunk these tropes as stereotypes. Scandinavian design's promotional engines, however, successfully transmitted these principles to the United States, where they were embraced by a broad public.

"Scandinavia" customarily refers to a region in Northern Europe encompassing Denmark, Norway, and Sweden that shares cultural and linguistic ties, while the "Scandinavian Peninsula" refers to Norway and Sweden only. For the purposes of this catalogue, "Scandinavia" also includes Finland, in order to reflect how that country often promoted its design alongside the Scandinavian nations, which led to Finland becoming linked with Scandinavia in the American imagination. It also includes Iceland, as that country remained a Danish dependency until 1944, and its small design industry enjoyed moments of American exchange. Alternatively, this entire geographic region is referred to as "the Nordic countries." This tendency to conflate the Nordic countries has historical roots. Design historians Kjetil Fallan and Christina Zetterlund have noted that Nordic culture has often been considered homogenous, identifying the region's nineteenth-century open-air museums (and their attendant vernacular objects rooted in a folk past) as a foundation for the collective "modern Nordic identity."[3] This strategy of emphasizing heritage was reinforced at the turn of the twentieth century in Norwegian and Swedish world's fair presentations in the United States, and in later museum exhibitions and promotional efforts (p. 15).

While we use the phrase "Scandinavian design" to capitalize on the term's continuing currency, we acknowledge its shortcomings and limitations.[4] "Scandinavian design" is a cultural construct that relies upon several myths propagated by numerous actors: the organizations that promoted design in each country and were responsible for generating messaging, coordinating marketing, and organizing overseas exhibitions; the Scandinavian companies that produced goods; the American retailers who sold them; journalists and curators who introduced this work to the public; and not least the designers and makers who participated in selling the narrative. As a term that emerged following World War II, "Scandinavian design" represents only a portion of what was conceived and made in Scandinavia—it excludes objects that did not conform to the stereotypes of organicism and naturalism and those made before or after the postwar period. This concept even extended to people who were not considered Scandinavian, such as the indigenous Sámi of the northern regions of Norway, Sweden, and Finland, who have only recently seen their cultural production considered part of the broader category. These cultural constructions functioned as exclusionary mechanisms that conveyed a narrow understanding of Scandinavian design to American audiences.[5] This project offers a wider narrative, incorporating industrial design and folk art along with the traditional craft media and covering the era from the late nineteenth century to 1980, resulting in a broader conception of "Scandinavian design."

Swedish Section, Women's Pavilion,
Centennial International Exposition,
Philadelphia, Pennsylvania, 1876

The *Viking*, a replica of a ninth-century
Norwegian ship, en route to the
World's Columbian Exposition, Chicago,
Illinois, 1893

Before "Scandinavian design" became consolidated as a category in the mid-twentieth century, Nordic and Nordic-inspired luxury goods had appealed to Americans seeking refined products, such as Georg Jensen silver (p. 68) or Gustavsberg ceramics (p. 16). Additionally, immigrants and their descendants expressed nostalgia for their home country through objects and experiences. For instance, when greeting the replica of a ninth-century Viking ship that sailed from Norway to Chicago for the 1893 World's Columbian Exposition (p. 15), the *Chicago Tribune* noted that "Swedes, Norwegians, and Danes of Chicago, loyal to the heart's core to the United States, are also overflowing with affection for their old homes and for everything which recalls the memory of them."[6] Scandinavians were considered model immigrants, balancing their loyalty to their new nation with connections to their home countries. As Charles C. Moore, president of San Francisco's 1915 Panama-Pacific International Exposition, explained at the Danish Brotherhood Day celebration in front of the Danish Pavilion, "This little piece of Denmark you have created here on the shores of the Pacific… is indeed a beautiful testimonial of your loyalty to your mother country. At the same time it proves that the Danes in this country are good American citizens, inasmuch as the Denmark building forms a part of an American undertaking, the Panama Pacific International Exposition. The idea of erecting this beautiful Danish pavilion was first advanced by members of the Danish Brotherhood."[7]

Scandinavian design soon began to appeal to a broader segment of the American population. In 1932, interior design journalist Walter Rendell Storey remarked: "The growing popularity of Scandinavian decorative art, as attested by the frequent exhibitions held last season, such as those at the Home Making Centre and at the Roerich Museum, will doubtless be increased as the public becomes more familiar with the remarkable collection at the Brooklyn Museum. There important additions have recently been made to the three galleries which are devoted to the craftwork of Sweden, Norway, and Denmark, so that they now house what is considered the finest and most extensive collection of Scandinavian decorative art in the country."[8] Just over a decade later, in 1945, *New York Times* home editor Mary Roche noted Swedish design's appeal to Americans, expressing that "in furniture or fabrics, glass or pottery, Swedish design seems peculiarly adaptable to American modes and mores and many a contemporary American designer is frank to acknowledge its influence."[9] *House Beautiful* proclaimed in 1959 that "Scandinavian design influences are now so intermingled with American that it takes a bit of perceptive experience to distinguish the pure from the mixed. Some furniture, for instance, is imported

in toto; some is partially made abroad and assembled in American factories; some is made here from designs created in Scandinavia. And there are copies which plagiarize the superficial form of Scandinavian design without reference to its organic nature or the craftsmanship it demands."[10]

By 1962 Scandinavian design had become so ubiquitous that the *New York Times* wrote that "Danish modern… is the one furniture style that everyone understands."[11] Even places not typically associated with Nordic settlement were touched by the long reach of Scandinavian design. For example, American architect and designer Charles Eames recalled that Alvar Aalto and Swedish modernism were well known in St. Louis in the mid-1930s, and residents of Dallas could buy the work of Scandinavian designers Bjørn Wiinblad, Tapio Wirkkala, and Erik Höglund at the luxury retailer Neiman-Marcus.[12] When First Lady Jacqueline Kennedy wore a Marimekko dress on the cover of *Sports Illustrated* in 1960, it was a high-profile endorsement of the nonconformist Finnish clothing brand (p. 18).

Why did Scandinavian design resonate so deeply with American audiences? The pervasive and persuasive rhetoric of savvy salespeople spoke to an American longing for what Scandinavian goods offered—both literally and metaphorically. But Scandinavian design's intensifying popularity in the United States over the twentieth century resulted from the convergence of several historical, political, and commercial factors. The popular understanding of Scandinavian design was premised on the mythic unity of the Scandinavian countries and their perception as peaceful and prosperous nations. The ideology of "Pan-Scandinavianism" has roots in the late eighteenth century during the birth of national movements, as Mirjam Gelfer-Jørgensen has traced.[13] It was propagated in the United States in such popular books as Marquis Childs' 1936 bestselling analysis of Sweden's cooperative movement, *Sweden: The Middle Way*, which portrayed the Nordic nations as having "an ancient integration, a fundamental coherence," and "remarkable homogeneity."[14] Even the Museum of Modern Art (MoMA) defined Scandinavia collectively when it issued a 1959 press release detailing the museum's activities in the region as part of its program in worldwide cultural exchange.[15] The unity myth was so ingrained that by the mid-twentieth century, some figures chafed against the assumption of regional conformity: Arthur Hald, the editor of the Swedish design magazine *Form*, insisted in 1954 that "in many respects Scandinavia is a unit, but there are large internal differences. Generally, a Dane, a Finn, a Norwegian, or a Swede does not feel that he is considered a Scandinavian until he travels beyond the borders of this region."[16] Moreover, the five Nordic nations have a centuries-long history of territorial disputes, occupations, and campaigns for independence.

And contrary to the myth of prosperity, large segments of their populations lived in poverty in the nineteenth and early twentieth centuries, triggering substantial migrations to the United States. Nevertheless, the efforts to promote unity persist, with models of Nordic collaboration proliferating in several sectors today.[17]

Advertising for Scandinavian objects emphasized quality craftsmanship, often suggesting that goods were carefully made by an individual craftsperson, when, in fact, most were produced by a division of labor in small factories. A journalist writing about "Viking" silversmith Peer Smed in 1936 noted that "the Scandinavian countries, famed for clean streets… and tremendous progress in the social scheme… are at the same time leaders of the world in the ancient crafts, where handwork triumphs over the machine."[18] Scandinavian design was often advertised as "distinguished" and "handcrafted" (p. 70); one poster promoting Danish furniture suggested that a single skilled craftsman cut down the oak tree and fashioned the wood into an elegant chair (p. 21). For Americans, Scandinavian objects offered an appealing alternative to increasingly ubiquitous mass-produced goods, conferring on their owners a sense of refinement and distinction.

This narrative was bolstered by official propaganda that linked the United States and the Nordic nations politically. Scandinavian organizations noted the similarities between their countries and the United States as part of a strategy to align themselves with the democratic, capitalist power during decades of global instability. On the eve of World War II, Folke Bernadotte, the commissioner general of the Swedish Pavilion at the 1939 New York World's Fair, remarked that "Sweden, like the United States, believes in democracy and the freedom of the individual, freedom of enterprise, and also in the equality of opportunity for all."[19] In the midst of the Cold War, Gotthard Johansson, the president of Svenska Slöjdföreningen (Swedish Arts and Crafts Society), expressed the same sentiments, writing in 1954 that "the four [Nordic] countries concerned belong to the sphere of Western culture. The design of the day is created for the people of to-day, people who live under conditions which are essentially much the same as those of the average American."[20] Others in the design world echoed these views, such as when Georg Jensen, Inc. president Just Lunning claimed that "the acceptance of Scandinavian design in the United States is based on a deep similarity in the way of life of the people, in respect for the individual and in the need to supplement mass products with individualized work."[21] Ultimately, these figures contended that Scandinavians and Americans shared not only material tastes, but also fundamental values of freedom, democracy, and individuality. An American buying Scandinavian design objects affirmed these similarities while engaging in an act of consumption that supported all of the actors.[22]

IB ANTONI
Vang Rasmussen
Denmark: Famous for Fine Furniture
poster, designed 1964. CAT. 5

Design ideas traveled both ways, and while this project does not examine the American impact on Nordic design as extensively, it does acknowledge the many ways that American technology and taste shaped Scandinavian material production. For example, at the turn of the twentieth century, at the encouragement of an American importer, the Finnish ceramic firm Arabia produced a line of tableware expressly designed for the American market, of which the *Fennia* vase is one example (p. 23).[23] Furthermore, countless figures, including Swedish designers Olle Eksell (below) and Edward Hald, Finnish designer Kaj Franck, Norwegian designers Arne and Grete Prytz Korsmo, IKEA founder Ingvar Kamprad, and BabyBjörn founder Björn Jakobson all traveled to the United States during the postwar period to learn about American design industry and management practices. After spending six months in the U.S., Swedish designer Bruno Mathsson returned home to report that Swedish production lagged behind that of the U.S. because Americans could experiment; he also cautioned about Swedish export to the U.S., noting that "we must realize that they want typically Swedish goods, and that we shall do well if we give our products a certain good form and quality which they can rely on."[24] Acknowledging the importance of the American export market, Sweden's leading design magazine, *Form*, devoted an entire issue to American taste, and several articles in various other issues to American design.[25] Exhibitions of American design in the Nordic countries also broadcast the latest developments, particularly *American Design for Home and Decorative Use*, which traveled to several Nordic

OLLE EKSELL
Ögon Cacao **packaging**, designed
1956–57. Large box: 4 ⅞ × 2 ½ × 1 ⅜ in.
(12.4 × 6.2 × 3.4 cm). Nationalmuseum,
NMK 222/1999

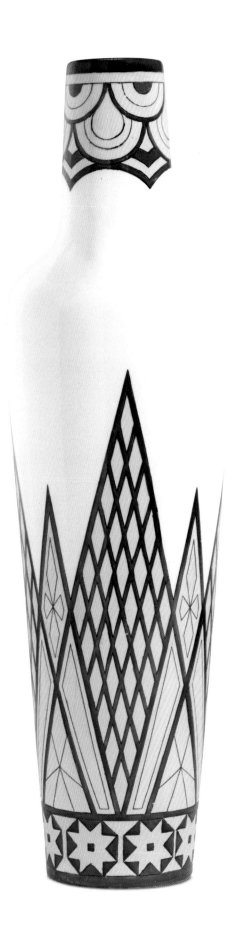

museums between 1953 and 1955 under the auspices of the United States Information Agency and the Museum of Modern Art (below).[26] At the opening in Oslo, a journalist noted that "names like Charles Eames, Eero Saarinen and many others have been known almost as well here as in the U.S.A. The new aspect is to be able to see the things themselves, study their appearance, trace their development and attempt to penetrate the thoughts and ideas which lie behind each individual object."[27]

In 1980, a number of Norwegian designers and students led by Terje Meyer, president of ID-gruppen (Norwegian Group of Industrial Designers), proclaimed the end of Scandinavian design's dominance when they carried a coffin marked "Scandinavian Design" through Oslo and sank it in the Oslo Fjord to declare the concept's lack of relevance to contemporary design.[28] Scandinavian design

in the United States as a market category had already begun to weaken in the 1970s as countries such as Italy and Japan assumed greater international prominence. More fundamentally, though, the design field faced a reckoning, with a new generation of practitioners asking how their work could better address the world's most pressing problems rather than meet the material needs of the most affluent, an issue with which today's designers continue to grapple. This exhibition shows how even during the turbulent decade of the 1970s, when many orthodoxies of the design field were being questioned, Scandinavian and American designers continued to collaborate and exchange ideas on such topics of mutual interest as design for sustainability and accessibility. Sometimes these designers worked together and at other times independently in pursuit of shared aims. While such collaborations continue to the present, this exhibition concludes in 1980. The dynamics of contemporary globalization, which proliferated after this date, mean that dual-region comparisons oversimplify an increasingly complex phenomenon. While earlier methodological models that relied on nationalism as a framework were useful for understanding culture and identity, by the end of the 1970s, national identity within the context of design culture was starting to be viewed as a constructed, imagined category.[29]

A major theme of *Scandinavian Design and the United States* is the valuable contributions made by immigrant artists, designers, and craftspeople to their adopted societies and the myriad ways they have shaped American design and visual culture. Immigrants have also been key players in promoting Scandinavian design not only as creators and consumers, but also as importers, marketers, and shop owners, making these goods accessible to a broad American populace. At this moment, when both the United States and the Nordic countries are engaged in fierce immigration debates, this exhibition argues for the importance of welcoming immigrants and nurturing their talents.[30] Although he was writing exclusively about European immigration, President John F. Kennedy's sentiments still resonate: "each wave of immigration has left its own imprint on American society" and "each made its distinctive 'contribution' to the building of the nation and the evolution of American life."[31] Admittedly, narratives of Scandinavian immigration do not represent the experiences of all immigrants, as the predominantly white, Protestant arrivals from the Nordic countries did not encounter the same discrimination, prejudice, and even violence that immigrants, refugees, and enslaved peoples from other parts of the world have faced when entering the United States.[32]

The fundamental inquiry of *Scandinavian Design and the United States* is the underexamined question of why there was an extensive exchange between the American and Scandinavian design communities in the modern era, and how this exchange shaped the trajectory of American design. While this exhibition is the first to examine this topic, it relies on scholarship that has examined the influence of Scandinavian design on other European countries and British Commonwealth nations.[33] It also builds upon recent scholarship that reframes the history of Scandinavian design by revealing ingrained stereotypes.[34] Furthermore, the exhibition presents an alternative to the canonical history of modern American design, which has largely been a story of Central Europeans immigrating to the United States in the 1930s (figures such as Walter Gropius, Marcel Breuer, Ludwig Mies van der Rohe, and Josef Albers) to become leaders at architecture and design schools across the country, thereby shaping the course of design in the United States. This history has obfuscated, for example, the critical role played by Cranbrook Academy of Art—specifically through Finnish architect Eliel Saarinen and a dynamic group of Scandinavian instructors—in shaping what is arguably the most important generation of American designers, which included Charles and Ray Eames, Eero Saarinen, and Florence Knoll. This project seeks to correct the prevailing narrative, which neglects the long, extensive influence of Scandinavian design in the United States.

Like the exhibition it accompanies, the book is divided into six sections, each representing one dimension of Scandinavian-American design exchange. **Migration and Heritage** demonstrates the artistic contributions of Scandinavian immigrants to their American communities, highlighting the positive impact that immigrants made to their adopted homes while preserving their culture and ethnicity. **Selling the Scandinavian Dream** illustrates how Scandinavian and Scandinavian-inspired goods perpetuated myths about the Nordic region in order to satisfy the desires and expectations of American consumers. **Design for Diplomacy** examines how nations have used design to advance their political goals through both traditional diplomatic tactics and the "soft power" of cultural propaganda. **Teachers and Students** traces how lineages of instructors and pupils at several institutions compounded the influence of Scandinavian artists and designers living in the United States. **Travel Abroad** considers how designers exchanged knowledge and ideas with their international counterparts through academic programs, apprenticeships, and travel fellowships. **Design for Social Change** explores how consumer and environmental critiques emerging in the 1960s and 1970s shifted the international design discourse from the production of "better things for everyday life" (a translation of Swedish design theorist Gregor Paulsson's phrase *vackrare vardagsvara*) to critical discussions about sustainable design, ergonomic design, and social applications of design.[35] These issues are some among several—alongside immigration, cultural mythmaking, and critical analysis of advertising and marketing—that are as relevant today as in the period covered by the exhibition, demonstrating design's continuing role in engaging with contemporary issues.

1 *Red Crocus* was originally published in Arthur Hald and Sven Erik Skawonius, *Contemporary Swedish Design: A Survey in Pictures* (Stockholm: Nordisk Rotogravyr, 1951), 146; see also *The Wonders of Thread: A Gift of Textiles from the Collection of Elizabeth Gordon*, exh. cat. (New York: Cooper Union Museum, 1964). Our thanks to Susan Brown, curator, Cooper Hewitt, Smithsonian Design Museum, for sharing this story with us.

2 Hald and Skawonius, *Contemporary Swedish Design*, 5.

3 Kjetil Fallan and Christina Zetterlund, "Altering a Homogenized Heritage: Articulating Heterogeneous Material Cultures in Norway and Sweden," in *Designing Worlds: National Design Histories in an Age of Globalization*, ed. Kjetil Fallan and Grace Lees-Maffei (New York and Oxford: Berghahn Books, 2016), 173–74.

4 In Nordic design history, "Scandinavian Design" (with a capital *D*) refers to a specific stylistic category prominent from roughly 1950 to 1970 when the overseas promotion of this material was at its height. The term has not typically been used in English-language design history to designate a style category, though "Scandinavian design" (with a lowercase *d*) generally refers to the subset of post–World War II objects from these countries that fit the stereotypes of organic modernism. For more on this distinction, see Kjetil Fallan, "Introduction," in *Scandinavian Design: Alternate Histories*, ed. Kjetil Fallan (London and New York: Berg, 2012), 2–3.

5 For a case study on inclusion and exclusion in the design canon, see Mark Ian Jones, *Vicke Lindstrand on the Periphery: Mid-Twentieth Century Swedish Design and the Reception of Vicke Lindstrand* (Uppsala, Sweden: Uppsala Universitet, 2016). Also see Fallan and Zetterlund, "Altering a Homogenized Heritage."

6 "A Welcome to the Norseman," *Chicago Tribune*, July 13, 1893.

7 "Ancient Lurs Blown by Danes," *San Francisco Chronicle*, June 8, 1915.

8 Walter Rendell Storey, "Utility and Art Combined in the Home," *New York Times*, September 4, 1932.

9 Mary Roche, "Designs from Sweden," *New York Times*, July 8, 1945.

10 "Designed and Made in the U.S.A.," *House Beautiful* 101, no. 7 (July 1959): 89.

11 Rita Reif, "Cooper Union Offers Danish Exhibition," *New York Times*, October 19, 1962.

12 "St. Louis Oral History Project: Interview with Charles Eames," in *An Eames Anthology*, ed. Daniel Ostroff (New Haven and London: Yale University Press, 2015), 373–74. Stanley Marcus initiated buying trips to Scandinavia for Neiman-Marcus in 1956; see Stanley Marcus, "How We Made the Christmas Catalogue a Success," *D Magazine*, July 1979, https://www.dmagazine.com/publications/d-magazine/1979/july/how-we-made-the-christmas-catalogue-a-success/.

13 Mirjam Gelfer-Jørgensen, "Scandinavianism—a Cultural Brand," in *Scandinavian Design beyond the Myth: Fifty Years of Design from the Nordic Countries*, exh. cat., ed. Widar Halén and Kerstin Wickman (Stockholm: Arvinius, 2003), 16–25. This myth of unity persisted, for example, in the exhibition *Design in Scandinavia*, which toured the United States and Canada in 1954–57; see Jørn Guldberg, "'Scandinavian Design' as Discourse: The Exhibition *Design in Scandinavia*, 1954–57," *Design Issues* 27, no. 2 (Spring 2011): 41–58.

14 Marquis W. Childs, *Sweden: The Middle Way* (New Haven: Yale University Press, 1936), xi–xii.

15 "The Museum of Modern Art and Scandinavia," Museum of Modern Art press release, November 18, 1959, https://www.moma.org/shared/pdfs/docs/press_archives/2568/releases/MOMA_1959_0134_104K.pdf. The press release mentions the 1938 Alvar Aalto exhibition and the 1950 Edvard Munch exhibition shown at MoMA, and several exhibitions of American art, design, and architecture sent to the Nordic countries.

16 Arthur Hald, "A Fresh Breeze from the Northeast," *House Beautiful* 96, no. 2 (February 1954): 154.

17 For example, the Nordic Council, founded in 1952 to promote cooperation among the various Nordic governments, still advocates for cooperation through policy and initiatives across many fields.

18 Alice Cogan, "Craftman: Model 1936, Peer Smed Pursues a Medieval Craft against a Medieval Background in the Heart of Brooklyn," *Brooklyn Daily Eagle*, November 29, 1936.

19 Folke Bernadotte, "Greetings," in Naboth Hedin, *Sweden at the New York World's Fair* (New York?: Royal Swedish Commission, New York World's Fair, 1939), 3, https://digital.wolfsonian.org/WOLF071805/00001/pageturner#page/3.

20 Arne Remlov, ed., *Design in Scandinavia: An Exhibition of Objects for the Home from Denmark, Finland, Norway, Sweden*, exh. cat. (Oslo: Kirstes Boktrykkeri, 1954), 12. Iceland did not participate in the exhibition.

21 Olga Gueft and Just Lunning, "Young Americans/Young Scandinavians," *Craft Horizons* 17, no. 1 (February 1957): 30–31; quoted in Claire Selkurt, "Scandinavian Modern Design in Postwar America," *Form Function Finland* 2 (1990): 42–43.

22 The connection between democracy and consumption has been explored by Lizabeth Cohen, *A Consumers' Republic: The Politics of Mass Consumption in Postwar America* (New York: Knopf, 2003).

23 Marianne Aav, *Arabia: Ceramics, Art, Industry* (Helsinki: Designmuseo, 2009), 53. It is not recorded which aspects of the *Fennia* vase line particularly appealed to American buyers.

24 English summary of Dag Widman, "A Fresh Beginning: An Interview with Bruno Mathsson," *Form* 46, no. 1 (1950): n.p.

25 *Form* 45, nos. 4 and 5 (1949).

26 Widar Halén, "The Flow of Ideas USA–Scandinavia," in Halén and Wickman, *Scandinavian Design beyond the Myth*, 46–55.

27 Quoted in *Verdens Gang* (Oslo), Press Analysis, American Design for Home and Decorative Use, May 1, 1956, International Council and International Program Records, I.B.28, The Museum of Modern Art Archives, New York.

28 Kjetil Fallan, "How an Excavator Got Aesthetic Pretensions— Negotiating Design in 1960s' Norway," *Journal of Design History* 20 (Spring 2007): 53–54.

29 Of course, the seeds of globalism have been arguably present for centuries; see Grace Lees-Maffei and Kjetil Fallan, "Introduction," in *Designing Worlds*, 2.

30 Today in the Nordic countries, and in the United States as well, right-wing political groups have co-opted Viking rhetoric and visual motifs to promote a racially divisive nationalism. See Dorothy Kim, "White Supremacists Have Weaponized an Imaginary Viking Past. It's Time to Reclaim the Real History," *Time*, April 12, 2019.

31 John F. Kennedy, *A Nation of Immigrants* (New York: Harper and Row, 1964; rev. ed., New York: Harper Perennial, 2008), 32. The concept of America as "a nation of immigrants" has come to be recognized as part of a discursive framework that obscures the conquest of Native Americans as central to the history of settler colonialism in the United States. These debates about immigration, citizenship, and national identity are taken up by Bonnie Honig, *Democracy and the Foreigner* (Princeton, NJ: Princeton University Press, 2003).

32 Though Swedes and Norwegians did experience some anti-immigrant discrimination, especially during World War I, when all immigrant communities (particularly those with cultural ties to Germany) were subject to increased suspicion, Nordic immigrants were largely welcomed by the Anglo-American majority. See Daron W. Olson, *Vikings across the Atlantic: Emigration and the Building of a Greater Norway, 1860–1945* (Minneapolis: University of Minnesota Press, 2013), 115–21; and Jørn Brøndal, "'The Fairest among the So-Called White Races': Portrayals of Scandinavian Americans in the Filiopietistic and Nativist Literature of the Late Nineteenth and Early Twentieth Centuries," *Journal of American Ethnic History* 33, no. 3 (Spring 2014): 5–36.

33 Rachel Gotlieb and Michael Prokopow, *True Nordic: How Scandinavia Influenced Design in Canada*, exh. cat. (London: Black Dog Publishing, 2016); Simon Jackson, "Blonde Wood among the Gum Trees: Scandinavian Influences in Furniture Design in Australia, 1930–1975," *Scandinavian Journal of Design History* 13 (2003): 36–51; Paul Caffrey, "The Scandinavian Ideal: A Model for Design in Ireland," *Scandinavian Journal of Design History* 8 (1998): 32–43; Kevin Davies, "Norwegian Wood?: Scandinavian Design in Britain 1950–65," *Scandinavian Journal of Design History* 8 (1998): 80–93; Ingeborg Glambek, *Sett Utenfra: Det Nordiske i Arkitektur og Design* (Oslo and Copenhagen: Norsk Arkitekturforlag and Arkitektens Forlag, 1997); Lesley Jackson, "A Positive Influence: The Impact of Scandinavian Design in Britain during the 1950s," *Scandinavian Journal of Design History* 3 (1993): 41–60.

34 Per H. Hansen, *Danish Modern Furniture, 1930–2016: The Rise, Decline and Re-emergence of a Cultural Market Category*, trans. Mark Mussari (Odense: University Press of Southern Denmark, 2018); Fallan, *Scandinavian Design: Alternate Histories*; Jones, *Vicke Lindstrand on the Periphery*.

35 Lucy Creagh, Helena Kåberg, and Barbara Miller Lane, "General Introduction," in *Modern Swedish Design: Three Founding Texts*, ed. Lucy Creagh, Helena Kåberg, and Barbara Miller Lane (New York: Museum of Modern Art, 2008), 12.

MIGRATION AND HERITAGE

BOBBYE
TIGERMAN

MIGRATION AND HERITAGE

Scandinavian immigrants and their descendants made myriad contributions to the artistic and cultural life of their adopted communities. Beginning in the mid-nineteenth century, Danes, Finns, Icelanders, Norwegians, and Swedes began moving to the United States in increasing numbers, seeking economic opportunity and religious freedom. By the 1920s, as many as 2.3 million had arrived in America. While they settled all over the country, concentrated communities developed in the upper Midwest (Michigan, Minnesota, Wisconsin, Illinois, and Iowa) and the Pacific Northwest, as well as in major cities. Many were highly skilled artists and craftspeople, some carefully preserving traditional motifs and techniques, and others adapting these traditions to American tastes. In some cases, designers invented original forms for their new nation. Like all immigrants, Scandinavians faced choices about whether and how to conform to their new society's customs. As historian April Schultz has shown, assimilation is not a linear process, but occurs to different degrees in different aspects of life, taking different forms with each successive generation, and indeed, with each individual.[1]

Scandinavian immigrants largely avoided the systemic discrimination encountered by other ethnic groups, though there were instances of targeted prejudice, especially during World War I, when anti-German bias was mistakenly directed at them.[2] In an effort to combat anti-immigrant sentiment during a period of immigrant restrictions, craft advocate Allen H. Eaton spearheaded a number of projects intended to "suggest some of the contributions of our foreign-born citizens to American culture."[3] His *Arts and Crafts of the Homelands* exhibitions (1919) and related book *Immigrant Gifts to American Life* (1932) aimed to encourage tolerance and familiarize native-born Americans with European immigrants' artistic achievements. For these exhibitions (held in Buffalo, Rochester, and Albany, New York, and several locations in the Northeast and Midwest), Eaton invited European immigrant groups in each city to contribute handmade objects from their nation of origin. The objects were shown in dense, multimedia displays organized by country and complemented by programs of live performances and craft demonstrations.[4] At the Albright Art Gallery in Buffalo, the Norway, Sweden, and Denmark sections were shown together, demonstrating how Americans have tended to associate these countries with one another since the early twentieth century (p. 33). One of the exhibition's most popular objects, which was both discussed in press coverage and illustrated in *Immigrant Gifts to American Life,* was an antique painted Swedish trunk (p. 33). The trunk sparked the imagination of visitors with its delicately painted flowers and inscribed initials of past owners. It bore the dates 1739 (perhaps when it was made in Sweden) and 1805 (the conjectured date of its most recent decoration), indicating its long life in the United States.[5] The nearby Finnish section featured ships in bottles and engagement jewelry, and was accompanied by a Finnish American woman in native costume who explained the objects to visitors. A Danish woman also demonstrated the weaving of colorful parade towels.[6]

Scandinavian Americans, like other immigrant groups, were involved in a wide variety of these sorts of heritage activities, which included participating in cultural festivals and the performing or visual arts, preparing traditional foods, speaking native languages, and wearing traditional costumes. These activities could even encompass urban-scale projects like Lindsborg, Kansas ("Little Sweden"), and Solvang, California ("a Danish village").[7] Within Scandinavian communities, making traditional crafts or reviving extinct traditions remained an important way for immigrants and their descendants to maintain connections to their cultural heritage. Crafts offered an especially potent way to identify with one's ethnic past, as the making of furniture, woodwork, and textiles became an outlet for both cultural identification and artistic expression. For example, Norwegian immigrant Per Lysne launched the modern interest in rosemaling (traditional Norwegian folk art painting) from his home in Stoughton, Wisconsin. Lysne inspired second- and third-generation immigrant artists such as American-born Violet Christophersen, who made rosemaled objects using techniques and motifs from an instructional folio brought to the United States after World War II.[8] Rosemaled objects were often not functional, but used decoratively to signal the homeowner's Norwegian heritage. Christophersen's monumental platter commemorated two nearly concurrent celebrations: the sesquicentennial of the first arrival of Norwegians to the United States in 1975, and the United States' Bicentennial in 1976, allowing the artist to express her bicultural identity through a distinctively Norwegian form (p. 34).

For some immigrants and their descendants, identifying with Nordic heritage meant collecting and displaying objects made in their native countries, such as Swedish Dala horses. These small hand-painted wooden horses

Installation view of Norway-Denmark-Sweden section of *Arts and Crafts of the Homelands*, Albright Art Gallery, Buffalo, New York, 1919

Swedish immigrant's trunk, made 1739, decorated 1805. Illustrated in Allen H. Eaton, *Immigrant Gifts to American Life*, 1932

Swedish Pavilion entrance showing the large-scale Dala horse, New York World's Fair, 1939

VIOLET CHRISTOPHERSEN
Platter, 1976. CAT. 20

GRANNAS A. OLSSONS HEMSLÖJD
NILS OLSSON HEMSLÖJD
Dala horses, these examples produced
c. 1970. CAT. 49

34

were made in Dalarna, a largely rural region of the country associated with "authentic," preindustrial Swedish culture (p. 34).[9] Dala horses had been produced since at least the seventeenth century, but became popular tourist souvenirs in Sweden in the second half of the nineteenth century. The mania for Dala horses in the United States began at the 1939 New York World's Fair, where an eight-foot painted horse was placed in front of the Swedish Pavilion (p. 33). Demand for the horses was overwhelming, with more than twenty thousand sold at the fair and the Swedish producers receiving orders for twenty thousand more in the following year. They remain a popular staple of Scandinavian gift shops in the U.S., with the horse motif applied to a variety of consumer products such as upholstery fabrics, tablewares, and napkins.[10]

Nordic immigrants to the United States worked as both independent designers and collaborative craftspeople, bringing valuable skills acquired in their native countries. The armchair for the Robert R. Blacker House in Pasadena, designed by Southern California architects Charles Sumner Greene and Henry Mather Greene in 1907, and made in the workshop of the Swedish-born brothers Peter and John Hall, is one such collaboration (p. 37). After the Greenes designed the chair, the Halls and their European (including Swedish) immigrant employees executed the work. Furniture scholar Edward S. Cooke, Jr. has noted that the level of craftsmanship and joinery of the Greenes' furniture increased after they hired the Halls in 1906. This advance has been attributed to the knowledge of woodworking practices found in the Hall workshop.[11] Similarly, Loja Saarinen employed exclusively Swedish designers and weavers in her studio at Cranbrook Academy of Art from the late 1920s through the early 1940s.[12]

Immigrant designers also worked for industry, such as architect and designer Greta Magnusson Grossman, who created pieces for several U.S. manufacturers after moving from Sweden to Los Angeles in 1940. Her desk for the firm Glenn of California exemplifies her combination of Scandinavian and Californian design influences (p. 36). Its asymmetrical forms, juxtaposition of light and dark, and use of Formica contribute to the piece's modern California aesthetic. At the same time, the use of walnut reflects her knowledge of traditional materials, while the skillful way she engineered the desk for small-batch production points to the cabinetmaker's training she acquired in Sweden.[13]

GRETA MAGNUSSON GROSSMAN
Glenn of California
Desk, designed 1952, this example
c. 1952–54. CAT. 54

CHARLES SUMNER GREENE
HENRY MATHER GREENE
Peter Hall Manufacturing Company
Armchair for the Robert R.
Blacker House, 1907. CAT. 52

Other immigrants, such as Erik Gronborg, became independent artists. Unlike earlier arrivals fleeing hardship, Gronborg arrived in the United States in 1959 seeking artistic opportunity and believing he could better realize his potential in the United States: "I did not come to USA for the *freedom*, Denmark had all the civil liberties plus a much better, more progressive, social welfare system. I came to become an artist. The art world in Denmark was a small closed group and the Royal Academy was the only art school and rigid and old, so I came here looking for a more creative environment. And it worked out well."[14] He studied sculpture with Peter Voulkos and Ron Nagle at the University of California, Berkeley, in the early 1960s. Gronborg uses vivid color and popular imagery on his ceramics, making subversive sculptural work that challenges long-held expectations about pottery's functional purpose. Works such as his bowl are characterized by vibrant glazes and the appropriation of newspaper imagery of distinctively American motifs such as cowboys, cars, and computers (p. 39). Gronborg found that combining these pop culture images with art-historical representations of the female nude produced the provocation he desired.

The Scandinavian immigrant experience was far from monolithic; Danes, Finns, Swedes, and Norwegians faced significantly different social and political pressures in their homelands, and therefore these groups adapted differently as they settled in the United States. This section—indeed, this catalogue—reflects on some of the commonalities among Nordic immigrant artists, designers, and craftspeople who came to America and influenced American design without underplaying the profound differences in each country's disparate traditions and mores.[15] The collective contributions of these designers and craftspeople demonstrate the myriad and ongoing ways that Scandinavian immigrants have shaped art and design in the United States and speak to the value that all immigrants bring to their adopted communities.

1 April Schultz, "'The Pride of the Race Had Been Touched': The 1925 Norse-American Immigration Centennial and Ethnic Identity," *Journal of American History* 77, no. 4 (March 1991): 1265–95.

2 Dag Blanck, "'A Mixture of People with Different Roots': Swedish Immigrants in the American Ethno-Racial Hierarchies," *Journal of American Ethnic History* 33, no. 3 (Spring 2014): 37–54; Jørn Brøndal, "'The Fairest among the So-Called White Races': Portrayals of Scandinavian Americans in the Filiopietistic and Nativist Literature of the Late Nineteenth and Early Twentieth Centuries," *Journal of American Ethnic History* 33, no. 3 (Spring 2014): 5–36; Daron W. Olson, *Vikings across the Atlantic: Emigration and the Building of a Greater Norway, 1860–1945* (Minneapolis: University of Minnesota Press, 2013), 115–58.

3 Allen H. Eaton, "Author's Preface," in *Immigrant Gifts to American Life: Some Experiments in Appreciation of the Contributions of Our Foreign-Born Citizens to American Culture* (New York: Russell Sage Foundation, 1932), 13.

4 Diana Greenwold, "'The Great Palace of American Civilization': Allen Eaton's *Arts and Crafts of the Homelands, 1919–1932*," *Contemporaneity* 3, no. 1 (2014): 99–115.

5 Eaton, *Immigrant Gifts to American Life*, opp. p. 40.

6 Eaton, *Immigrant Gifts to American Life*, 47–50.

7 Lizette Gradén, Hanne Pico Larsen, and Susanne Österlund-Pötzsch, "Nordic Spaces in the U.S.: Three Examples of the Performance of Nordic-American Identity," *American Studies in Scandinavia* 44, no. 1 (2012): 67–96.

8 Philip Martin, *Rosemaling in the Upper Midwest: A Story of Region & Revival* (Mount Horeb, WI: Wisconsin Folk Museum, 1989), 32. The portfolio was created by Norwegian artist Knut Hovden and published in 1938.

9 Rune Bondjers, "The Wooden Horse That Became a National Symbol," in *Swedish Wooden Toys*, ed. Amy F. Ogata and Susan Weber (New Haven and London: Yale University Press, 2014), 167.

10 Bondjers, "The Wooden Horse," 178–81.

11 Edward S. Cooke, Jr., "Scandinavian Modern Furniture in the Arts and Crafts Period: The Collaboration of the Greenes and the Halls," in *American Furniture*, ed. Luke Beckerdite (Hanover, NH: Chipstone Foundation, 1993), 55–74.

12 Christa C. Mayer Thurman, "Textiles," in *Design in America: The Cranbrook Vision, 1925–1950*, exh. cat., ed. Robert Judson Clark and Andrea P. A. Belloli (New York: Detroit Institute of Arts and the Metropolitan Museum of Art, 1983), 180. For more on Saarinen and Swedish designers, see Erica Warren in this volume, 209–15.

13 For one explanation of how immigrant designers adapt to their new societies, see Bobbye Tigerman, "Fusing Old and New: Émigré Designers in California," in *California Design, 1930-1965: Living in a Modern Way*, exh. cat., ed. Wendy Kaplan (Los Angeles and Cambridge, MA: Los Angeles County Museum of Art and MIT Press, 2011), 91–115.

14 Erik Gronborg, email message to author, August 10, 2018.

15 I thank Diana Jocelyn Greenwold for this observation.

Making Scandinavian Americans

DIANA JOCELYN GREENWOLD

In 1898, Swedish American farmer Olof Ohman reported a miraculous discovery: a runestone unearthed in his fields in Douglas County, Minnesota, that allegedly provided evidence of a Viking presence in fourteenth-century North America (right). The monolith, which became known as the Kensington Runestone, dated the arrival of Scandinavians on the continent to 1362, a full 130 years before the arrival of Christopher Columbus. Despite skepticism as to the stone's authenticity, Ohman's monument was first put on view in the window of a bank in Kensington, Minnesota, then at the Smithsonian Institution in Washington, DC, in 1949, and finally at the 1964 New York World's Fair.[1] There, in the Minnesota pavilion, an enormous fiberglass Viking guarded the stone bearing a shield that read, "Minnesota, Birthplace of America?" From the moment it emerged, the stele became a tangible marker of a Nordic presence in North America predating Anglo-American settlement by centuries.

While scholars have nearly always doubted the age and origin of the Kensington Runestone, the sentiments that account for its allure were entirely genuine. Its nationwide popularity reflects Scandinavian Americans' efforts to stake their claim in the foundational mythology of this country. As historians Orm Øverland and Daron W. Olson have suggested, immigrant communities across North America created histories for themselves to cement their early presence and their affinities with important American historical moments and figures.[2] Øverland, in particular, has described the potency of such "homemaking myths" as helping immigrant communities retain a sense of identity, rooting them both to their countries of origin and to their new homes.[3] Norwegian, Swedish, Finnish, and Danish Americans, like so many ethnic groups settling in

Kensington Runestone from the Runestone Museum, Alexandria, Minnesota

this country, used art and material culture to make these connections and to assert their presence in America's past and its present.

Scandinavians arrived in the United States in waves throughout the nineteenth and twentieth centuries and worked to maintain their native traditions in the face of dominant Anglo-American cultural norms as they adapted ideas and objects to conform to prevailing tastes. Many who made their living as craftspeople and designers navigated the presentation of dual Scandinavian American identities by linking themselves to the history of their adopted country. They accentuated their ingenuity and knowledge of modern styles and techniques while also translating traditions from their countries of origin in ways that were legible and appealing to American consumers. Textiles and metalwork were particularly important fields for Scandinavian artists and designers who cleverly walked the line between introducing designs and patterns unique to their own cultures and associating their work and practice with tropes familiar to Anglo-American consumers.

Throughout the twentieth century, Scandinavian American artists and designers utilized three principal narratives to integrate their work into the broader history of American culture: they connected their handmade products to colonial America and its small-scale producers; they recalled their important role in the settlement of the frontier as rugged and self-sufficient pioneers; and they designed and created works that embedded themselves within modern, urban, and cosmopolitan America.[4] In doing so, they distanced themselves from Southern and Eastern Europeans who were then arriving in the United States in large numbers and encountering overt hostility from American nativists. Scandinavians pointed to their shared faith (Protestantism) and shared physical attributes (whiteness) as ways to associate with Anglo-American culture.[5] Linking themselves to early Americans and the country's most recent accomplishments allowed Nordic immigrants to elevate their status in the United States over those Southern and Eastern Europeans considered categorically different from Anglo-Americans and in some cases inherently unsuited to American citizenship.[6]

This essay addresses a select group of craftspeople and designers whose experiences represent larger trends in the story of twentieth-century Scandinavian immigration to the United States. From Valborg "Mama" Gravander's traditional weavings to Erik Magnussen's modern designs in silver for the Gorham Manufacturing Company, Nordic artists impacted the material culture of the United States through selective adaptation and astute assimilation of American tastes and proclivities that embedded them in American life. Examining their careers and the means through which they presented their objects in the commercial sphere helps shed light on how Norwegians, Swedes, Danes, and Finns fundamentally reshaped modern American culture.

Scandinavian Immigration to the United States

Scandinavian immigration to the United States occurred in three large waves, beginning in the mid-nineteenth century, increasing again toward the end of the 1800s, and peaking once again in the early decades of the twentieth century.[7] Migrants left home largely due to lopsided population growth as landless peasant classes ballooned in regions where social structures made it very difficult for them to become independent farmers.[8] The passage of the U.S. Homestead Act in 1862, which gave citizens and newly arriving immigrants alike the opportunity to settle up to 160 acres in the West, lured many farmers from Norway, Sweden, Finland, and Denmark.[9] Though their numbers were relatively small compared to many other nineteenth- and twentieth-century groups, Nordic immigrants significantly impacted the populations and local cultures of certain regions of the country, particularly the upper Midwest.[10] Unlike other immigrant groups arriving in the United States in the second half of the nineteenth century, much settlement of Scandinavians was rural, not urban. These groups established small towns that fanned out westward across Illinois, Wisconsin, Iowa, Minnesota, Michigan, and the Dakotas.[11] Immigrants from the Scandinavian countries continued to arrive into the twentieth-century, although the closing of the American frontier caused more to congregate in urban centers than rural outposts.

Successive waves of immigrants from across Europe altered the country's social and cultural makeup in fundamental ways. For some early twentieth-century Anglo-Americans, influxes of new citizens, particularly from Southern and Eastern Europe, posed an apparent threat to the fundamental values and ethnic makeup of the nation. Slavs, Italians, and Eastern European Jews made up a large portion of new arrivals during the early twentieth century, and were targeted by writers and politicians fearful that their way of life was in danger of disappearing.[12] American nativists such as eugenicist Madison Grant welcomed immigrants from Scandinavian countries and felt a sense of shared kinship between those they referred to as the "Nordic races," as they were allegedly of "higher intelligence" and provided "the best material for American citizenship."[13]

Based on social Darwinist theories ranking the relative status of ethnic groups, Scandinavian immigrants fared better than Southern and Eastern European arrivals and worked in concerted ways to accentuate the distance between themselves and those that nativists deemed less suitable for citizenship. Historian Kendric Charles Babcock related this version of Scandinavians as hearty American pioneers: "The prospective joys of owning a farm and of expanding its acreage, with the prosperity of the years and with the growth of the family, made the hardships of pioneering and the isolation of the frontier seem as very little things to the strong-limbed, sound-hearted, land-hungry Swedes, Norwegians, and Danes in the middle Northwest, as compared with their more gregarious cousins of western and southern Europe, who sought American cities, construction gangs, or mining camps."[14] Conceptualized as categorically apart from other new Americans, Scandinavians frequently enjoyed a more seamless integration into cultural and political spheres, and artists of Scandinavian descent visualized this perceived gap in their designs and modes of production.

The Folk in Scandinavian American Textiles

Textiles were a key means through which Scandinavian craft entered into the American mainstream and an important way that Nordic American weavers and needleworkers established themselves as the descendants of the settlers who populated the West and Midwest.[15] Scandinavian American lace and embroidery flourished in the United States in the early twentieth century, both as an imported commodity and as a pastime for American women who incorporated aspects of traditional patterns into hybridized designs. Works such as Karen Marie Jensen and Lillian Poulsen's hedebo lace doily (above) represent a traditional form of needlework from rural Denmark transported to this country and celebrated as skilled handiwork in the Arts and Crafts tradition. The consummate representation of small-scale labor, traditional lace could only be produced with ample time by trained artists using either a needle or a series of wooden dowels called bobbins. Originally associated with European court culture, the work of lacemaking had, by the late nineteenth century, largely migrated to rural homes and workshops. These industries appealed to Arts and Crafts enthusiasts eager to associate products with rural life lived in concert with the natural world.[16]

Lacemaking enjoyed a renaissance in America in the early twentieth century, both as contemporary fashion and a collectible item replete with European associations and connections to self-sufficient American makers of the past. Collectors, largely women, purchased antique and revival pieces from lace dealers, and museums such as the Metropolitan Museum of Art, the Museum of Fine Arts, Boston, and the de Young Museum built extensive antique lace collections.[17] In the early twentieth century, American women traveling abroad began to

KAREN MARIE JENSEN
LILLIAN POULSEN
Doily, started by Jensen c. 1908; finished later by Poulsen. CAT. 70

collect lace in large quantities or to purchase fragments from dealers who proffered examples at prices that rivaled those of old master paintings.[18] While Italy and France served as the primary sites for collectors and dealers selling antique laces, patterns from across Europe, including Scandinavia, became popular and proliferated in books and manuals that enabled American women to integrate designs gleaned from European cultures into new forms.

Hedebo lace (named after the region where the embroidery was popular) originated in Zealand, Denmark, in the seventeenth century, but gained popularity in the nineteenth century when folk revival proponents brought the designs to Copenhagen and then the United States.[19] Akin to Italian *reticella*, or cutwork, hedebo lace makers used white thread on white fabric, removing strands from the linen to form a base grid, into which they inserted tiny buttonhole stitches to create symmetrical patterns of flowers, leaves, droplets, and other designs drawn from nature.[20] Hedebo lace enthusiasts lauded both the individual works and the skilled labor required to produce the textiles. As one writer remarked, "the pieces that have been brought to this country are so exact that they do not look as if they could have been made by hand, but rather by machine."[21] Manuals designed to teach hedebo patterns to American needlewomen stressed both the ancient origins of the patterns and their applicability to contemporary fashion: "Careful study of the illustrations and instruction will enable the worker to produce many beautiful effects in this ancient Danish Art Needle Work that is now in the front rank of modern style in hand embroidery."[22] For American consumers, that such delicate workmanship might emerge from such modest circumstances was an identifying feature that linked Scandinavian lace makers with works produced by other enterprising pioneer settlers. Remarking on the nature of fine craftsmanship that emerged from humble origins, *Ladies' Home Journal* reported that "all the spare time of the peasant women of this country is given to this needlework, and the marvel is how they can execute this most tedious and dainty work with their clumsy fingers—used, as they are, to rough and heavy work."[23]

Scandinavian weavers also adapted stylistic tropes that linked them to their Scandinavian roots and to the ancestors who had settled the Midwest. Ida Laituri Nevala's rag rug (p. 46) is the consummate emblem of frugality. Comprising scraps and remnants, the rag rug exists in many cultures as a textile made from the leftovers of other projects.[24] A Michigan newspaper noted of rag rug weaver Laina Lampf that "like all Finnish American weavers, she is the consummate recycler.... Recycling these discards into beautiful rugs is her special art."[25] These textiles, created for the home, helped link producers to the virtues of pioneer life and to those who had utilized scant resources to create their homesteads on the range. Writings by Scandinavian American historians lauded early nineteenth-century settlers and proposed that the temperament of their countrymen made them uniquely suited to the task of settling the lands of the American Midwest. One principal mythology around the temperament of the Scandinavian was her innately rural proclivities, her insatiable desire to foster growth and prosperity in inhospitable climates, and her success in cultivating the wilderness. Scandinavians related themselves in fundamental ways to these ideals as they applied to American pioneers. Historian Frederick Jackson Turner's Frontier Thesis, for instance, contended

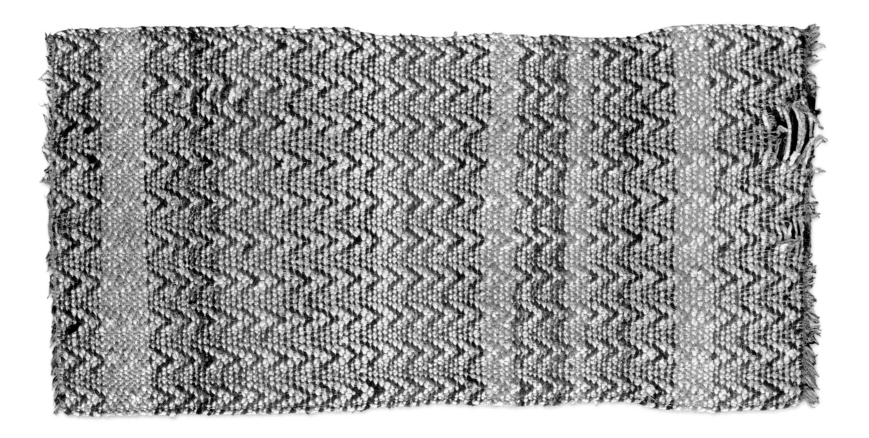

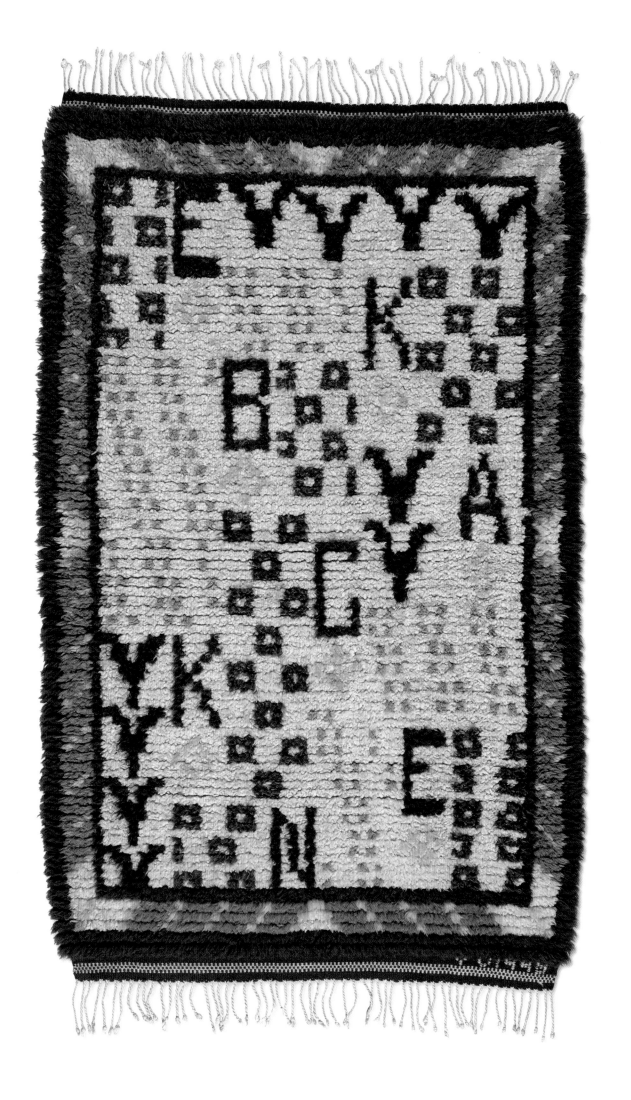

Valborg "Mama" Gravander at her loom at Ekbacken in Mill Valley, California, c. 1953

that a uniquely American temperament of independence and grit had been forged by continuously encountering and subjugating new peoples and terrains in the push across the continent.[26]

Valborg "Mama" Gravander epitomized that pioneer spirit as she brought the ethos of both Swedish rural life and American frontier living to U.S. audiences. Gravander produced handwoven Swedish textiles, such as the rug that bears the name of Ekbacken, her homestead in Mill Valley, California (p. 47). She and her husband, Axel, immigrated to San Francisco from Gävle, Sweden, in the 1920s. Their San Francisco home, which they called Sveagard, became a communal gathering place for local Swedes and a center for dances and festivals. Also referred to as the Swedish Applied Arts, it was a space where Axel built looms and Valborg taught students traditional weaving techniques.[27] In 1945, the Gravanders moved from San Francisco to Mill Valley, where they built their compound in the style of Swedish country cottages. At Ekbacken, which

was described as "a hand-weaving center and treasure house of arts and crafts products from Sweden," Valborg continued to teach weaving and also ran a boardinghouse.[28]

Gravander herself, who often wore traditional Swedish costume, was as much the attraction as the wares she produced or the lessons she provided (above). As one reporter noted, "The beautiful things she has brought from Sweden, the fabrics she has woven and her home and museum are certainly worth a visit, but the woman herself, a warm, perceptive, and inspirational individual is what really makes it all worthwhile."[29] For some, the performance of traditional Swedish weaving in costume marked Gravander as an immigrant who had managed to deter assimilation and maintain the customs of her homeland: "Mrs. Gravander has been in this country some 14 years—long enough, think you, to become quite Americanized. Yes and no to that one, for Mrs. Gravander has accomplished that difficult feat of transplanting successfully the traditions of

PEER SMED
Cocktail shaker, 1931. CAT. 144

her native country to the country of her adaption [*sic*]."[30] Others saw in Gravander's folk weaving, cooking, and dress an amalgamation of both her native land and a tribute to the Swedish American pioneers of the western United States: "Valborg 'Mama' Gravander spins on an old spinning wheel and weaves on an old loom while she impersonates the 'Pioneer Mother' at the Yuba county exhibit at the state fair."[31] Reenacting Scandinavian dances, folk crafts, and meals meant not only connecting back to Sweden, Norway, Denmark, or Finland, but also connecting to other immigrants who had brought those customs and traditions to the New World and maintained them here.

The Colonial and the Modern in Scandinavian American Silver

Scandinavian American silversmiths in the twentieth century linked themselves to the small-scale working methods of traditional European and early American workshops, frequently by comparing their practices with the most well-known American colonial artisan, Paul Revere. At the same time, Peer Smed, Erik Magnussen, and Nordic immigrant artists of the Kalo Shop also fashioned objects and participated in exhibitions that celebrated the aesthetics of modern design and cosmopolitanism. In 1937, the Brooklyn Museum mounted *Contemporary Industrial and Handwrought Silver*, an exhibition that included two Danish silversmiths, Peer Smed and Erik Magnussen. The show crystallized these dual motivations on the part of Scandinavian silversmiths and the companies that marketed their wares. Curators paired works by early American silversmiths such as Revere with contemporary objects that immigrant artists created by hand and machine to establish a clear lineage between the eighteenth-century Boston silversmith and present-day Scandinavian American artisans.[32] Organizers in Brooklyn further visualized affinities between colonial wares, contemporary handmade objects, and those wrought by machine in the exhibit catalogue, wherein hand and machine production received equal attention.[33] The exhibition suggested a smooth continuum from the handwork of Revere to the industrial production of works in silver.

GREENWOLD

Contextualizing immigrant silversmiths using Revere also featured in press related to Peer Smed, an artist who apprenticed at a young age to a Danish court silversmith before moving to New York in 1903.[34] His designs often included rounded, organic forms, such as his owl-shaped cocktail shaker (p. 49). Part of a larger group of animal shakers, this work evokes zoomorphic vessels popular in German-speaking countries in the fifteenth and sixteenth centuries.[35] Astute in his efforts to align his work with both European production and with the best aspects of American colonial wares, Smed fashioned works with antique Germanic roots while speaking admiringly of Revere, the quintessential American silversmith and patriot. Smed lauded the simplicity and care with which the Boston silversmith approached his craft: "His designs were simple and in excellent taste."[36] Smed's works straddled the divide between the classic and the modern by borrowing aspects of each. His objects were described as being "in the so-called classic-modern fashion, in which the ornamentation, though modern, is reminiscent of the fine work of the past."[37] Notably hostile to machines, Smed aligned himself both with traditional production methods and, by extension, those of the colonial era. He asserted that machines had no place in hand silversmithing, stating that "they are in the way."[38]

Correspondingly, Smed carefully configured his workshop to evoke Europe or early America, creating an air of time travel to a mythical golden age of craft production; writer Guy Hickok described visiting Smed's studio as stepping "into the middle ages."[39] The physical space seemed to impress writers nearly as much as the craftsman's Nordic features. "He is a Viking of a man, tall, powerful, calm," wrote one critic.[40] Hickok described the experience: "You find a forge, an anvil mounted on the stump of a tree, and a big blue-eyed blond-bearded Dane heating not gold but silver into forms that ravish the eye and cause the muscles to quiver."[41] Smed leveraged the interest in his physical attributes and his quaint surroundings by re-creating his own workshop in 1936 as a bronze diorama that went on view in the Fifth Avenue window of jeweler E. M. Gattle and Co., a store that also sold his wares.[42] This performative emphasis on traditional production conjured associations not only with Europe but also with the bygone age of hand production in America, thus linking Smed's present production to the country's past.

Artists working in Chicago's Kalo Shop similarly marketed a particular vision of collective handcraftsmanship suggestive of a much earlier age. The enterprise was founded in 1900 by Clara Barck Welles, along with Bertha Hall, Rose Dolese, Grace Gerow, Ruth Raymond, and Bessie McNeal, all graduates of the decorative design course at the Art Institute of Chicago. Inspired by the Arts and Crafts movement and organized along the lines of Charles Robert Ashbee's Guild and School of Handicraft in Britain, the shop operated with the motto "Beautiful, Useful, and Enduring" and employed artists who produced handmade products on a small scale.[43] Like Ashbee's move from London to rural Chipping Camden, Welles moved the Kalo Shop in 1905 to nearby Park Ridge, a more idyllic suburban setting for the workshop and school that began to specialize in silver and jewelry.[44]

Many of the works produced by the shop were the result of collaborations, such as the shared work of silversmith Peter Berg and goldsmith Yngve Olsson.[45] Berg designed a pair of organically inspired five-armed candelabra, and Olsson embellished them with chasing and repoussé to create the silhouettes of chrysanthemum blossoms and leaves encircling the base (p. 50).[46] Berg and Olsson were both immigrants—from Norway and Denmark, respectively. Like many small-scale industries of the early twentieth century, the Kalo Shop recognized the expertise of makers trained abroad, and immigrants' work defined Kalo's aesthetic. Welles and her colleagues valued both men's knowledge of traditional European forms as well as their willingness to adapt and innovate these to meet the needs of consumers in the United States. The Kalo Shop's objects represented a "blending of past tradition, early American or European, with the modern attitude."[47] For the artists, the small-scale rural workshop suggested images of craftsmen in Europe as well as colonial America, while the works these artisans created were reminiscent of the past but also embraced modernity.

Erik Magnussen, who was also included in the Brooklyn Museum's *Contemporary Industrial and Handwrought Silver* exhibition, arrived in the United States from Denmark in 1925. Trained by his uncle as well as Norwegian sculptor Stephan Sinding and Danish silversmith Viggo Christian Hansen, Magnussen worked in Sweden and then Berlin before opening his own shop in Copenhagen in 1907.[48] In 1925, the Gorham Manufacturing Company in Rhode Island hired Magnussen to modernize

their tableware designs. Like fellow Scandinavian silversmith Georg Jensen, whose work was known through a New York shop opened in 1924, Magnussen incorporated aspects of Nordic patterns into his designs for American audiences that were distinct from Gorham's emphasis on colonial revival forms.[49] Gorham invested heavily in Magnussen, providing him with his own workshop and free rein to create new products for the American market. His first effort for Gorham, the *Cubic* coffee service, took inspiration from Cubist painters Braque and Picasso as well as the reflective planes of the modern American city (p. 236). The *New York Times* deemed the service "the Lights and Shadows of Manhattan," but the avant-garde set was not commercially successful, and Magnussen's next effort, the *Modern American* line, incorporated aspects of Art Deco architecture with less aggressively geometric forms (p. 53).[50]

With the *Modern American* line, Magnussen adapted the curling and sloping silhouettes of existing Gorham designs into a stepped pattern. Horizontal and vertical scored lines constitute the only decorative element on the surface of the vessels.[51] Magnussen also designed cocktail sets, coffee sets, candlesticks, bowls, service plates, and salt and pepper shakers for the line. Sets such as this one also made use of new materials, such as Bakelite, in place of more costly ivory or ebony. Gorham stated that the immigrant maker had created "something of America, and for America."[52] The company advertised the set in an illustrated brochure that featured a pair of sleekly dressed connoisseurs who admire the *Modern American* compote with the city skyline outlined in a window beyond.[53] Gorham marketed Magnussen's designs as sharing an affinity with early American silver, though the works appear seemingly divorced from the rounded shapes of colonial revival silver or the work of craftsmen such as Revere. A 1930 *New York Times* article explained of Magnussen's offerings that

ERIK MAGNUSSEN
Gorham Manufacturing Company
Modern American **cocktail set**, designed
1928, this example 1930. CAT. 97

Erik Magnussen photographed for
a Gorham Manufacturing Company
advertisement, 1926

JOHN SINGLETON COPLEY
Paul Revere, 1768. Oil on canvas,
35 ⅛ × 28 ½ in. (89.2 × 72.4 cm).
Museum of Fine Arts, Boston,
Gift of Joseph W. Revere, William B.
Revere and Edward H. R. Revere, 30.78

"while they do not follow in the footsteps of Paul Revere and other early Colonial craftsmen, they still show the austere refinement that set apart American silver from the more ornate European models of that time."[54] To the *Times*, at least, there was something fundamentally American in the way that Magnussen eschewed excess ornament in favor of austere silhouettes and minimal decoration.

Rather than distance themselves from industrial production, some Scandinavian artists and artisans defined themselves by embracing the machine aesthetic in pursuit of pure, pared-down modernist forms. However, despite efforts to provide strong ties to the ideal of Scandinavian and American modernism, even those seemingly committed to streamlining also incorporated aspects of traditional cultural production, and associated themselves and their work with both their European heritage and America's historical roots. A photograph of Magnussen published by Gorham in 1926 shows the silversmith poised with a chasing hammer and punch in his hands (top left). Arrayed before him are a variety of tools and objects. Magnussen himself is as polished as his silver, with carefully combed hair and a white work coat. His smile and direct gaze exude a sense of confidence and mastery of his materials. Comparing this image to John Singleton Copley's 1768 portrait of Paul Revere, the inspiration for Magnussen's photographic portrayal is immediately recognizable (bottom left). Like Magnussen, Copley's Revere appears serene and stoic, and also holds the fruits of his creative genius with his tools strewn before him. Though he wears the clothing of a workman, Revere, like Magnussen, is immaculately presented, all shine and surface, even in the reflection of his bright white shirtsleeves on the gleaming wood desk. The association provides another means by which Gorham visualized this foreign artist in the guise of the nation's most famous silversmith.

Conclusion

Immigrants from Denmark, Finland, Norway, and Sweden arrived with traditions from their home countries that they selectively integrated into new lives in the United States. In doing so, they and those who marketed their work associated them with their Scandinavian heritage as well as with the proudest moments in America's past and present. Broadly speaking, Scandinavians assimilated with more ease than Southern and Eastern European immigrants of the nineteenth century, thanks to the perception of religious and ethnic attributes shared with Anglo-Saxons. While it would be comforting to assume such racialized assumptions faded over the last century, in January 2018, President Donald Trump decried the immigration of Haitians and Africans to the United States, declaring that he would rather see more new Americans arriving from nations such as Norway.[55] Far from a randomly selected nation, in this context Norway and its citizens represented a specific set of ideals and values. As nativist rhetoric seeps back into mainstream political discourse, it is worth recalling that the ideal of the Nordic immigrant did not emerge in 2018. Rather, this preference represents a long-standing interest in valorizing the peoples and material cultures of Scandinavia as well as a concerted effort on the part of Scandinavian Americans to place themselves at the heart of narratives about their character as colonists, pioneers, and innovators. Exploring artists and objects that supported these ideas provides an entrée into how notions of the so-called "ideal immigrant" emerged a century ago, and how they continue to inform contemporary political and social discourse.

1 Adam Hjorthén, "A VIKING in New York: The Kensington Runestone at the 1964–1965 World's Fair," *Minnesota History* 63, no. 1 (2012): 8. The trope of the Viking discovery of America was also widely promoted through the early twentieth-century Viking Revival style. See Graham C. Boettcher in this volume, 81–91.

2 Orm Øverland, *Immigrant Minds, American Identities: Making the United States Home, 1870–1930* (Urbana: University of Illinois Press, 2000); Daron W. Olson, "Norwegian-American Historians and the Creation of an Ethnic Identity," *Scandinavian Studies* 79, no. 1 (2007): 41–56.

3 Øverland, *Immigrant Minds*, 18–19.

4 Daron W. Olson describes four slightly different community mythologies Norwegian Americans used to place themselves at the center of the continent's discovery, its colonial period, its frontier society, and throughout its wars and conflicts; Olson, "Norwegian-American Historians and the Creation of an Ethnic Identity," 43.

5 H. Arnold Barton, "Where Have the Scandinavian-Americanists Been?," *Journal of American Ethnic History* 15, no. 1 (1995): 48.

6 John Higham, *Strangers in the Land: Patterns of American Nativism, 1860–1925*, 2nd ed. (New Brunswick, NJ: Rutgers University Press, 1988); Matthew Frye Jacobson, *Whiteness of a Different Color: European Immigrants and the Alchemy of Race* (Cambridge, MA: Harvard University Press, 1998).

7 Odd S. Lovoll, *The Promise of America: A History of the Norwegian-American People*, rev. ed. (Minneapolis: University of Minnesota Press, 1999), 8.

8 Lovoll, *The Promise of America*, 14.

9 Jon Gjerde, *From Peasants to Farmers: The Migration from Balestrand, Norway, to the Upper Middle West* (Cambridge: Cambridge University Press, 1989), 4–5.

10 Between 1820 and 1920, one million Norwegians immigrated to the United States, and more than one million Swedes between 1880 and 1930; "Immigration Timeline," The Statue of Liberty–Ellis Island Foundation, https://www.libertyellisfoundation.org/immigration-timeline#1880.

11 Gjerde, *From Peasants to Farmers*, 4–5.

12 Jacobson, *Whiteness of a Different Color*, 80.

13 Jacobson, *Whiteness of a Different Color*, 83.

14 Kendric Charles Babcock, "The Scandinavian Element in American Population," *American Historical Review* 16, no. 2 (1911): 302.

15 Anglo-American settlers displaced Native populations in significant numbers as they pushed across the continent. This subjugation is not the subject of this essay but should nonetheless be acknowledged.

16 Edvige Giunta and Joseph Sciorra, "Introduction," in *Embroidered Stories: Interpreting Women's Domestic Needlework from the Italian Diaspora*, ed. Edvige Giunta and Joseph Sciorra (Jackson, MS: University Press of Mississippi, 2014), 10.

17 Diana Greenwold, "Crafting New Citizens: Art and Handicraft in New York and Boston Settlement Houses, 1900–1945" (PhD diss., University of California, Berkeley, 2016), 58.

18 Greenwold, "Crafting New Citizens," 54. By the late nineteenth century, wealthy Americans such as Isabella Stewart Gardner, Arabella Huntington, Jane Norton Morgan, Madeleine Astor, and Mary Stillman Harkness all maintained extensive lace collections.

19 "Hedebo Embroidery," Textile Research Centre, Leiden, https://trc-leiden.nl/trc-needles/regional-traditions/europe-and-north-america/embroideries/hedebo-embroidery-an-introduction-denmark.

20 Mary Gostelow, *A World of Embroidery* (New York: Charles Scribner's Sons, 1975), 58; Hattie Simpkins, "A Lamp Mat in Hedebo Work," *Pictorial Review* 8, no. 1 (October 1906): 23.

21 "Hedebo Needlework: New Lacework Designs," *Pictorial Review* 7, no. 8 (May 1906): 30.

22 *Hedebo Embroidery* (Chicago: T. Buettner & Co., 1911), 2.

23 Bessie Berry Grabowskii, "'Hedebo': A Danish Embroidery," *Ladies' Home Journal*, August 1904, 29.

24 Ruth Fitzgibbons, "Finnish Rag Rugs Gaining U.S. Fans," *The Republic*, December 2, 1978.

25 "Laina Lampf," *Lansing State Journal*, August 2, 2003.

26 Frederick Jackson Turner, "The Significance of the Frontier in American History," *Annual Report of the American Historical Association for the Year 1893* (Washington, DC, 1894), 197–227.

27 Virgil Morton, "'Dear Guest, the Pleasure Is All Ours,'" *Let's Dance: The Magazine of Folk & Square Dancing*, August 1954, 4.

28 "Mama Gravander Hostess for Celebration of Santa Lucia Festival," *Mill Valley Record*, December 16, 1949.

29 Nancy Swadesh, "Mama Gravander Returns Home from Sweden and Tells of Her Weaving and Travels," *Mill Valley Record*, June 18, 1954.

30 Martha Lee, "Swedish Arts Dishes to be Forum Theme: Mrs. Valborg Gravander of Svegard [*sic*] in S.F. to Be Guest of Homemakers," *Oakland Tribune*, April 24, 1936.

31 "Mama Gravander Is 'Pioneer Mother,'" *Mill Valley Record*, September 3, 1948.

32 On the use of the colonial past to educate immigrant communities, see Barbara Miller Solomon, *Ancestors and Immigrants: A Changing New England Tradition* (Boston: Northeastern University Press, 1989). For Revere and immigrant makers in the twentieth century, see Greenwold, "Crafting New Citizens," chap. 1; *Contemporary Industrial and Handwrought Silver*, exh. cat. (Brooklyn, NY: Brooklyn Museum of Art, 1937), 21.

33 *Contemporary Industrial and Handwrought Silver*, 10.

34 Alice Cogan, "Craftman: Model 1936, Peer Smed Pursues a Medieval Craft against a Medieval Background in the Heart of Brooklyn," *Brooklyn Daily Eagle*, November 29, 1936.

35 Rosie Mills, correspondence with Monica Obniski, June 25, 2018.

36 Cogan, "Craftman: Model 1936."

37 "Old and New in the Silver Craft of Today," *New York Times*, April 18, 1937.

38 "Silversmith Seeks to Spread His Art," *Daily News*, April 10, 1935.

39 Guy Hickok, "Dane Hammers Miracles in Silver Here in Middle Ages' Studio," *Brooklyn Daily Eagle*, March 31, 1935.

40 "Brooklyn Cellini," *Brooklyn Daily Eagle*, December 9, 1935.

41 Hickok, "Dane Hammers Miracles."

42 Cogan, "Craftman: Model 1936."

43 Barbara K. Schnitzer, "Necklace and Earrings, 1911/12," in *American Silver in the Art Institute of Chicago*, ed. Elizabeth McGoey (Chicago: Art Institute of Chicago, 2017), cat. 77.

44 Barbara K. Schnitzer, "Candelabra, 1920/21," in McGoey, *American Silver*, cat. 82.

45 Schnitzer, "Candelabra, 1920/21."

46 Schnitzer, "Candelabra, 1920/21."

47 Mary Moore, "New Silhouettes in Silver," *Craft Horizons* 9, no. 1 (Spring 1949): 17.

48 Patricia E. Kane, "Master of Modern Silver: Erik Magnussen," *Antiques and Fine Art*, Summer 2014, https://www.incollect.com/articles/master-of-modern-silver-erik-magnussen.

49 Jewel Stern, *Modernism in American Silver*, exh. cat., ed. Kevin W. Tucker and Charles L. Venable (New Haven and London: Yale University Press, 2005), 26–27.

50 Charles L. Venable, *Silver in America, 1840–1940: A Century of Splendor*, exh. cat. (Dallas: Dallas Museum of Art, 1995), 278.

51 Venable, *Silver in America*, 280.

52 Gorham Manufacturing Company, *The Modern American* (New York: Gorham, 1928), in Stern, *Modernism in American Silver*, 31.

53 Stern, *Modernism in American Silver*, 33.

54 Walter Rendell Storey, "Fine Art and Design in New Furnishings," *New York Times*, September 28, 1930.

55 Josh Dawsey, "Trump Derides Protections for Immigrants from 'Shithole' Countries," *Washington Post*, January 12, 2018.

Making Scandinavian Americans

57

PER LYSNE AND THE BIRTH OF NORWEGIAN AMERICAN ROSEMALING

HANNAH PIVO

Norwegian American rosemaling has long served as a vehicle for the preservation, adaptation, and celebration of Norwegian cultural identity in the United States, due in large part to the influence of Per Lysne, a Norwegian immigrant to Wisconsin who developed a national reputation beginning in the 1930s. Rosemaling is decorative folk painting that developed in Norway in the eighteenth century.[1] Regional variations abound, but generally it consists of scrolls, vines, and abstracted florals painted on wooden surfaces in churches and domestic interiors, as well as on objects, such as furniture and bowls.

 Lysne was born in Os, Norway, and learned rosemaling from his father before immigrating to the United States in 1907 at the age of twenty-seven.[2] He settled in the rural town of Stoughton, Wisconsin, and found employment at the Stoughton Wagon Company, where his work included painting decorative designs on the sides of wagons. He soon began painting independently, often redecorating wooden trunks that fellow immigrants brought from Europe. He also decorated new items, many of them Norwegian in form, such as three-legged chairs, called *jorestols* or *bandestols*, with semicircular seats and narrow bentwood backs. Frequently, the front of the chairs' arms were carved and painted to resemble dragons, furthering their association with Scandinavian (specifically Viking) heritage (p. 59). Lysne developed a national reputation, and was particularly celebrated in Wisconsin, receiving commissions to decorate homes throughout the state, including one for actors Lynn Fontanne and Alfred Lunt.[3]

 Lysne's rosemaling was celebrated as an authentic Norwegian craft "skillfully adapted to American living."[4] This adaptation was accomplished, in part, by freely mixing regional styles, thereby relaying a unified image of Norwegian heritage in lieu of a more complex representation of regional variations. Lysne also often used colored backgrounds, rarely seen in Norway but preferred by American consumers.[5] The popular appeal of this approach is evidenced by the inclusion of rosemaling patterns in *The American Home* magazine

PIVO

in the late 1940s; an illustration of the designs applied to cabinets in a gleaming white kitchen portrayed rosemaling as fitting decoration for the modern American home.[6]

Lysne's most popular product was also his most innovative: smorgasbord plates intended for display (p. 60). Lysne generally decorated them with one of four stock patterns, though each was individualized with detailing. His plates were available in Chicago's Marshall Field's department store, and Lysne also received orders directly from as far away as California. The plates typically featured a Norwegian phrase across the rim, most often *Smørgaasbordet er nu dækket—Vær saa god!* ("The smorgasbord is now ready—help yourself!").

Though Lysne died in 1947, rosemaling remained popular in the Midwest and beyond throughout the postwar period. However, American rosemalers who came after Lysne returned to traditional regional styles, learning from books, classes, and lectures. The Vesterheim Norwegian-American Museum in Decorah, Iowa, supported this approach, hosting instructors from Norway and holding an annual national competition beginning in 1967. Rosemaling continues to serve as an expression of Norwegian American identity, especially in Lysne's adopted hometown of Stoughton, which hosts a rosemaling competition and exhibition as part of its annual Norwegian heritage festival.

1 Philip Martin, *Rosemaling in the Upper Midwest: A Story of Region and Revival* (Mount Horeb, WI: Wisconsin Folk Museum, 1989), 15.
2 Kristin Margaret Anderson, "Per Lysne: Immigrant Rosemaler" (master's thesis, University of Minnesota, 1985), 10–14.
3 United Press International, "Man Is Expert at 'Rosemaling'," May 1933; Allen Eaton and Lucinda Crile, *Rural Handicrafts in the United States* (Washington, DC: U.S. Department of Agriculture, 1946), 30; United Press International, "Lunt-Fontanne Home Has Norwegian Art," June and July 1936.
4 Severa Boylen, "Rosemaling in Wisconsin," *School Arts* 47, no. 7 (1948): 223.
5 Bjarne Romnes, "Rosemaling in America," *Sons of Norway* 50, no. 3 (March 1956): 48.
6 "Authentic Norwegian," *The American Home* 40, no. 6 (1948): 128.

WEAVING A BRIDGE ACROSS THE ATLANTIC

Frida Hansen and Berthea Aske Bergh

HANNAH PIVO

In 1929, a Brooklyn newspaper proclaimed, "The Vikings are again in possession of the seas, woolen seas, of vegetable dyed blue—they sail their sturdy ships on legendary tapestries."[1] This association between ancient Norse history and modern Norwegian tapestry was made often in the first half of the twentieth century as works by Norwegian weaver Frida Hansen were exhibited widely in the United States, thanks to the efforts of Norwegian American immigrant Berthea Aske Bergh.

In her own country, Hansen's work was framed differently. Though credited with reviving medieval tapestry weaving, she was also seen as a remarkable innovator who ran her own studio in Oslo, developed new techniques for dyeing and weaving, and departed from tradition by infusing Norwegian weaving techniques with Art Nouveau aesthetics.[2]

Hansen's work was first shown in the United States at the 1893 World's Columbian Exposition in Chicago, but had

its greatest impact on American design culture when Bergh acquired several of her weavings and began exhibiting them in the mid-1920s.[3] Bergh (like Hansen) was born in Stavanger, Norway, and arrived in the United States in 1886 at age nineteen. She soon married fellow Norwegian immigrant John Bergh, and the couple eventually settled in New York. Bergh returned to Norway on several occasions, meeting and possibly studying with Hansen.[4] Bergh ultimately became the primary authority on Norwegian weaving in the United States, lecturing, instructing, and creating many tapestries of her own.

In 1915, Bergh arranged a display of Hansen's work at the Carnegie Institute in Pittsburgh, including *Sommernattsdrøm* (Summer Night's Dream) (p. 63).[5] This weaving employed her inventive "transparents" technique (patented in 1897), which incorporated unwoven areas to create a sense of transparency and lightness; it was also Hansen's first design to rely heavily on silver

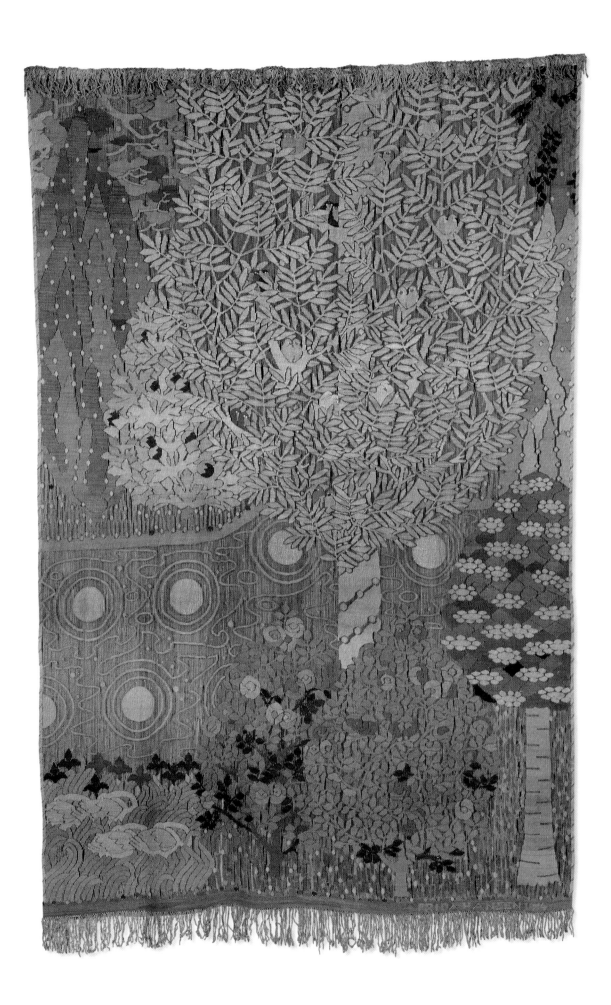

thread, which imparted a mystical quality to the nocturne scene.[6] Bergh's collection of Norwegian tapestries was regularly shown at the annual Women's Exposition of Arts and Industries in New York.[7] Hansen's *Sørover* (Southward) tapestry, picturing seven Norse goddesses sailing on swans, met with particular acclaim. In 1925, it was exhibited at the Norse-American Centennial at the Minnesota State Fairgrounds (right), and was illustrated in *House Beautiful* in 1929.[8]

Also in 1929, Bergh became founding director of The Weavers, an organization dedicated to distributing Norwegian handicraft in the United States. Though various wares were stocked, tapestry remained central to the organization's activities. As Bergh described, "the women of Norway are weaving a bridge, a fantastical bridge you may call it, from the Norse country to reach over to the women of America."[9] Bergh herself had laid the foundations of that bridge, introducing Hansen's work—and Norwegian weaving more broadly—to a new American audience.

1 "Vikings Still Sail the Seas on Legendary Tapestries at Women's Art Exposition," *Brooklyn Daily Eagle*, October 5, 1929.
2 Hanne Beate Ueland, ed., *Frida Hansen: Art Nouveau i full blomst* (Stavanger, Norway: Stavanger Kunstmuseum, 2015).
3 *Catalog of the Exhibit of Norway at the World's Columbian Exposition, Chicago, 1893* (Chicago: John Anderson Publishing, 1893), 56, 83.
4 Newspapers present conflicting accounts of Bergh's relationship to Hansen; she may have studied with Hansen as a girl in Stavanger or as a young woman visiting from the United States, or perhaps Bergh simply consulted Hansen as she built her collection.
5 "Exhibit Tapestries of Famous Weaver," *Pittsburgh Daily Post*, January 13, 1915.
6 Ueland, *Frida Hansen*, 70.
7 "Women's Institute Opens Exposition," *New York Times*, October 28, 1941.
8 *Norse-American Centennial: Catalog of Exhibits Exclusive of Fine Arts* (St. Paul, MN: n.p., 1925); Miriam Ott Munson, "An Old Art for the New World," *House Beautiful* 66, no. 1 (July 1929): 42.
9 V. A. Maura, "Brings Vivid Norse Art," *Brooklyn Daily Eagle*, December 29, 1929.

PIVO

64

SELLING THE SCANDINAVIAN DREAM

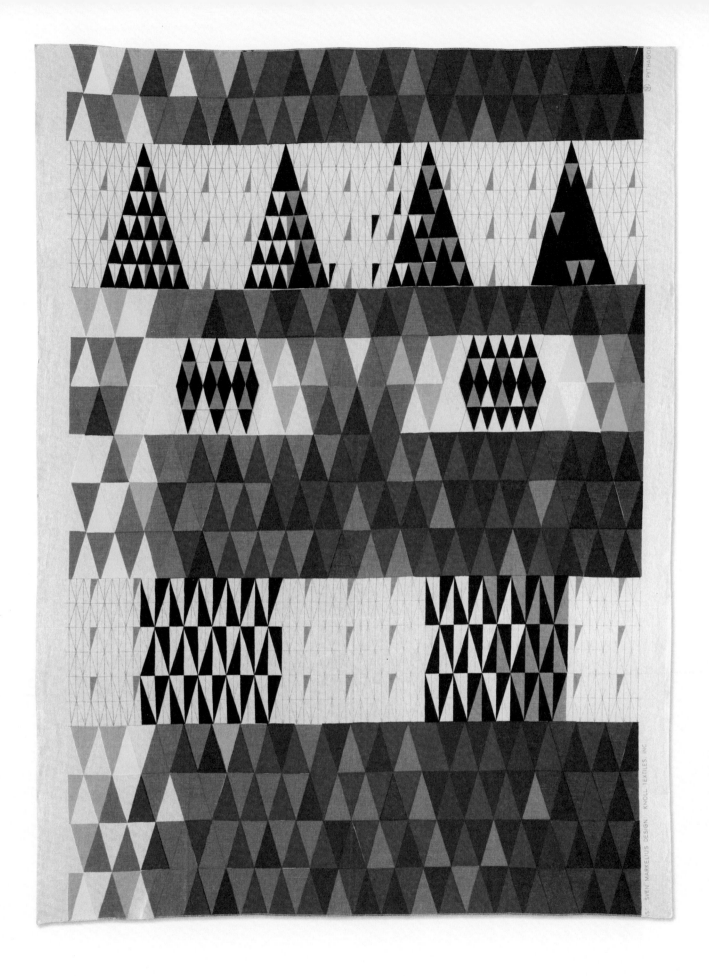

MONICA
OBNISKI

SELLING THE SCANDINAVIAN DREAM   Since at least the mid-twentieth century, Americans have associated Scandinavian design with such adjectives as "honest," "organic," and "handcrafted." Goods were sold to American consumers by evoking a constructed "Scandinavian dream" that paralleled the mythic "American dream," linking the ownership of such objects with comfortable, modern living. In the United States, Scandinavian design also benefitted from the expansion of leisure time and air travel during the mid-twentieth century. Fundamentally, consumption shaped American postwar society, and the American dream was founded on consumer capitalism and class mobility.[1] For many Americans, including those who read magazines like *House Beautiful*, these goods were sold as aspirational and indicative of middle-class values, reinforcing the relationship between purchasing power and specific principles. Through their selection of goods and advertising, retailers like Design Research helped forge the "recognized truth that Scandinavian design has become so much a fact of American life as to be nearly synonymous."[2] For Americans, who were usually bound by individualistic expression as opposed to a more collective social model present in the Nordic countries, the qualities associated with Scandinavian design were nonetheless appealing because they resonated with progressive ideals of freedom and democracy that were promoted after World War II. The Nordic countries were allied with the U.S. on many fronts, including the belief that we can consume our way into a better (designed) world—that is, until the turbulent late 1960s challenged social norms, calling into question the selling of a Scandinavian dream.

Scandinavian firms began to sell modern design to Americans in the early twentieth century; these objects were often depicted as luxurious and exclusive. Georg Jensen silver became the first sustained retail venture when Frederik Lunning, a successful salesman in the Copenhagen Georg Jensen shop since 1918, brought his business acumen to the American market, appealing to a desire for quality craftsmanship. Lunning opened his New York City shop in 1924, and moved to a prestigious address on Fifth Avenue in 1935.[3] Holding the exclusive right to sell Georg Jensen in the United States, he purveyed silver and jewelry alongside other Danish decorative arts.[4] In 1929, Beatrice Winser, acting director of the Newark Museum, bought two pieces of jewelry and four pieces of hollowware from Lunning's shop, including a silver and labradorite necklace designed by Jensen himself (p. 68).[5] Lunning was not the only agent working to persuade the American market to buy Scandinavian products at this time; in New York, J. H. Venon, Inc.

GEORG JENSEN
Georg Jensen Silversmithy
Necklace, designed 1904. CAT. 68

promoted Swedish glass and Sigfrid K. Lonegren introduced Swedish wallpaper, while the Swedish Arts and Crafts Company was active in Chicago for some years.[6] The shop Sweden House, Inc. opened in Rockefeller Center in 1934, importing Swedish goods such as Bruno Mathsson's work chair, which was advertised as possessing "luxurious ease" (cat. 103).[7]

Some consumers looked for alternatives to mass-produced objects that suggested high quality, craftsmanship, and individuality. In response, Scandinavian craftspeople, manufacturers, and retailers engaged several stereotypes and myths that persist today in marketing their goods—namely that these objects were tied to Nordic history and made by hand using natural materials, and that they achieved comfort through organic form. While in the early twentieth century many Americans associated the Nordic nations with Viking Revival style, the marketing of Scandinavian design soon adopted the rhetoric of organicism, comfort, and tempered modernity. This can be seen in an advertisement for the DUX furniture firm, which imported Scandinavian furniture and manufactured designs for the U.S. market, and offered "distinguished designs handcrafted to famous perfection" (p. 70).

By midcentury, there were countless options for buying Scandinavian goods in the U.S. Zacho in Los Angeles, Cargoes in San Francisco, and Frank Bros. in Long Beach offered a broad array of products for California consumers, while in the Midwest several architects opened shops, including Contemporary Backgrounds in Detroit and Baldwin Kingrey in Chicago.[8] In New York, Bonniers (owned by the Swedish publishing firm) was a venue for books, periodicals, and imported Nordic home goods.[9] Finland House sold Finnish crafts and design, including Paavo Tynell's captivating lighting fixtures.[10] Tynell's chandelier resembles a fountain, featuring slim brass branches that spray from a central core with stylized shimmering snowflakes on the ends (p. 70). Critics hoped that Tynell's remarkable designs would inspire American lighting designers to create more original fixtures.[11]

Norway, too, desired to enter the U.S. market. Conceived by Per Tannum when he traveled to Chicago for a trade fair in 1950, Norway Designs for Living was a business endeavor by Tannum and Torolf Prytz, Jr. (the fifth-generation head of the jewelry firm J. Tostrup), with support from both the Landsforeningen Norsk Brukskunst (National Association of Norwegian Applied Art) and the Norwegian government. Originating as a selling exhibition in 1951, the organization sought to create a permanent home for Norwegian crafts in Chicago (p. 73). Journalists employed the idealizing terminology surrounding Scandinavian design, noting that the Norwegian material was "good modern… not extreme… more of an impression of warmth."[12] After two successful months in Chicago, Tannum returned to Oslo and formed Norway Designs, Inc.

Advertisement for DUX from *Interiors* magazine, October 1959

PAAVO TYNELL
Taito Oy
Chandelier, designed 1948, this example c. 1953. CAT. 159

MAIJA ISOLA
Marimekko
Unikko **textile**, designed 1964, this example 1965. CAT. 62

OBNISKI

to coordinate marketing and production for Norwegian companies. In 1952, the Norway Designs for Living sales exhibition moved to Minneapolis, and subsequently to Seattle, Washington; Grand Forks, North Dakota; and Moorhead, Minnesota. Ultimately, however, the U.S. market proved too large for Norway's production capacity, and this short-lived export experiment was discontinued.[13]

Shops such as Design Research fared better. Established by architect Ben Thompson in 1953 in Cambridge, Massachusetts, the store offered a colorful range of objects, including Scandinavian design, in service of good taste and better contemporary living for all.[14] Significantly, it was the first U.S. retailer to carry the Finnish clothing brand Marimekko. Thompson's colleagues, the architects Robert and Margaret Eskridge, became friends with Marimekko's founder Armi Ratia while on a Fulbright to Finland in 1957–58. Upon their return, they showed Thompson several Marimekko dresses, which he included in a Finnish design exhibition at the shop.[15] Afterward, Design Research introduced Marimekko's colorful hand-printed textiles and loose-fitting dresses to its inventory in September 1959, helping to popularize patterns like *Unikko,* in which enormous, brightly colored graphic poppies dominate a white ground (p. 71).[16] Success in the U.S. was guaranteed when Jacqueline Kennedy appeared on the December 26, 1960 cover of *Sports Illustrated* wearing one of the unconventional Finnish dresses (p. 18). Despite its iconic status today, Marimekko was radical at the time, with dresses cut in simple shapes to accommodate all body types and to encourage freedom and mobility.

Aside from the varied success and failure of these endeavors, it was the marketing and retailing surrounding the touring exhibition *Design in Scandinavia* (1954–57) that cemented national appeal for Scandinavian design in the United States. The project was a concerted effort of Nordic cooperation, with the various participating nations coordinating publicity. Additionally, it was embraced by U.S. partners; Leslie Cheek, Jr., director of the Virginia Museum of Fine Arts (VMFA) in Richmond and coordinator of the American committee of the exhibition, believed that it would have "an enormous influence on the taste of the American public."[17] *Design in Scandinavia* was closely tied to commercial interests of department stores and design shops, with related retail exhibits planned to stimulate sales. For example, the front window of Richmond department store Thalhimers featured the exhibition's logo—a hand-painted rendering of Tapio Wirkkala's leaf tray—along with objects that could be seen at the museum, forging an explicit connection between culture and commerce (p. 73).

While *Design in Scandinavia* was staged at the Brooklyn Museum, the New York City shop Georg Jensen, Inc. mounted *Scandinavian Design in Use,* a series of related exhibitions that included objects featured in the museum display, such as Herbert Krenchel's *Krenit* bowls (p. 75). The store also sponsored

Installation view of Norway Designs
for Living, Chicago, Illinois, 1951

Design in Scandinavia promotion
at Thalhimers department store,
Richmond, Virginia, 1954

Scandinavian design through the Lunning Prize, a five-thousand-dollar award for young Scandinavian designers to study abroad, inaugurated by the company's owner Frederik Lunning in 1951. By exhibiting the award winners' work at the shop, the prize also promoted Scandinavian design in the United States. Many prominent designers, including Ingrid Dessau, Grete Prytz Korsmo, Hans Wegner, and Tapio Wirkkala, were recipients.

Further demonstrating Nordic cooperation, the Scandinavian Design Cavalcade began in 1955 as a coordinated series of museum exhibitions, store displays, tours, and other programs in Denmark, Finland, Norway, and Sweden to encourage American tourists to buy Scandinavian design.[18] Copenhagen was a key destination; as Ib Antoni's poster declares, Denmark was "Famous for Fine Furniture" (p. 21). The "most rewarding single showplace for the traveler" was Den Permanente, the premier outlet for Danish design in the mid-twentieth century, which supported both Danish design specifically and the Scandinavian Design Cavalcade more generally.[19] As a result of generous export laws, many Americans visited the Scandinavian countries and brought home souvenirs of their travels, such as Kay Bojesen's wooden toy monkeys, which were aimed at developing creativity and were among Den Permanente's most popular objects (p. 76).[20] These and other Scandinavian designs for children were also exported widely to the United States.

Iceland was not part of the broader Scandinavian marketing coalition in the 1950s, but it benefited from the goodwill that *Design in Scandinavia* engendered. Opened in New York City in 1965, the Icelandic Arts and Crafts shop was the country's first sales effort in the U.S.[21] Iceland's reputation for excellence in ceramics was forged through exhibitions such as *The Eighth International Exhibition of Ceramic Art* in 1961 at the Smithsonian Institution. Journalists emphasized how the country's volcanic landscape was evoked by the handmade quality of Icelandic ceramics, a familiar rhetorical trope of Scandinavian design.[22]

By that time, although Norway continued to export design, such as enamelwork and Luxo lamps, a new endeavor was formed. After Norway Designs for Living folded, Tannum found other ways to promote his country's craft and design in the U.S.; in 1958, he helped found the artists' colony PLUS (officially known as the Craftsmen's National Association of Norway) in Fredrikstad, outside of Oslo.[23] PLUS glassware, ceramics, silver, and textiles were sold at several American galleries and stores, including Carson Pirie Scott & Company in Chicago.[24]

As Scandinavian design gained in popularity stateside, many American manufacturers and makers contributed to the creation of a stereotypical "Scandinavian style," producing objects that suggested Scandinavia in their formal characteristics and marketing them in ways consistent with the ideals of modernity, organic form, and comfort. Sometimes a Scandinavian

KAY BOJESEN
Monkey toys, designed 1951,
these examples 1955. CAT. 16

76

OBNISKI

designer was involved in producing these goods, but the mere choice of name for the product was often enough to make the connection for the public. Scandinavian furniture—especially that from Denmark, which had the largest furniture export economy—made an indelible mark on U.S. furniture production, with American manufacturers quickly seizing the opportunity to manufacture so-called Scandinavian design locally.[25] In September 1950, Danish designer Finn Juhl visited Grand Rapids, Michigan, to discuss a new modern line with Hollis S. Baker, president of Baker Furniture. Baker had been impressed by Juhl's work in a 1949 *Interiors* magazine and, after visiting his Copenhagen studio in 1950, invited the designer to create a furnishings line suitable for Americans (p. 78).[26] Though Baker maintained that the furniture should not be artificially styled, he certainly desired to capitalize on it to some degree, as Danish modern was gaining currency as a brand that signified hand-craftedness, simplicity, and democracy.[27] With their design pedigree, Baker's offerings did not need to resort to the usual marketing rhetoric: alongside the furniture, the advertisements simply noted: "Designed by Finn Juhl."

THIS IS
DANSK
For living in today's world with color, taste and basic simplicity.

Advertisement for Dansk Designs, c. 1958

OBNISKI

For many Americans, the housewares company Dansk was the epitome of Scandinavian design, to the point that many did not realize it was technically an American company. In 1954, New York entrepreneur Ted Nierenberg established the firm and introduced flatware by the Dane Jens Quistgaard, followed by a line of tableware. Through extensive advertising (p. 77), Dansk exploited popular notions of Scandinavian design—that it was colorful, simple, and tasteful. Other products from American companies, such as Philco Predicta's *Danish Modern* television and Heywood-Wakefield's *Swedish Modern* line of furniture, took advantage of Scandinavian associations without any true connection. Similarly, Anchor Hocking Glass Corporation of Lancaster, Ohio, made a set of turquoise nested *Swedish Modern* glass bowls that traded on associations of beauty and convenience connected to Swedish goods, but which had no authentic link to Sweden (below).[28]

The marketing of Scandinavian design made claims about its modern, organic, and handcrafted qualities, but these stereotypes reflect American taste more than the heterogeneous nature of the subject. These explicit constructions did not accurately indicate the broader range of design produced in the Nordic countries, as many were mass-produced in factories and combined aspects of tradition and modernity in their design and fabrication. Only recently have scholars worked to redress the imbalances in the narrative of Scandinavian design by considering a wider range of objects and more diverse perspectives.[29]

ANCHOR HOCKING GLASS CORPORATION
Swedish Modern **mixing bowls,**
designed c. 1957. CAT. 3

1 Lizabeth Cohen, *A Consumers' Republic: The Politics of Mass Consumption in Postwar America* (New York: Knopf, 2003).

2 "Finnish Exhibition in Cambridge," *Interiors* 119 (August 1959): 14.

3 "Manufacturing Firm Leases on West Side," *New York Times,* May 16, 1935.

4 Susan Weber Soros, "Building an International Reputation: The Georg Jensen Phenomenon in the United States, 1915–1973," in *Georg Jensen Jewelry*, exh. cat., ed. David A. Taylor (New Haven and London: Yale University Press, 2005), 107.

5 Ulysses Grant Dietz, "Ahead of the Curve: The Newark Museum Now and Then," *The Magazine Antiques*, January 16, 2015, http://www .themagazineantiques.com/article /ahead-of-the-curve-newark-museum/.

6 Robert Hessby, "The American Market for Swedish Industrial Art," *American Swedish Monthly,* March 1935, 15.

7 "New Swedish Firm Rents in Midtown," *New York Times*, April 25, 1934; Sweden House advertisement, *American Swedish Monthly*, August 1940, 23.

8 Cara Mullio and Jennifer M. Volland, *Frank Bros.: The Store That Modernized Modern*, exh. cat. (London: Black Dog Publishing, 2017); John Brunetti, *Baldwin Kingrey: Midcentury Modern in Chicago, 1947–1957* (Chicago: Wright, 2004).

9 "Scandinavia in New York," *Interiors* 108 (June 1949): 78–87.

10 The Finnish-American Trading Company operated a restaurant and store on the ground floor and a trade organization on the second floor; "Remodel Two Homes: Finnish Interests Occupying Space on 50th Street," *New York Times,* August 25, 1948.

11 Lois Wagner, "Light and Shadow— for Function and for Fun," *Interiors* 114 (February 1955): 110–11; Dan Cooper, "Interiors: An Opportunity for Craftsmen," *Craft Horizons* 8, no. 22 (August 1948): 14–15.

12 Anne Douglas, "Norway Shows City Her Finest in Furnishings," *Chicago Tribune*, May 27, 1951.

13 Kjetil Fallan, "Love and Hate in Industrial Design: Europe's Design Professionals and America in the 1950s," in *The Making of European Consumption: Facing the American Challenge*, ed. Per Lundin and Thomas Kaiserfeld (Basingstoke, UK: Palgrave Macmillan, 2015), 134–56.

14 "Craftsman's Choice," *Architectural Forum* 111 (September 1959): 139.

15 Jane Thompson and Alexandra Lange, "A 'Uniform for Intellectuals': Marimekko Arrives," in *Design Research: The Store That Brought Modern Living to American Homes* (San Francisco: Chronicle Books, 2010), 76.

16 Thompson and Lange, "Experiencing the Store," in *Design Research*, 61.

17 "Scandinavia: Tableware Design Is a Natural Resource," *Crockery and Glass Journal*, March 4, 1954, 35.

18 Louise Sloane, "Scandinavian Design Cavalcade," *Progressive Architecture* 37 (April 1956): 147–53.

19 Mitchell Goodman, "An All-Scandinavia Show: Designers Plan to Open Shops to Tourists This Summer," *New York Times*, April 22, 1956.

20 Jean A. Givens, "Craft, Commerce and Den Permanente," *Design and Culture* 7, no. 3 (2015): 335–56; Robert Shaplen, "Letter from Copenhagen," *New Yorker*, May 18, 1957, 145.

21 "Market Spotlight," *Interior Design*, January 1965, 27.

22 "Glit Ceramics of Iceland," *Harper's Bazaar*, September 1965, 343.

23 It was called PLUS because the logo is a plus sign; *Et PLUS i Norsk Designhistorie: Brukskunstorganisasjonen PLUS 1958–1978*, exh. cat., ed. Marianne Yvenes et al. (Oslo: Nasjonalmuseet in collaboration with the Fredrikstad Museum, 2008).

24 "Calendar of Events," *Chicago Tribune*, May 2, 1966.

25 Kevin Davies, "Markets, Marketing and Design: The Danish Furniture Industry c. 1947–65," *Scandinavian Journal of Design History* 9 (1999): 56–73.

26 "Baker Modern Furniture by Finn Juhl Is Introduced in Dramatic Showing," *Baker Bugle and Market Journal* 7 (January 1951): 1, 206/16/1, Baker Furniture Company Collection, History and Special Collections, Grand Rapids Public Library, Grand Rapids, MI.

27 Per H. Hansen, "Cobranding Product and Nation: Danish Modern Furniture and Denmark in the United States, 1940–1970," in *Trademarks, Brands, and Competitiveness*, ed. Teresa da Silva Lopes and Paul Duguid (New York: Routledge, 2010), 77–101.

28 Jeff Werner, "What Was So Swedish about Swedish Modern?," in *Mind and Matter: Selected Papers of Nordik 2009 Conference for Art Historians*, ed. Johanna Vakkari (Helsinki: Taidehistorian seura, 2010), 199–215.

29 For example, *Scandinavian Design: Alternative Histories*, ed. Kjetil Fallan (London: Berg, 2012); Lasse Brunnström, *Swedish Design: A History* (London: Bloomsbury Visual Arts, 2018); and *Scandinavian Design beyond the Myth: Fifty Years of Design from the Nordic Countries*, exh. cat., ed. Widar Halén and Kerstin Wickman (Stockholm: Arvinius, 2003).

Dragons in America

GRAHAM C. BOETTCHER

In the late 1830s, a scattershot movement emerged in the United States with the goal of crediting the Viking explorer Leif Eriksson as America's "true discoverer."[1] In 1000 CE, "Leif the Lucky" is believed to have explored and briefly settled the grape-rich terrain he called Vinland, the area around the Gulf of St. Lawrence in eastern Canada. Advocates of Viking discovery were bolstered by purported archaeological evidence, such as the Old Stone Mill of Newport, Rhode Island, believed by some to be an ancient Norse structure; Dighton Rock, a four-hundred-ton boulder inscribed with strange markings resembling Norse runes, originally located in the Taunton River at Berkley, Massachusetts; and the 1831 discovery of skeletal remains with remnants of copper ornaments near Fall River, Massachusetts, immortalized in Henry Wadsworth Longfellow's 1841 poem, "The Skeleton in Armor."[2] Among the movement's earliest proponents was Asahel Davis, a self-proclaimed historian who beginning in the late 1830s traveled the East Coast delivering "A Lecture on the Discovery of America by the Northmen Five Hundred Years before Columbus." Davis's work seems to have resonated with the American public; first published in 1838, by 1854, it was in its thirtieth edition.[3] In 1877, Rasmus B. Anderson, a professor of Scandinavian languages and literature at the University of Wisconsin, published his emphatically titled *America Not Discovered by Columbus*, in which he entreated, "Let us remember Leif Erikson, the first white man who planted his feet on American soil!... Let us erect a monument to Leif Erikson worthy of the man and the cause."[4] On October 29, 1887, a group of Bostonians did exactly that, dedicating sculptor Anne Whitney's monument to Leif Eriksson—an eight-and-a-half-foot-tall idealized bronze likeness atop a nine-foot-high sandstone base resembling a Viking ship—at the end of Commonwealth Avenue (right).

Statue of Leif Eriksson, sculpted by Anne Whitney and erected on Commonwealth Avenue, Boston, 1887. Photographed c. 1887–95

For Boston's Brahmins—the aristocratic scions of the city's prominent Protestant families—Eriksson provided a foil to Columbus, who had been embraced as a hero by Roman Catholics, particularly recent Italian and Irish immigrants. In 1878, the *Connecticut Catholic* ran an editorial declaring, "As American Catholics we do not know of anyone who more deserves our grateful remembrance than the great and noble man—the pious, zealous, faithful Catholic, the enterprising navigator, and the large-hearted and generous sailor: Christopher Columbus."[5] In 1882, an Irish American Catholic priest organized the Knights of Columbus, today the world's largest Catholic fraternal organization. While Boston Brahmins stopped short of organizing the "Knights of Eriksson," the zeal with which they sought to commemorate the Viking explorer is revealing. For Brahmins, Eriksson was an adopted ancestor. Embodying qualities of strength, industriousness, and curiosity, the Viking explorer could effectively be celebrated as the prototypical Yankee, thereby permitting Boston's Protestant Anglo-Saxon ruling class to connect themselves with America's discovery nearly five hundred years before the Italian Catholic Christopher Columbus ever set sail. As art historian Janet Headley has observed, "This reading thinly disguised ethnic tensions and unease with the waves of new immigrants arriving in late-nineteenth-century Boston."[6]

Among Boston's elite, Eriksson had no greater champion than Eben Norton Horsford, a Harvard chemistry professor famous for the invention of double-acting baking powder. An earlier effort to erect the Eriksson monument had faltered, but was revived in the 1880s thanks to Horsford, who authored seven books promoting Eriksson as America's true discoverer, claiming "Norumbega" (present-day Cambridge, Massachusetts) as Viking America's first great settlement.[7] On November 15, 1887, two weeks following the dedication of Boston's Eriksson monument, a replica of the sculpture with a more modest base was erected in Milwaukee's Juneau Park in the middle of the night at the request of the publicity-shy donor Mrs. Joseph T. Gilbert. Dubbed the "Norse Columbus" by the *Weekly Wisconsin*, the sculpture became a locus of pride and identity for Wisconsin's burgeoning community of Scandinavian immigrants.[8]

Whitney's sculpture touched off a brief but intense Viking moment in American fine and decorative arts, typically referred to as the Viking or Norse Revival. The profusion of Viking imagery likely carried varying associations depending upon the beholder. For those who ascribed to the teachings of Horsford, such motifs may have constituted a colonial revival of sorts. For Scandinavian immigrants, Viking decoration probably stirred feelings of ethnic pride. For still others, the Norse idiom may have simply been one among many revival styles popular in the late nineteenth and early twentieth centuries. Influenced by late nineteenth-century Scandinavian design in the traditional *dragestil* ("dragon style")—so called because of the predominance of dragon motifs—the Viking Revival in the United States found its primary expression in silver, ceramics, and furniture.[9] The movement's apex coincided with the 1893 World's Columbian Exposition, which served as an unofficial showdown between factions on both sides of the discovery debate; a cartoon by Charles W. Saalburg published during the fair entitled "Who Did Discover America?" depicted Eriksson and Columbus duking it out in a boxing match refereed by Lady Chicago, who asks, "Gentlemen, you are now in your 401st round. How long is this controversy going to last?"[10] (p. 83).

Charles W. Saalburg, "Who Did Discover America?," *Inter-Ocean Illustrated Supplement*, July 30, 1893

WHO DID DISCOVER AMERICA?

Chicago to Discoverers Columbus and Ericson—Gentlemen, you are now on your quest round. How long is this controversy going to last?

Some works exhibited at the exposition seemed to stoke the controversy. A full-size bronzed plaster replica of Whitney's statue was prominently shown alongside maps drawn by Eben Horsford at the Norway Building, a sixty-by-twenty-five-foot facsimile of a twelfth-century *stavkirke* (stave church) constructed of Norway pine (p. 142).[11] William Walton, a chronicler of the Columbian Exposition, commented that Norway's exhibit in the Fine Arts Building was "perhaps the most eminently national in its characteristics."[12] At the center of the exhibit was a nine-by-eighteen-foot canvas by Realist painter Christian Krohg entitled *Leif Ericksson Discovers America*. By far the most noted Norwegian contribution to the exposition, however, was the *Viking*, a replica of the Gokstad ship, a ninth-century Viking vessel discovered in a burial mound in Norway in

1880. The *Viking* sailed from Bergen to Chicago for the exposition, where it remained throughout the fair, providing a spectacular counterpoint to the replicas of Columbus's three caravels contributed by Spain (p. 15). The *Viking*, noted Walton, "represent[ed] with suitable dignity the nation that maintains, amidst this Columbian Exposition, a prior claim to the discovery of America."[13]

On July 17, 1893, the *Viking*'s crew was celebrated with a dinner at Chicago's Mecca Hotel, hosted by the Society de Sancto-Claro, professed descendants of Rollo, the Viking who became the first Duke of Normandy in 911 CE.[14] For the occasion, the Milwaukee ceramist Susan Stuart Frackelton was commissioned to create thirteen loving cups, which were used in ceremonial drinking rites during the banquet, then gifted as keepsakes to attending dignitaries, including the *Viking*'s captain, Magnus Anderson. Only one of the cups has been located (p. 84). On one side, its incised decorations include a Viking ship and the names of various Viking explorers and the dates of their voyages to North America. The other side is decorated with thirteen shields and three dragons encircling a symbol for the Norse god Odin. A poem surrouding the cartouche reads: *Slaves cannot drink from me—/If once their lips receive my wine/That moment they are free!/They drink God's bounty—/And their shackles fall!*, while the inscription below the spout declares *Skald* ("praise") *to the Viking*. That same month, Frackelton—perhaps wishing to remain impartial—also presented a loving cup to Captain Concas, the Spanish commander of the replicas of Columbus's ships.[15]

Among the most striking manifestations of the Viking style at the fair was Tiffany & Company's *Viking* punch bowl, designed by Paulding Farnham and exhibited in the Manufactures and Liberal Arts Building (p. 85). The eight-handled iron bowl inlaid with gold and silver has a rim embellished with finials inspired by the prow of a Viking ship. Tiffany exhibited several other pieces fashioned in the "Viking style," including a second punch bowl; a sixteen-piece silver library set encrusted with lapis lazuli with a sealskin blotter; a coffeepot inset with Labrador spar; and a sealskin belt with a chased gold buckle.[16] While the Viking style was one of many that Farnham employed, its use demonstrated the prominence of Norse imagery in the American imagination in the late nineteenth century. The

SUSAN STUART FRACKELTON
Viking Loving Cup, 1893. Salt-glazed
stoneware, 11 ½ × 8 ¾ × 8 in.
(29.2 × 22.2 × 20.3 cm). Leeds Art
Foundation

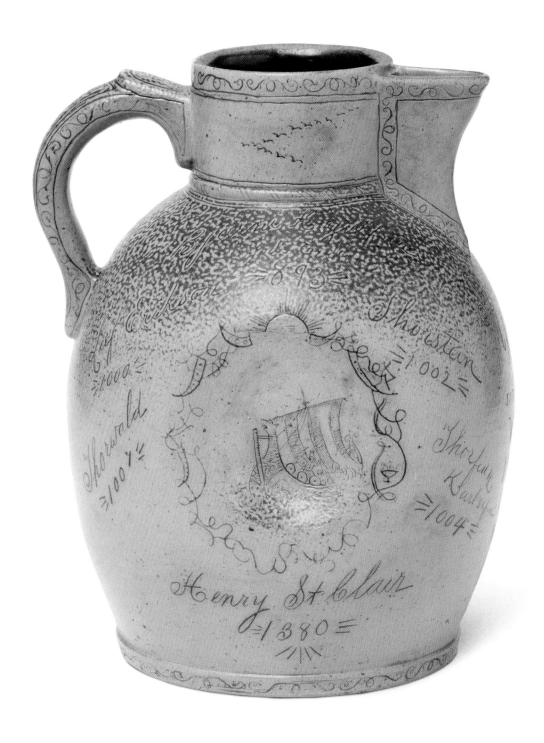

KARL VON RYDINGSVÄRD
Armchair, c. 1905. CAT. 131

PAULDING FARNHAM
Tiffany & Co. (maker)
Dressing table and chair, 1903–4.
Silver, narwhal ivory, mahogany; table:
75 × 38 × 20 in. (190.5 × 96.5 × 50.8 cm);
chair: 47 × 19 ½ × 19 in.
(119.4 × 49.5 × 48.3 cm). Maymont
House Museum, Richmond, Virginia

punch bowl even attracted international attention, noted as a "beautiful and effective work" in a Danish report of the fair.[17]

While it is uncertain the extent to which the Scandinavian *dragestil*—a concurrent movement in Scandinavian decorative arts with nationalist overtones—influenced Farnham's designs, he likely encountered the Viking-inspired work of Norwegian silversmiths when he attended the opening of the Exposition Universelle in Paris in May 1889. Owing to the success of the *Viking* punch bowl, he designed additional pieces in this style, which Tiffany exhibited at the 1901 Pan-American Exposition in Buffalo and the 1902 International Exposition of Modern Decorative Arts in Turin (cat. 35).[18] Farnham's most elaborate achievement in the Viking fashion was his extraordinary silver and narwhal tusk vanity and chair, embellished with dragon's-head finials and accompanied by a twenty-two-piece Viking-style toilette set fashioned of silver and narwhal ivory (p. 86). Designed and manufactured between 1903 and 1904, the elaborate ensemble may have been exhibited at the 1904 Louisiana Purchase Exposition in St. Louis before being purchased by a prominent family in Richmond, Virginia.[19] Literary critic Annette Kolodny has noted that Farnham's narwhal tusk chair recalls a passage in Herman Melville's *Moby-Dick*, in which Captain Ahab is likened to royalty

as he sits on an ivory stool: "In old Norse times, the thrones of the sea-loving Danish kings were fabricated, saith tradition, of the tusks of the narwhale."[20] In the case of Farnham's dressing table and chair, the unusual materials and Norse design may have made its owner feel like a Viking queen. For those without the means to live like Norse royalty, the Gorham Manufacturing Company of Providence, Rhode Island, offered consumers a more affordable expression of the idiom in the form of a *Viking Boat Centerpiece* (below). Originally manufactured by Durgin, which became a division of Gorham in 1905, the silver ship with dragon-head prows and applied shields was sometimes part of a three-piece garniture, accompanied by two smaller ships made of pressed glass with applied silver ornaments.

After 1900, the leading American practitioner of the Viking style was Swedish-born, Philadelphia-based master carver and furniture maker Karl von Rydingsvärd. Unlike Frackelton and Farnham, who claimed no Scandinavian origins, for Rydingsvärd, the Viking style was an expression of his native heritage. Though he worked in several revival styles, including Gothic and Tudor, his carved bas-relief panels and sturdy wooden furniture depicting Viking sagas and embellished with dragons, coiling bands, and knotwork received the most attention, perhaps because of their connection with Rydingsvärd's own

GORHAM MANUFACTURING COMPANY, DURGIN DIVISION
Viking Boat Centerpiece, designed c. 1905. CAT. 48

BOETTCHER

SCANDIA RESTAURANT
Bjørg Larsen, cover artist
Menu, designed c. 1962. CAT. 188

Scandia

heritage.[21] One armchair, typical of Rydingsvärd's work, has dragon-shaped ears and a splat and arms carved with scenes from the Viking saga of the dragonslayer Sigurd (p. 86).[22] In 1918, one author referred to Rydingsvärd as "a descendant of the Danish Vikings" (he was Swedish) and "of a powerful stature characteristic of his Northern stock," further noting that "the furniture he makes displays great manual force as well as artistic judgment."[23]

The Viking Revival in the United States also made its way into the literary realm, most notably in the work of Ottilie Liljencrantz, the Swedish American author whose Norse-themed novels included titles such as *The Thrall of Leif the Lucky: A Story of Viking Days* (1902) and *Randvar the Songsmith: A Tale of Norumbega* (1906). So successful was her work that in 1928, *The Thrall of Leif the Lucky* was adapted for the first feature-length Technicolor film to feature a soundtrack, entitled *The Viking*.[24] Norse imagery also permeated the pages of the deluxe Christmas annual *Jul i Vesterheimen* (Christmas in the Western Home), published from 1911 to 1957 by Minneapolis's Augsburg Publishing House, which was popular in Norwegian American homes during the holidays. The cover of the 1916 album features a Viking in a winged helmet standing proudly at the prow of his ship (p. 88). Despite the image's questionable relationship with Christmas, Norse themes were popular in the pages of *Jul i Vesterheimen* because "Vikings link Norwegian-Americans to both Norwegian roots and American history and identity," since nineteenth-century American writers "had already helped to popularize the Norsemen as sources of original American character."[25]

While there is no precise end to the Viking Revival, its popularity was waning by the time of the 1925 Norse-American Centennial, which celebrated the one hundredth anniversary of the first organized emigration from Norway on October 9, 1825 (later designated by Congress as Leif Erikson Day). The few Viking Revival pieces made for the occasion employed cheap materials such as spelter (a zinc alloy) or celluloid, a far cry from the glorious goods presented at the World's Columbian Exposition. Nevertheless, Viking motifs persisted well into the twentieth century, often as part of the décor or graphic identity of the large number of Scandinavian restaurants and lounges that sprang up in cities and towns from coast to coast from the late 1940s through the 1960s. Among the most famous of these was Scandia, an upscale Hollywood eatery from 1947 to 1989, whose menu featured such items as the "Viking Sword" (a flaming skewer of turkey, beef, and pork) and the "Crepe of the Amorous Viking" (p. 89). Despite the persistence of Viking motifs in the popular realm, by the mid-twentieth century the style had lost its more serious early associations with the debate over the discovery of America, becoming a playful expression of ethnic pride used by Scandinavian Americans around the country or those wishing to conjure a romantic association with these hardy seafaring explorers of the past.

1 For more on the ongoing debate concerning America's Viking discovery, see Annette Kolodny, *In Search of First Contact: The Vikings of Vinland, the Peoples of the Dawnland, and the Anglo-American Anxiety of Discovery* (Durham, NC: Duke University Press, 2012). See also Geraldine Barnes, *Viking America: The First Millennium* (Cambridge: D. S. Brewer, 2001). On the use of Viking imagery in contemporary culture, see Bobbye Tigerman and Monica Obniski in this volume, 27n30. There are various accepted spellings of Leif the Lucky's surname, including Eriksson, Erikson, and Ericson; I use the first variation here, except in quoted material.

2 Edmund Burke Delabarre, "Recent History of Dighton Rock," in *Transactions 1917–1919*, Publications of the Colonial Society of Massachusetts 20 (Boston: Colonial Society of Massachusetts, 1920), 285–461.

3 Delabarre, "Recent History of Dighton Rock," 321.

4 Rasmus B. Anderson, *America Not Discovered by Columbus: An Historical Sketch of the Discovery of America by the Norsemen in the Tenth Century* (Chicago, 1877), 93.

5 "Christopher Columbus—Discoverer of the New World," *Connecticut Catholic*, no. 3 (May 25, 1878): 4, in Christopher J. Kaufmann, *Faith and Fraternalism: The History of the Knights of Columbus*, rev. ed. (New York: Simon and Schuster, 1992), 17.

6 Janet A. Headley, "Anne Whitney's 'Leif Eriksson': A Brahmin Response to Christopher Columbus," *American Art* 17, no. 2 (Summer 2003): 42.

7 Headley, "Anne Whitney's 'Leif Eriksson,'" 47–48.

8 "The Norse Columbus," *Weekly Wisconsin* (Milwaukee), October 1, 1887.

9 *Dragestil* has been analyzed in Ethan Robey, "Kings, Peasants, Dragons, and Flowers: National Symbolism in Decorative Arts at the World's Fairs," in *Inventing the Modern World: Decorative Arts at the World's Fairs, 1851–1939*, exh. cat., ed. Jason T. Busch and Catherine L. Futter (New York: Skira Rizzoli in association with the Carnegie Museum of Art and Nelson-Atkins Museum of Art, 2012), 179–85; Elisabet Stavenow-Hidemark, "Viking Revival and Art Nouveau: Traditions of Excellence," in *Scandinavian Modern Design 1880–1980*, exh. cat., ed. David Revere McFadden (New York: Abrams in association with the Cooper-Hewitt Museum, Minnesota Museum of Art, and Renwick Gallery, 1982), 47–85; Widar Halén, "The Dragon Style in Norwegian Decoration," *The Magazine Antiques* 152, no. 3 (September 1997): 334–45; and Widar Halén, *Dragons from the North: Norwegian Silver Around 1900 Including an Article on the Neoceltic Art in Ireland*, trans. Virginia Siger, 3rd ed. (Dublin and Bergen, Norway: National Museum and West Norway Museum of Applied Art, 1995).

10 *Inter-Ocean Illustrated Supplement* (Chicago), July 30, 1893.

11 Headley, "Anne Whitney's 'Leif Eriksson,'" 57, 59n27.

12 William Walton, *Art and Architecture*, 3 vols. (Philadelphia, 1893), 2:56.

13 Walton, *Art and Architecture*, 2:56.

14 May Whitney Emerson, "Our Loving Cup," *American Monthly Magazine* 7 (July–December 1895): 134–39.

15 "Lady Managers Receive Capt. Concas," *Chicago Tribune*, August 12, 1893.

16 *Catalogue of Tiffany & Co.'s Exhibit, Manufactures and Liberal Arts Building, World's Columbian Exposition, Chicago, 1893* (New York, 1893), 28, 47, 57, 60.

17 "Fra Udstillingen i Chicago," *Tidsskrift for Kunstindustri* 9 (1893): 199.

18 John Loring, *Paulding Farnham: Tiffany's Lost Genius* (New York: Abrams, 2000), 133, 148.

19 Dale Cyrus Wheary, "Vanity of Vanities: A Tiffany and Company Rediscovery," *The Magazine Antiques* 173, no. 4 (April 2008): 102–3.

20 Herman Melville, *Moby-Dick* (1851), Norton Critical Editions, 2nd ed. (New York: Norton, 2009), 113, quoted in Kolodny, *In Search of First Contact*, 210–11.

21 "Norse Legends Carved in Wood to Decorate Commodore James's Yacht, *Aloha II*," *International Studio* 161 (July 1910): xxi–xxiv.

22 Carrie Hogan, *Flowers & Monsters: Hand-Carved Furniture by Karl von Rydingsvärd*, exh. guide (Philadelphia: American Swedish Historical Museum, 2016), n.p.

23 "Current News and Comment: The National Society of Craftsmen," *Good Furniture: The Magazine of Decoration* 10, no. 1 (January 1918): 22.

24 For an excellent discussion of the film, see Arne Lunde, *Nordic Exposures: Scandinavian Identities in Classical Hollywood Cinema* (Seattle: University of Washington Press, 2010), 16–37.

25 Kristin A. Risley, "Christmas in Our Western Home: The Cultural Work of a Norwegian-American Christmas Annual," *American Periodicals: A Journal of History & Criticism* 13 (2003): 60–62.

Elizabeth Gordon, *House Beautiful,* and the Scandinavian Look

MONICA PENICK

In 1950, Elizabeth Gordon, editor of *House Beautiful* magazine, launched a decade-long effort to promote modern Scandinavian furniture, textiles, and housewares to American consumers as good design for everyday living. She positioned Scandinavian home goods within her larger editorial campaign to shape consumer taste and influence buying habits, suggesting—rather uncritically—that imported designs from Denmark, Finland, Norway, and Sweden could improve the contemporary American home. Gordon argued that Scandinavian designers, unlike many of their modernist counterparts (for example, designers from Germany and the Bauhaus school), prioritized utility *and* beauty, and sought to bring artful and well-crafted goods into the homes of ordinary people. Gordon's advocacy, with its embedded criticism of German modernism, took many forms and engaged multiple media: in just ten years, she published more than thirty editorials and feature articles, edited a dedicated magazine issue (July 1959), and launched two design exhibitions, *The Arts of Daily Living* (1954) and *Design in Scandinavia* (1954–57). Through these efforts, Gordon and *House Beautiful* helped to shape American consumers' understanding and reception of Scandinavian design, and profoundly influenced its surging popularity in the 1950s.

In February 1951, *House Beautiful* published one of its first stories on Scandinavian design: a sixteen-page article titled "If Your Home Is Your Hobby… Take a Trip to Scandinavia." Marion Gough, the magazine's features and textile editor, offered readers a "home-conscious travel guide" carefully compiled during the staff's visits to Copenhagen, Stockholm, and Oslo.[1] Gough was impressed by a "common way of life" that she had observed there, where people were inclined to "live intimately and unself-consciously with good design, to *use* art as well as look at it."[2] This attitude and lifestyle resonated with the magazine's editors; as they "discovered" Scandinavia, they felt they had found a kindred culture. Gough encouraged her audience to travel overseas to experience this culture firsthand, and to bring back some of the "uncommonly lovely things" that accessorized Scandinavian life. She advised *House Beautiful* readers on how to get there, where to stay, where to eat, what to wear, where to shop, and, most importantly, which home goods to buy. For consumers

and connoisseurs of domestic design, the magazine's "what to buy" lists offered an edited (if decidedly biased) selection, with the assurance that these items met the high standards of *House Beautiful*'s trusted and discerning editors.

To illustrate Gough's endorsements, the magazine ran a full-color staged photograph of twenty-nine "home furnishings" (and black-and-white snapshots of more than two dozen other objects) acquired during staff travels (above), complete with a keyed sketch crediting each designer. Only a few of these designers' names would have been familiar to American readers in 1951, such as Swedish glassmaker Orrefors or Swedish designer Bruno Mathsson, but Gough's article provided an introduction to Scandinavian design and an overview of what *House*

Beautiful called (somewhat generically and without regard to regional variations) the "Scandinavian look." It was not unusual for *House Beautiful* to publish staff-tested travel itineraries and shopping guides, but Gough's article carried an embedded critique: the magazine's editors suggested that Americans who were "home-conscious," who sought good design that was useful, beautiful, and current, and who truly wanted to master "the art of good living" would need to look beyond their local markets.[3]

Gordon and her staff led by example, and continued to look abroad for emerging trends in good design. Three months after publishing Gough's article, Gordon traveled to Italy to see the 1951 Milan Triennial. This international design exhibition was a watershed moment for many Scandinavian designers, and their emergent success garnered the attention of *House Beautiful*.[4] Gordon was particularly impressed with the superb quality of what she saw, including Tapio Wirkkala's leaf tray (p. 94). The elegant tray, handcrafted from birch laminate and likened to sculpture, earned Wirkkala a Grand Prix, and subsequently, *House Beautiful*'s designation as "The Most Beautiful Object of 1951." In a January 1952 profile, the magazine praised Wirkkala for his accomplishment: "Here is the marriage between ancient craftsmanship and modern engineering. Here is something lovely as a work of art, as handy as a kitchen stool. Here is simplicity, the eloquence of understatement, the art that knows when to stop. We find the happy blend of beauty with utility, of motion with poise. We see the multiplicity of parts resolved into the unity of the whole. In a larger sense we read how man, the designer and the builder, can work in agreement with the world around him. Not in revolt."[5]

Gordon's visit to the Triennial and the magazine's publication of Wirkkala's leaf tray marked a turning point for *House Beautiful*: afterward, Scandinavian design appeared with more frequency in the magazine's featured content and in its advertisements. With increasing fanfare, Scandinavian design had entered the world stage, and, through *House Beautiful*, the living room of millions of Americans.

Gordon's discoveries in Milan certainly influenced her editorial choices in subsequent years, but the trip proved serendipitous in another way: she met Herman Olof (H.O.) Gummerus. Gummerus was the managing director of the Suomen Taideteollisuusyhdistys (Finnish Society of Crafts and Design), and was involved in promoting design from his

PENICK

home country. Gordon shared her enthusiasm with Gummerus for the work on display at the Triennial, and for the homewares she had seen (and bought) during her trips to Finland, Denmark, Norway, and Sweden. Visiting well into the night (which indicated the energy of the exchange, as Gordon famously never stayed awake past nine o'clock), they devised a potential collaboration: an exhibition of Scandinavian design to travel the United States. Gordon, through *House Beautiful,* offered to sponsor it. Later that year, Gummerus, along with the Swedish designer Elias Svedberg, visited Gordon in New York to put a plan into action. Gordon clearly recognized the potential of a traveling exhibition: it could enhance the reputation of any hosting institution (American museums, for example); it could serve as a "tangible public relations device" for the Scandinavian countries; and, citing the commercial success of Italian design following the *Italy at Work: Her Renaissance in Design Today* (shown at the Brooklyn Museum, and merchandised by Macy's), Gordon believed a successful show could boost the

Scandinavian export business. The idea, though, was larger than *House Beautiful* could support alone. According to Gummerus, Gordon (who had a large professional network) "made a telephone call to Leslie Cheek [Jr.,]: *Design in Scandinavia* was born!"[6]

Cheek, a former *House Beautiful* editor and then-director of the Virginia Museum of Fine Arts in Richmond, would eventually take the lead in organizing the traveling exhibition, but generative conversations and correspondence continued through 1951 and 1954 between Cheek, Gordon, Gummerus, Svedberg, and another of Gordon's colleagues, the Swedish journalist Mac Lindahl.[7] As Gordon's initial concept for a Scandinavian design show evolved into a large-scale, multi-year collaboration between representatives from twenty-four museums and five nations, her involvement tapered. Cheek and Gummerus assumed major roles (Cheek as the exhibition's American coordinator, and Gummerus as part of the Scandinavian Organizing Committee)— but not without acknowledging Gordon's formative influence. Cheek wrote frequently to keep her

DESIGN IN SCANDINAVIA
Tapio Wirkkala, layout and cover
designer
Exhibition catalogue, 1954. CAT. 181

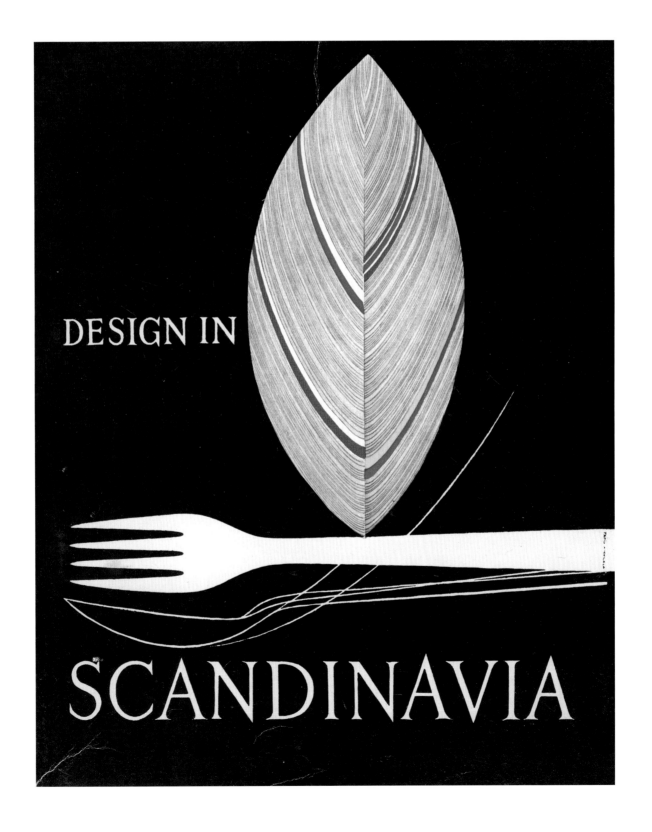

abreast of his progress and sometimes to seek advice, and, before the exhibition opened in 1954, suggested that *House Beautiful* might receive first publication rights (it didn't). Gummerus likewise kept Gordon informed of his activities in Finland, calling her (in 1952) the "spiritual mother of Scandinavian exhibitions."[8]

Design in Scandinavia launched three years later, and though Gordon's name was absent from the exhibition's official credits, her role in initiating the project was indisputable. Cheek, decades later, wrote "thanks to you [Gordon], the American museum world got its first thorough look at design in Scandinavia."[9] Gordon unabashedly claimed credit for the idea, informing *House Beautiful* readers upon the show's opening in 1954 that "we" had "set in motion the great effort" that became *Design in Scandinavia*.[10] The exhibition, with more than seven hundred objects, was indeed a great collaborative effort. Much of the selection and design work came from members of the participating craft and design associations from Denmark, Finland, Norway, and Sweden.[11] Danish architect Erik Herløw designed the traveling installation, which was widely lauded as "ingenious" and elegant.[12] Tapio Wirkkala designed the cover and layout for the catalogue, illustrating it with a rendering of his 1951 leaf tray (p. 95). The show opened at the Virginia Museum of Fine Arts in January 1954, and traveled to twenty-four venues in the United States and Canada before it closed in May 1957.

Design in Scandinavia broke attendance records at several museums, and the total number of visitors at all venues was estimated at 660,000, though its influence was even greater than these numbers suggest: the exhibition was a nationwide event that included not only the static display of designed objects, but also an active program of lectures, films, and merchandising.[13] The organizers—just as Gordon had anticipated in 1951—clearly leveraged the show's commercial potential. In nearly every host city, local stores stocked both mass-produced and handcrafted Scandinavian home goods from the exhibition (p. 73), and the organizers published a directory to indicate where visitors could buy the goods on display.[14] In New York, for example, while the exhibition was on view at the Brooklyn Museum, the Georg Jensen shop organized a thematically linked display, *Scandinavian Design in Use*, and offered many of the objects for sale.[15] This was the first large-scale buying opportunity for Scandinavian goods in the United States, and by all accounts, it was an enormous success.[16]

Local and national press coverage was extensive and positive (if abbreviated), as were reports in popular magazines and professional journals.[17] Most sources printed only short reviews with little critical reflection or editorial stance, but *House Beautiful* emerged as a vocal proponent. Gordon, who never shied from voicing her editorial point of view (on this or any other topic), clearly saw *Design in Scandinavia* as a significant event that would shape the future of American design.[18] In a February 1954 article, written to publicize the exhibition's January opening in Virginia, she suggested that Scandinavian design, although intimately tied to its national origins, could be readily adopted and adapted to fit the American home. In her view, the material qualities and aesthetic characteristics that she observed in Scandinavian domestic crafts aligned well with American values and buying interests.[19] In the four years that preceded *Design in Scandinavia*, she had identified, through quantitative sales data and qualitative observations, increased consumer demand for what she saw in the show: a "shift to naturalism" (a preference for nature-based color palettes, patterns, textures, and materials, first reported in November 1950);[20] a "growing love of soft, rounded flowing forms" (reported in 1952, with illustrations of a Wirkkala plate and a Hans Wegner chair);[21] and a more general interest in "humanism" in design.[22]

A keen observer of *House Beautiful* might have seen Gordon's editorials as boosterish. That there may have been *other* approaches to Scandinavian design, or a "Scandinavian look" that contrasted with what she had identified, seemed to pass without mention. Her strategy was one of careful curation: she selected certain objects and certain designers that told the story she wanted to tell. She rarely wrote or published material that did not fit her definition of good design, but she was well aware of the broad range of contemporary design, and of consumer interest in industrial materials and machine forms (rather than the natural materials and organic forms that she favored). Indeed, this juxtaposition—which Gordon framed as "bad" design versus "good" design—was the subject of great controversy within the American design discourse in the late 1940s and 1950s, and Gordon herself was at the center of the debate.[23]

She may have offered a biased and sometimes limited view, but millions of Americans were swayed by her reporting. Her message, printed without qualification in 1954, must have resonated: "Why are [Scandinavian] home furnishings so well designed and so full of meaning for us? Because they are so well designed and so meaningful for the Scandinavians themselves. Aimed at Scandinavian home life, their designs have a natural beauty and usefulness for our own, for we are both deeply democratic people. Home is their center—and people are the center of their home. Their design is human and warm. Therefore it is personal, national, and universal."[24] This emphasis on the "universal" sidelined any potential criticism of Scandinavian design as "foreign," and therefore inappropriate for American use. This last point was critical for Gordon's credibility: in her April 1953 "Threat to the Next America" article, she had railed against the "imported" International Style as "totalitarian," and advocated instead for "homegrown," regionally sensitive "democratic" designs of figures like Frank Lloyd Wright.[25] In her later reporting, Gordon sidestepped glaring inconsistencies (including the fact that Alvar Aalto had been included in the Museum of Modern Art's genre-defining 1932 International Style exhibition), and argued that the similarities in cultural and political *outlook* made Scandinavian design uniquely compatible with American tastes and lifestyles.[26]

As *Design in Scandinavia* was touring the United States, Gordon launched a *House Beautiful*–sponsored exhibition that explored similar themes of good design for the home. In September 1954, *The Arts of Daily Living* opened at the Los Angeles County Fair in Pomona, California. Gordon, working with Millard Sheets (the fair's Fine Arts director), commissioned architects, designers, artists, and craftspeople to create twenty-two model rooms. Each room was a three-sided stage set, carefully constructed and accessorized to demonstrate what *House Beautiful* described as a "modern way of living" that integrated beautiful and useful objects into everyday life. Two of these vignettes, showcased in the October 1954 print issue of *House Beautiful*, underscored the relevance and influence of Scandinavian design: a Scandinavian American dining alcove and a living room.

The dining alcove incorporated objects imported from Scandinavia alongside American-made furnishings that Gordon claimed were influenced by Scandinavian design (p. 98). For example, in its expansive reporting, the magazine argued that Swedish designer Barbro Nilsson's wall hanging had inspired the design of the rug made by New York–based Edward Fields Co. and that the Hans Wegner chairs and table were "sympathetic to the American-made settee [pictured], thanks to their mutual use of a tapering spindle."[27]

Several Scandinavian objects from the dining alcove
were Gordon favorites, and she frequently reused
them to stage other *House Beautiful*–designed vignettes.
The Wegner chair, for example, first introduced in
Gough's February 1951 travel article, reappeared
in dozens of magazine spreads of designed interiors
and in *House Beautiful* advertisements (which
Gordon's staff frequently designed or art-directed).
The Nilsson wall hanging, featured so prominently
in the dining alcove, was the focal point of at least
four other *House Beautiful* features, including
the November 1953 cover (where it appeared behind
a set of Wegner chairs), Gordon's February 1954
Design in Scandinavia review, and an essay on textiles
arranged for the July 1959 issue.[28]

For *The Arts of Daily Living*'s living room
vignette, Swedish designer Ann-Mari Forsberg's *Röd
Krokus* (Red Crocus) hanging (p. 12) became the
focal point. The space was planned around this wall
hanging, using a strategy that Gordon encouraged
her readers to employ in their own homes: "splurge"

on "one glorious something" and finish the room with
inexpensive pieces.[29] To Gordon's credit, she acknowledged the expense of Forsberg's piece (323 dollars,
the equivalent of slightly more than three thousand
dollars today), yet explained that "it was…the most
vivid, dynamic thing in the room, [and] that it would
pay to subordinate all the other elements…to the
vibrant colors of the tapestry."[30] As an endnote to
the *Arts of Daily Living*, the magazine called out
two designs as "The Most Significant Objects in this
Exhibition."[31] The first, shown in a full-page black-
and-white image, was Timo Sarpaneva's *Orkidea*
(Orchid) vase (p. 99). It was noted for its "liquid, drop-
like grace" and superb use of material. The second,
a hand-carved wooden plate by Ronald Senungetuk
(a native Alaskan who was then a student at the
School for American Craftsmen, and later studied
in Oslo on a Fulbright fellowship), clearly recalled
the work of Wirkkala.

House Beautiful focused considerable attention on Scandinavian design in 1954, as *Design
in Scandinavia* and *Arts of Daily Living* continued to
draw media attention and visitors. In subsequent
years, Gordon's editorial lens shifted (most notably
toward Japanese design), but her support of specific
designers and design ideas remained remarkably
consistent. She demonstrated this decisively in July
1959, when she devoted a full issue of *House Beautiful*
to "The Scandinavian Look in U.S. Homes" (p. 101).
This 124-page publication marked the height of
Gordon's interest in Scandinavia (and perhaps the
postwar zenith for the popularity of Scandinavian
design itself). In twenty-one articles, her staff
described Scandinavian design, its craft-based ideals,
and its nature-based inspirations. The magazine
also chronicled the contributions made by all four
Nordic countries, and the impact of designers
who the editors considered "masters" of their craft
(including Jens Risom, Finn Juhl, and Hans Wegner).[32]
Gordon underscored the international influence that
Scandinavian design had achieved during the 1950s,
as evidenced by the prizes from the Milan Triennials
and the increased availability of Scandinavian
goods on the American market.[33] Several articles
informed, or perhaps reminded, readers of what
Scandinavian design—at least in Gordon's estimation—added to American homes: freshness, utility,
integrity, timelessness, and the "poetic exploration
of raw material."[34]

In the same July 1959 issue, the magazine endorsed the Scandinavian Design Cavalcade, a two-month, four-country "festival of home furnishings" that, as Marion Gough wrote, "might well have been expressly planned for *House Beautiful* readers."[35] Indeed, Gordon and her staff (who claimed to "have been virtually commuting to Scandinavia for ten years") may have exerted some influence on the conceptualization of this annual event aimed, in part, at American visitors.[36] *House Beautiful*'s coverage of the 1959 Cavalcade, written mostly by Gough, followed the same model as her 1951 travel guide article, and served as a bookend to the magazine's decade-long promotional campaign. Gough enthusiastically recommended the Cavalcade as an opportunity to see exhibitions and displays of contemporary products, to get "behind the design scenes" by meeting designers and craftspeople, and to buy goods not yet available in the United States (*House Beautiful* even published advice on how to get Scandinavian goods through U.S. Customs).[37] If readers were unable to make the recommended twenty-five-day itinerary, they could see special exhibits of Scandinavian goods in New York shops, including Georg Jensen, Inc., Bonniers, and Lord & Taylor.[38]

Gordon's own 1959 editorial, "The Beauty That Comes with Common Sense," was by far the most critical, revisiting themes that she had introduced earlier in the decade.[39] She reminded readers that *House Beautiful* had long championed Scandinavian design ideas, specifically the underlying "proposition that beauty and utility should not be separated, that they *can* be made features of the same object."[40] As she outlined the characteristics that made contemporary Scandinavian design so compelling for her (including craft-based production methods), she positioned these as a counterpoint against which her readers should judge contemporary American design, and more specifically, what she derided as "the gibberish of Modernism."[41] Her frustrations with a pervasive austerity and sterility in some versions of modernism, which had surfaced repeatedly over the previous decade, persisted (these had come to a zenith in 1953 with her infamous anti-International Style essay, "The Threat to the Next America").[42] In 1959, using Scandinavian design as a foil, she again railed against "functional" products that didn't function, against "honest design" that lied, against misused materials, against the "contradiction between the words and the realities in design."[43]

TIMO SARPANEVA
Iittala Glassworks
Orkidea (Orchid) vase, designed 1953.
CAT. 141

Functionalism, at least as Gordon narrowly defined it, had failed. "The Modern movement has lost its way," she wrote, but Scandinavian design, along with compatible American developments, provided a humane alternative.[44]

With such a good model in Scandinavia, Gordon seemed perturbed that much of American design still remained "bad." She faulted the "drawing-board designer" who practiced theory and no craft, and the "snobbish" designer who worked not for "the people" (as she believed Scandinavian designers did) but for his fellow professionals. She blamed American consumers for debasing contemporary design by remaining uninformed, uninterested, and passive. They were too easily swayed, she argued, by the "celebrity-ism of the publicized name-designer" and were too readily consumed by fads (she claimed, without qualification, that Scandinavians preferred timeless design that would last generations).[45] If American designers and consumers were guilty, American retailers were more so, as stores attempted to meet their customers' constant demand for the new, and as industry "[pressured] designers to produce too much, too fast," while "Scandinavian manufacturers can wait."[46]

Gordon had found in Scandinavia, or at least in her idealized version of these four nations, all that she missed in 1950s American design culture: what she described as an "atmosphere of confidence, of respect, of honor, of freedom, of informed, critical understanding from both public and manufacturer." This, she argued, was what had "brought about a real flowering of contemporary design."[47] Yet the design culture that she described was mostly myth, and Gordon was among the most powerful of mythmakers.

On the eve of her retirement from *House Beautiful*, Gordon donated part of her personal textile collection to the Cooper Union Museum (now the Cooper Hewitt, Smithsonian Design Museum). In December 1964, the museum opened the exhibition *The Wonders of Thread*, drawn exclusively from her gift. The cover of the catalogue featured a detail of Ann-Mari Forsberg's *Red Crocus* (p. 12), which had been displayed prominently at *House Beautiful*'s *Arts of Daily Living* exhibition as the focal point of the "inexpensive" living room. Of the seventy-eight textiles listed in *The Wonders of Thread* checklist, thirty-two were Scandinavian.[48] Many of the designs had played operative roles within *House Beautiful* between 1951 and 1959 (including *Red Crocus* and Nilsson's *Yellow Ovoids*), offering themselves as beautiful, useful, everyday objects that Gordon hoped would convince American homeowners and designers alike to bring "art" into their daily living.

Gordon's introduction to *The Wonders of Thread* revealed little of her previous editorial zeal, but rather turned the power of discovery over to her audience. As she withdrew from her post as editor, critic, and tastemaker, she seemed satisfied that she had done her work, perhaps convinced that American consumers were ready to "start investigating this area of life" for themselves. Her last words to the public assured Americans that, even in her absence, they could forge ahead, with confidence in their own good taste: "Nothing but your own good sense and artistic awareness need be your guide."[49]

HOUSE BEAUTIFUL
Special issue: "The Scandinavian Look in U.S. Homes"
Magazine, July 1959. CAT. 183

PENICK

House Beautiful

The Scandinavian Look in U.S. Homes

See inside for more about
five-way child's chair from Denmark

Elizabeth Gordon, *House Beautiful*, and the Scandinavian Look

1 For the travel guide generally, see Marion Gough, "If Your Home Is Your Hobby…Take a Trip to Scandinavia," *House Beautiful* (hereafter cited as *HB*) (February 1951): 102–4, 106, 108, 110, 113–14, 116–18, 124–26, 145–46; for "home-conscious," 103; for documentation of *HB* staff travels, 103, 125. Gough visited in April 1950, and home furnishings editor Frances Taylor Heard traveled in August and September. For a personal account of Gordon's travels, see Gordon's "Dear Elizabeth," a collection of personal letters to Gordon on the occasion of her sixty-fifth birthday [August 8, 1971], collected by her husband, Carl Norcross, author's collection.

2 Gough, "If Your Home Is Your Hobby," 103.

3 "The Art of Good Living," a guide or educational tool for readers, was introduced in the March 1951 issue.

4 On the Milan Triennials and the international promotion of Scandinavian design, see Kjetil Fallan, "Milanese Mediations: Crafting Scandinavian Design at the Triennali di Milano," *Konsthistorisk tidskrift/Journal of Art History* 83, no. 1 (2014): 1–23; Harri Kalha, "'The Miracle of Milan': Finland at the 1951 Triennial," *Scandinavian Journal of Design History* 14 (2004): 61–71; and Kerstin Wickman, "Design Olympics—The Milan Triennial," in *Scandinavian Design beyond the Myth: Fifty Years of Design from the Nordic Countries*, exh. cat., ed. Widar Halén and Kerstin Wickman (Stockholm: Arvinius, 2003), 32–45.

5 "The Most Beautiful Object of 1951," *HB* (January 1952): 67.

6 For "public relations" and Gordon's full account of the meeting with Gummerus and Svedberg, held at her home in Dobbs Ferry, New York, see Gordon to Mac Lindahl, October 19, 1951, Virginia Museum of Fine Arts, Directors' Correspondence, 1933–1977 (bulk 1934–1976), Accession 33863, State Government Records Collection, The Library of Virginia, Richmond, Virginia (hereafter cited as VMFA), box 25, folder 4. For Gordon's call to Cheek, see [Herman] Olof Gummerus to Gordon, August 8, 1971, in "Dear Elizabeth" [sixty-fifth birthday album].

7 See, for example, Gordon to Lindahl, October 19, 1951; Cheek to Gordon, October 30, 1951; Lindahl to Gordon, November 6, 1951; Gordon to Cheek, telegram, January 14, 1952; and Cheek to Gordon, April 3, 1953; all at VMFA, box 25, folder 4.

8 Gummerus to Gordon, October 3, 1952, VMFA, box 25, folder 4.

9 Gummerus to Gordon, October 3, 1952, VMFA, box 25, folder 4; for "thorough look," see Cheek to Gordon, July 11, 1971, in "Dear Elizabeth" [sixty-fifth birthday album].

10 Elizabeth Gordon, "Why the New Scandinavian Show Is Important to America," *HB* (February 1954): 94.

11 For a complete listing of committees and patrons, see Arne Remlov, ed., *Design in Scandinavia: An Exhibition of Objects for the Home from Denmark, Finland, Norway, Sweden*, exh. cat. (Oslo: Kirstes Boktrykkeri, 1954), 4–8. For recent scholarship, see Jørn Guldberg, "'Scandinavian Design' as Discourse: The Exhibition *Design in Scandinavia*, 1954–57," *Design Issues* 27, no. 2 (Spring 2011): 41–58; Harri Kalha, "'Just One of Those Things': The Design in Scandinavia Exhibition 1954–57," in *Scandinavian Design beyond the Myth*, 66–75; and Hildi Hawkins, "Finding a Place in a New World Order: Finland, America, and the 'Design in Scandinavia' Exhibition of 1954–57," in *Finnish Modern Design: Utopian Ideals and Everyday Realities, 1930–1997*, exh. cat., ed. Marianne Aav and Nina Stritzler-Levine (New Haven: Yale University Press and New York: Bard Graduate Center for Studies in the Decorative Arts, 1998), 232–51.

12 "Packing Cases Unfold into Display Cases for Traveling Exhibit," *Architectural Forum* 100, no. 1 (January 1954): 146–49; for "ingenious," 147.

13 For a summary of the show's impact, see Guldberg, "'Scandinavian Design' as Discourse."

14 Viggo Sten Møller, *Scandinavian Design: Directory of Arts and Crafts Resources in Denmark, Finland, Norway, Sweden* (Copenhagen: Langkjærs Bogtryk, 1953).

15 Betty Pepis, "Scandinavian Gets Museum Display: Stores Duplicate Some of the 700 Items in Show of Design in Brooklyn," *New York Times*, April 21, 1954. The Georg Jensen shop even published a lengthy brochure: *Georg Jensen Inc. Presents: "Scandinavian Design in Use"* (New York: Georg Jensen, 1954).

16 Åke H. Huldt and Per A. Laurén, eds., *Design in Scandinavia: USA-Canada 1954–1957*, exh. cat. (Stockholm: AB Egnellska Boktryckeriet, 1958).

17 See, for example, "Scandinavians in America," *American-Scandinavian Review* 42, no. 2 (June 1954): 158; and Anne Douglas, "Scandinavian Design Show at Best," *Chicago Daily Tribune*, May 20, 1956.

18 Gordon, "Why the New Scandinavian Show Is Important," 90, 94, 155, 170. Gordon commented that in February, she and her staff had not yet seen the show. Marion Gough had planned to attend the VMFA opening, but illness kept her in New York; see Gough to Leslie Cheek, Jr., telegram, January 14, 1954, VMFA, box 1, folder 1. Gordon did not attend the VMFA opening but was present at the VIP opening event in New York; see "Guest List New York Cocktail Party for Virginia Museum," November 19, 1953 (Hotel Dorset), VMFA, box 2, folder 1.

19 Gordon, "Why the New Scandinavian Show Is Important," 94.

20 Jean Murray Bangs and Ralph Linton, "Naturalism," *HB* (November 1950): 190–93, 292; see also "Naturalism Is the Core of the Emerging American Style," *HB* (November 1950): 196–203; and Joseph Wood Krutch, "The American Predilection for Naturalism as Old as It Is New," *HB* (March 1951): 112–15, 125–26, 128.

21 Mary Roche, "The Growing Love of Soft, Rounded Flowing Forms," *HB* (October 1952): 184–85; and Elizabeth Gordon, "The Editor's Forecast of the New Taste Cycle," *HB* (October 1952): 182–83, 269.

22 Joseph A. Barry, "The Architecture of Humanism," *HB* (November 1953): 224–27, 326, 329–30.

23 On Gordon's career, see Monica Penick, *Tastemaker: Elizabeth Gordon,* House Beautiful *and the Postwar American Home* (New Haven and London: Yale University Press, 2017).

24 Gordon, "Why the New Scandinavian Show Is Important," 94.

25 Elizabeth Gordon, "The Threat to the Next America," *HB* (April 1953): 126–31, 250–51.

26 For a discussion of Scandinavian social structure and "democratic outlook," see also Remlov, *Design in Scandinavia*, 15.

27 "Rooms for a Lively Life / The Scandinavian-American Dining Alcove," *HB* (October 1954): 170.

28 For Nilsson and Fields credits from *Arts of Daily Living*, see *HB* (October 1954): 242.

29 "How Inexpensively—and Nicely—Can You Furnish a Living Room in 1955?," *HB* (January 1955): 58–61; for "splurge" and "glorious," 60.

30 "How Inexpensively," 60. In print, the piece was wrongly attributed to Barbro Nilsson.

31 "The Most Significant Objects in this Exhibition," *HB* (October 1954): 202–3, 232.

32 "Designed and Made in the U.S.A.," *HB* (July 1959): 88–89; "Masters of Their Art and Craft," 90–91; and Marion Gough, "Hans J. Wegner: Poet of Practicality," 64–71, 114. See also "What Is the Scandinavian Look?," 51.

33 See "A New World-wide Influence," *HB* (July 1959): 82–83; and "Where to Find Scandinavian Merchandise," 122.

34 "Exploit the Nature of the Material to Its Fullest," *HB* (July 1959): 60.

35 Marion Gough, "The Scandinavian Design Cavalcade," *HB* (July 1959): 46.

36 Gough, "The Scandinavian Design Cavalcade," 106.

37 "How to Bring Home Your Scandinavian Purchases," *HB* (July 1959): 121.

38 "Scandinavian Exhibits in the USA," *HB* (July 1959): 77.

39 Elizabeth Gordon, "The Beauty That Comes with Common Sense," *HB* (July 1959): 54–57.

40 Gordon, "The Beauty," 54.

41 Gordon, "The Beauty," 55.

42 Gordon, "The Threat to the Next America," 126–31, 250–51. For a complete discussion of this article and the controversy surrounding Gordon's vocal critique of the International Style, see Penick, *Tastemaker*.

43 Gordon, "The Beauty," 55.

44 Gordon, "The Beauty," 54, 55.

45 Gordon, "The Beauty," 122.

46 Gordon, "The Beauty," 57, 122.

47 Gordon, "The Beauty," 122.

48 For a complete list of objects, see *The Wonders of Thread*, exh. cat. (New York: Cooper Union Museum, 1964).

49 Elizabeth Gordon, introduction to *The Wonders of Thread*, 3.

Free to Be… Scandinavian: Postwar Nordic Design for Children

ALEXANDRA LANGE

Free to Be…You and Me was first broadcast on the ABC network on March 11, 1974. The musical special, based on the best-selling album and book created by Marlo Thomas, was one of the most visible manifestations of a sea change in children's media in the United States in the early 1970s. With songs such as "William's Doll," materials such as Barbara Sprung's posters and toys showing women as construction workers and African Americans as doctors, and resources such as *Non-Sexist Education for Young Children: A Practical Guide*, educators and parents acknowledged the need for children's media to combat stereotypes about which toys were appropriate for boys, what careers were open to girls, and who should be doing the day-to-day parenting.[1] But Americans were behind the times in this realization. Long before the 1970s, products imported from Denmark, Finland, Norway, and Sweden showed a different way to be a parent, through one's choice of toys, furniture, play equipment, and even baby carriers. The first run of postwar Scandinavian products, from tiny plastic bricks to weighty playground sculpture, introduced gender-neutral abstraction, honest materials, and child-led play to the American scene.[2]

"Small children have never understood why they are not allowed to climb around on sculptures," Danish-Swedish architect and sculptor Egon Møller-Nielsen told an interviewer in 1954.[3] Møller-Nielsen was motivated, like so many parent-designers, by his own child—in this case, his three-year-old daughter—whom he observed climbing rocks, hiding in caves, and sliding down stones. Why should urban playgrounds not mimic these nature experiences in action, if not in material? In 1949 his *Tufsen* play sculpture was installed in the People's Park in Stockholm as part of a city-wide effort to make Stockholm's parks greener as an antidote to rapid postwar industrialization.[4]

The sculpture's prominent location led to international publicity. Copies of *Tufsen*, as well as Møller-Nielsen's *Spiral Slide* (p. 104) and *Ägget* (The Egg), proliferated in Sweden and made their way to the United States. In 1953, Frank Caplan, the founder of educational toy company Creative Playthings, met Møller-Nielsen in Sweden.[5] They struck a deal for the *Spiral Slide* to be added to the company's new Play Sculptures Division. One of their catalogs describes it

View of Egon Møller-Nielsen's *Spiral Slide*, designed c. 1956

in poetic and kinetic terms: "The Spiral Slide of polished stone is an exciting adventure. Enter a cave-like entrance at its base, discover a ladder, climb to its summit, and there find the opalescent, satiny toboggan-like slide spiraling downward and widening as it descends."[6] In 1954 the Museum of Modern Art held its own Play Sculpture competition, cosponsored by Creative Playthings and *Parents' Magazine*, intended to spur American design thinking in this area.[7] When Aline Saarinen reviewed the results in the *New York Times*, she was less than impressed. "Few have the evidence of the Scandinavian achievements in this field of plastic play equipment," she wrote.[8]

A Philadelphia playground designed by landscape architect Cornelia Hahn Oberlander used several pieces from the Creative Playthings catalog, including the *Spiral Slide* and half-hoop climbers in graduated sizes.[9] Images of this playground would appear in subsequent Play Sculpture catalogs, as well as a December 1955 feature in *Progressive Architecture*.[10] The magazine text drew a dramatic contrast between the classic urban play lot and the new sculptural forms, celebrating the "passing of the stereotyped, cindery city 'playground' with its rigid rows of iron-and-wood exercise equipment

behind spiked fences" in favor of "city play centers that entire families can enjoy." Like Møller-Nielsen, Danish artist Tom Lindhardt Wils noticed that children enjoyed playing on his large public outdoor sculptures and decided to develop a playground equipment business. An early design was the *Mudderkliren* (Sandpiper) springer (now called the Hen springer), an adaptation of the classic indoor rocking toy (p. 106). Its primary colors and abstracted shape appealed to children and adults alike. Lindhardt Wils's company, Multikunst Legepladser (now KOMPAN), applied for an American patent for the spring technology in the late 1970s, and began to install its moving animals in the United States in the early 1980s.[11]

Opportunities for children's physical play were not only available outdoors. In 1963, *Design Quarterly* editor Anna Campbell Bliss used one of Danish architect Kristian Vedel's child's chairs to illustrate a point about the advantages of playable furniture (p. 106): "In the hands of a creative designer, it will open up new avenues for his imagination. A table may be a chair or a hiding place, a tunnel or a house."[12] Vedel's system combined half-cylinders of bentwood notched up the sides with flat wooden sections that slot into those notches.

Free to Be…Scandinavian

The hardware-free system allowed children to adjust the height of their seat, link two half-cylinders with a larger oval to make a table, or tip the whole thing over on its side to make a rocking cradle or cave.[13] In 1957 Vedel's furniture was featured in the *At Home with Scandinavian Design* exhibition at Bloomingdale's in New York.[14] The pieces came in "natural," red, and blue, which would become the default colors for Nordic unisex children's gear, and retailed for thirty dollars. The red version appeared on the cover of *House Beautiful* in July 1959 in an issue devoted to "The Scandinavian Look in U.S. Homes" (p. 101), where the editor described it as "cheerful" and explained that its "simple, direct approach is typical of the Scandinavian designer."[15] Versatility of function and adjustability in size would become a leitmotif in Scandinavian and American children's furniture of this era.[16] Other examples include American architect Anne Tyng's 1947 Tyng Toy, whose wooden pieces could be assembled to form a rocking horse or a desk, and Danish designer Nanna Ditzel's 1962 *Trissen* (The Toadstool) tables and stools (p. 107). Ditzel said at the time that children's furniture should be distinct from that for adults, for "children do not sit still, they move and run around."[17]

LEGO, perhaps Denmark's most famous design export, elaborated on the simple act of stacking, adding its patented stud-and-tube system to make children's creations easier to build. LEGO arrived in the United States in time for Christmas 1961, imported by luggage manufacturer Samsonite (above). Over the next few years, LEGO promoted its toy in a wide range of American popular magazines. Its graphic advertisements, which almost always featured both a boy and a girl, used language intended to draw a contrast between LEGO and other toys. One 1965 ad assured parents that "There is, in this nervous world, one toy that does not shoot or go boom or bang or rat-tat-tat-tat. Its name is Lego. It makes things."[18] This ad featured the LEGO *Town-Plan*, the first system developed by Godtfred Kirk Christiansen, son of founder Ole Kirk Christiansen, as a comprehensive set to encourage imaginative play (p. 109).[19] Later ads pitched it as "Lego… the thoughtful toy… Why not give them a gift that lets them create something? A gift that stretches the imagination, that widens the world they live in. A gift that lasts."[20]

KRISTIAN VEDEL
Torben Ørskov & Co.
Child's chair, designed 1957. CAT. 161

TOM LINDHARDT WILS
Multikunst Legepladser (now KOMPAN)
Mudderkliren (**Sandpiper**) **springer**,
designed 1971–72, this example 2017.
CAT. 92

Nanna Ditzel's *Trissen* (The Toadstool)
children's stools, promotional image,
1962

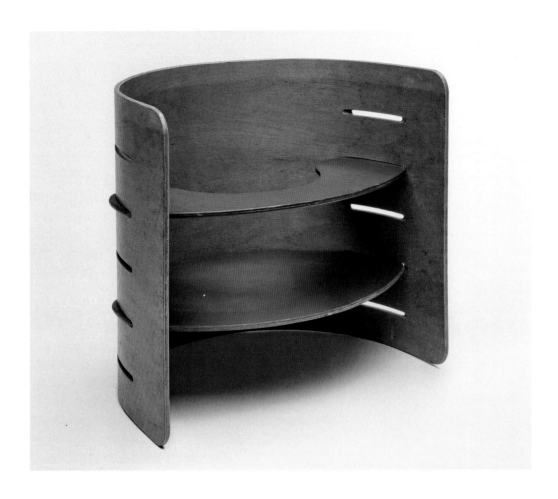

This framing of LEGO as a creative toy was part of a broader international postwar emphasis on children's creativity.[21] LEGO had to work to position its plastic product as a "good" toy, since it was not made of a natural material such as wood, stone, or cotton like the other objects discussed here. Emphasizing its quiet nature and open-ended play brought the engineered plastic bricks closer to the wooden blocks of old, and the wooden furniture Nordic designers such as Ditzel and Vedel were producing for children. The playrooms that proliferated in American suburban houses following World War II had wide-open floors, ideal for building projects, and checklists for decorating such rooms emphasized "space for free play" as well as "colorful surroundings" and "a wall to mark and pin." Scandinavian designs, with their sturdy materials, bright colors, and interchangeable parts, easily met all the criteria.[22]

Norwegian designer Peter Opsvik's *Tripp Trapp* chair (p. 110), manufactured by Stokke, used many of the same structural principles and conceptual strategies as Vedel's chair. When Opsvik's son Thor was about three, his father observed that he was too small for a standard chair, yet too big for a high chair. He needed a lift to see eye to eye with the adults at the table but wanted to be able to get up and down on his own. The result was a chair created to bridge the transitions between infancy, toddlerhood, and childhood, and which remains a model for adaptive design.[23] The *Tripp Trapp* consists of two beech supports shaped like upside-down 7s, connected by two roughly rectangular platforms also made of beech, which slide into notches along the supports. The top platform functions as a seat, the bottom as a footrest, and the wide base adds stability. In addition to being easily adjustable, the chair can also be used as a stepladder. In his book *Rethinking Sitting*, Opsvik explained that "mealtimes may become more relaxed, and children find it easier to concentrate on the activities taking place around the table when the physical environment has been adapted to their size and needs."[24] The chair debuted in 1972 and was first sold in the United States by specialty stores, including Design Research and Scandinavian Design Inc. in 1975.[25] Articles in American publications at the time echoed Opsvik's language of adaptability.[26]

Scandinavian designers created products specifically for children in many media beyond furniture and toys. Although Finnish fabric house Marimekko had been producing playful prints and children's clothing and toys since 1951, the company did not have a textile specifically for children until 1975, when Japanese designer Katsuji Wakisaka created *Bo-Boo*, which features brightly colored cars, trucks, and buses, racing in two directions (p. 111). Like Marimekko's cotton shift dresses, which were imported by Design Research in 1959, Marimekko's children's bedding filled a niche for bright, modern, well-designed goods.[27] The introduction of Wakisaka's children's prints coincided with an explosion in the manufacture and marketing of soft goods for children in the United States, and led to Marimekko's partnership with textile producer Dan River Mills in Danville, Virginia.[28] Girls and boys alike enjoyed *Bo-Boo*'s design, described as "the most crayon colorful parade of cars, trucks, and buses in just about the most mixed-up traffic jam since the invention of the wheel."[29] The Marimekko designs were always promoted as unisex: a Robinson's department store ad from 1980, for example, showed boys and girls jumping on a *Bo-Boo* bed together.[30]

Designers were concerned not only with the domestic needs of children but also with how they moved around in the world. The BabyBjörn carrier, which debuted in the United States in 1979, was originally called the *Hjärtenära*,

PETER OPSVIK
Stokke
Tripp Trapp **chair**, designed 1972.
CAT. 111

KATSUJI WAKISAKA
Marimekko
Bo-Boo **textile**, designed 1975. CAT. 165

LANGE

meaning "close to the heart" (cat. 67). It was designed in Sweden in 1973 by Björn Jakobson, who developed a structured sack that would support babies' necks and spines, and his wife, Lillemor Jakobson, who styled it as something fashionable parents would want to wear.[31] Like other examples of Scandinavian design for children that preceded it, the carrier was simple (a pouch with spidery straps), plain (made of cotton in solid colors and window pane patterns), and freeing (allowing for no-hands parenting). A 1979 Swedish promotional photo shows a family of four (plus dog) standing at the edge of a forest (right). With the carrier, the advertisement suggested, the birth of a baby meant there would be no interruption in their healthy outdoor lifestyle.

The Jakobsons had originally been intrigued by research on so-called "attachment parenting" by physicians at Cleveland's Rainbow Babies and Children's Hospital, showing that close parental contact early in life made for more secure emotional bonds later. (Rainbow physicians continue to consult on the company's products today.) To foster strong attachment, the carrier and its American counterpart, the Snugli, allowed parents to wear their babies on their bodies. The Snugli, patented by Ann and Mike Moore in 1969, was a twentieth-century Western update of the wraps, rebozos, and mei-tai carriers the Moores had seen in Africa, East Asia, and Mexico—an example of "co-opting [that] has signaled a bohemian attitude toward childrearing in postindustrial countries since the 1960s."[32] The two carriers, developed separately, took different routes to a similar end: the Snugli emerged from cultural traditions in the developing world, while the *Hjärtenära* was inspired by Western medical research. The latter was initially anticipated as a boon for stay-at-home mothers trying to do housework with an infant, but its combination of dark colors, sturdy fabrics, and lack of baby animal decorations made it an early unisex parenting product; by the 1990s, the carrier's heyday in the United States, it was explicitly marketed to fathers.[33] Since the era of the *Hjärtenära*'s development, Sweden has been a leader in many aspects of progressive parenting, including gender-neutral schooling for young children and equal parental leave.[34]

Each of these Scandinavian imports, from the LEGO brick to the *Tripp Trapp* chair, made a version

Advertisement for BabyBjörn's *Hjärtenära* baby carrier, 1979

of the claim that their simple design and (in most cases) natural materials offered greater happiness and freedom for the whole family. Aesthetic choices brought these children's products closer in appearance to their adult counterparts, while also ridding them of traditional gender codes. American playtime trends in the 1990s and 2000s, however, largely cycled back to traditional binaries—pink/blue, dolls/action figures, ballet/baseball—in bedding, toys, clothes, and television programs.[35] The past decade has brought a second reckoning with the destructive nature of stereotypes embodied in toys, paired with data showing how little progress women in the United States have made toward professional economic and gender parity.[36] Nothing quite approaches the heady optimism of *Free to Be...You and Me*, but Scandinavian policy and design continue to serve as a model.

1 Marlo Thomas and friends, *Free to Be…You and Me*, Arista Records AL 4003, 1972; *Free to Be…You and Me*, ed. Carole Hart, Letty Cottin Pogrebin, Mary Rodgers, and Marlo Thomas (Philadelphia: Running Press, 1974); *Free to Be…You and Me*, directed by Bill Davis, Len Steckler, and Fred Wolf, first aired March 11, 1974, on ABC; Barbara Sprung, *Non-Sexist Education for Young Children: A Practical Guide* (New York: Citation Press, 1975); Laura L. Lovett, "Child's Play: Boys' Toys, Women's Work, and 'Free Children,'" in *When We Were Free to Be: Looking Back at a Children's Classic and the Difference It Made*, ed. Lori Rotskoff and Laura L. Lovett (Chapel Hill: University of North Carolina Press, 2012), 111–26.

2 Amy F. Ogata, "Good Toys," in *Century of the Child: Growing by Design, 1900–2000*, exh. cat., ed. Juliet Kinchin and Aidan O'Connor (New York: Museum of Modern Art, 2012), 173.

3 E. Muller-Kraus, "Der Bildhauer, der Spielen Kann," in *Abstrakte Kunst: Querschnitt 1953*, Das Kunstwerk 43/44 (Baden-Baden, Germany: Woldemar Klein, 1954), 83, translated and quoted in *The Playground Project*, exh. cat., ed. Gabriela Burkhalter (Zurich: JRP Ringier, 2016), 139–40.

4 Fred M. Hechinger, "Sculpture to Play On," *New York Herald Tribune*, November 25, 1951.

5 Susan G. Solomon, *American Playgrounds: Revitalizing Community Space* (Lebanon, NH: University Press of New England, 2005), 27–29.

6 Creative Playthings, Play Sculptures Division catalog (1954), n.p., Loeb Library, Harvard Graduate School of Design.

7 "A New Look for Playgrounds," *Parents' Magazine*, July 1954, 42–43; Amy F. Ogata, *Designing the Creative Child: Playthings and Places in Midcentury America* (Minneapolis: University of Minnesota Press, 2013), 61–63.

8 Aline B. Saarinen, "Playground: Function and Art," *New York Times*, July 4, 1954.

9 Solomon, *American Playgrounds*, 33–34.

10 "Neighborhood Playground," *Progressive Architecture* 36, no. 12 (December 1955): 102–3.

11 Ning de Coninck-Smith, "Mudderkliren (The Sandpiper)," in *Century of the Child: Nordic Design for Children 1900 to Today*, exh. cat., ed. Hedvig Hedqvist and Elna Svenle (Värnamo, Sweden: Museum Vandalorum, 2014), 122–23.

12 Anna Campbell Bliss, "Children's Furniture," *Design Quarterly* 57 (1963): 13.

13 Alexander Von Vegesack, ed., *Kid Size: The Material World of Childhood*, exh. cat. (Milan: Skira in association with Vitra Design Museum, 1997), 261.

14 Rita Reif, "Room Settings Have the Accent of Scandinavia," *New York Times*, October 16, 1957.

15 *House Beautiful* (July 1959): 4. (The reference to "the Scandinavian designer" was not to Vedel specifically but to the general category of Scandinavian designers.) For more on *House Beautiful*'s coverage of Scandinavian design, see Monica Penick in this volume, 92–102.

16 Alexandra Lange, "Toys as Furniture/Furniture as Toys," in *Serious Play: Design in Midcentury America*, exh. cat., ed. Monica Obniski and Darrin Alfred (New Haven and London: Yale University Press, 2018), 139ff.

17 Von Vegesack, *Kid Size*, 268.

18 The ad appeared several times, including in the *Los Angeles Times* (November 28, 1965), the *New York Times* (December 5, 1965), and *The New Yorker* (December 11, 1965).

19 Colin Fanning, "Building Kids: LEGO and the Commodification of Creativity," in *Childhood by Design: Toys and the Material Culture of Childhood, 1700–Present*, ed. Megan Brandow-Faller (New York: Bloomsbury Visual Arts, 2018), 91.

20 LEGO ad, *Parents' Magazine*, December 1967, 69.

21 Fanning, "Building Kids," 89ff. See also Ogata, *Designing the Creative Child*, chap. 2.

22 Ogata, *Designing the Creative Child*, 83–84.

23 Alexandra Lange, *The Design of Childhood: How the Material World Shapes Independent Kids* (New York: Bloomsbury, 2018), 74–77.

24 Peter Opsvik, *Rethinking Sitting* (New York: W.W. Norton, 2009), 158.

25 "Scandinavian Design: A Beautiful and Easy Way to Live," *Better Homes and Gardens*, November 1976, 113; Lisa Hammel, "New & Useful: A Chair That Grows," *New York Times*, November 17, 1977.

26 "Scandinavian Design: A Beautiful and Easy Way to Live," 113.

27 Jane Thompson and Alexandra Lange, *Design Research: The Store That Brought Modern Living to American Homes* (San Francisco: Chronicle Books, 2010), 70.

28 Jane Geniesse, "Home Beat," *New York Times*, November 16, 1978.

29 Bloomingdale's ad, *New York Times*, February 7, 1982.

30 Robinson's ad, *Los Angeles Times*, December 4, 1980.

31 Sadie Stein, "Who Made That Baby Bjorn?," *New York Times Magazine*, June 29, 2012.

32 Michelle Millar Fisher, "S-087: Snugli," in *Items: Is Fashion Modern?*, exh. cat., ed. Paola Antonelli and Michelle Millar Fisher (New York: Museum of Modern Art, 2017), 219–20.

33 Maria Fagerström (communications manager, BabyBjörn), email message to author, August 21, 2018.

34 Ellen Barry, "In Sweden, Preschools Teach Boys to Dance and Girls to Yell," *New York Times*, March 24, 2018.

35 Elizabeth Sweet, "Guys and Dolls No More?," *New York Times*, December 21, 2012; Elizabeth Sweet, "Boy Builders and Pink Princesses: Gender, Toys, and Inequality over the Twentieth Century" (dissertation, University of California, Davis, 2013); Jo Paoletti, *Pink and Blue: Telling the Boys from the Girls in America* (Bloomington: Indiana University Press, 2012), 114–16.

36 Anne-Marie Slaughter, "Why Women Still Can't Have It All," *The Atlantic*, July/August 2012, https://www.theatlantic.com/magazine/archive/2012/07/why-women-still-cant-have-it-all/309020/; Let Toys Be Toys, http://lettoysbetoys.org.uk; GoldieBlox, https://www.goldieblox.com.

A TROLL
IN
THE WHITE
HOUSE

DANIELLE CHARLAP

Despite their modest origins in the late 1950s, by 1963 troll dolls were an international craze—even making their way to the Oval Office (right). These wild-haired, impish-grinned dolls originated in Denmark. After including his handmade trolls as decoration in a 1956 Christmas window display, Danish woodcarver Thomas Dam found himself inundated with orders. To keep up with demand, Dam used a plastic mold to create rubber trolls stuffed with sawdust. By the time he incorporated Dam Things Establishment in 1962, he had switched to PVC plastic, employing rotational molding to produce hollow but durable versions of the figure.[1] Dam branded his dolls Good Luck Trolls, rehabilitating the troll's reputation in Scandinavian lore as an unfriendly, isolated creature.[2] By 1959, troll sales in Denmark exceeded ten thousand a month, prompting expansion into foreign markets.[3]

Inge Dykins, a Danish-born, Florida-based entrepreneur, began importing them into the U.S. in 1961.[4] When Dam Things decided to manufacture its trolls in the U.S. through a licensee, Dykins obtained an exclusive buying agreement with the company.[5] She debuted the trolls at the 1963 International Toy Fair in New York City, selling nearly three million dolls by 1964.[6] "The Trolls Take Over,"

declared *Life* magazine in 1964, bewildering critics and retailers alike (p. 116).[7] "We just took a chance people would like them," one toy shop owner recounted, "and our first shipment sold out by 1 p.m. the first day we put them on the counter."[8] Dykins maintained that "the secret of their charm is that they're so ugly you have to laugh."[9]

President John F. Kennedy, pilot Betty
Miller, and Dammit the troll in the
Oval Office, White House, Washington,
DC, July 19, 1963

THOMAS DAM
Dam Things Establishment
Dammit troll doll, this example
manufactured c. 1963. CAT. 22

When Betty Miller brought a troll with her to the Oval Office, even President John F. Kennedy could not escape the fad. The first woman to fly solo across the Pacific from California to Australia, Miller enlisted Dammit the troll as her flight companion (p. 115). Dubbed a "flying housewife," Miller was actually an experienced pilot who ran a flight school in Santa Monica, California, with her husband, and she relied on Dammit to deflect the press's incessant attention.[10] "He's my good luck charm," she told reporters, "[a]nd we made it together."[11] Upon receiving the Federal Aviation Administration's Decoration for Exceptional Service, Miller visited the White House with Dammit in tow.

A lawsuit in 1965, however, revealed the complex business of international trade. Despite patents in both Denmark and the United States, Dam lost proprietary rights in the U.S. to his original design on the grounds of failure to notify customers of his copyright.[12] The loss cut into Dam Things' sales as the market flooded with imitators, until the 1996 Uruguay Round Agreement precipitated a change. In an effort to protect U.S. interests abroad, the U.S. government agreed to reinstate international copyrights lost to technicalities, including failure to notify.[13] The troll's years of ubiquity had not diminished the popularity of Dam's creations; a resurgence in the 1990s and new interest created by DreamWorks' *Trolls* movies in the 2010s prove the mischievous creature's enduring international appeal.

1 Tim Walsh, *The Playmakers: Amazing Origins of Timeless Toys* (Sarasota, FL: Keys Publishing, 2004), 188–89. The company is now known as Dam Things from Denmark. See Dam Things from Denmark v. Russ Berrie & Co., 173 F. Supp. 2d 277 (D.N.J. 2001).

2 Dam was not the only one to cast the troll in a more positive light. In 1952, Finnish company Fauni Trolls produced a soft, handmade troll it marketed as friendly; see Eileene Harrison Beer, *Scandinavian Design: Objects of a Life Style* (New York: Farrar, Straus and Giroux and the American-Scandinavian Foundation, 1975), 196–98.

3 Sven Hauerbach, "De Laver Trolde På Samlebånd-!," *Se Og Hør*, September 4, 1959, 20–21.

4 Jean Sprain Wilson, "She's Importing Good Luck," *Lubbock Avalanche-Journal*, June 13, 1962.

5 Scandia House Enterprises v. Dam Things Establishment, 243 F. Supp. 450 (D.D.C. 1965).

6 *Scandia House*, 243 F. Supp. 450 (D.D.C. 1965); Mike Haggerty, "How Danes Troll for Money," *Miami News*, April 12, 1964.

7 "Army of Imps Invade U.S.: The Trolls Take Over," *Life*, April 24, 1964, 107–8.

8 Joan Beck, "Now Kids Are Going for Trolls," *Chicago Tribune*, August 27, 1963.

9 "Dammit All," *Newsweek*, February 3, 1964, 68.

10 "Woman Flier Mobbed as Pacific Solo Trip Ends," *The Age* (Melbourne, Australia), May 13, 1963; Patty Jeys (Miller's cousin), phone conversation with author, September 29, 2017.

11 Ted Kurrus, "First Woman to Fly Alone to Isles Makes Trip in 17 Hours, 3 Minutes," *Honolulu Star-Bulletin*, May 1, 1963.

12 *Scandia House*, 243 F. Supp. 450 (D.D.C. 1965).

13 Copyright cases were settled in the early 2000s. See 17 U.S.C. § 104A (h) (6); see also Dam Things from Denmark Troll Co. v. Russ Berrie & Co., 290 F.3d 548 (3d Cir 2002).

"Army of Imps Invade U.S.: The Trolls Take Over," *Life*, April 24, 1964

Army of imps invade U.S. **The Trolls Take Over**

Parents may feel themselves in the same Gulliver-style predicament as the little girl seen here. All over the U.S. dresser tops and blue-jean pockets are being jammed with tiny mop-haired invaders that are called trolls. These popeyed Lilliputians are inspired by the gremlinlike imps that abound in Nordic folklore, living in caves, tunnels and under bridges, and working mischief on unsuspecting mortals. Like all make-believe sprites, they kept out of sight—until a Danish wood-carver named Thomas Dam caught the eye of a toy merchant with a troll he had made for his daughter. In less time than it takes to say Billy-Goat Gruff, plastic copies were flooding the U.S. by the millions. The tiny trolls come in several grimacing varieties including Dammits, Heniks, Sheniks and Big Baby Wishniks. Despite the devilment blamed on the trolls back home in Scandinavia, the ones sold in this country are supposed to bring good luck. For rabbits, at least, they are very lucky indeed: the rabbit's-foot charm is on the way out.

CONTINUED

DESIGN FOR DIPLOMACY

JENS RISOM
Knoll Associates, Inc.
Chair, designed 1941, this example
c. 1947. CAT. 128

This chair bears a metal tag inscribed
"Central Post Fund Property, Clarksville
Base, Tennessee," indicating that it
likely came from Clarksville Base,
a purpose-built nuclear weapons stor-
age facility on the grounds of Fort
Campbell in Tennessee, built in 1947.
Knoll Associates had many government
contracts, so it is conceivable that the
company furnished the new facility.

MONICA
OBNISKI

DESIGN FOR DIPLOMACY   The theme of promoting the United States and the Nordic nations through cultural diplomacy binds together several modes of design display, including national pavilions at world's fairs, museum exhibitions, and diplomatic projects, all of which may be seen to demonstrate how design as "soft power" persuasively communicated cultural ideas.[1] Design has also been used to advance political goals through traditional diplomatic tactics. Within the Nordic pavilions at world fairs, the various countries exhibited products and other cultural exports while presenting themselves as they desired to be seen on the world stage. Design has also served as a form of cultural propaganda in museum exhibitions—staged in the United States as well as in the Nordic countries—in which government support was often instrumental. Finally, in the years following World War II, a number of diplomatic building projects in both the U.S. and Scandinavia can be understood as symbols of the United States and as persuasive instruments of Cold War diplomacy.

World's fairs were constructed environments that displayed objects, commodities, and people within national pavilions, government buildings, and corporate edifices. While The Great Exhibition of the Works of Industry of All Nations held in London in 1851 is generally considered the first world's fair, these events occurred regularly around the globe until the mid-twentieth century, and continue to be organized through the Bureau International des Expositions. Under the guise of educating the public, manufacturers marketed objects and countries organized presentations, displaying national achievements and using goods to symbolize national identity. As historian Robert Rydell has noted, world's fairs professed the ideas and values of a country's political, economic, corporate, and intellectual leaders.[2]

In the United States, the 1876 Centennial International Exposition in Philadelphia opened in a country still recovering from the Civil War, and accordingly, emphasized national unity.[3] By comparison, although politically unified under one king in 1876, Norway and Sweden created separate presentations; each had a pavilion with displays emphasizing Scandinavian folk life.[4] Some of the most-discussed objects at the fair were located in the Swedish section, including the Swedish Schoolhouse (p. 138) and the lifelike wax figures illustrating peasant life, organized by Swedish scholar Artur Hazelius (p. 15).[5] The American fascination with Scandinavia was commencing; in this early period, these objects and people captured the imagination of Americans and forged the early identity of Scandinavians in America.

For the World's Columbian Exposition of 1893 in Chicago, several Nordic nations participated, including Denmark, with displays that featured individual firms, such as A. Michelsen and Royal Copenhagen. As the sole manufacturer of Danish porcelain, Royal Copenhagen displayed its *Blue Fluted* dinnerware and its *Flora Danica* service alongside the unique under-glazed vessels that designer Arnold Krog and others had been refining for many years (p. 121). Norway's presentation at the fair was made as the country was campaigning for independence from Sweden, and its use of a re-created Viking ship—sailed by a Norwegian crew across the Atlantic—was important to proclaiming its independent political and cultural identity (p. 15). A wooden footed drinking horn elaborately carved by Lars Kinsarvik was displayed in Norway's Court, within the Manufactures and Liberal Arts Building (below). It featured *dragestil* ("dragon style") imagery, which incorporated Viking motifs and interlace patterns. Frequently, Kinsarvik's work also included gnomes and trolls from Norwegian fairytales, as exemplified by the seated figure on the drinking horn.[6]

Despite more well-known associations, a robust military arms industry belies the more familiar cultural and political identity of the region, and armaments should also be understood as "Scandinavian design."[7] Originally designed in Norway in 1887, an updated model of the Krag-Jørgensen rifle was shown at the World's Columbian Exposition (cat. 80).[8] Adopted by the

LARS KINSARVIK
Drinking horn, 1890. CAT. 76

(FROM LEFT TO RIGHT)
ARNOLD KROG
OLUF JENSEN
Royal Copenhagen Porcelain
Manufactory
Ginger jar, 1891. CAT. 85

ARNOLD KROG
GERHARD HEILMANN
Royal Copenhagen Porcelain
Manufactory
Vase, 1890. CAT. 83
Vase, 1892. CAT. 84

DESIGN FOR DIPLOMACY

ALVAR AALTO
Karhula-Iittala Glassworks
"Savoy" vase, designed 1936,
this example late 1930s. CAT. 2

Aino Aalto gave this "Savoy" vase to
Aline Goldstone in the late 1930s.
Goldstone was a poet and the mother
of Harmon Goldstone, an architect
who visited the Aaltos in Finland in 1936.
Aline and Aino likely met during
the Aaltos' visits to New York, in either
1938 or 1939.

THORVALD BINDESBØLL
A. Michelsen (manufacturer)
Vase, designed 1899, this example 1925.
Silver, 12 13/16 × 10 3/16 × 10 3/16 in.
(32.51 × 25.91 × 25.91 cm).
Designmuseum Danmark

U.S. Army in 1892, it went into production in 1894. While the rifle doesn't neatly fit into the prevailing Scandinavian cultural identity, it highlights that this was an ideological construction, and part of a larger diplomatic endeavor.

The next fair of consequence for the Nordic nations was the New York World's Fair in 1939. Each country—Denmark, Finland, Norway, and Sweden—exhibited in separate pavilions. In addition, Iceland, still in union with Denmark, sent its own pavilion (p. 160). Alvar and Aino Aalto's Finnish Pavilion and Sven Markelius' Swedish Pavilion particularly stood out because "Scandinavian architects and designers had developed a cohesive modern style that went beyond the clinical austerity of German functionalists."[9] The Aaltos' building positioned Finland's cultural identity as an artful union of nature and industry.[10] Called a "symphony in wood," the pavilion encompassed a multi-tiered undulating wall that formed the backdrop for large-scale photographs of Finnish landscapes, factories, and products.[11] Also on view, and possessing a similarly rippling form, the "Savoy" vase became a symbol of Finnish design (p. 122).

Writing about the fair for an American audience, Swedish designer G. A. Berg used the country's pavilion to illustrate his ideas about Swedish Modern, describing the movement as a "hurricane" of harmonious, clean, and delightful interiors sweeping the United States, indicative of a new attitude toward living—simplicity without pretentiousness.[12] Indeed, the Sven Markelius–designed pavilion was called the "most civilized piece of modern architecture" at the fair.[13] Displays demonstrated the country's arts and industries, including impressive glass installations and Bruno Mathsson's work chair (cat. 103). Outside were several large sculptures, including an enormous Dala horse (p. 33), the Carl Milles horse-and-rider sculpture *Sunglitter*, and an Orrefors glass fountain designed by Vicke Lindstrand.

World's fairs were not the only sites for national promotion through cultural diplomacy; exhibitions in the United States and Scandinavia promoted the artistry and crafts of the organizing nations. Exhibitions extolling the work of Norwegian weaver Frida Hansen at the Carnegie Institute of Art in 1915 (p. 63) and the Danish silversmithy Georg Jensen at the Art Institute of Chicago in 1921 were early statements of the value of handcrafted Nordic goods. The Brooklyn Museum opened galleries devoted to Norway, Sweden, and Denmark in 1926, and hosted such exhibitions as the *Swedish Art Exhibition* (1916) and the *Danish National Exhibition of Applied Art, Paintings, and Sculpture* (1927), which toured the United States.[14] The idea for the latter originated with Meta Lassen, a Danish immigrant businesswoman and design promoter.[15] Visitors and critics were impressed by works like the vase designed by Thorvald Bindesbøll, whom the silversmithy A. Michelsen had hired to apply his moody, dramatic illustrative style to silver (p. 122). The Danish organizers deemed the exhibition highly successful, and tried to replicate the model several times in subsequent years: first in the 1950s with *Design in Scandinavia*, and again in 1960 with *The Arts of Denmark*.

The Metropolitan Museum of Art hosted *Swedish Contemporary Decorative Arts* in 1927, with material organized by the Svenska Slöjdföreningen (Swedish Arts and Crafts Society). It was the first showing of modern decorative arts by a foreign country at the museum and traveled to Chicago and Detroit.[16] Following this show, the Metropolitan Museum of Art acquired many works, including Swedish glass.

During the 1920s, Swedish *graal* and engraved glass gained visibility in the U.S. through exhibitions and publications. Similarities between Swedish examples and American pieces by the Steuben division of Corning Glass Works are too related to be coincidental. Steuben's designers would have been aware of engraved Swedish glass through world's fairs and museum exhibitions, and designer Sidney Waugh visited Orrefors in 1930.[17] For instance, Edward Hald's *Vindrosen* (Wind Rose) plate for Orrefors and Waugh's *Mariner's Bowl* for Steuben both feature arrangements of engraved classical figures around a central compass (p. 125).[18] Additionally, Steuben hired Swedish glassblowers to supervise production in the 1930s.[19]

The United States government actively supported displaying American culture abroad by mounting art and design exhibitions in the Nordic countries during the postwar years.[20] The exhibition *American Design for Home and Decorative Use* (1953–55), which traveled to seven Nordic cities and continued on to continental Europe, was arranged as a reciprocal gesture for the *Design in Scandinavia* exhibition, which toured the United States and Canada in 1954–57.[21] It was organized by the Museum of Modern Art and circulated by the United States Information Agency (USIA), a federal body established in 1953 that used cultural propaganda as a weapon against Cold War enemies. Opening in Helsinki, the exhibition was viewed by more than twenty thousand Finns during its eight-day run (p. 24).[22] The Norwegian press dispatched the optimistic message: "We must get to know each other and exchange ideas," following the zeitgeist of the time, which encouraged unity and collaboration among anti-Communist nations.[23]

EDWARD HALD
Orrefors
Vindrosen (Wind Rose) plate, designed 1925, this example 1957. CAT. 57

SIDNEY WAUGH
Steuben Glass, division of Corning Glass Works
Mariner's Bowl, designed 1935, this example 1939. CAT. 167

OBNISKI

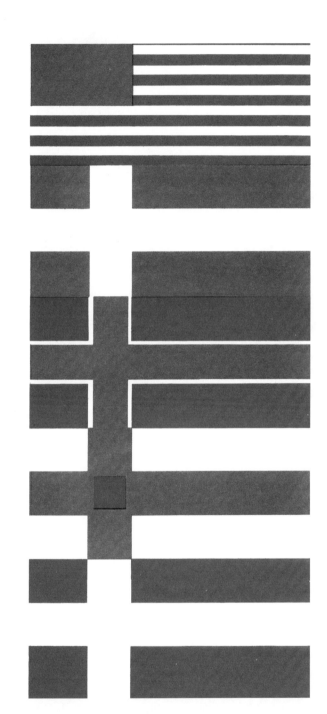

The Museum of
Contemporary Crafts
cordially invites you
to a Preview Opening
of the exhibition
"Young Americans and
Young Scandinavians"
Thursday
November 8th, 1956
from 9 to 11 o'clock
Dress Optional
This card admits two
29 West 53rd Street
New York City

DESIGN FOR DIPLOMACY

GUTTORM GAGNES
David Andersen
Beverage set, 1939. CAT. 44

SIMON GATE
Orrefors
Vase, 1938. CAT. 45

Earlier exhibitions about Scandinavian crafts and design may be seen as precursors for the greatest act of Scandinavian cultural diplomacy—the *Design in Scandinavia* exhibition.[24] Spearheaded by *House Beautiful* editor Elizabeth Gordon and first opened in Richmond, Virginia, at the same time that *American Design for Home and Decorative Use* opened in Oslo, this major endeavor was organized jointly by the national craft and design societies of Denmark, Finland, Norway, and Sweden. The kings of Denmark, Norway, and Sweden, the president of Finland, and President Eisenhower served as the exhibition's honorary patrons, signaling the political importance of this cultural and economic venture. The desired outcome of the touring exhibition was for an "expanding exchange of ideas between designers and producers on both sides of the Atlantic."[25]

The exhibition—with more than seven hundred objects ranging from everyday wares to luxury goods—portrayed a specific cultural image of Scandinavian design.[26] The Scandinavian countries aligned themselves with the democratic, capitalist side of the Cold War divide by appealing to American tastes and associating their products with values of freedom and openness. The exhibition was effusively reviewed in newspapers and magazines. Writing about Norwegian Grete Prytz Korsmo's bowl in *House Beautiful*, for example, Swedish author Arthur Hald described "the enameled bowl from Norway, with a blue arabesque on a white surface, as clear and bold as a reckless Norwegian mountain stream or the equally reckless Norwegian teen-age girl," equating the piece with purity and freedom (p. 126).[27]

Exhibitions of Scandinavian crafts and design, organized by many different groups, continued during the 1950s and 1960s. The American Craftsmen's Council had sponsored a competition for American craftspeople under the age of thirty for several years, but in 1956—at the peak of Scandinavian design enthusiasm—it added Scandinavian design to the mix. With an invitation that suggested unity, the Museum of Contemporary Crafts in New York organized *Young Americans and Young Scandinavians* (p. 127).

Designed objects play a specific role within the diplomatic networks of allied countries, as exemplified by several gifts from Scandinavian countries to President Franklin Delano Roosevelt shortly before the onset of World War II. Sweden, Denmark, and Norway presented Roosevelt with gifts indicative of each country's design expertise: Danish silver, Swedish glass, and Norwegian enamel. During a 1938 visit, Crown Prince Gustaf Adolph and Princess Louise of Sweden presented a Simon Gate–designed Orrefors vase engraved with a depiction of the ship carrying the first Swedes to the Delaware River Valley in 1638 (p. 128). In 1939, Crown Prince Frederik and Princess Ingrid of Denmark gave the Roosevelts a silver urn designed by Sigvard Bernadotte (the Swedish brother of Princess Ingrid) and made by the firm Georg Jensen (cat. 14). That same year, Norway's Crown Prince Olav and Crown Princess Martha offered a beverage set designed by Guttorm Gagnes for David Andersen (p. 128). The set was similar to one shown at the 1939 New York World's Fair, which served as the pretense for these visits—but the encroaching war was perhaps more significant motivation. Writing to the president several months later, Crown Prince Olav explained: "The war between Germany and Great Britain & France was bad enough for us in the Nordic Countries, but the brutal and unprovoked attaque [sic] of Russia on Finland is of course from our point of view very much more serious."[28]

Design was also used in overtly political diplomatic endeavors. U.S. embassies abroad were fundamentally intended to project American influence, and employed International Style modernism as the building form to proclaim the ideals of democracy—stability and transparency, for example—in the postwar era.[29] Nevertheless, the practical execution of these building projects suggests the U.S. government's awareness that imposing one's values would be less advantageous than harnessing local support, as seen in the projects for the Stockholm and Copenhagen embassies, where the American designers worked closely with Swedish and Danish architects.

The greatest diplomatic project of the postwar era was the United Nations headquarters (1946–52), built in New York City as a place for nations to gather peacefully.[30] As with U.S. embassies abroad, International Style modernism was proposed as the appropriate building language. Led by Wallace K. Harrison, ten architects from around the world offered ideas for the building complex. Sven Markelius was the only Scandinavian on the advisory committee, though the interiors were coordinated by Danish-born Abel Sorensen. As symbols of Scandinavia's diplomatic and political position in the world and its design prowess, the three most important UN chambers were entrusted to architects and designers from Denmark, Norway, and Sweden.

Norway's Arnstein Arneberg designed the most important of the three chambers, the Security Council Chamber (p. 131).[31] The wallcovering created by Else Poulsson featured a richly textured blue rayon and gold linen damask design (pp. 132–33). Its motifs of anchors, hearts, and wheat, symbolizing faith, charity, and hope, continued on the curtains, which framed a large mural by artist Per Krohg. Sweden's Markelius furnished the Economic and Social Affairs Council Chamber.[32] The room's focal point was Marianne Richter's tapestry curtain, which featured vibrant tones of magenta, orange, and plum in a geometric pattern, adding color, warmth, and texture to the otherwise neutral modernist palette, materially supporting the diplomatic

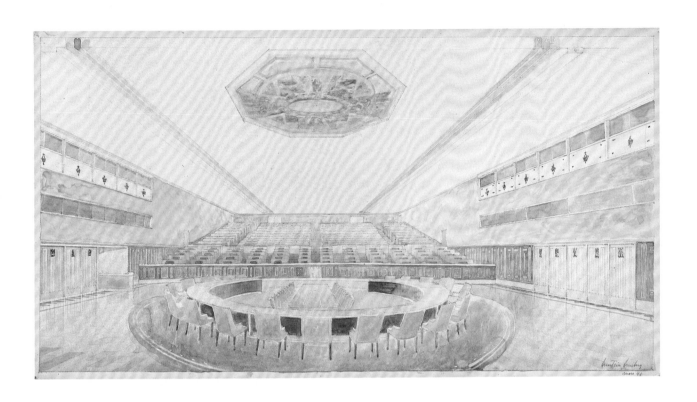

MARIANNE RICHTER
Sketch of tapestry for United Nations
Economic and Social Council Chamber,
c. 1951. CAT. 124

132

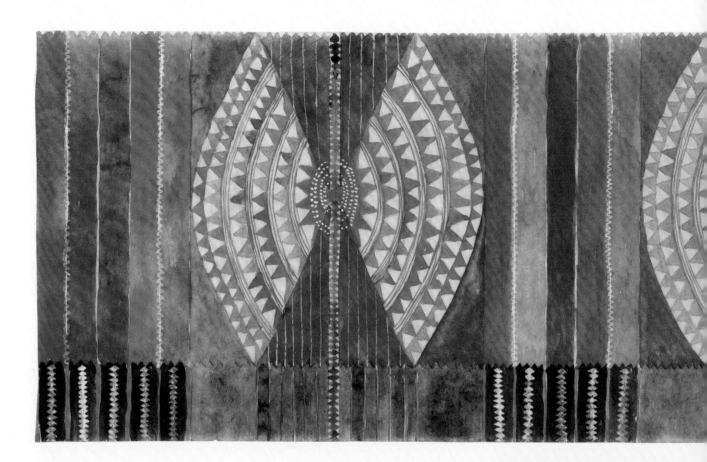

mission (pp. 132–33). Denmark's Finn Juhl was responsible for the Trusteeship Council Chamber. Juhl created visual interest on the ceiling with rows of battens and colorful boxes installed at varying intervals.[33] Juhl also designed the tables and chairs of walnut and sycamore and upholstered in dark blue, teal, and chartreuse for delegates and secretaries (p. 135).

While Juhl's chairs were designed expressly for the diplomatic sphere, Hans Wegner's chair became known because of a political event. For the first televised presidential debate—held in Chicago on September 26, 1960, between Senator John F. Kennedy and Vice President Richard M. Nixon—CBS used two Hans Wegner chairs (below).[34] Critics noted Nixon's tired and anxious appearance (he had undergone surgery a few weeks earlier), compared to Kennedy's relaxed look. While the chairs had nothing to do with the candidates' performance, Republican strategists blamed Nixon's lackluster showing on the "atmosphere created by the Chicago stage set."[35] The chair's role in these debates renders it a part of a larger narrative of design and diplomacy, and a powerful symbol of the exchange between the United States and the Nordic countries.

Hans Wegner chairs used at the first televised United States presidential debate between Senator John F. Kennedy and Vice President Richard Nixon, September 26, 1960

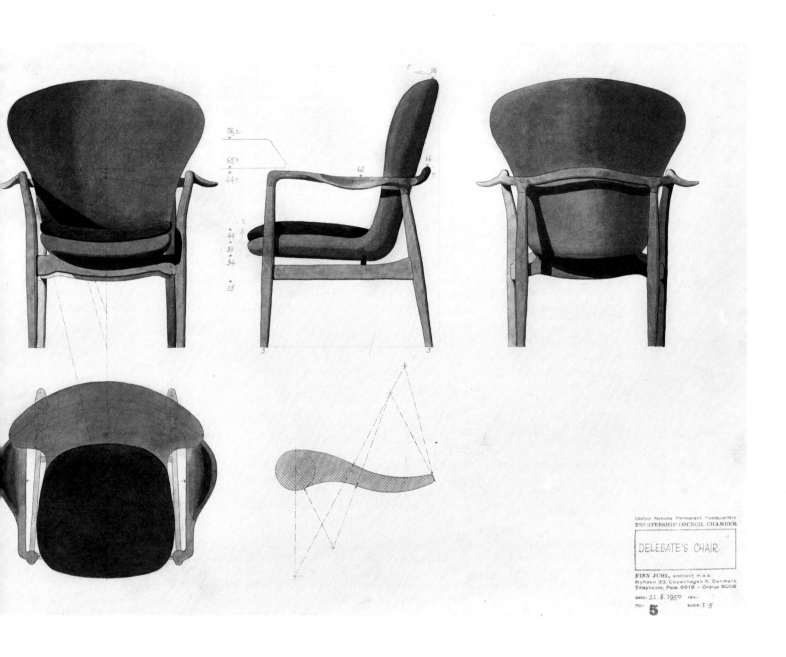

United Nations Permanent Headquarters
TRUSTEESHIP COUNCIL CHAMBER

DELEGATE'S CHAIR

FINN JUHL, architect m.a.a.
Nyhavn 33, Copenhagen K, Denmark
Telephones; Palæ 6616 - Ordrup 6009

date: 21. 8. 1950   rev.:
no.: 5   scale: 1:5

DESIGN FOR DIPLOMACY

1 Harriet Atkinson and Verity Clarkson, "Editors' Introduction," in "Design as an Object of Diplomacy Post-1945," ed. Harriet Atkinson and Verity Clarkson, special issue, *Design and Culture* 9, no. 2 (2017): 117–22; Fredie Floré and Cammie McAtee, "Introduction: The Politics of Furniture," in *The Politics of Furniture: Identity, Diplomacy and Persuasion in Post-War Interiors*, ed. Fredie Floré and Cammie McAtee (London: Routledge, 2017), 1–11. For the origin of the term "soft power," see Joseph S. Nye Jr., "Soft Power," *Foreign Policy*, no. 80 (1990): 153–71.

2 Robert W. Rydell, *All the World's a Fair: Visions of Empire at American International Expositions, 1876–1916* (Chicago: University of Chicago Press, 1984).

3 Rydell, *All the World's a Fair*, 11.

4 Bruno Giberti, *Designing the Centennial: A History of the 1876 International Exhibition in Philadelphia* (Lexington: University Press of Kentucky, 2002), 145.

5 *Frank Leslie's Illustrated Historical Register of the Centennial Exposition*, ed. Frank H. Norton (New York, 1877), 87. For more on Hazelius, founder of the Nordiska Museet and Skansen, see Daniel Alan DeGroff, "Artur Hazelius and the Ethnographic Display of the Scandinavian Peasantry: A Study in Context and Appropriation," *European Review of History* 19 (2012): 229–48.

6 Inger-Marie Lie, "Furniture," in *The Art of Norway, 1750–1914*, exh. cat., ed. Louise Lincoln (Minneapolis: Minneapolis Institute of Arts, 1978), 184–86.

7 Kjetil Fallan, "Nordic Noir: Deadly Design from the Peacemongering Periphery," in "The Influence of Scandinavian Design," ed. Bobbye Tigerman, special issue, *Design and Culture* 7 (2016): 377–402.

8 *Official Catalogue of Exhibits: World's Columbian Exposition, U.S. Government Building* (Chicago, 1893), 69.

9 Arthur J. Pulos, *The American Design Adventure, 1940–1975* (Cambridge, MA: MIT Press: 1988), 29.

10 Kerstin Smeds and Peter MacKeith, *The Finland Pavilions: Finland at the Universal Expositions, 1900–1992*, trans. John Arnold (Helsinki: Kustannus Oy City, 1992), 53–61.

11 "'Symphony in Wood' of Finns Has Debut: Finnish and Netherlands Pavilions Dedicated at Fair," *New York Times*, May 5, 1939.

12 G. A. Berg, "What Swedish Modern Is in Sweden," *American Home*, July 1939, 22–23, 65–67.

13 "Foreign Nations," *Architectural Forum* 70 (June 1939): 444.

14 "Scandinavian Rooms on View," *Brooklyn Daily Eagle*, April 18, 1926; Exhibition: Paintings, Sculpture and Arts & Crafts of Denmark (Danish National Exhibition) and Exhibition: Swedish Art, Records of the Office of the Director, Brooklyn Museum Archives.

15 November 4, 1927 press release, Brooklyn Museum Archives.

16 Robert W. De Forest, "The Opening of the Swedish Exhibition of Arts and Crafts" (opening statement, January 17, 1927), Loan Exhibitions-Held-1927-Swedish Contemporary Art-Publicity, Metropolitan Museum of Art Archives, New York.

17 Mary Jean Smith Madigan, *Steuben Glass: An American Tradition in Crystal* (New York: Abrams, 1982), 70.

18 Derek E. Ostergard, "Modern Swedish Glass in America, 1924–1939," in *The Brilliance of Swedish Glass, 1918–1939: An Alliance of Art and Industry*, exh. cat., ed. Derek E. Ostergard and Nina Stritzler-Levine (New Haven and London: Yale University Press in association with the Bard Graduate Center, 1996), 136–55.

19 Madigan, *Steuben Glass*, 71.

20 For examples beyond Scandinavia, see Greg Castillo, *Cold War on the Home Front: The Soft Power of Midcentury Design* (Minneapolis: University of Minnesota Press, 2010).

21 Gay McDonald, "The Modern American Home as Soft Power: Finland, MoMA and the 'American Home 1953' Exhibition," *Journal of Design History* 23, no. 4 (2010): 388–89.

22 "Summary Report on *American Design for Home and Decorative Use*" (dated in pencil, September 16, 1954), International Council and International Program Records, I.B.22, The Museum of Modern Art Archives, New York.

23 "Translation of Article in *Morgenavisen*, February 20, 1954," IC/IP, I.B.22, MoMA Archives, New York.

24 Arne Remlov, ed., *Design in Scandinavia: An Exhibition of Objects for the Home from Denmark, Finland, Norway, Sweden*, exh. cat. (Oslo: Kirstes Boktrykkeri, 1954); Jørn Guldberg, "'Scandinavian Design' as Discourse: The Exhibition Design in Scandinavia, 1954–57," *Design Issues* 27, no. 2 (Spring 2011): 41–58.

25 Ambassador Wilhelm Morgenstierne, "A Significant Venture," *Norwegian American Commerce* 17 (March 1954): 7.

26 For Norway's rationale, see Kjetil Fallan, "Crafting Scandinavian Design: Craft vs. Industrial Design in the Norwegian Contributions to the *Design in Scandinavia* and *X Triennale di Milano* Exhibitions," in *Design and Craft: A History of Convergences and Divergences: 7th Conference of the International Committee of Design History and Design Studies*, ed. Javier Gimeno-Martinez and Fredie Floré (Brussels: Koninklijke vlaamse academie van België voor Wetenschappen en kunsten, 2010), 420–24.

27 Arthur Hald, "A Fresh Breeze from the Northeast," *House Beautiful* 96 (February 1954): 97.

28 Crown Prince Olav to President Roosevelt, December 6, 1939, Norway 1935–39, Diplomatic Correspondence, President's Secretary's File, Franklin D. Roosevelt Presidential Library and Museum.

29 Beyond nationalistic zeal, the economic argument was also made that by building abroad, rental costs would be lowered, thus saving valuable taxpayer dollars. The building program was financed mainly by the use of foreign currency credits under the Marshall Plan, Lend-Lease, and Surplus Property; "For Your Information: America Abroad," *Interiors* 113 (November 1953): 8–15.

30 Ingeborg Glambek, "The Council Chambers in the UN Building in New York," *Scandinavian Journal of Design History* 15 (2005): 8–39.

31 *The Security Council Chamber*, exh. cat., ed. Jørn Holme (Oslo: Forlaget Press, 2018).

32 Eva Rudberg, *Sven Markelius, Architect*, trans. Roger Tanner (Stockholm: Architekturmuseet, 1989), 127–31.

33 Anne-Louise Sommer, *Watercolors by Finn Juhl*, trans. James Manley (Berlin: Hatje Cantz, 2016), 12. His assistant Marianne Riis-Carstensen developed the colors.

34 Per H. Hansen, *Danish Modern Furniture 1930–2016: The Rise, Decline and Re-emergence of a Cultural Market Category*, trans. Mark Mussari (Odense: University Press of Southern Denmark, 2018), 251–52.

35 Russell Baker, "Nixon Aides Fret about 2D Debate: But Hope 'Warmer' Setting Will Bar 'Tired' Look on TV Tomorrow Night," *New York Times*, October 6, 1960.

OBNISKI

Transatlantic Exchange: Performing Scandinavia at American World's Fairs

CHARLOTTE ASHBY

People and objects were not the only things that traveled back and forth between the United States and the Nordic countries in the late nineteenth and early twentieth centuries; whole buildings also made that journey. This essay will explore the design and afterlife of a few notable buildings that were presented as examples of Scandinavian culture at American world's fairs. The United States was a highly sought-after market for European goods, making it an important audience to reach and impress. The three buildings discussed here, unlike most exhibition structures, found long-term homes in the United States after the exhibitions for which they were constructed had closed. These buildings raise questions about the projection of national identity in an international arena and the role of architecture in communicating ideas of place, kinship, and cultural specificity.

The first of these was the Swedish Schoolhouse built for the 1876 Centennial International Exposition in Philadelphia, which became a recreational building in New York City's Central Park. The building blended messages of modern scientific education reform with more romantic associations of an ideal, rural Swedish community. The second structure under discussion is the Norway Building from the 1893 World's Columbian Exposition in Chicago, which reflected the high point of National Romanticism in the form of the Viking Revival known as *dragestil* ("dragon style"). Norwegian heritage was celebrated, with a particular nod to the Viking Age connections between Norway and North America. The intertwined issues of authenticity and invented tradition can be traced over the long life of this building, recently returned to Norway. The final building considered here is the Swedish Pavilion from the 1904 Louisiana Purchase Exposition in St. Louis, now located in Lindsborg, Kansas. The motivation for moving the building and its subsequent uses reveal how it functioned to meet the needs of Swedish Americans seeking to express their immigrant identity as well as raise the profile of their small town.

Exhibition Architecture
The latter half of the nineteenth century and the first decades of the twentieth were punctuated by a series of international exhibitions that reflected the rise of nationalism and global competition as well as the growth of internationalism and cooperation. These world's fairs brought scores of nations together in

SCHWEDISCHES SCHULHAUS.   EDIFICIO DE ESCUELA DE SUÉCIA.   ECOLE SUEDOISE.

SWEDISH SCHOOL HOUSE.

events that showcased technological innovations, natural resources, colonial ties, military might, and cultural achievements.[1] Events focused on competition and the fostering of excellence, with prizes and medals awarded in every conceivable category. They were, in a sense, an Olympics of objects, through which the political, economic, and cultural strengths of nations might be measured.

Participating countries competed for prestige on the international stage. These exhibitions—which combined public relations, trade, entertainment, and education—have been the subject of much scholarly attention, particularly as they functioned as vehicles for state-sponsored ideology.[2] World's fairs bombarded visitors with new sensory experiences and information presented in multiple formats. Within these huge events it was challenging for smaller nations to get noticed, as the size and location of displays were dictated by the priorities of the host nation. In each participating country, committees lobbied government and industry for funds, which in turn determined the size and scope of national displays. Small nations had to make judicious choices

if they were to have any hope of catching the public eye and securing a return on the high costs involved in shipping and installing their displays. The success of a country's showing could be measured in medals won, footfall through the door, and reviews in the international press. All this information was carefully gathered and reported back home, to be taken into consideration for the next fair.

National committees and pavilion architects agonized over decisions about a pavilion's form and content in order to create the most favorable impression upon visitors. Ultimately, though, the meaning of each country's presentation was created through the encounter between their designs and the visitors.[3] The three structures discussed here represent three attempts to present two Scandinavian nations—Sweden and Norway—to the American public, revealing some foundational ideas that shaped North American views on Swedish and Norwegian identity. By considering the long lives of these buildings in the United States, we can trace how these associations shifted over time.

Swedish School House, 1876, depicted by Thompson Westcott. Lithograph from *Centennial Portfolio: A Souvenir of the International Exhibition at Philadelphia*, 1876

The Swedish Schoolhouse: Philadelphia, 1876

The Swedish Schoolhouse was built for the 1876 Centennial International Exposition in Philadelphia (p. 138). This was the first of the major world's fairs in the United States, and Sweden's contribution marked a determined effort on the country's part to distinguish itself in the area of public education. The Swedish Schoolhouse was the culmination of a series of increasingly extensive and ambitious displays of Swedish educational expertise at international exhibitions.[4] Swedish education reforms in the mid-nineteenth century had yielded the successful, nationwide public elementary school system called the *folkskola*, followed by a national schoolhouse design standard in 1865. Simultaneously, educational theory was featured as a distinct category within international exhibitions starting in the 1860s.[5] Sweden's contributions were praised in the international press; in response the country devoted increasing resources to educational displays at subsequent fairs, which garnered further praise and attention. The expense of sending an entire schoolhouse was significant, and few countries went to these lengths, but Sweden presented one in London in 1871, in Vienna in 1873, and again in Philadelphia in 1876.[6]

This trajectory of bigger and better displays illustrates the positive feedback loop that so often shaped the presentation of national identity in the international arena. The presentation of a schoolhouse in the United States had particular cachet, as it was one of the few other countries prominent in educational theory and practice. Per A. Siljeström, the Swedish theorist central to the development of new thinking on schoolhouse design, had formed many of his ideas while traveling in the United States in the 1840s.[7] Sweden's 1876 schoolhouse was intended to be even more well-designed and appealing than the one shown in 1873 in Vienna in order to create the strongest impression of a nation with the highest educational standards.

The nationally standardized building plans for schoolhouses in Sweden were based on a single-story wooden building; one large rectangular room functioned as the schoolroom and the remaining section of the building served as a small apartment for the teacher. The schoolhouse shown in Vienna largely replicated this design, though with more attention to decorative detail and an attic story. In Philadelphia the design was further adapted. In place of the wooden frame with weatherboards, the schoolhouse shown in Philadelphia was constructed out of round logs, in a manner that reflected the contemporary trend for National Romantic architecture. The log construction, deep eaves, and projecting upper story evoked the traditional form of the rural Swedish grain store, or *stuga*, which was one of the core forms used in Swedish National Romanticism.[8] This revaluation of folk culture and crafts as unique national markers reflected a new cultural turn across Europe, as seen in national revivals and other Arts and Crafts movements.[9] This log cabin character also helped the schoolhouse tie in with other Swedish displays, notably Artur Hazelius's arrangements of mannequins in folk dress, mounted in scenes of everyday life that were also exhibited in Philadelphia to great effect (p. 15).[10] These types of displays would later appear in Stockholm in the Nordiska Museet, a museum dedicated to preserving Nordic culture, and Skansen, the world's first open-air museum.[11]

Why did Sweden make these changes in 1876 to present a building that differed so much from the prototype for Swedish schools? The shift allowed Sweden to link different elements of its fair presentation together, essentially creating a stronger national brand. It also reflects something of the way fair architecture functioned, blending fact and fiction, theater and science. Unlike other vehicles for the dissemination of information, such as printed material, images, or film, buildings are entered physically. They thus have a different potential to transport the visitor, who must approach and step inside the structure. The impact of these spaces lay not in factual authenticity, but in the power to give visitors an immediate sense of experiencing a true insight into another country.

Unlike displays located within exhibition halls, pavilions are distinct entities that function as capsules of experience. Postcards of exhibition buildings frequently depicted these structures relocated into imagined landscapes of the nations they represented, capturing the extent to which visiting a country's pavilion was understood as a proxy-visit to the country itself. As one commentator noted, "Few who visited the exhibition, would likely visit Sweden; she, therefore in effect, transported to Philadelphia, as it were, a little shady nook of a rural village, with its quaint, but tasteful Schoolhouse."[12] The Swedish Schoolhouse thus transported American visitors to the Swedish countryside. Through its clean and airy interior, thoughtful provision of different-sized desks for children of different ages, and array of stimulating educational apparatus for drawing, making, studying, and physical exercise, the schoolhouse represented an outstanding example of state provision for public education. International and American audiences were suitably impressed, and the building won a gold medal. In reality, while some new schools had been built following the proposed school building reforms, many old, poorly lit, and ill-furnished buildings remained.[13] That the schoolhouse presented in Philadelphia was not what

schoolhouses in Sweden necessarily looked like was unimportant. The image of Sweden as a nation in which all children were responsibly cared for was established in the public arena, and inspired pride and affirmation for these efforts.

The image was a desirable one and, like nearly all the material on display at these international exhibitions, it was also for sale. After the 1871 exhibition in London, the South Kensington library purchased nearly all the education materials from the Swedish section, forming the basis for a library of education. After the 1873 exhibition in Vienna, the Romanian government made special requests to the Swedish government for their schoolhouse plans.[14] The 1876 Philadelphia pavilion itself cost between twenty-five and thirty thousand Swedish krona and was purchased for fifteen hundred dollars (about thirty-five thousand dollars today) by the City of New York.[15] At the suggestion of landscape architect Frederick Law Olmsted, it found a place in Central Park in 1877 (left). This occurred despite the financial pressures the park was under as the city sought to cut expenses during the depression of the 1870s.[16] (Olmsted himself was to lose his job with the Parks Department the following year.)

As a landscape architect, Olmsted was driven by his aesthetic vision for the park, to which the building made a picturesque addition; there was little thought given to how it would actually be used. Initially it functioned as a toolshed and later as a public restroom. In the 1910s local Swedish Americans, who felt a sense of ownership or connection to the building, lobbied for it to be repurposed to something more respectable.[17] Park commissioner Charles Stover acquiesced and, as part of his wider project to make the park into a recreation area that welcomed the city's working people, it became a center for the study of entomology in 1912.[18] However, tensions surrounding the allocation and use of space in Central Park continued to surface, and the *New York Times* took issue with the new plan: "The place [for the school] is to be the shanty on the edge of the Ramble, which has been called the Swedish schoolhouse, and has a history which would be more respectable if it had never been dumped in Central Park. Mr. Stover proposes to have a perpetual exhibition of bugs in that shanty. The study of bugs

Swedish Cottage Marionette Theatre, Central Park, New York City. Photographed in 2006

is edifying, but Central Park is no place for schools."[19] The Swedish community took issue with the description of it as a "shanty," and a letter to the editor was published a few days later: "In the issue of THE TIMES of June 30 you speak of the Swedish schoolhouse as a 'shanty,' which is hardly fair when we consider it constituted a valuable Swedish educational exhibit at the World's Fair held in Philadelphia in 1876. The Swedish people of New York value it on this account and it certainly deserves a place somewhere in the public domain."[20]

The schoolhouse functioned as the civil defense headquarters during World War II, and in 1947 it assumed its present role as home to the park's Marionette Theatre. Though it is occasionally referred to incorrectly as a Swiss Cottage, a Central Park website currently notes the building's Swedish identity: "In a show of patriotism, both Swedish and American flags fly from the roof of what was once a traditional schoolhouse."[21] The building's afterlife intriguingly perpetuates the blurred lines between its character as both educational and theatrical: its picturesque qualities, intended to catch the eye of exhibition crowds, contributed to its second life within the park landscape. The fantasy evocation of Swedish schoolchildren, diligently arriving each morning, continues to echo in the suggestion that it was once a traditional schoolhouse and in the ongoing association with childhood that stems from its current role as a children's theater. The building thus communicated Swedish progress in Philadelphia while subsequently projecting rustic, rural charm in New York.

The Norway Building: Chicago, 1893

The idea of exhibition architecture-as-voyage is also captured in the Norway Building presented at the next major American world's fair, the World's Columbian Exposition in Chicago in 1893 (p. 142). The 1890s were the high point of the various national revivals across Europe, and Norway's contribution to this trend was *dragestil*.[22] The style drew on folk culture and architectural heritage in the form of wooden buildings and objects decorated with elaborate carvings, often depicting dragons in particular. In Norway, this was a reflection of the country's desire for political independence from Sweden, and was further stimulated by archaeological discoveries such as the Gokstad ship. The first major Viking vessel to be excavated was the Tune ship in 1867, followed in 1880 by the Gokstad ship. These ships became part of the University of Oslo's Collection of National Antiquities (Universitetets Oldsaksamling) and were exhibited in Oslo, attracting national and international attention.[23]

Dragestil was particularly popular in Norway for holiday villas and hotels, where it performed another sort of architectural transportation: a voyage into the past. Norwegian tourists could imagine themselves transported to the feasting halls of their ancestors in buildings such as the Holmenkollen Hotel.[24] *Dragestil* also had international currency. Public fascination with Viking archeology was widespread, including in the United States.[25] Norwegian architectural heritage in the form of stave churches also achieved international renown, following increased interest in historic craft and wooden architecture starting in the mid-nineteenth century.[26] These wooden buildings, which dated from the eleventh century, represented the survival of a unique architectural tradition, distinct in construction and ornament from anywhere else in Europe. National distinctiveness was always at a premium in the crowded

Gol stave church at the Norsk
Folkemuseum, Bygdøy, Norway,
c. 1880–90

The Norway Building at the 1893 World's
Columbian Exposition, designed by
Albert Waldemar Hansteen.
Photograph from *Picturesque World's
Fair: An Elaborate Collection of Colored
Views*, 1894

THE NORWEGIAN BUILDING.—Despite their political connection, Norway and Sweden had separate buildings at the World's Fair, each a credit to its country. The Norwegian Building was situated near the lake front and east of the North Pond, amid a group of trees familiar to those who have visited Jackson Park before an Exposition was thought of. In size the building was sixty by twenty-five feet, and was constructed almost entirely of Norway pine. All the workmen employed and all the material used were Norwegian, the house being made at Drontheim, put together with screws to enable transportation, and then taken apart again and shipped to this country. It had gables surmounted by conventional "dragons' heads," such as those which appeared on the Viking Ships, and quaint oriel windows which gave a most picturesque effect. No attempt at a display of products was made in this building, Norway being well represented elsewhere, but a large map of Norway, a few banners and a picture of the Viking Ship were among the decorations of the interior. The Viking Ship, with the great Norse discovery it suggested, was, in itself display enough for one nation, and the Scandinavians, as descendants of the daring race who first learned that America existed, had splendid recognition at the Fair. In the Norwegian Building, the race who have been sea-rovers from time immemorial, gathered and were as merry as were their ancestors returning after a raid along the southern coasts of Europe.

114

and competitive arena of world's fairs and the decision to build the small Norwegian pavilion emulating a stave church capitalized on the form's recent rise in popularity.

The building was commissioned from the firm M. Thams & Co., which produced crates and flat-packed wooden buildings in Orkdal, Norway. The architect Albert Waldemar Hansteen had experience in designing flat-pack buildings for M. Thams & Co. He had also been responsible for the architectural restoration of the Gol stave church (p. 142).[27] Both areas of experience fed into his design for the Norway Building. The pavilion was not a replica of the Gol church, but fidelity to the original source of inspiration remained important in its design, which had a similarly evocative silhouette. Details such as the carved heads of Norse kings and queens on the staves in the interior and the carved dragon heads of the ridge crests on the exterior explicitly referred to the Gol church, though here the dragons were made larger than the original. This practice of rendering ornamental details more prominent in exhibition architecture was well established. For example, the installation of the Alhambra court at the 1851 Great Exhibition in London was reduced in scale, but ornamental details were retained at full size.[28] For many fair visitors, ornament was the point of interest and was also particularly regarded as a bearer of national identity.[29]

Just as the Swedish Schoolhouse in Philadelphia was visually aligned with the other Swedish displays to create a stronger overall impression, the Norwegian contribution in Chicago sought a similar cumulative impact. Norway's displays in the Manufactures and Liberal Arts Building also included *dragestil* woodwork by M. Thams & Co. The highlight of the country's presence at the fair was a full-scale replica of the Gokstad ship, named *Viking*, which a Norwegian crew had sailed across the Atlantic in a bid to prove the assertion that America was first "discovered" by (Norwegian) Vikings.[30] It was a bold move, considering that the fair was framed as a celebration of the "discovery" of America by Christopher Columbus.[31] The feat played well to a strand of American thinking enchanted by the idea of Vinland and the possibility of proto-Protestant, Viking origins of the United States.[32]

The national identity advanced in these pavilions was undoubtedly of the top-down variety.[33] The craftsmen who actually made the buildings or the schoolchildren who contributed their work to displays had no say in how either Sweden or Norway was represented. Instead, such contributions were used to reaffirm an image of their nation that they were themselves presented with in textbooks, national pageants, almanacs, and other sources. The nation-building education project was so effective in Norway that the ship that sailed to Chicago was funded by a country-wide public subscription. Connections between the old countries and the new communities of Scandinavians in the United States, fostered especially by the circulation of printed materials, ensured that nation-building ideologies and mythologies were also readily recognized by expatriate communities.

Cornelius Kingsland Billings, president of the People's Gas Light and Coke Company of Chicago and a member of the board of directors for the Columbian Exposition, was proud of his Norwegian heritage and of his contributions to the success of the fair—which he commemorated by buying the Norway Building and re-erecting it on the grounds of his rural retreat on the shores of Lake Geneva, Wisconsin.[34] The wooden construction of both the Swedish Schoolhouse and the Norway Building lent themselves to disassembly and reassembly. This ease with which such wooden buildings could be transported was a factor in the preservation of many of them, such as the Gol stave church, which had been transported from Hallingdal to the antiquities collection of King Oscar II, later the Norsk Folkemuseum (Norwegian Museum of Cultural History) at Bygdøy. Another example was the stave church of Valdres, which the famous Norwegian landscape painter and antiquarian Johan Christian Dahl persuaded King Friedrich Wilhelm IV of Prussia to save from destruction by purchasing and re-erecting it on one of his estates.[35]

This was not the end of the Norway Building's journey. The estate on Lake Geneva passed through the hands of various owners for whom the building had less significance. It was converted into a private movie theater in 1917;[36] in some disrepair, it was finally bought in 1932 by Isak Dahle, a Chicago businessman whose ambition was to build a museum celebrating the Norwegian heritage of his family, the state of Wisconsin, and the United States. The Norway Building was again disassembled and rebuilt to become the centerpiece of the Little Norway museum, also called Nissedahle, located outside Mt. Horeb, Wisconsin (p. 143). It stood alongside a collection of buildings erected following traditional techniques used by early Norwegian settlers of the area. In this manner the site captured the intersection of Norwegian heritage and American immigrant culture. Dahle furnished the buildings with Norwegian craft objects from his family collection, objects purchased directly from Norway, and also via appeals to the local Norwegian American community. A notice was placed in the local paper, which read: "Have You Any Norse Antiques to Sell? If so, bring them to Dahle's Store. Am especially anxious to get old furniture, paintings, dishes, wooden bowls, etc. In fact any Norwegian antiquity that will add to the interest of 'Little Norway' (as it is being called)."[37]

The collection had parallels with the phenomenon of open-air museums, which had originated in 1891 with Skansen in Sweden and which was swiftly replicated across the Nordic countries and further afield. The open-air museum, like exhibition architecture, transports visitors across time and geography. Both Skansen and the Norsk Folkemuseum presented a journey around their respective nations in miniature as well as a journey back in time through the display of traditional ways of life and craft practices that were rapidly becoming obsolete. In the face of assimilation into broader American society and rapid social change, the memorialization of Norwegian immigrant heritage in Little Norway sought to capture the distinctiveness of that community and its connection to the past. After Little Norway closed in 2012, the Norway Building made a return journey in 2016 to Orkdal, Norway, where it had originally been manufactured. In Orkdal, it is in the process of again being restored, this time as an artifact of Norwegian cultural and industrial history.[38] Residents of Orkdal led the campaign to retrieve the building, whose future in America had become uncertain. The name of their campaign, Prosjekt Heimatt (Project Heimatt, in English) uses the difficult-to-translate term *heimatt*, meaning home or homeward-bound, conveying the emotive sense of belonging and longing for return.

Heritage, identity, and belonging are complex issues. Dahle's grandfather emigrated from Norway; Dahle did not visit the country himself until adulthood, but his emotional connection to the idea of Norway played a significant role in his life and identity. His dedication to Little Norway and the transfer of this dedication to his family members over three generations is testament to that. Additionally, Dahle was a member of the American Scandinavian Foundation, the Norwegian American Society, and the Chicago Norske Klub. The very existence of such societies indicates the wider importance of this heritage to the identities of many Americans of Nordic descent. In a fitting parallel, Sigrid Stenset and Olav Sigurd Kvaale, residents of the Orkdal municipality and active as part of the Project Heimatt campaign, are the grandchildren of Peder Hvaale, the M. Thams craftsman who executed the artistic centerpiece of the Norway Building, the hand-carved entrance portal.[39] Over the course of its lifetime, the building has retained powerful, if shifting, meanings. Whether as a symbol of independent eleventh-century Norway, the burgeoning nineteenth-century flat-pack industry, or the ancestral homeland of a twentieth-century American, the Norway Building has been able to transport these meanings back and forth across the ocean and through time.

The Swedish Pavilion: St. Louis, 1904

The Swedish Pavilion at the Louisiana Purchase Exposition in St. Louis in 1904 was intended as a gathering place and hospitality venue for Swedish organizers, exhibitors, and visitors from Sweden and of Swedish heritage (p. 147). It was designed by Ferdinand Boberg, considered Sweden's premier exhibition architect after executing much of the 1897 Stockholm Exhibition. Following common practice, Boberg's design for the St. Louis fair evoked a historical type, in this case an eighteenth-century manor house. Like the other buildings discussed above, it was constructed of wood, prefabricated in Sweden, and shipped to the United States. Rather than suggesting rustic or folkish associations, the building was painted yellow with white trim and a red tile roof. This color combination and subdued classicism of the composition were familiar from the manor houses and large farmhouses of the Swedish countryside; from the 1890s they were also seen in middle-class villas. In this way the design alluded to Swedish high culture and heritage, suggesting that Sweden was not interested in presenting herself as a backwoods nation.

Additionally, Boberg planned for Swedish native plants (and the gardeners to care for them) to be brought over to surround the building.[40] At the end of the fair the building was purchased by the United States Minister to Sweden and Norway, W. W. Thomas Jr., for two thousand dollars (about fifty-five thousand dollars today).[41] This recouped a small amount of the seventeen thousand dollars the building originally cost.[42] The building was donated to Bethany College, a Swedish Lutheran school established in 1881 in Lindsborg, Kansas, in memory of the college's founder, Carl Aaron Swensson. Swensson, a second-generation Swedish American, had been a member of the committee that helped to plan and finance the Swedish section of the Louisiana Purchase Exposition.[43] Lindsborg itself had been founded in 1869 by Swedish immigrants, and it maintained strong connections to Sweden. Boberg's building was used by the college from 1905 to 1960 for a range of functions, including as a classroom, library, museum, and art studio (p. 147).

The first generation of American settlers often held complex and ambivalent attitudes toward the nations they had left behind. Immigration to the United States had frequently been driven by necessity, with the majority of nineteenth-century Swedish immigrants drawn from the class of landless

Swedish Pavilion at the 1904 Louisiana Purchase Exposition, designed by Ferdinand Boberg

Swedish Pavilion from the 1904 Louisiana Purchase Exposition as part of McPherson County Old Mill Museum, Lindsborg, Kansas. Photographed in 2015

rural laborers. Subsequent generations often regarded "the old country" with greater affection and through a veil of nostalgia, as seen with Dahle in relation to Norway. It was typically second- or third-generation Americans who traveled back to their ancestors' home countries and reestablished connections with extended family, and it was these later generations who embraced the Swedish Pavilion and its place in their community as a symbol of Sweden.[44] But in doing so, it became a part of local history and memory.

Bethany College, which was closely tied to the church, played a central role in the community life of Lindsborg through the first half of the twentieth century.[45] Between social, fundraising, and educational activities, a great number of the inhabitants of Lindsborg would have passed through the Swedish Pavilion's doors during these years. These functions were intertwined in the Swedish community festivals that were enacted in and around the building. The Svensk Hyllningsfest, which has celebrated the founding of the town by Swedish immigrants since the 1940s, is the largest of a series of celebrations, which also include St. Lucia Day, Midsummer, and *julotta* (Christmas matins). As an authentically Swedish house, the building was regarded as the appropriate home for such festivals and other community gatherings. Anthropologist Lizette Gradén has commented on the distinctions between the way Midsummer is celebrated at the Swedish Pavilion in Lindsborg and how it is celebrated in Sweden, and the tensions between those who want to maintain "the Lindsborg way" and those who have visited or come from Sweden more recently.[46] For example, the garlands of greenery preferred by Lindsborg traditionalists are more reminiscent of those Boberg used to decorate the original pavilion, thereby preserving Swedish tastes of 1904 rather than reflecting contemporary Sweden. The Swedish character cultivated in the building has become the Swedishness of the immigrant community and increasingly extends to encompass Lindsborg residents who identify with the town's Swedish brand, whether or not they have Swedish heritage.

In 1969 the building was donated to the Smoky Valley Historical Association, and was moved to become part of the McPherson County Old Mill Museum complex. This was accompanied by a restoration process that returned the building to Boberg's design. As part of this local history museum, which contains other buildings relating to the industrial and social history of Lindsborg, the pavilion is museologized as both a Swedish building and an American one. Originally a representation in 1904 of Sweden as a cultured and sophisticated nation, the building now represents a connection to a Swedish past and the persistence of traditional values.

Heritage and history are valuable building blocks in the formation of identity. Just as the late nineteenth-century Norwegians used artifacts from the tenth through twelfth centuries to define their national identity, so twentieth- and twenty-first-century Americans use elements of history to establish their own identities. This happens not only on an individual and familial level, but also on a civic level. Swedishness was something that made Lindsborg distinctive, and as tourism became increasingly important to the economy, it was actively used as part of the town's self-branding from the 1960s onwards. This occurred despite the fact that an ever-declining fraction of Lindsborg's population claim Swedish ancestry. Participation in celebrations of Swedishness is increasingly not about the past, but about a present sense of belonging to the town.[47] The town was nicknamed "Little Sweden USA" and the Dala horse was made the official town symbol. It remains so today, with the town website greeting visitors: *Välkommen till Lindsborg!*[48]

These three buildings all reflect the power of architecture to function as a vessel for ideas and emotions, even contradictory ones. The Swedish Schoolhouse was both an ambassador for a modern education system and a symbol of a charming, timeless, rural idyll. The Norway Building conveyed first the proud history of the ancient independent kingdom of Norway, and then the personal success of a prominent Chicago businessman. It went on to form the centerpiece of two labors of love—first as a celebration of Norwegian immigrant heritage in Wisconsin, and then as a commemoration of the achievements of local craftsmen in Norway. The Swedish Pavilion represented the trim elegance of a modern yet traditional Sweden. It then became a monument to the efforts of a Swedish immigrant educator. Over time, as it became a community building, its meaning shifted to represent the community's Swedishness, whether that meant its residents' actual heritage or simply residents' sense of affiliation with the town's identity. As a museum object, it continues these functions, while also representing the educational aspirations of the town and the immigrants who founded it. The long histories of these buildings, and their adoption by individuals and communities, reveal the ties that continue to stretch across the Atlantic, generation after generation.

1 Paul Greenhalgh, *Ephemeral Vistas: The Expositions Universelles, Great Exhibitions and World's Fairs, 1851–1939* (Manchester: Manchester University Press, 1988); Robert Rydell, *All the World's a Fair: Visions of Empire at American International Expositions, 1876–1916* (Chicago: University of Chicago Press, 1984).

2 Marta Filipová, ed., *Cultures of International Exhibitions 1840–1940: Great Exhibitions in the Margins* (Farnham, UK: Ashgate, 2015); David Raizman and Ethan Robey, eds., *Expanding Nationalisms at World's Fairs: Identity, Diversity, and Exchange, 1851–1915* (London: Routledge, 2017).

3 Elfie Rembold, "Exhibitions and National Identity," *National Identities* 1, no. 3 (1999): 222.

4 Christian Lundahl, "Swedish Education Exhibitions and Aesthetic Governing at World's Fairs in the Late Nineteenth Century," *Nordic Journal of Educational History* 3, no. 2 (2016): 3–30; Christian Lundahl and Martin Lawn, "The Swedish Schoolhouse: A Case Study in Transnational Influences in Education at the 1870s World Fairs," *Paedagogica Historica* 51, no. 3 (2015): 319–34; Christian Lundahl, "The Swedish Schoolhouse at the Centennial Exposition in Philadelphia, 1876: World's Fairs and Innovation in Policy and Practice" (paper presented at the annual meeting of the American Educational Research Association, Philadelphia, April 5, 2014), http://www.aera.net/Publications/Online-Paper-Repository/AERA-Online-Paper-Repository/Owner/935052.

5 Lundahl, "Swedish Education Exhibitions," 3–5.

6 Lundahl, "Swedish Education Exhibitions," 7–9.

7 Lundahl, "Swedish Education Exhibitions," 9–11.

8 Barbara Miller Lane, *National Romanticism and Modern Architecture in Germany and the Scandinavian Countries* (Cambridge: Cambridge University Press, 2000), 64–65.

9 Karen Livingstone and Linda Parry, eds., *International Arts and Crafts*, exh. cat. (London: V&A, 2005); Wendy Kaplan, ed., *The Arts and Crafts Movement in Europe and America: Design for the Modern World, 1880–1920*, exh. cat. (Los Angeles and London: Los Angeles County Museum of Art and Thames & Hudson, 2004); Nicola Gordon Bowe, ed., *Art and the National Dream: The Search for Vernacular Expression in Turn-of-the-Century Design* (Dublin: Irish Academic Press, 1993).

10 Bruno Giberti, *Designing the Centennial: A History of the 1876 International Exhibition in Philadelphia* (Lexington: University Press of Kentucky, 2002), 145–46.

11 Edward N. Kaufman, "The Architectural Museum from World's Fair to Restoration Village," *Assemblage*, no. 9 (June 1989): 27–28.

12 G. J. Hodgins, *The School House: Its Architecture, External and Internal Arrangements, etc.* (Toronto, 1876), 59; quoted in Lundahl, "The Swedish Schoolhouse at the Centennial Exposition," 11.

13 Lundahl, "The Swedish Schoolhouse at the Centennial Exposition," 17–18.

14 Lundahl, "The Swedish Schoolhouse at the Centennial Exposition," 9.

15 Mike Gregory, *Expo Legacies: Names, Numbers, Facts & Figures* (Bloomington, IN: AuthorHouse, 2009), 19.

16 Roy Rosenzweig and Elizabeth Blackmar, *The Park and the People: A History of Central Park* (Ithaca, NY: Cornell University Press, 1992), 281–83.

17 John S. Berman, *Central Park* (New York: Barnes and Noble Books, 2003), 33.

18 Rosenzweig and Blackmar, *The Park and the People*, 424.

19 "Central Park Bugs," *New York Times*, June 30, 1912.

20 "X. Y. Z.," letter to the editor, *New York Times*, July 2, 1912.

21 "Swedish Cottage," https://www.centralpark.com/things-to-do/attractions/swedish-cottage.

22 For more on *dragestil* in the United States, see Graham C. Boettcher in this volume, 81–91.

23 Nicolay Nicolaysen, *Langskibet fra Gokstad ved Sandefjord* (Kristiania [Oslo], 1882); Ingvald Martin Undset, *A Short Guide for the Use of Visitors to the Viking-ship from Gokstad* (Kristiania [Oslo], 1887), available in Norwegian, English, and German editions.

24 Jan Kokkin, *Gerhard Munthe: Norwegian Pioneer of Modernism* (Stuttgart: Arnoldsche Art Publishers, 2018), 146–51.

25 Donald Macleod, "The Viking Ship," *Good Words* 22 (1881): 759–66; J. Harris Stone, "The Viking Ship," *Potter's American Monthly* 18, no. 123 (1882): 304; F. York Powell, "The Viking-Ship Discovered at Gokstad in Norway," *The Academy* 21, no. 528 (1882): 428; "The Viking Ship at Gokstad," *The American* 4, no. 111 (1882): 378.

26 Johan Christian Dahl, *Denkmale einer sehr ausgebildeten Holzbaukunst aus den frühesten Jahrhunderten in den innern Langschaften Norwegens* (Dresden, 1837); Franz T. Kugler, *Geschichte der Baukunst*, vol. 2 (Stuttgart, 1859), 568–69; Rudolph Gottgetreu, *Lehrbuch der Hochbau-Konstruktionen*, vol. 2, *Die Arbeiten des Zimmermannes* (Berlin, 1882), 9–11.

27 Brian J. Bigler and Lynn Martinson Mudrey, *The Norway Building of the Chicago World's Fair: A Building's Journey from Norway to America; An Architectural Legacy* (Blue Mounds, WI: Little Norway, 1992), 13–19.

28 Kaufman, "The Architectural Museum," 32.

29 Many studies were undertaken in the latter half of the nineteenth century to tabulate national "languages" of ornament. See, for example, Owen Jones, *The Grammar of Ornament: Illustrated by Examples from Various Styles of Ornament* (London, 1856); Vladimir V. Stasov, *Russkij Narodnyj Ornamenti* (St. Petersburg, 1872); Jószef Huszka, *Magyar Ornamentika* (Budapest, 1891); and Theodor Schvindt, *Suomalaisia Koristeita: Finnische Ornamente* (Helsinki, 1894).

30 See Boettcher in this volume, 83.

31 Replicas of Columbus's three ships were constructed in Spain for the fair; they set out on August 6, 1892, the 400th anniversary of the commencement of his voyage.

32 Erin Leary, "'The Total Absence of Foreign Subjects': The Racial Politics of US Interwar Exhibitions of Scandinavian Design," in "The Influence of Scandinavian Design," ed. Bobbye Tigerman, special issue, *Design and Culture* 7, no. 3 (2015): 283–312; Axel Andersson and Scott Magelssen, "Performing a Viking History of America: The 1893 Voyage and Display of a Viking Longship at the Columbus Quadricentennial," *Theatre Journal* 69, no. 2 (2017): 175–95.

33 Javier Gimeno-Martínez, *Design and National Identity* (London: Bloomsbury, 2016), 93–145.

34 Bigler and Mudrey, *The Norway Building*, 29–31.

35 Miller Lane, *National Romanticism*, 27.

36 Bigler and Mudrey, *The Norway Building*, 32–33.

37 *Mount Horeb Mail*, June 7, 1928; notice reproduced in Bigler and Mudrey, *The Norway Building*, 48.

38 "Little Norway," https://romrepair.no/repair-prosjekter/little-norway-2.

39 "Project Heimatt: The Norway Building Returns Home," *Norwegian American Weekly*, January 15, 2016, https://www.norwegianamerican.com/featured/project-heimatt-the-norway-building-returns-home.

40 Ann Thorson Walton, *Ferdinand Boberg, Architect: The Complete Work* (Cambridge, MA: MIT Press, 1994), 59–60.

41 Walton, *Ferdinand Boberg*, 62.

42 Diane Rademacher, *Still Shining: Discovering Lost Treasures from the 1904 St. Louis World's Fair* (St. Louis, MO: Virginia Publishing, 2003), 56.

43 Lizette Gradén, "Christmas in Lindsborg," *Creating Diversities: Folklore, Religion and the Politics of Heritage*, ed. Anna-Leena Siikala, Barbro Klein, and Stein R. Mathisen, Studia Fennica Folkloristica 14 (Helsinki: Finnish Literature Society, 2004), 282.

44 Wayne Wheeler, *An Analysis of Social Change in a Swedish-Immigrant Community: The Case of Lindsborg, Kansas* (New York: AMS, 1986), 129–31.

45 Wheeler, *Social Change*, 230–33.

46 Gradén, "Christmas in Lindsborg," 285–86.

47 Steven M. Schnell, "Creating Narratives of Place and Identity in 'Little Sweden, U.S.A.,'" *Geographical Review* 93, no. 1 (2003): 23–24.

48 https://www.lindsborgcity.org.

Edgar Kaufmann, jr.: Design Diplomat

BOBBYE TIGERMAN

In the late 1940s, while serving as director of the department of industrial design at the Museum of Modern Art (MoMA) in New York, Edgar J. Kaufmann, jr. bought several chairs by the Swedish architect Bruno Mathsson (cat. 102).[1] Most went to Fallingwater, his parents' Frank Lloyd Wright–designed retreat in western Pennsylvania (right), though one was donated to MoMA. Beyond reflecting Kaufmann's own taste, these purchases were emblematic of his zeal to promote modern design in his own home and in the broader world. Kaufmann used all of the tools at his disposal, including curating exhibitions, publishing articles, and parlaying his many design-world connections in pursuit of this mission. In his lifetime, he was most celebrated for the preservation of Fallingwater and for organizing the *Good Design* exhibitions at MoMA (1950–55).[2] While he promoted modern design and craft from many countries, he was an especially strong advocate of Scandinavian design. This essay outlines some of the ways that Kaufmann promoted Scandinavian design in the United States, as well as American design in the Nordic countries. It argues that he was a key force in spreading knowledge about this field, and should be considered alongside *House Beautiful* editor Elizabeth Gordon, entrepreneurs Frederik and Just Lunning, and design activist Victor Papanek as one of the chief advocates of Scandinavian design in the United States.[3]

Kaufmann was driven to spread the gospel of good design—and of Scandinavian design in particular—because he believed that it had the power "to implement the lives of free individuals," thus linking modern design to ideals of democracy and freedom.[4] He defined his version of "good design" through exhibitions and writings in order to both educate the broader public and shape buying habits. He also declared that each individual must determine it for themselves: "no one will envisage better

Interior view of Fallingwater, showing Bruno Mathsson's chair ("Easy Chair No. 1")

human values than he wishes for himself.... If this private insight is increased by sympathetic observation of people, practices, and ideas, so much the better."[5] Thus, what might now be considered a patriarchal or elitist approach, Kaufmann framed as an effort to liberate individuals by encouraging them to exercise their freedom of choice and powers of discernment.

His determination to make Scandinavian design better known in the United States stemmed from the belief that it was especially suited to American lifestyles, and that its practitioners should be better known among Americans. He declared that "the United States in particular has been benefitted by the presence of Saarinen and Aalto and their works," elaborating that "the public on this side of the Atlantic needs to know whose are the artistic energies that give Finnish glass its most beautiful forms, challenging in their originality. We need to know who has guided the exceptional program of Arabia, a great factory supporting an artistic studio of first rank. And which artists have given it that rank?"[6] Elsewhere he wrote that Scandinavian designs "could slip without much strain into many American homes right now; they are directly acceptable and enjoyable here."[7]

Even before World War II, Kaufmann had many contacts in Scandinavia. He had known Finnish architects Alvar and Aino Aalto since Alvar's 1938 MoMA exhibition, and when the couple came to the United States in 1940, they visited Fallingwater twice.[8] He was also friendly with Swedish architect Bruno Mathsson, trying to help Mathsson find U.S. retailers and organize an exhibition at MoMA in 1946, though the latter did not materialize.[9] Two years later, when Mathsson visited the United States, Kaufmann arranged a series of visits and parties to introduce him to the luminaries of the American design community in New York and throughout the country.[10] Kaufmann was a renowned host and connector, and many Scandinavian designers have similar stories of his hospitality. Norwegians Arne and Grete Prytz Korsmo visited Fallingwater (which Kaufmann also used as a weekend retreat), as did Danish designer Finn Juhl.[11]

In 1948, Kaufmann traveled to Denmark, Finland, Norway, and Sweden to forge connections with Nordic museum colleagues and members of each nation's arts and crafts organization.[12] He began planning an exhibition of Scandinavian design to be shown at MoMA in 1950. The exhibition was abruptly cancelled in 1949, to the great

disappointment of the Nordic design community. According to Norwegian press reports, Nordic organizers assumed that their offerings did not meet the level of quality required for MoMA.[13] While this may have been true, the cancellation could also be attributed to other causes. The news article indicated that each nation's arts and crafts organization wished to select objects, but Kaufmann insisted on choosing the objects himself; the museum may have been deterred by the organizations' assumption of playing a curatorial role. In 1949 Kaufmann was also preparing the first *Good Design* exhibition, which opened in November 1950, and so the museum's stated reason for the cancellation—lack of space—may have in fact been true. Nevertheless, Kaufmann's 1948 trip had substantial impact. He met Finn Juhl and became his most vigorous advocate, publishing the first English article on him and inviting him to install the *Good Design* exhibition in 1951 (below).[14] As a result of the relationships Kaufmann established on the trip, Scandinavians were well represented in all of the *Good Design* exhibitions, more so than any other country besides the United States.[15]

Edgar Kaufmann, jr. at the 1951 *Good Design* exhibition designed by Finn Juhl, Museum of Modern Art, New York. Kaufmann is placing his hand on a Hans Wegner chair.

In 1954, the Nordic arts and crafts organizations mounted *Design in Scandinavia*, the major exhibition of Scandinavian design in the United States that they had hoped to realize at MoMA in 1950. It traveled to twenty-four venues in the U.S. and Canada between 1954 and 1957 and attracted huge crowds, only coming to an end when one of the trucks transporting objects from Los Angeles to Indianapolis had a catastrophic accident, destroying much of the exhibition material.[16] While Kaufmann was not directly involved in *Design in Scandinavia*'s organization, he was friendly with many of its key players, including *House Beautiful* editor Elizabeth Gordon and the Virginia Museum of Fine Arts director Leslie Cheek, Jr., who led the American committee overseeing the exhibition. Kaufmann wrote a rave review of the exhibition, gushing that "I wonder if any area of the world other than the Scandinavian North could muster such a list, could find industry and commerce ready to back them, governments ready to sponsor them, and the ultimate ability to assemble them in so attractive an exhibition? The exhibition 'Design in Scandinavia' is an impressive and heartening demonstration of true culture."[17] In articulating why this material resonated so much with Americans, Kaufmann pointed to architect Eric Herløw's demountable displays: they were "clean, well-finished, unobtrusive, carefully considered, ingenious, sensible, and elegant," all terms synonymous with how Scandinavian design was marketed to Americans, as well as the ideals of the *Good Design* program.

Kaufmann not only advocated for Scandinavian design in the United States but also promoted American design abroad. In 1953, under MoMA's auspices, he curated *American Design for Home and Decorative Use*, an exhibition that traveled to seven Nordic cities and additional destinations in continental Europe.[18] The show was sponsored by the United States Information Agency, a federal body organized in 1953 to promote American interests abroad through the "soft" power of radio broadcasts, movies, books, and art exhibitions. With the propagandistic intentions of the project clear, the exhibition demonstrated "the best in contemporary American design and workmanship," and suggested that these goods demonstrated the superiority of the American way of life.[19] Many objects, such as the lamp designed by Olga Lee (p. 154), had appeared in previous *Good Design* exhibitions, though others like Eva Zeisel's *Museum* dinner service (p. 155) and Charles and Ray Eameses' *DAX* chair (p. 188) came from MoMA's collection. Because the United States' achievements in mass production were well known abroad, Kaufmann emphasized the skillfulness of American craftspeople, including unique work by such figures as jeweler Betty Cooke, ceramists Gertrud and Otto Natzler, woodturner James Prestini (p. 155), and Finnish American textile designer Marianne Strengell. As Kaufmann explained to a press junket attending a staged display in a New York warehouse prior to shipping the exhibition to Finland, "Europeans are inclined to believe that because we long ago committed ourselves as a nation to mass production, we thereby killed off individual talent and lost the chance to make beautiful things. We believe otherwise."[20]

Kaufmann's extensive connections translated into other opportunities to support Scandinavian design. The *Design in Scandinavia* exhibition had originated as a project of the Landsforeningen Dansk Kunsthåndværk (National Association of Danish Arts and Crafts), but was expanded to include the three other Nordic countries. The organization's desire for a solely Danish exhibition had persisted, however, and when they wanted to circulate an ambitious exhibition of Danish art and design to major American museums, they turned to Kaufmann for help.[21] Kaufmann approached James J. Rorimer, the director

TIGERMAN

EVA ZEISEL
Castleton China Company
Museum coffeepot,
designed c. 1942–45. CAT. 176

JAMES PRESTINI
Bowl, 1933–53. CAT. 115

Edgar Kaufmann, Jr.

of the Metropolitan Museum of Art, who was enthusiastic. *The Arts of Denmark: Viking to Modern* opened there in October 1960 with Kaufmann serving as the intermediary between the Danish organization and the museum (p. 157).[22] The show comprised two parts: the first devoted to archaeological and historical objects and the second consisting of new pieces by contemporary designers and craftspeople. Danish design's appeal reached its zenith in 1960, and *The Arts of Denmark* capitalized on its popularity. When the Metropolitan Museum of Art made the rare move of acquiring several pieces from the exhibition, including the gold and turquoise necklace by Jens Andreasen (p. 158), the *New York Times* sniffed that the museum had "broken down" and was "the latest American buyer to succumb to modern Danish designs."[23] But Rorimer asserted that building the collection of modern design was a museum priority, and that he hoped to allocate permanent display space for twentieth-century design objects in the near future. Following its New York showing, the exhibition traveled to the Art Institute of Chicago and the Los Angeles Municipal Art Gallery in 1961.[24]

Much like *Design in Scandinavia*, *The Arts of Denmark* served both commercial and diplomatic functions. In his foreword to the exhibition catalogue, Danish prime minister Viggo Kampmann used Cold War rhetoric that aligned Denmark with the United States, explaining that, "in all matters—not only in the spheres of art and culture—we Danes have the freedom of speech....Today Denmark, with her sister nations throughout the North, raises her voice for the cause of liberty, tolerance, and cooperation."[25] But the project also had commercial benefit, boosting the international profile and presumably sales for the objects shown. *The Arts of Denmark* allowed Kaufmann to test his thesis that "a deeper cause exists for American enthusiasm for Danish modern design." He posited that there were three kinds of design: correct design that seeks perfection, expressive design that "aims for maximum effect," and organic design that "blends form, structure and utility into a vivid whole." He continued: "I believe that Americans naturally and by tradition lean toward the third kind of design, however much they may on occasion be pushed toward the other two. And I believe the Danes feel the same way. If I am right that is why Americans, like so many others, feel firmly drawn to even daring examples of Danish design."[26]

Kaufmann was arguing for a fundamental similarity between Danes and Americans (and considering how the Nordic nations were conflated in the American mindset, this similarity may apply to all Scandinavians).[27] He had been developing this argument for some time. As early as 1947, he defined the contemporary sensibility as a synthesis of the "strictness and purity of the great modern work of the 20's and early 30's" with the "freely curved lines and forms neglected since the turn of the century, and [the] traditional craft materials and processes."[28] These competing tendencies came together in the work of his longtime Nordic friends Alvar and Aino Aalto and Bruno Mathsson, and especially in the work of Frank Lloyd Wright. Kaufmann explained that "modern design and modern rooms have shown a consistent trend, blending craft with industry, free curves with stricter shapes, still guided by the same principles that have prevailed ever since the earliest modern efforts—honesty of means, simplicity, clarity, lightness, unity."[29] For him, the ideals of modern design, which he had advocated in the MoMA *Good Design* exhibitions, equally described the work of these Nordic figures.

ROLF MIDDELBOE
Landsforeningen Dansk
Kunsthåndværk
***The Arts of Denmark: Viking to Modern*
poster**, 1960. CAT. 105

The Arts of Denmark

VIKING TO MODERN

Second Floor   **South Wing**

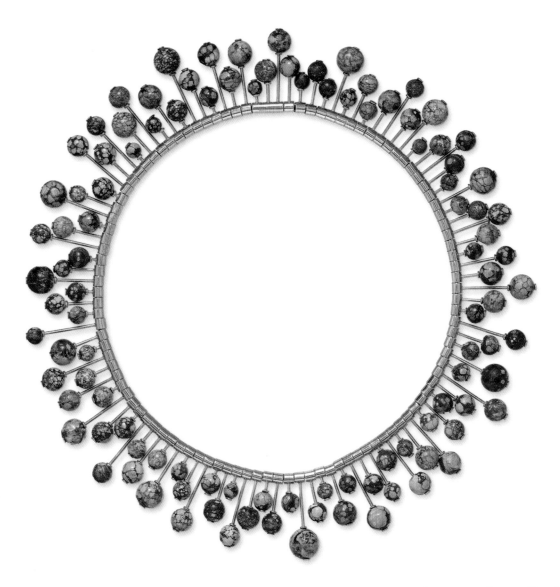

Kaufmann's securing an important commission for Alvar Aalto provides a final example of his enduring support of Scandinavian design. In 1961, he invited Aalto to create the penthouse conference room (now known, after his father, as the Edgar J. Kaufmann Conference Rooms) for the newly constructed Institute of International Education (IIE) building in New York City (p. 159).[30] Founded in 1919, the IIE facilitated international exchanges of students and teachers, most notably the Fulbright fellowship program. Kaufmann had been a supporter of the organization, and when the IIE requested a donation for the construction of the new building, he agreed, suggesting that a prominent international architect create an attractive top-floor conference suite for the rather mundane building designed by Wallace K. Harrison. Located across the street from the United Nations, the site had special significance for Aalto. While Denmark, Norway, and Sweden had furnished the UN Council chambers, Finland did not participate in the complex's design, as it did not become a member of the UN until 1955.[31] The IIE project would allow Aalto to define his own space

in proximity to that storied set of buildings. Aalto's brief was the interior—the furnishings and the surface treatments—for which he chose laminated birch, blue ceramic tile, and his own furniture and lighting. *New York Times* architecture critic Ada Louise Huxtable raved that it was "the most beautiful and distinguished interior that New York has seen in many years."[32] The IIE rooms were Aalto's fourth realized project in the United States, and represented the appropriate collaborative spirit for an organization devoted to the exchange of international ideas.

Following the IIE project with Aalto, Kaufmann continued to write and teach about contemporary architecture and design, devoting his life to circulating progressive ideas across the Atlantic. By both promoting Scandinavian design in the United States and American design in the Nordic countries, he argued for their fundamental similarities and compatibility. In this unofficial diplomatic role, Kaufmann was a principal protagonist in nurturing and reinforcing the bonds between American and Scandinavian design.

JENS ANDREASEN
Necklace, 1960. CAT. 4

Edgar J. Kaufmann Conference Rooms,
Institute of International Education,
New York City, 1961–65, designed
by Alvar Aalto. Photo: Jari Jetsonen,
Alvar Aalto Museum, 2001

1 Kaufmann preferred to use the lower-case suffix after his surname.
2 Franklin Toker, *Fallingwater Rising: Frank Lloyd Wright, E. J. Kaufmann, and America's Most Extraordinary House* (New York: Knopf, 2012); Terence Riley and Edward Eigen, "Between the Museum and the Marketplace: Selling Good Design," in *The Museum of Modern Art at Mid-Century: At Home and Abroad*, Studies in Modern Art 4 (New York: Museum of Modern Art, 1994), 150–79.
3 In addition to the activities outlined here, Kaufmann wrote several articles and book chapters about Scandinavian design, including "New Lamps Are Lit in Europe," *Arts and Architecture* 65, no. 10 (October 1948): 28–30; "Finland Designs Glass for 1949," *Art News* 47, no. 9 (January 1949): 36–37; "Wonderworks of Tapio Wirkkala," *Interiors* 111, no. 4 (November 1951): 94–99; "Great Danes in Silver," *Art News* 51, no. 3 (May 1952): 39–41, 61–63; "Jensen and Silver," in *Fifty Years of Danish Silver in the Georg Jensen Tradition* (New York: Georg Jensen, 1956), 2–9; and "A True Artist: Finland's Tapio Wirkkala, 1915–1985," *Interior Design* 56, no. 8 (August 1985): 197–201. Additionally, Kaufmann was guest director of the 1958 *Fulbright Designers* exhibition at the Museum of Contemporary Crafts in New York, which included three Americans who received fellowships to the Nordic countries.
4 Edgar Kaufmann, Jr., *What is Modern Design?* (New York: Museum of Modern Art, 1950), 8.
5 Kaufmann, *What Is Modern Design?*, 9.
6 Edgar J. Kaufmann, Jr., "Letter for Art and Industry of Finland," *Suomen Koristetaidetta* (Helsinki: Suomen Koristetaiteiljain Liitto Ornamo, 1949), 16–17.

7 Edgar Kaufmann, Jr., "Scandinavian Design in the U.S.A.," *Interiors* 113, no. 10 (May 1954): 108.
8 "Chronology," in *Aalto and America*, ed. Stanford Anderson, Gail Fenske, and David Fixler (New Haven and London: Yale University Press, 2012), vii–viii.
9 Edgar Kaufmann to Bruno Mathsson, September 18, 1946, Museum of Modern Art, Architecture and Design Department Acquisition Files, cited in Nina Stritzler-Levine, "Thou Shall/Not Be Branded," in *Bruno Mathsson: Architect and Designer* (Malmo: Bokförlaget Arena, 2006), 208n28.
10 Karin Winter, "The Path to the Glass Houses," in *Bruno Mathsson*, 121–26.
11 Karianne Bjellås Gilje, ed., *Grete Prytz Kittelsen: emalje design,* exh. cat. (Oslo: Gyldendal, 2008), 59; Per H. Hansen, *Finn Juhl and His House* (Ostfildern, Germany: Hatje Cantz, 2014), 49.
12 Kjetil Fallan, "Love and Hate in Industrial Design: Europe's Design Professionals and America in the 1950s," in *The Making of European Consumption: Facing the American Challenge*, ed. Per Lundin and Thomas Kaiserfeld (Basingstoke, UK: Palgrave Macmillan, 2015), 140–41.
13 "New York avlyser den nordiske brukskunstutstilling," *Aftenposten*, January 10, 1949. A clipping of this article is preserved in the archive of Foreningen Brukskunst (the Norwegian Applied Art Association), National Archives of Norway, in the 1946–48 annual report.
14 "Finn Juhl of Copenhagen," *Interiors* 108 (November 1948): 96–99; Edgar Kaufmann, Jr. and Finn Juhl, "Good Design '51 As Seen by Its Director and by Its Designer," *Interiors* 110, no. 8 (March 1951): 100–103, 160, 162.
15 Riley and Eigen first observed this in "Between the Museum and the Marketplace," 160.

16 More than 660,000 people visited the exhibition in total, with many museums noting that it broke attendance records; Åke H. Huldt and Per A. Laurén, eds., *Design in Scandinavia: USA-Canada 1954–1957* (Stockholm: AB Egnellska Boktryckeriet, 1958). See also Monica Penick in this volume, 93–97. On the truck accident, see Leslie Cheek, Jr. to Hans Aanestad, May 30, 1957, 1956–1957, Box 1, IMA Exhibition Records (EXH001), Indianapolis Museum of Art at Newfields, Indianapolis, IN.
17 Edgar Kaufmann, Jr., "Scandinavian Design in the U.S.A.," *Interiors* 113, no. 10 (May 1954): 108–13, 182–85.
18 See Gay McDonald, "The Modern American Home as Soft Power: Finland, MoMA and the 'American Home 1953' Exhibition," *Journal of Design History* 23, no. 4 (2010): 387–408. The exhibition traveled to Helsinki, Gothenburg, Oslo, Bergen, Stavanger, Copenhagen, Aarhus, and nine European cities. Also see International Council and International Program Records, I.B.11–29, The Museum of Modern Art Archives, New York.
19 "Not to Last," Talk of the Town, *New Yorker,* August 22, 1953, 17.
20 "Not to Last," 17.
21 In the catalogue foreword, Danish prime minister Viggo Kampmann expressed that "the similarities of culture, general outlook and democratic form of government between Denmark and our sister nations in the North are so great that the stranger may sometimes fail to notice the differences. But we *are* different, of which THE ARTS OF DENMARK is manifestation"; *The Arts of Denmark*, exh. cat. (Copenhagen: Landsforeningen Dansk Kunsthaandværk, 1960), 7.

22 Edgar Kaufmann, jr. to James J. Rorimer, October 1, 1958, and Agreement between Landsforeningen Dansk Kunsthaandværk and the Metropolitan Museum of Art, March 9, 1960, Loan Exhibition 1960: The Arts of Denmark, The Metropolitan Museum of Art Archives.
23 "Museum's Own Exhibit Source of Acquisitions," *New York Times*, December 28, 1960.
24 Abbey Johnson, "Artistry in 'Danish Modern,'" *Chicago Tribune*, February 23, 1961; "Superior Craftsmanship Marks Arts of Denmark Exhibition," *Los Angeles Times*, October 15, 1961.
25 Kampmann, "Foreword," *The Arts of Denmark*, 8.
26 Edgar Kaufmann, jr., "An American View of the Arts of Denmark and Danish Modern Design," in *The Arts of Denmark*, 106.
27 Both *House Beautiful* editor Elizabeth Gordon and several Scandinavian political figures also proclaimed the cultural and even moral similarities between Americans and Scandinavians. See Bobbye Tigerman and Monica Obniski, 20, and Monica Penick, 97, both in this volume.
28 Edgar Kaufmann, jr., "Modern Rooms of the Last Fifty Years," *Interiors* 106 (February 1947): 77.
29 Kaufmann, "Modern Rooms," 77.
30 Matthew Postal, "Alvar Aalto and the Edgar J. Kaufmann Conference Rooms," in Anderson, Fenske, and Fixler, *Aalto and America*, 262–73; and Edgar J. Kaufmann, Jr., "Aalto on First Avenue," *Interior Design* 55, no. 9 (September 1984): 270–73.
31 See Monica Obniski in this volume, 130–35.
32 Ada Louise Huxtable, "Alvar Aalto, Finnish Master, Represented Here," *New York Times*, November 30, 1964.

ICELAND AT THE 1939 NEW YORK WORLD'S FAIR

ARNDÍS S. ÁRNADÓTTIR

The government of Iceland made an ambitious decision to take part in the 1939 New York World's Fair, the first time that the country organized an independent pavilion at such an event. The main reason for participating was so that the small sovereign island nation, at the time still in union with Denmark, could improve commercial relations as well as exchange cultural ideas with the United States.[1] The event was proclaimed "our greatest effort so far at introducing the culture and economy of Iceland."[2]

The invitation to participate came through Danish diplomatic channels in December 1936, and the government set up exhibition and fundraising councils in late 1937.[3] Funding was secured from the state, banks, private and public enterprises, and individuals. Prominent Icelanders in the United States and Canada were involved in the preparations as well; the Reverend Rögnvaldur Pétursson of Winnipeg and Judge Guðmundur Grímsson of North Dakota signed the tentative agreement in New York in November 1937, and enlisted public relations support of Icelandic-Canadian explorer and ethnologist Vilhjálmur Stefánsson. Early in the planning stages, the arts became a central issue, as the League of Icelandic Artists pointed out that they were "the most

important factor in drawing attention to Iceland and Icelandic export goods."[4]

The Iceland Pavilion was located in a fair-built structure, one of several adjoining pavilions in the Hall of Nations, part of the fair's Government Zone.[5] Icelandic architects made the initial interior plans and opted for an airy, two-story structure with balconies and linoleum floor covering (below).[6] An American design consultant, Leonard Outhwaite, recommended the use

Interior view of the Iceland Pavilion,
New York World's Fair, 1939

GUÐMUNDUR EINARSSON
LYDIA PÁLSDÓTTIR
Listvinahús
Vase, 1939. CAT. 32

of dioramas, then a fashionable method for museum display, depicting various aspects of Iceland's main industries—agriculture and fishing—"against a naturalistic background."[7] Outhwaite also chose the distinctive blue color of the interior walls, while Icelandic artist Jón Þorleifsson painted and executed the dioramas and a landscape mural running along the second-floor balcony. Visitors reacted favorably to the dark colors, finding them a repose for the eye from the overall white-beige effect of the fair and the heat of summer.[8]

The cases for Icelandic manuscripts, literature, and fine and decorative arts were located on the second-floor balcony over-looking the great open vault of the modern building. Borghildur Fenger, the daughter of Vilhjálmur Þór, Commissioner General of the Executive Committee, described an impres-sive setting that included streamlined walls, curving stairs, niches, and indirect lighting.[9] The Listvinahús ceramic studio in Reykjavík exhibited several objects on the balcony, inclu-ding a pierced, ochre-glazed double-walled ceramic vase decorated in the manner of traditional woodcarving (p. 161).[10] The vase, made of clays indigenous to Iceland, was designed by studio founder Guðmundur Einarsson and his wife, Lydia Pálsdóttir, and represented modern art industry in Iceland at that time.[11]

The Iceland Pavilion attracted two million visitors during the 1939 season.[12] For the first time the five Nordic countries were represented in five separate pavilions, an unprecedented and groundbreaking event in terms of Icelandic trade, tourism, and diplomatic history. An American reviewer noted, "Iceland is no doubt the smallest independent nation that has a building of its own at the World's Fair. The Commission, with very small means at its disposal, has limi-ted itself to what could be done excellently."[13] The event had a long-term impact in Iceland, creating new opportunities in trade and cultural exchange and leading to the com-mencement of scheduled air travel between Iceland and the United States in 1948.

1 *Iceland in the New York World's Fair 1939* (Reykjavik: n.p., 1939), 8. Iceland gained sovereignty from Denmark in 1918, sharing a king and foreign policy until it became an independent republic in 1944.

2 Hörður Bjarnason, "Heimssýningin mikla í New York 1939: Sýningar Norðurlandaþjóðanna" (The Great New York World's Fair 1939: The Pavilions of the Nordic Countries), *Vísir*, November 29, 1939, 2.

3 Þjóðskjalasafn Íslands (National Archives of Iceland), Utanrrn (Ministry for Foreign Affairs) 1967 65-b, Sýningar (Exhibitions) II.

4 Jón Leifs (President of the League of Icelandic Artists) to the Minister for Foreign Affairs, October 3, 1937, Þjóðskjalasafn Íslands, Utanrrn, 1967 65-b, Sýningar (Exhibitions) II.

5 "Tilhögun sýningarinnar: Skýrsla sýningarráðs og framkvæmdastjórnar" (Exhibition planning: Report of the exhibition advisory council and board of directors), *Morgunblaðið*, February 7, 1939, 3–6.

6 It was possibly the office of architect Sigurður Guðmundsson.

7 "At the World's Fair," *American-Scandinavian Review* 27, no. 2 (June 1939): 121–23.

8 "Íslenska sýningin í New York er sjerstæð. Fellur sýningagestum vel í geð. Frásögn Jóns Þorleifssonar" (The Icelandic exhibition in New York is unique. Well received by visitors. Interview with Jón Þorleifsson), *Morgunblaðið*, May 31, 1939, 3, 7.

9 Borghildur Fenger, interview with author, January 2002.

10 The Listvinahús (House of the Friends of the Arts) ceramic studio was the first of its kind in Iceland, in operation since 1927.

11 Yngvi Guðmundsson (son of Lydia and Guðmundur Einarsson), interview with author, September 5, 2018.

12 *Vísir*, November 1, 1939, 1. The Iceland Pavilion reopened for the second season of the fair in May 1940.

13 "At the World's Fair," 123.

Astrid Sampe, the United States, and the United Nations

HELENA KÅBERG

Astrid Sampe was one of Sweden's most influential and innovative textile designers. Focusing on handwoven and hand-printed fabrics at the beginning of her career, she gradually shifted to industrially manufactured textiles, developing modern and abstract patterns with new technologies that helped give machine-made textiles the artistic and material qualities normally found only in handcrafted objects. Although she shared this ambition with many other designers, Sampe was exceptionally successful thanks to her profound knowledge of techniques and materials and her aptitude for building networks in Sweden and abroad. She adopted many technical innovations from the United States, and her U.S. projects reflected the impact of design as both an economically important export product and a means of promoting shared cultural, social, and ideological values. Her most prominent commission in the United States was for the Jacquard-woven *flossa* rugs for the United Nations Dag Hammarskjöld Library in 1961.

Sampe enrolled at Konstfack (the University of Arts, Crafts, and Design) in Stockholm in 1928. She continued her education in 1932 at the Royal College of Art in London. In 1938 she was recruited to head Nordiska Kompaniet's new textile studio, NK Textilkammare. Nordiska Kompaniet (NK) was Sweden's leading department store, which produced its own lines of furniture, interior design, and hand- and machine-woven textiles. Sampe's new role afforded her the resources to develop her ideas and the opportunity to collaborate with architects, artists, and designers in a series of high-profile national and international projects. In her first year, she participated in the Golden Gate International Exposition in San Francisco and was part of the team that designed the Swedish Pavilion at the 1939 New York World's Fair. In addition, her printed curtains with a glass object motif were displayed in the glass section.[1] Numerous other exhibitions in the United States included her work, such as *Design in Scandinavia* (1954–57) and *Swedish Textiles Today* (1958). Sampe was featured on her own merits, but also represented Sweden as part of a concerted effort to promote the Swedish export industry and international relations.

Sweden and Swedish companies had taken part in world's fairs in Europe and the United States since the nineteenth century; in the first years of the twentieth century, however, a national crisis prompted more deliberate and concerted efforts to promote Swedish industry and trade. Concern about slowing population growth and population loss due to immigration to the United States meant that social development risked stagnating as Swedish industry struggled. A parliamentary committee | was appointed to study how mass emigration could be prevented. The result was the Emigration Report, published in 1908–13. One of its findings was that the standard of living was generally higher in the United States due to higher wages. According to American engineer Frederick Winslow Taylor, who pioneered principles of scientific management, rational mass production was a key to success. In Sweden, this strategy was called "Americanism," which meant adapting industry to enable mass production of more profitable and affordable products. A department for industry and trade was created, Swedish ambassadors and consulates were instructed to promote Swedish exports, and chambers of commerce were established, including the Swedish Chamber of Commerce of the United States, founded in 1907.[2] After World War II, many Swedes traveled to the United States to network and further study the American market. *The American-Swedish Monthly*, published in the United States by the American-Swedish News Exchange, contained countless examples of initiatives launched by Swedish companies and the Swedish Chamber of Commerce to boost American interest in Sweden and Swedish products. Articles and advertisements spoke of friendship, common purposes, and resuming contacts as soon as the war was over.[3]

In 1948, Sampe made the journey with Swedish businessman Rudolf Kalderén, a financial director at NK who represented the producers section of the Svenska Slöjdföreningen (Swedish Arts and Crafts Society).[4] She visited California to meet with designers Paul Williams, Greta Magnusson Grossman, Dorothy Liebes, and Maria Kipp. At Cranbrook Academy of Art she met Swedish sculptor Carl Milles, Finnish American architect and designer Eero Saarinen, and Finnish American textile artist Marianne Strengell.[5] The tour ended in New York, where she opened an exhibition of NK textiles produced by Knoll. Her friendship with Saarinen proved especially significant. Sampe

Astrid Sampe and Dorothy Liebes at Liebes's New York studio in the 1960s

later said that he taught her the basic principles of interior design—that textiles can contribute greatly to a room, but can also counteract the architecture. He also suggested that the floor should be one material, curtains should preferably run from ceiling to floor, and the line where floor and wall meet should be as unbroken as possible, which meant that pedestal tables and one-legged chairs like Saarinen's were preferred.[6]

On their return, Sampe and Kalderén shared their views about how to increase export opportunities with the Swedish press.[7] The market was vast, so Swedish companies needed to collaborate. Initiatives such as exhibitions should be restricted to the most influential cities for design: New York, Chicago, Los Angeles, and possibly New Orleans. Moreover, something had to be done about the exorbitant packing and shipping costs. In Chicago, Kalderén had been to a hotel decorated with NK's flat-packed furniture series *Triva* (cat. 151), which prompted him to consider whether flat-packing could perhaps cut the cost of furniture exports. Another option was licensed manufacturing; NK had given Knoll sole rights to produce its textiles in the U.S., for instance.[8]

Fiberglass fabric ball gown, designed
and worn by Sampe at the
centennial celebration of the Svenska
Slöjdföreningen, 1945

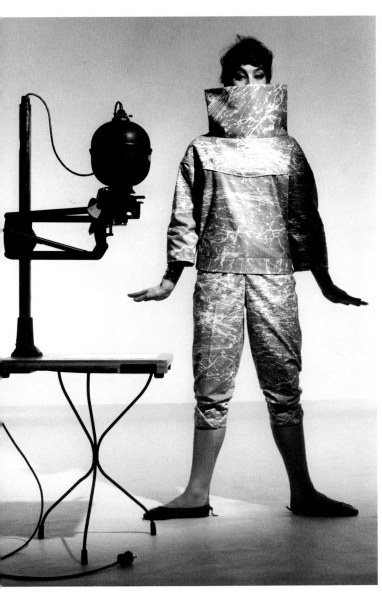

Diver-inspired beach outfit
by Göta Trädgård, made from Sampe's
Spontanism textile, 1954

Sampe also noted that Sweden had nothing resembling Eero Saarinen's progressive furniture made of resin, rubber, and metal, and proposed experimentation with new technologies as another way to increase exports. Regarding American experiments with new materials, she noted that "Europeans might find much of it harsh or garish, unnecessary or totally absurd—but it shouldn't be laughed at. For without experiments there will be no progress."[9] She further observed that the range of products was huge in the United States, where shiny fabrics were the current fashion: "there is a golden glow over most newly decorated American homes... emanating from the glass, plastic, and metal threads that manufacturers enthusiastically weave into every kind of interior textiles, even the printed ones."

Sampe herself had already followed this principle and continued to do so for decades. She imported fiberglass technology from the United States before World War II (p. 165).[10] In 1946, she imported nylon, which she printed and sold as fabric for dressmaking and curtains.[11] Two years later she designed machine-woven Tensolite fabrics for Knoll, which were durable textiles with a plastic-coated fiberglass weft that could be easily cleaned.[12] She also worked with American photographer Arthur Siegel on a technique to print photographs on textiles in the early 1950s.[13] Fabrics were impregnated with a photosensitive substance, then photographic negatives were projected on them. This technology made it possible to print complicated patterns with fine lines and details that could not be reproduced with conventional techniques such as screenprinting (p. 165). In the 1960s, she participated in a computer-aided design collaboration with IBM.[14] With assistance from Sten Kallin at IBM in Sweden and a pen plotter controlled by the IBM 1130 computer, she experimented with patterns that were generated when simple graphic forms or pictures of mathematical functions were repeated, moved, and modified.

In 1961, Sampe landed the prestigious assignment to design rugs for the Dag Hammarskjöld Library at the United Nations (below). Founded immediately following World War II, the United Nations aimed to prevent future wars and promote global understanding and collaboration. In 1947, American architect Wallace K. Harrison led an international team (including Swedish architect Sven Markelius) to design the organization's New York headquarters. The project reflected the organization's values and embodied its vision of global community, cooperation, and understanding. Dag Hammarskjöld, the Swedish diplomat who had been appointed the second Secretary-General of the United Nations in 1953, had personally campaigned for a new library to replace the small existing one in the original UN Secretariat building. Following his death in a plane crash while on a peace mission to the Congo in September 1961, the library was named in his honor.[15]

Main Reading Room, Dag Hammarskjöld
Library, United Nations, c. 1962

Astrid Sampe, the United States, and the United Nations

Although American architectural firm Harrison & Abramovitz was given the contract and U.S. firms dominated the long list of subcontractors, the intention was for the library to represent the entire world.[16] In a letter from early 1961, Hammarskjöld had noted that the library's interior design would require balance, explaining, "We should try to break up a too dominant American style, while avoiding the typically Danish."[17] The solution was to install wall panels of African and Australian woods, carpets from Hong Kong, Italian marble, and furniture, art, and crafts from several countries, including the United States, the United Kingdom, and France. There were also many Swedish elements. The penthouse included a mural by Bo Beskow and a hand-woven *rya* rug by Viola Gråsten. The Woodrow Wilson Reading Room on the second and third floors had blond pine wall panels leading up to an undulating pine ceiling, and blond oak furniture by Swedish designer Karl Erik Ekselius. Ekselius chairs and NK armchairs and a sofa table were found on the first floor and in the periodicals reading room on the upper basement level.

Sampe designed five *flossa* rugs for the Main Reading Room on the first floor. In 1963, she explained that Hammarskjöld had wanted the rugs to represent international motifs and that Sampe should avoid emphasizing her Swedish nationality.[18] They agreed that each continent would be represented by a kind of tree: the Americas by pine (p. 167), Europe by oleander, Asia by cypress, Africa by olive, and Australia by eucalyptus. This symbolism was free of political or ideological associations, and also echoed Hammarskjöld's passion for nature and outdoor life. Additionally, Hammarskjöld specified the fourteen shades of green for the rugs. Swedish color expert Perry Marthin, who had designed the color scheme for the Secretariat Building and the Library, was also involved, asserting that green was a soothing color for reading.[19] Skilled weavers at the Swedish rug firm Kasthall converted these drawings into punch cards to control the Jacquard looms. The rugs were installed in spring 1962. To contemporary Swedes, the library interiors looked typically American in their large scale and mainly industrial materials, while non-Swedes most likely saw the blond wood and rugs as typically Scandinavian. In fact, they are both: they reflect the international popularity of Scandinavian design in the 1950s, while also embodying the multicultural, international modernism of the time.

Translated by Gabriella Berggren

1 "Till Gyllene Västern och Golden Gate," *Ny Daglig Allehanda*, November 26, 1938; Barbro Alving, "Vad är det… Konstindustrin ett lyckligt grepp. NK:s sportstugerum får lovord," *Dagens Nyheter*, May 11, 1939, both in Nationalmuseum, NK Textilkammare archives, AS1:29.

2 Helena Kåberg, "Rationell arkitektur. Företagskontor för massproduktion och masskommunikation" (diss., Uppsala University, 2003), 49–51, 61–62.

3 Due to Sweden's neutrality, its industry was intact when the war ended; consequently, Sweden had a considerable head start over other European countries, and exports to war-ravaged Europe meant that Swedish industry experienced rapid growth. See *Amerika bygger* (America Builds), Nationalmuseum exhibition catalogue 100 (Stockholm: Haeggström, 1944); Kåberg, "Rationell arkitektur," 62.

4 "Nytt USA-hem skimrar av guld, experimentmaterial favoriter," *Dagens Nyheter*, July 25, 1948.

5 Rolf Lamborn, "Glöggdrickande negerarkitekt expert på svensk konsthantverk," *Stockholms-Tidningen*, July 7, 1948; "Sweden's Leading Textile Designer Guest of Friends Here," *Worcester Sunday Telegram*, July 4, 1948; "Vad människor är uppfinningsrika!," Nationalmuseum, NK Textilkammare archives, AS1:31, press cuttings, p. 98.

6 Helena Dahlbäck Lutteman, "Astrid Sampe—Half a Century of Up-to-Dateness," *Astrid Sampe: Svensk Industritextil*, exh. cat. (Stockholm: Nationalmuseum, 1984), 45–46.

7 "Nytt USA-hem skimrar av guld, experimentmaterial favoriter"; "Goda möjligheter för export till USA av svenska möbler," *Svenska Dagbladet*, July 25, 1948.

8 Lamborn, "Glöggdrickande negerarkitekt expert på svensk konsthantverk."

9 "Nytt USA-hem skimrar av guld, experimentmaterial favoriter."

10 "Glass. The first dress made of glass recently danced in the City Hall, and Gunnar Myrdal has glass curtains and furniture in his newly-decorated study," *Idun*, January 1946; *Astrid Sampe*, 5.

11 "Från Amerika," *Bonniers*, July 1946.

12 "Swedish Fabrics Go on Exhibition," *New York Times*, July 9, 1948; Ann Pringle, "New Fabrics from Sweden Displayed Here. Knoll Associates' Collection Includes Upholstery of Plastic, Glass Threads," *New York Herald Tribune*, July 9, 1948; "Goda möjligheter för export till USA av svenska möbler"; "Vad människor är uppfinningsrika!."

13 In 1947, AB Alf Stigens Fabriker acquired the U.S. patent with sole rights for Scandinavia; Gunnar Johansson, "Fotografiskt textiltryck," *Fotografisk årsbok*, 1956, 137–46.

14 Nationalmuseum, NK Textilkammare archives, AS3: 3–4, IBM; Anna Orrghen, "Driven by Visualization: Sten Kallin's Collaboration with Astrid Sampe, Sture Johannesson, and Mats Amundin as Explorations of Computer Technology," *Konsthistorisk tidskrift/Journal of Art History* 84, no. 2 (2015): 93–107.

15 Rebecka Tarschys, "Svensk medverkan i FN-biblioteket," *Dagens Nyheter*, October 25, 1961. The Ford Foundation donated the required funds; General Assembly resolution 1625 (XVI), Memorial to the late Dag Hammarskjöld.

16 "The Dag Hammarskjöld Library. Notes on its construction and furnishings. United Nations. New York. 1961," Nationalmuseum, NK Textilkammare archives, AS1:107.

17 Letter cited in Tarschys, "Svensk medverkan i FN-biblioteket."

18 Transcript for a radio lecture broadcast by Swedish Radio on February 22, 1963, Nationalmuseum, NK Textilkammare archives, AS1:107.

19 Tarschys, "Svensk medverkan i FN-biblioteket"; Rebecka Tarschys, "FN-biblioteket," *Form*, 1963, 216–19; Ulf Hård af Segerstad, "Svensk inredning i FN-biblioteket," *Svenska Dagbladet*, October 25, 1962.

REPRESENTING THE U.S. ABROAD

Ralph Rapson in Scandinavia

MONICA OBNISKI

After World War II, the U.S. State Department's Office of Foreign Buildings Operations (FBO) made International Style modernism the official building language of U.S. embassies abroad, including in Scandinavia.[1] As symbols of an architectural modernism that projected American values, these embassies were designed to exude democratic ideals and an American identity, but also remained mindful of local conditions and functioned for diplomatic tasks. As noted by *Architectural Forum*, "No country can exercise political world leadership without exercising a degree of cultural leadership as well."[2]

Ralph Rapson studied architecture at the University of Michigan before attending Cranbrook Academy of Art, where he experimented with modern materials, such as bentwood, designing a rocking chair that was eventually produced by Knoll Associates, Inc. (p. 171). His association with Knoll was an entrée to the FBO program, as Hans Knoll was selling furniture to the FBO when he learned of jobs in Scandinavia. Rapson, then teaching at MIT, was summoned to Washington, DC, in 1951 and FBO director Leland W. King invited him to design the

Stockholm, Copenhagen, Oslo, and the Hague embassies. Rapson accepted and asked his architecture school friend and Chicago colleague John van der Meulen to be his partner.

For the Stockholm and Copenhagen projects, the pair worked out of the office of Swedish architect Anders Tengbom, and were aided by Swedish and Danish architects.[3] Located on the city's eastern edge, the U.S. Embassy in Stockholm rises from a rocky base near a large park. Rapson had to receive clearance for his plans from Swedish architect Sven Markelius, who controlled urban planning in Stockholm (and whom Rapson affectionately called a "bull-headed Swede").[4] Initially, Rapson and van der Meulen proposed a taller building (p. 172), but Markelius wanted to maintain the integrity of the residential neighborhood. The final building, completed in 1954, consisted of a three-story tower with courses of fenestration. Cubic volumes hovered on piers; the upper block, containing offices for the U.S. ambassador and military attachés, protruded forward, shielding the transparent aluminum and glass entrance lobby. A glass-walled ground floor

RALPH RAPSON
Perspective drawing, United States Embassy, Stockholm (unbuilt proposal), 1951. CAT. 120

RALPH RAPSON
Perspective drawing, United States Embassy, Copenhagen, c. 1951. CAT. 121

RALPH RAPSON
Drawing of United States Embassy staff housing, Oslo (unbuilt proposal), c. 1953. Graphite on tracing paper, 9 × 10 in. (22.9 × 25.4 cm.). Ralph Rapson Collection, Cranbrook Archives, Cranbrook Center for Collections and Research, Gift of Rip Rapson

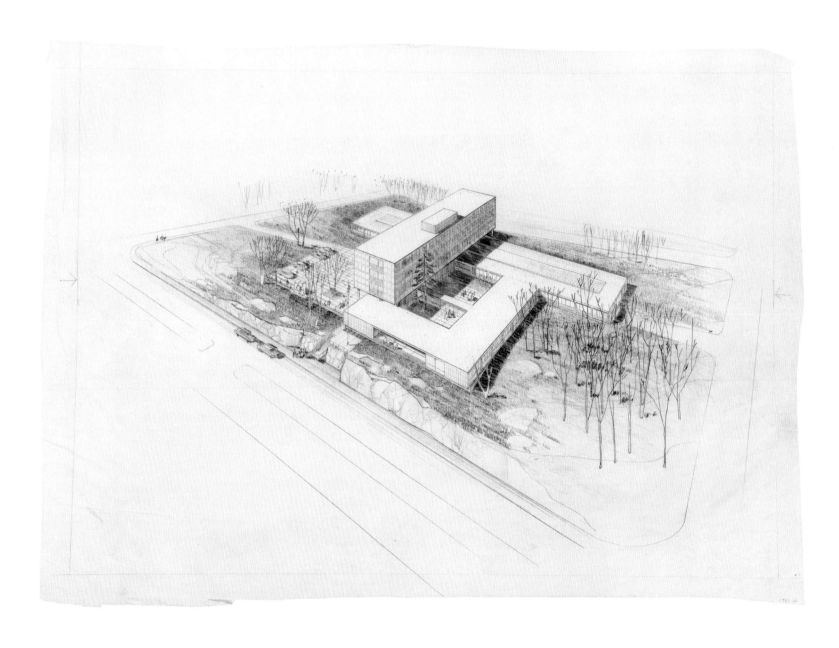

U.S. STAFF
HOUSING
OSLO
NORWAY

enclosed courtyards and housed the public-facing embassy offices, auditorium, lunchroom, and reception hall.

Press reception of the Stockholm embassy was split along national lines. Apart from Markelius' approval, Rapson and van der Meulen had little oversight during the design process, and the building was viewed as too unconventional by the Swedes, who deemed it an "architectural Marilyn Monroe."[5] American opinions proved more positive, with journalist Aline Louchheim complimenting the project for "maintaining a look of friendliness important in the Scandinavian environment," a comment that perpetuated the language of warmth that was intrinsic to the American perception of Scandinavia.[6] Around this time, Museum of Modern Art curator Arthur Drexler organized the exhibition *Architecture for the State Department* (1953), which included the Stockholm and Copenhagen buildings among the photographs and models representing nine projects.

The U.S. Embassy in Copenhagen was also designed by the pair in collaboration with other architects (p. 173).[7] The modern building was distinct from its traditional neighbors, such as the Canadian Embassy next door. The architects located public zones on the ground floor, while placing secure areas on upper floors. This resulted, as in Stockholm, in a building with deliberate massing floating above the ground. The architects used local materials and building techniques, when appropriate. Rapson's interest in experimenting with materials was evidenced in the building's reinforced concrete structure and light gray local stone facing. Designed only months apart, the structure, materials, and ventilating systems in Stockholm and Copenhagen were consistent, a reflection of similar local conditions.[8] The *New York Times* acknowledged that the Danes were "skeptical about the resistance of the light, glass structure to the damp, grim Danish winters," but the paper's primary message was one of nationalist rhetoric, as captured in the headline: "Modernistic U.S. Embassy in Denmark Is a Sensation."[9]

Rapson and van der Meulen began designing the Embassy building in Oslo, as well as staff housing, but these projects were abandoned (p. 173). The change in political climate in Washington, DC, coupled with MIT's demand to return, caused the architects to leave in 1954.[10] In 1955, Eero Saarinen was selected to design the U.S. Embassy for Oslo, completed in 1959.

1 Ada Louise Huxtable, "Sharp Debate: What Should an Embassy Be?," *New York Times*, September 18, 1960; Jane C. Loeffler, *The Architecture of Diplomacy: Building America's Embassies*, 2nd ed. (New York: Princeton Architectural Press, 2011).
2 "U.S. Architecture Abroad," *Architectural Forum* 98 (March 1953): 101.
3 "U.S. Embassy Buildings," *Architectural Review* 118 (October 1955): 240–48; Loeffler, *Architecture of Diplomacy*, 72.
4 Loeffler, *Architecture of Diplomacy*, 73.
5 Ides van der Gracht to Leland King, November 2, 1954, Ralph Rapson Collection (1935–1954), Cranbrook Center for Collections and Research, Bloomfield Hills, MI.

6 Aline B. Louchheim, "State Department Opens Show Today," *New York Times*, October 7, 1953.
7 Construction was supervised by the U.S. government under Leland W. King; head architect Ides van der Gracht, responsible for all U.S. buildings in northern Europe, was assisted by Swede Anders Tengbom; Danish architects Erik Herløw and Jørgen Juul-Møller and interior architect Susanne Wasson-Tucker contributed to the project.
8 "U.S. Embassy Buildings," 244.
9 "Modernistic U.S. Embassy in Denmark Is a Sensation," *New York Times*, June 8, 1954.
10 Loeffler, *Architecture of Diplomacy*, 78.

STRENGTHENING BONDS

Eero Saarinen's U.S. Chancery in Oslo, 1955–59

DENISE HAGSTRÖMER

"As the American Embassy begins its operations in its new home," Frances E. Willis, the United States ambassador to Norway, wrote in her inaugural greetings, "it is our hope that we shall be able to provide greater service to the public. Just as the construction of this building was a joint Norwegian-American undertaking, so we hope that in using it together day by day we may strengthen the close bonds which so happily already exist between our two countries."[1] Norway paid for the project using credit from U.S. financial aid after World War II. The embassy's new home, located in central Oslo south of the Royal Palace Park (p. 176), did not supersede the old one; while it promoted a new image of openness and collaboration with local industry, the resi-dence continued its original and crucial role in diplomacy.[2]

Saarinen adapted the building to the local cityscape by placing a triangular volume on a triangular site, with its height matching the neighboring rooflines. Made of precast concrete panels using a 90 percent aggregate of Norwegian emerald pearl granite, the façade was pierced with teak-framed windows that reflected the sky and the park's trees.[3] Inside, visitors found a welcoming, light-filled, airy space (p. 176). The chancery was conceived as a three-sided Renaissance palace surrounding a skylit, four-level rectangular atrium, with beige Roman travertine paving and teak benches around a central pool. The walls were made of light-toned brick grilles and high screens of louvered teak. One of the two public side entrances led to a set of quasi-public spaces, which included a library, a soundproof listening room, and a hexagonal auditorium with a stage. Susanne Wasson-Tucker, of Knoll Associates, designed the interiors, which were furnished mainly with Knoll designs manufactured locally by the furniture firm Tannum, adding a Norwegian accent to a unified U.S. design identity.[4]

Norwegian media reported on every stage of the project, showing Nordic pride at the choice of Saarinen and noting the controversies in the U.S. surrounding his appointment.[5] The official Oslo tourist guide ranked the new addition as one of the city's major attractions, and nine out of ten Oslonians reportedly liked it.[6] Noted architect Berent Moe's extensive review in *Byggekunst* praised the "primacy of aesthetics and psychological values over early Modernism's function and logic," while *Morgenbladet* noted the skylight's historical references.[7]

The new chancery (the embassy office building) marked a significant change in practice, since prior to its construction, the ambassador's residence was the usual site of diplomatic activity. Ambassador Willis's new suite was only a ten-minute walk from Villa Otium, her palatial residence

United States Embassy, Oslo, 1955–59, designed by Eero Saarinen. Photographed in 1959

Interior courtyard of United States Embassy, Oslo, 1955–59, designed by Eero Saarinen. Photographed in 1959

designed by Henrik Bull in 1911, which the U.S. government had bought in 1923.[8] Although Norwegians could listen to American jazz while sitting in Eames chairs at the chancery,[9] the residence's Parisian salon furniture continued (and still continues) to provide a traditional setting for Norwegians and Americans to meet for the exchange of ideas and information, or in Ambassador Willis's words, the strengthening of bonds.

1 *The New American Embassy Building in Norway* (Oslo, 1959). The Norwegian associate architects were John Engh and Henrik Kiær. "Den amerikanske ambassade i Oslo," *Byggekunst*, no. 5 (1959): 113–14.
2 Jane C. Loeffler, *The Architecture of Diplomacy: Building America's Embassies* (New York: Princeton Architectural Press, 1998); Denise Hagströmer, "In Search of a National Vision: Swedish Embassies from the Mid-20th Century to the Present" (PhD thesis, Royal College of Art, London, 2011). The chancery moved to the suburb of Huseby in 2017.
3 "U.S. Embassy in Oslo," *Architectural Record* 126, no. 6 (December 1959): 107–13; Timo Tuomi, "Embassies and Chancelleries: The Necessity of Unity," in *Eero Saarinen: Shaping the Future*, exh. cat., ed. Eeva-Liisa Pelkonen and Donald Albrecht (New Haven: Yale University Press, 2006), 286–99; *Eero Saarinen on His Work: A Selection of Buildings Dating from 1947 to 1964, with Statements by the Architect*, ed. Aline B. Saarinen (New Haven: Yale University Press, 1968), 52.
4 "Amerikansk Sensasjon på Drammensveien!," *Dagbladet*, June 15, 1959.
5 Even Hebbe Johnsrud, "Suomis sønner skaper stil," *Aftenposten*, June 7, 1955; "Amerikansk bekymring: 'Til Oslo' for å få arkitekt?," *Morgenbladet*, February 26, 1959. Throughout the decade there were tensions between the progressive architectural community and some conservative members of Congress, one of whom threatened to withhold funds from the Office of Foreign Buildings Operations if Saarinen "ever got another job." "Exciting Embassy by Saarinen Opens Under Fire," *Progressive Architecture* (November 1959): 90–91.
6 "Norway's Precast Palazzo," *Architectural Forum* 3, no. 6 (December 1959): 130–33.
7 Berent Moe, "Eero Saarinen på Drammensveien," *Byggekunst*, no. 5 (May 1959): 115–28; "Uttrykk for en kommende epoke," *Morgenbladet*, September 25, 1959. The article noted similarity to the vaulted ceilings of the late fifteenth-century St. George's Church in Nördlingen, Germany.
8 On Villa Otium, see no.usembassy.gov /embassy/oslo/ambassadors-residence.
9 "Amerikansk Sensasjon på Drammensveien!"

TEACHERS AND STUDENTS

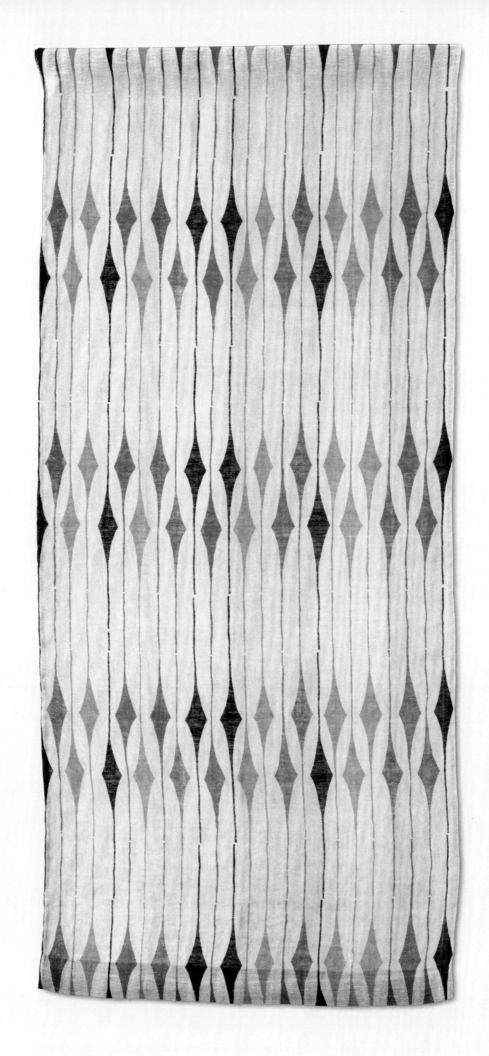

BOBBYE TIGERMAN

TEACHERS AND STUDENTS "Sloyd is the fad," announced the *Chicago Tribune* on January 21, 1892, referring to the handicraft curriculum that had originated in the Nordic countries and gained a substantial American following.[1] "Reading, writing, spelling, and the like have to take a back seat just now, and the sewing fad is coming next." In Swedish, *slöjd* translates literally as "skill" or "craft" and refers to the practice of making useful objects at home, both to fulfill domestic needs and provide additional income. Fearing the loss of traditional skills as children moved out of the workforce and into school during the Industrial Revolution, the Swedish government set up dedicated schools to preserve these skills by training teachers in *slöjd* curriculum. *Slöjd* education consisted of a series of progressively complex manual exercises that led to the creation of useful objects, from simple letter openers to elaborate cabinets.[2]

Gustaf Larsson, a graduate of the famous *slöjd* teacher training school in Nääs, Sweden, was largely responsible for promoting this educational model in the United States (where *slöjd* was anglicized as sloyd). Larsson arrived in Boston in 1888, where he met Pauline Agassiz Shaw, an influential social reformer.[3] Shaw invited him to implement a sloyd teacher training curriculum at the North Bennet Street Industrial School.[4] Larsson adapted the Swedish curriculum for his American students in several ways, including allowing more freedom in the design of their work and expanding the curriculum to include metalwork, bookbinding, printing, and other crafts. Larsson lectured throughout the country and published several books, especially on his adaptation of the program to American schools (opposite p. 336).

Sloyd classes were just one way that Nordic teachers influenced American design education. Throughout the twentieth century, many Scandinavian designers and craftspeople taught in American schools where they shaped the careers of American students, ultimately helping to determine the course of American design. One center for this pedagogical chain of influence was Cranbrook Academy of Art in Bloomfield Hills, Michigan, near Detroit, founded in 1927 by newspaper publisher and arts patron George G. Booth and his wife, philanthropist Ellen Scripps Booth. The Booths envisioned the school as the premier American institution for art and craft education, loosely based on the American Academy in Rome, which was originally founded as an art academy. Cranbrook's faculty included many

EVA-LISA (PIPSAN) SAARINEN SWANSON
Edwin Raphael Company, Inc.
Saratoga textile, designed 1952–62.
CAT. 152

TIGERMAN

leading Nordic artists, architects, designers, and craftspeople who in turn attracted promising American students. As a proving ground for the most important American designers of the twentieth century, Cranbrook profoundly influenced how Scandinavian design would shape American design.

In 1924, the Booths invited Finnish architect Eliel Saarinen to propose architectural plans for Cranbrook Academy of Art, and to advise on the new school's pedagogy.[5] Saarinen already enjoyed a prominent reputation in the United States, having won second place in the 1923 Tribune Tower competition.[6] His drawing of the Chicago Tower, Lakefront Development Project, was one of his first proposals after arriving in the United States (prior to his invitation to Cranbrook), and demonstrates his ambition to shape American cities and his prominent role in American architectural discourse (p. 180). Saarinen ultimately designed several buildings on the Cranbrook campus, including Cranbrook School for Boys, Kingswood School for Girls, Cranbrook Institute of Science, Cranbrook Art Museum, and homes for his own family and the Swedish sculptor Carl Milles, whom Saarinen recruited as the Academy's sculpture instructor in 1931. Many of these buildings appear in the "Cranbrook Map" hanging, woven in the studio of his wife, Loja, in 1935 (pp. 212–13). The hanging depicts not only existing buildings, but also Saarinen's aspirations for the campus's future growth; it even includes representations of Milles sculptures, such as the *Jonah and the Whale* fountain, visible in the center of the hanging (p. 182).[7]

In 1938 Saarinen hired the Finnish ceramist Maija Grotell to head Cranbrook's ceramic department, where she taught until 1966.[8] Her work is characterized by strong color contrasts and low-relief geometric decoration, as evident in her vase (p. 184). Grotell's student and assistant Toshiko Takaezu became an important teacher herself, renowned for perfecting the pinched neck form with pinhole opening, as she sought the largest possible surface area on her pots (p. 185).[9] When Grotell arrived at Cranbrook, ceramics classes were largely for recreational potters, but after World War II, she built a degree program that produced many professional ceramists and teachers. In addition to Takaezu, prominent students included Leza McVey, who made asymmetrical, biomorphic sculptures in the 1950s; Harvey Littleton, a seminal figure in the American studio glass movement; and Richard DeVore, who succeeded Grotell as ceramics instructor at Cranbrook.

TIGERMAN

CARL MILLES
Model for *Jonah and the Whale*
fountain, 1932. CAT. 106

The year before hiring Grotell, Saarinen invited Finnish textile designer Marianne Strengell to teach weaving, and she became the head of that department in 1942.[10] Strengell gradually updated the largely handweaving-based curriculum by adding instruction in power loom weaving and textile printing. Strengell's interest in new techniques and synthetic materials reflected the focus of her own professional work, which emphasized collaborations with industry and architectural firms. Her students acknowledged that the example she set—both her single-minded devotion to her career and the professional relationships she forged with industry—shaped their own professional aims and encouraged them to envision careers beyond traditional expectations. As the tapestry artist Alice Adams reflected, "she instilled in all of her students a sense of the particular responsibility of the designer-weaver to himself and to the public and a genuine professionalism in the very best sense of the word."[11] Strengell's students pursued careers in vastly divergent areas of the textile field, from one-of-a-kind sculptural hangings by Alice Kagawa Parrott (p. 253) to the production textile empire built by Jack Lenor Larsen (p. 187).

One of Strengell's most accomplished students was Ed Rossbach, who attended Cranbrook in 1946–47, majoring in ceramics and minoring in weaving before going on to establish his own influential teaching career at the University of Washington and the University of California, Berkeley.[12] Rossbach worked in many fiber techniques, including standard weaving, ikat, and basketry, and was known for using unconventional materials such as plastic tubing and raffia. Deviating from Strengell's model of designing for industry, he focused on technical investigation and artistic experimentation. His *Modular Construction* employs a tapestry weave structure with an ikat weft to create a composition of squares and rectangles, demonstrating the potential for variety within the grid format (p. 186). Furthermore, he extended his influence by writing several books, including *Baskets as Textile Art* (1973), *The New Basketry* (1976), and *The Art of Paisley* (1980).

In contrast to Rossbach's path, Jack Lenor Larsen followed closely in Strengell's footsteps, developing designs for mass production and forging strong relationships with industry. Larsen was Rossbach's teaching assistant at the University of Washington before Rossbach encouraged Larsen to enroll at Cranbrook, where he completed his master's degree in 1951.[13] A prolific designer and successful entrepreneur, Larsen built a vast line of furnishing textiles, as well as carpets and furniture. One of Larsen's most celebrated designs was *Magnum*, originally created as the curtain for the

TIGERMAN

ED ROSSBACH
Modular Construction hanging, 1968.
CAT. 130

JACK LENOR LARSEN
WIN ANDERSON
Jack Lenor Larsen, Inc.
Magnum textile, designed 1970.
CAT. 87

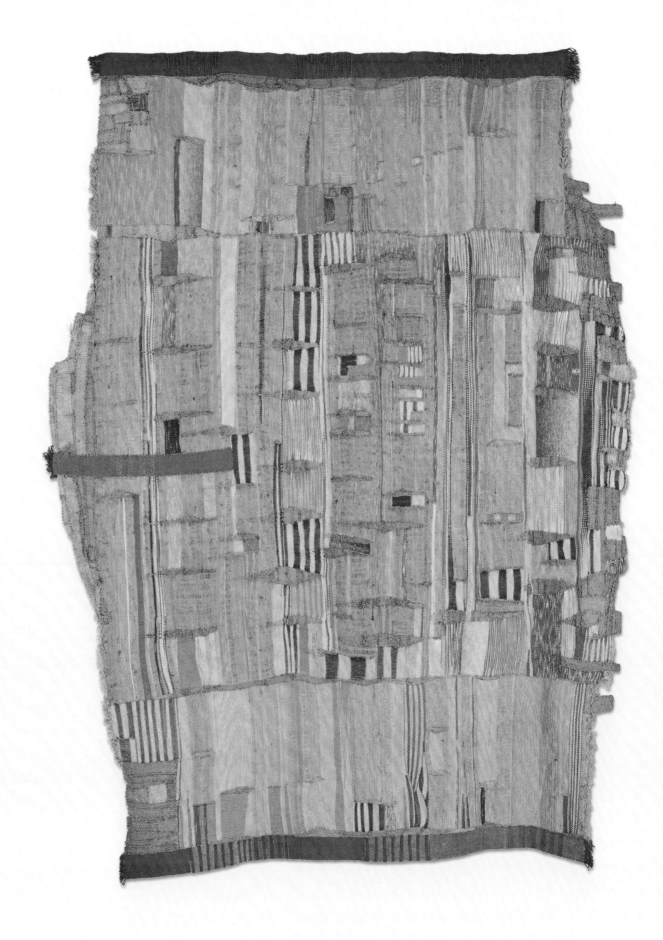

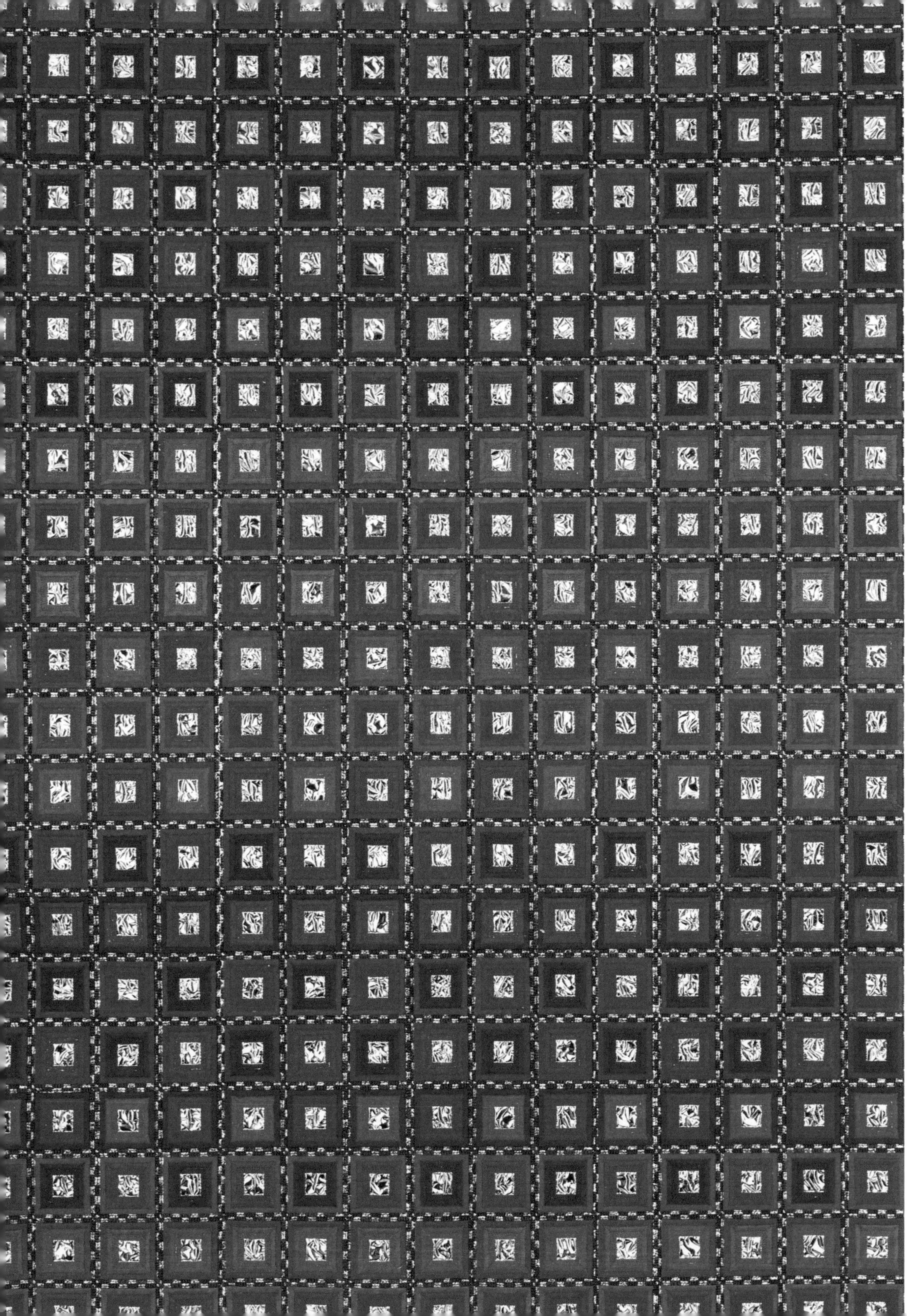

CHARLES EAMES
EERO SAARINEN
Haskelite Manufacturing Corporation
Chair, 1940. CAT. 28

CHARLES EAMES
RAY EAMES
Herman Miller Furniture Company
DAX (Dining Armchair X-base),
designed 1948–50, this example
c. 1951–52. CAT. 27

EERO SAARINEN
Knoll Associates, Inc.
Pedestal ("Tulip") side chair,
designed 1956, this example 1976.
CAT. 133

Phoenix Civic Plaza Symphony Hall and in production from 1972 to 1992 (p. 187).[14] Seeking to imitate Indian and Pakistani mirror embroidery, Larsen machine-embroidered brightly colored threads on a sheet of reflective Mylar film.[15] For this project, he worked with Win Anderson, whom he knew as a student at the University of Washington and at Cranbrook, and who later became his studio manager.[16]

Other Cranbrook alumni from the 1940s and 1950s rivaled their teachers in the extent of their influence on modern American design and became leaders in their respective fields, including Benjamin Baldwin, Harry Bertoia, Charles Eames, Ray Eames, Florence Knoll, Ralph Rapson, and Harry Weese. While Charles Eames was still a student at Cranbrook, he and Eero Saarinen collaborated on a suite of furniture for the Museum of Modern Art's 1940 Organic Design in Home Furnishings competition (p. 188). They used molded plywood to create a single-material seat, unlike predecessors that required multiple layers of support and upholstery. While the chair from the Organic Design competition did not ultimately go into mass production, both Eames and Saarinen continued to pursue this principle independently. Each achieved the goal of an integral single-material chair seat using plastic—the Eameses designed the *DAX* chair made by Herman Miller and Saarinen created the *Pedestal* furniture produced by Knoll Associates, Inc. (pp. 188–89).

Kingswood's most distinguished design alumnus was 1936 graduate Florence Knoll. Orphaned before she arrived at Cranbrook, Knoll became close with the entire Saarinen family, even spending vacations with them in Finland. Knoll studied architecture before moving to New York City in 1943 to pursue her design career. She met German furniture entrepreneur Hans Knoll, and together they built the firm Knoll Associates, Inc. Florence Knoll led one of its divisions, the Knoll Planning Unit, a design consultancy responsible for several modernist corporate interiors.[17] She often used the technique of the paste-up, adhering fabric swatches and wood chips to a miniature aerial plan of the space to convey the impression of the fully furnished room, as seen in the design for the office of Jack Heinz, CEO of the H. J. Heinz Company (p. 192). Knoll learned this technique from Loja Saarinen in 1935, when Saarinen gave Knoll the paste-up of a dress design as a Christmas present, and the fully realized dress shortly after (p. 193).[18] Additionally, Knoll commissioned many designers she knew through Cranbrook, including Harry Bertoia, Ralph Rapson, Eero Saarinen, and Marianne Strengell, to create furniture and textiles for the Knoll line.

Other U.S. institutions hired Scandinavian immigrants as permanent faculty, including the School for American Craftsmen (SAC).[19] In 1948, in response to a great influx of students attending on the G.I. Bill, SAC sought instructors in the fields of silversmithing and woodwork. The American-born silversmith John Prip, then living in Denmark, was offered the job. Having completed his five-year apprenticeship with Danish silversmith Evald Nielsen in 1942, Prip brought deep technical knowledge to the school, where he taught until 1954, while simultaneously designing for several firms.[20] Beginning in 1957, Prip served as designer-in-residence at Massachusetts-based Reed & Barton, where he created the *Denmark* tea and coffee service (p. 251). This set, along with his other designs for the company, embodied the elegant, organic forms associated with postwar Danish design, and allowed him to realize the Scandinavian ideal of craft alliance with industry.[21] When he left SAC, the school hired Hans Christensen, a similarly trained Dane who had apprenticed at the Georg Jensen Silversmithy, to continue the metal-work curriculum (p. 194).[22]

In 1948, SAC also sought a woodworking instructor, and Prip encouraged his longtime friend Tage Frid, a formally trained Danish cabinetmaker, to apply.[23] Together Prip and Frid adapted the school's curriculum to incorporate a more Scandinavian approach to design and fabrication. In 1963, they began teaching at Rhode Island School of Design (RISD), where both fostered dedicated followings, with Frid counting John Dunnigan, Hank Gilpin, Bill Keyser, Alphonse Mattia, Daniel Jackson, and Jere Osgood among his students who became professional furnituremakers.[24] Frid's legacy at RISD endures through his student Rosanne Somerson, who became a RISD furniture design professor and is now the school's president (pp. 229–31). Prip's students included Louis Mueller and Robin Quigley, both of whom succeeded him as RISD professors.

Not all craft and design instruction occurred in formal educational settings. Hobbyist classes, intensive workshops, and summer schools also served as outlets for Nordic immigrants to transmit their artistic knowledge. When the silversmith Margret Craver wanted to learn modern metalsmithing, she found no suitable program in the United States, so she cobbled together her education from several smiths around the country before traveling to Sweden in 1938 to study with Baron Erik Fleming, court silversmith to King Gustav of Sweden. There she learned how to raise hollowware, making a silver bonbonnière (p. 195).[25] In 1946, Craver became head of

FLORENCE KNOLL
Paste-up of the design for Jack Heinz's office, H. J. Heinz, c. 1960.
Mixed media, 7⅞ × 10¼ in. (20 × 26 cm).
Florence Knoll Bassett Papers,
1932–2000. Archives of American Art,
Smithsonian Institution

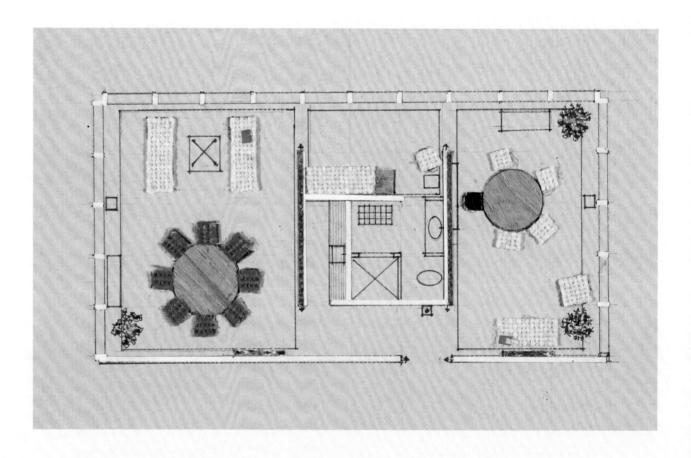

LOJA SAARINEN
Paste-up of a dress design, 1935.
Mixed media, 8 ¼ × 6 in. (21 × 15 cm).
Florence Knoll Bassett Papers,
1932–2000. Archives of American Art,
Smithsonian Institution

TEACHERS AND STUDENTS

HANS CHRISTENSEN
Coffeepot, designed c. 1956,
this example c. 1960. CAT. 18

195

TIGERMAN

the Craft Services Department of Handy & Harman, a New York precious metals firm, where she organized five summer silversmithing workshops between 1947 and 1951. The purpose of these month-long programs was to train the next generation of promising American craftspeople in advanced techniques, providing an education that could not be found elsewhere in the U.S. Craver invited Fleming to teach at the workshops in 1948, 1949, and 1951.[26] These short-term programs raised the skill level of American craftspeople; from the 1948 workshop alone, several students went on to become both influential figures and teachers, including Alma Eikerman, Frederick Miller, Arthur Pulos, and Richard Reinhardt.

Another significant example of Scandinavian influence in a workshop setting was the transformation of American artist Lenore Tawney from a painter and sculptor into a fiber artist. Tawney enrolled in a six-week tapestry workshop in 1954 with Finnish weaver Martta Taipale at the Penland School of Crafts in North Carolina. Taipale was known for brightly colored tapestries that incorporated a combination of natural and manmade materials (p. 196).[27] Tawney later declared the immersive weaving experience "the beginning of my real career."[28] Following the workshop, Tawney began to make her boundary-breaking art textiles, becoming a leader in the fiber art movement in the 1960s–70s (p. 197).

U.S. arts institutions sought Nordic instructors because of their specialized skills, catalyzing a migration of artists and craftspeople that would shape the course of American design. In both formal, degree-granting programs and short-term (but equally influential) courses, generations of American design students learned directly from these instructors, who did not just teach a style or technique, but imparted an approach that informed their students' work. When these students became teachers, they multiplied the influence of their mentors and further extended the reach of Scandinavian methods and knowledge in the United States.

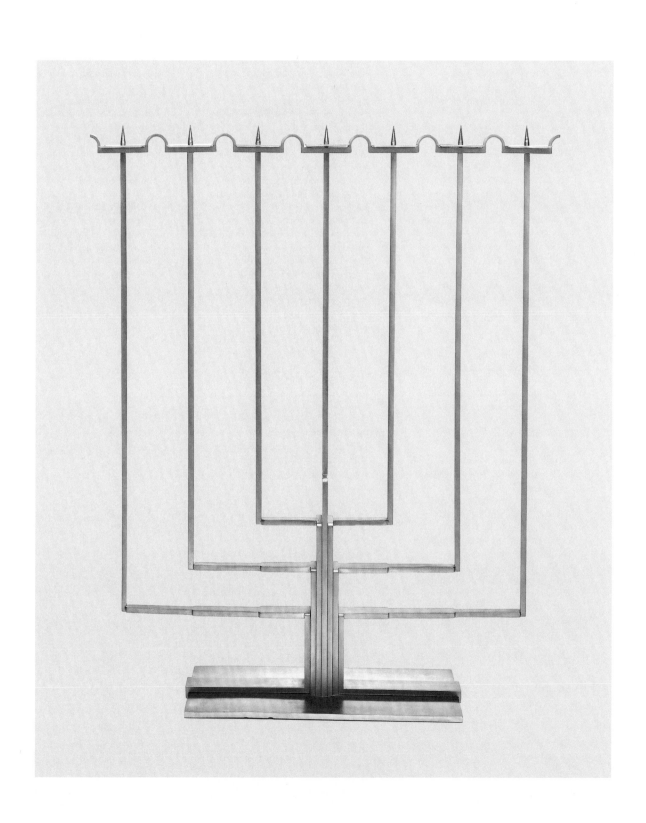

1 "Sloyd Is the Fad, Three Chicago Schools Industriously Teaching It," *Chicago Tribune*, January 21, 1892. Sloyd's origins are generally attributed to Sweden, although one of its earliest theorists was the Finn Uno Cygnaeus. There was also a Danish version of sloyd education promoted in the United States; see *The Danish Sloyd: Guide to the Exposition of the Danish Sloyd Association* (Copenhagen, 1893).

2 June E. Eyestone, "The Influence of Swedish Sloyd and Its Interpreters on American Art Education," *Studies in Art Education* 34, no. 1 (Autumn 1992): 29–31.

3 *Pauline Agassiz Shaw: Tributes Paid Her Memory at the Memorial Service Held on Easter Sunday, April 8, 1917, at Faneuil Hall, Boston* (Boston: privately printed, 1917), Internet Archive, https://archive.org.

4 Eyestone, "The Influence of Swedish Sloyd," 31–33.

5 At that time, Saarinen was teaching at the University of Michigan's School of Architecture, where the Booths' son Henry was his student; Davira S. Taragin, "The History of the Cranbrook Community," in *Design in America: The Cranbrook Vision, 1925–1950*, exh. cat., ed. Robert Judson Clark and Andrea P. A. Belloli (New York: Detroit Institute of Arts and the Metropolitan Museum of Art, 1983), 34–45.

6 Katherine Solomonson, *The Chicago Tribune Tower Competition: Skyscraper Design and Cultural Change in the 1920s* (Chicago: University of Chicago Press, 2001).

7 Leena Svinhufvud, "The *Cranbrook Map*: Locating Meanings in Textile Art," in *Imagining Spaces and Places*, ed. Saija Isomaa et al. (Newcastle upon Tyne, UK: Cambridge Scholars Publishing, 2013), 199–225. *Jonah and the Whale* was Milles' first work completed in the United States, commissioned by Cranbrook in 1932.

8 Martin Eidelberg, "Ceramics," in Clark and Belloli, *Design in America*, 221–22; *Maija Grotell*, exh. cat. (New York: New Era Lithograph, 1967).

9 Paul J. Smith, "Toshiko Takaezu—Her Life and Work," in *Toshiko Takaezu: Four Decades* (Montclair, NJ: Montclair Art Museum, 1989), 8–11.

10 Ann Marguerite Tartsinis, "Marianne Strengell," in *Knoll Textiles, 1945–2010*, exh. cat., ed. Earl James Martin (New Haven: Bard Graduate Center in association with Yale University Press, 2011), 381–83.

11 Alice Adams, "Marianne Strengell," *Craft Horizons* 23, no. 1 (January/February 1963): 34–36 at 36.

12 Ann Pollard Rowe and Rebecca A. T. Stevens, eds., *Ed Rossbach: 40 Years of Exploration and Innovation in Fiber Art*, exh. cat. (Asheville, NC, and Washington, DC: Lark Books and Textile Museum, 1990).

13 Jack Lenor Larsen, "Introduction," in *Ed Rossbach*, 8–10.

14 A detail from *Magnum* appeared on the cover of *Craft Horizons* in April 1971.

15 Larsen Design Studio, *Magnum*, 1973, cotton, vinyl, nylon, and polyester, backed with nylon scrim; 53 in. × 37 ¼ in. (134.6 × 94.6 cm); Cooper Hewitt, Cowtan and Tout Larsen Archive Collection, Gift of Longhouse Reserve (2016-32-15), https://collection.cooperhewitt.org/objects/673135633/.

16 Mary Schoeser and Whitney Blausen, "'Wellpaying Self Support': Women Textile Designers," in *Women Designers in the USA 1900–2000: Diversity and Difference*, exh. cat., ed. Pat Kirkham (New Haven and London: Yale University Press in association with the Bard Graduate Center for Studies in the Decorative Arts, 2000), 163–64.

17 Bobbye Tigerman, "'I Am Not a Decorator': Florence Knoll, the Knoll Planning Unit and the Making of the Modern Office," *Journal of Design History* 20, no. 1 (Spring 2007): 61–74.

18 Bobbye Tigerman, "The Heart and Soul of the Company: The Knoll Planning Unit, 1944–65," in Martin, *Knoll Textiles*, 181.

19 The School for American Craftsmen, founded by Aileen Osborn Webb, was located at Dartmouth College (1944–46), Alfred University (1946–50), and the Rochester Institute of Technology (1950–present); "School for American Craftsmen," in *Crafting Modernism: Midcentury American Art and Design*, exh. cat., ed. Jeannine Falino, History of Twentieth-Century American Craft 4 (New York: Abrams in association with the Museum of Arts and Design, 2011), 326. See also W. Scott Braznell, "The Early Career of Ronald Hayes Pearson and the Post–World War II Revival of American Silversmithing and Jewelrymaking," *Winterthur Portfolio* 34, no. 4 (Winter 1999): 185–213.

20 John Prip, oral history conducted October 20, 1980, and November 21, 1981, by Robert Brown, Archives of American Art, Smithsonian Institution; Jeannine Falino, "Restless Dane: The Evolving Metalwork of John Prip," *Metalsmith* 30, no. 1 (2010): 44–51.

21 John Prip, "John Prip and Reed & Barton," *Craft Horizons* 24, no. 2 (March/April 1964): 41–42.

22 "A Remembrance: Hans Christensen 1924–1983," *Metalsmith* 3 (Spring 1983): 6.

23 The Prip and Frid families were close. Prip's grandfather owned a silver-smithing shop, where Prip's father apprenticed and Frid's father also worked; Prip oral history.

24 Hank Gilpin, "Professor Frid," *Fine Woodworking*, Winter 2000/2001, 85.

25 "The Reminiscences of Margret Craver," oral history conducted September 11 and 30, 1987, by Richard Polsky, American Craftspeople Oral History Project, Columbia University Oral History Research Office. Craver made the cloisonné enamel insert the previous year while studying with British silversmith Arthur Nevill Kirk in Detroit.

26 Jeannine Falino and Yvonne Markowitz, "Margret Craver: A Foremost 20th Century Jeweler and Educator," *Jewelry: Journal of the American Society of Jewelry Historians* 1 (Spring 1997): 9–23; Lisa Hammel, "On Her Mettle: Margret Craver," *American Craft* 51, no. 3 (June/July 1991): 54–60.

27 Dorothy Liebes, "Tapestries by Martta Taipale," *Craft Horizons* 12, no. 5 (September/October 1952): 18–19.

28 Lenore Tawney, oral history conducted June 23, 1971, by Paul Cummings, Archives of American Art, Smithsonian Institution.

Intersecting Threads: Scandinavian Weaving Influences in the United States

ERICA WARREN

I n November 1892, Norwegian American author Hjalmar Hjorth Boyesen published "The Scandinavian in the United States," in which he criticized Swedish, Norwegian, and Danish immigrants for not assimilating quickly enough into American society. Boyesen proposed that "we have to grind alien grain in the national hopper. But the more homogeneous [nationality], which in time will issue forth, will, I doubt not, justify the turmoil and noise and discomfort of the grinding."[1] A few months later, in February 1893, a rebuttal was penned by George Taylor Rygh: "The fact is that the Scandinavians in the United States are not Norwegians, Swedes and Danes, strictly speaking, but American citizens first and always…. The vast majority of them are valuable accessions to our composite population."[2] Florid, impassioned, and often polarizing proclamations frequently appeared in a variety of American media at the turn of the century, but did not necessarily describe the breadth of options available to immigrants nor the actual attitudes of those born in the United States to those more newly arrived. Among the Scandinavian Americans that Boyesen and Rygh abstractly generalized and debated, but who defied the limits of their reductive narrative of citizenship, was Pauline Fjelde, a Norwegian woman who had immigrated to America in 1887. Fjelde's life as an artist and entrepreneur serves as an apt early example of the many exchanges that have shaped both the discourse and the aesthetics of weaving and textile design in America from the late nineteenth through the twentieth century.

Fjelde was just one of the 750,000 Norwegians who came to the United States between 1865 and 1915.[3] She had been a needlework instructor in Copenhagen and immigrated to the United States with her brother Jacob, a sculptor and wood-carver.[4] They joined their eldest brother in Minneapolis, and soon their younger sister Thomane arrived as well. In 1890 Pauline and Thomane opened a needlework shop, where they specialized in embroidered banners and monograms. In 1893, the sisters were commissioned to embroider the first Minnesota state flag (p. 202), which had been designed by Amelia Hyde Center and was exhibited in Chicago that same year at the World's Columbian Exposition, where it received a gold medal.[5] The medal further bolstered their reputation, and they also received the commission to make the

AMELIA HYDE CENTER
Pauline Fjelde
Thomane Fjelde Hansen
Minnesota state flag, 1893. CAT. 17

HANS ANDERSEN BRENDEKILDE
Pauline Fjelde (weaver)
Hiawatha **tapestry**, completed 1923.
Cotton, wool, and silk, 108 ¼ × 100 ½ in.
(275 × 254 cm). Minnesota Historical
Society

silk regimental battle flag that was carried in the Spanish-American War.[6] The Fjelde sisters' successful shop, coupled with their work on these state flags, demonstrates their participation in and contributions to early Minneapolis, and Minnesotan, culture and society. Moreover, the flags highlight their role in the production of state and national identity in the late nineteenth century. Although they did not design the flags, through their embroidery work, the sisters became quite familiar with the state seal, which features a farmer tilling the land in the foreground, while a Native American figure rides off on a horse in the distance.

This narrative of statehood present in the flag's design, which emphasizes the importance of settlers (a category that included immigrants) and an imagined harmony with idealized Native Americans, also informed Fjelde's major life work, the *Hiawatha* tapestry (above). Begun in 1912, it remained a work in progress for at least a decade. The tapestry illustrates a verse from Henry Wadsworth Longfellow's *Song of Hiawatha* (1855), an epic poem relating the fictional tale of Hiawatha, an Ojibwe warrior, and his

doomed love for Minnehaha, a Dakota woman. The central pictorial scene in Fjelde's tapestry depicts Hiawatha encountering Minnehaha and her father. A border that features the relevant stanza from the poem as well as discreet stylized and silhouetted figures, supposedly representing scenes of everyday life for Native Americans, frames the illusionistic tableau.[7] Fjelde, who lived close to Minnehaha Falls, had seen the public response to her brother Jacob's sculpture *Hiawatha and Minnehaha*. In 1902, the city's municipal art commission considered producing a bronze version of the plaster sculpture, which had been exhibited at the World's Columbian Exposition in front of the Minnesota building. The art commission rejected the sculpture for its poor design and "grave anatomical error" (according to the members of the commission, the frontal view of the sculpture, which emphasized Minnehaha, was not pleasing, and Hiawatha's legs were not bent sufficiently to accommodate the weight of Minnehaha).[8] However, ten years later (following Jacob Fjelde's death in 1896), the sculpture—now cast in bronze and placed in the stream above the falls—was declared "gallant."[9] Although the sculpture did find a public home, this was only after the Minneapolis municipal art commission had publicly critiqued it quite harshly. With her tapestry, Fjelde endeavored to produce a better interpretation of the poem that would enshrine her legacy in the artistic life of her adopted country. The tapestry received a warmer reception than Jacob's sculpture, lauded a few years after Fjelde's death in 1923 as "the great, final triumph" of "an extremely gifted human life."[10]

The *Hiawatha* tapestry is a product of cultural exchange on many levels. Although Fjelde was already familiar with her homeland's weaving traditions, the increasing popularity of tapestries in the United States prompted her to return to Europe in 1911 to study tapestry techniques in France and Norway.[11] Some of her weavings prior to *Hiawatha* combine tapestry methods characteristic of France with the interlocking weft technique common in Norway. However, in making *Hiawatha* Fjelde relied solely on the slit tapestry technique typically used in French workshops.[12] She did not design the tapestry herself, but instead the Danish painter Hans Andersen Brendekilde supplied the drawing. *Hiawatha* thus fuses the work of an American-born author, a Danish artist, and a Norwegian American weaver who possibly combined Norwegian warps and imported French wefts.[13] The tapestry demonstrates the complex nature of weaving in America and the rich variety of technical, aesthetic, and material knowledge that shaped the work of Scandinavian American weavers.

A contemporary of Fjelde, Edward F. Worst, the son of German immigrants and raised in Lockport, Illinois, gained his expertise in weaving as an educator in Chicago. Inspired by the ideals of the Arts and Crafts movement, Worst saw handicraft as a way to empower individuals by making them independent of industrial manufacture and its attendant dehumanizing labor practices as well as aesthetically inferior goods.[14] In order to teach advanced woven techniques to students (from the primary school level all the way through to high school and beyond) as well as other teachers, Worst sought additional training, first attending the Lowell Textile School in Massachusetts for two summers. Disappointed in Lowell's emphasis on mechanical and industrial methods of production, Worst traveled to Sweden to attend the Bronson Textile School in 1908.[15] Four years later, he enrolled in weaving classes at the Swedish handwork school at Nääs, whose progressive mission aligned with Worst's beliefs. The school, established in 1874, provided teachers with hands-on training in order to cultivate "a respect for manual toil, a dexterity of hand, and an appreciation for grace of line and form" at home and abroad.[16] Also in 1874, a group of women in Stockholm had founded Handarbetets Vänner (Friends of Handicraft), an organization that encouraged handwork in the home and promoted the idea that peasant women in particular should weave and sell goods for income. By the time Worst attended the school in Nääs, several additional handicraft societies had been established and "the crusade for handicrafts" had proved successful in Sweden.[17] This constellation of educational and cultural experiences prepared Worst for his next project, which extended beyond the classroom.

Back in Illinois, and eager to implement a craft industry, Worst received a shipment of spinning wheels and looms from Sweden and Norway and established the Lockport Home Industry in his hometown.[18] Worst's experiences in Sweden presumably guided his choice of a local Swedish immigrant community as the basis for his handicraft industry; moreover, the choice of location for his enterprise, thirty miles southwest of Chicago, suggests that he was aware of the efforts of influential Arts and Crafts practitioners such as

William Morris, Charles Robert Ashbee, and Ralph Whitehead, who each established rural outposts for production. Learning from his predecessors, Worst encouraged the weavers to make household goods that could be sold locally as well as in Chicago.[19]

Worst shared his knowledge beyond the Lockport endeavors, publishing *Foot-Power Loom Weaving* in 1918 as a guide for the amateur weaver.[20] The manual echoed his Arts and Crafts philosophy and demonstrated his understanding of the textile traditions that were shaping weaving in the United States. In the introduction to the volume, Worst extolls the virtues of weaving, confidently asserting: "The work is so full of possibilities and the results obtained have such a wonderful effect on the character of the worker that these alone afford ample reasons why weaving should be carried on in both school and community."[21] The perceived social benefits of weaving reinforced Worst's efforts in the local school systems as well as his engagement with the Lockport Home Industry.

The book is well illustrated and offers straightforward and detailed instructions intended to make weaving accessible. Chapters are dedicated to technical information about setting up a loom, the basics of pattern weaving and drafting, and an overview of dyeing. Beyond this, the volume also includes an extensive chapter on colonial patterns, a short one on Danish and Norwegian weaving, and a substantial chapter devoted to Swedish weaving. Clearly keeping the amateur weaver in mind, Worst opens his chapter on Swedish weaving with the following statement, "In many respects the Swedish way of writing a draft is more simple than any of the other ways described."[22] Indeed, Worst's appreciation for Swedish weaving stemmed in part from the fact that he found it to be readily comprehensible, and thus easier to learn and teach.

The juxtaposition of chapters dealing with colonial American patterns and Danish, Norwegian, and Swedish weaving signals Worst's attempt to negotiate a confluence of prevalent theories about decorative arts and design in America in the early twentieth century. When Worst published his book, collectors of colonial American textiles exhibited their objects to establish a lineage or pedigree of American identity, in part as a way to codify what it meant to be an American. The conservative thinking inherent in this collecting approach illuminates the presence of anti-immigrant sentiment at the time, and calls back to Boyesen's statement about assimilation that opens this essay.[23] With chapters devoted to Scandinavia, promoting the techniques as well as designs, Worst defied this insular sentiment, suggesting that it was not necessary to disown one's heritage to be an American. He also attempted to recuperate the immigrant status of colonial designs, remarking that "it is difficult to know just where they first originated." Furthermore, he advised weavers not to reproduce patterns exactly, but instead "to make such changes as will enable the finished products to find an appropriate place in the house furnishings of today."[24] Worst recognized the adaptability of these woven patterns and their potential to foster the production of textiles intended for the modern American home and the diverse interpretations of that ideal.

Worst himself produced woven textiles based on designs included in his book, such as a table runner woven in the rosepath pattern (p. 206), a design included in the "Pattern Weaving" chapter of his book. In the chapter, Worst notes that "the Rose Path is full of interesting combinations which may be used in borders for curtains, bags, table runners and pillow tops."[25] To illustrate his claim, he includes two border samples as well as a curtain featuring an adaptation of the design. Although the rosepath pattern appears in his general chapter on pattern weaving, he notes in the section dedicated to Swedish

WARREN

patterns that one of his illustrations "shows a threading which is the same as that of the Rose Path."[26] Worst thus indicates that he understands rosepath to be a popular Swedish pattern, and beyond that, a pattern central to the study and practice of weaving.

Worst furthered his already substantial efforts to promote the manual arts and expand his educational network through the development of the Lockport loom, which he designed around 1920 in association with his work with the Lockport Home Industry. Gustav Sandbloom, a Swedish American cabinetmaker, built Worst's design, which was easy to use and based on Swedish and Norwegian models.[27] Looms were sold to individuals and weaving schools across the United States, including Berea College in Kentucky, where Lucy Morgan studied before going on to direct the Penland Weavers and Potters in North Carolina.[28] During her studies at Berea, Morgan had obtained a copy of *Foot-Power Loom Weaving*, which she had been told was "the best book on hand weaving that had ever been written."[29] Morgan also had seen examples of Worst's weavings at a conference in Tennessee. In the hope that she might persuade him to come to North Carolina, Morgan wrote to Worst in 1928, initiating an enduring friendship and professional affiliation. After two informal summer sessions, Worst's weaving institute became a regular part of the Penland program.[30]

Worst was one of a number of weavers in the twentieth century who designed looms to facilitate teaching and domestic weaving. Hilma Berglund, a child of Swedish immigrants, grew up in Minnesota and attended several local art schools. In 1922, building on a short weaving course she had taken before World War I, Berglund traveled to Sweden and studied weaving at the Handarbetets Vänners Vävskole (Friends of Handicraft Weaving School). This foundational training prepared Berglund to enroll at the University of Minnesota, where she eventually became an instructor in art education while earning her master's degree, which she finished in 1939.[31] Berglund, like Worst, embraced the philosophy of the Arts and Crafts movement, and focused her attention on sharing the benefits of weaving with others.[32] For this reason, in 1955 she designed the "Minnesota loom," a twenty-inch portable loom that could be assembled easily and came with a floor stand.[33] Smaller than the Lockport loom, its scale suggests that Berglund intended it to be a practical introductory tool that could fit easily within a living space or educational setting rather than for use within a handicraft industry.

In addition to teaching at the university, Berglund cofounded the Weavers Guild of Minnesota (then the Twin Cities Weavers Guild) in 1940, and went on to organize an Institute of Weaving for guild members.[34] In her teaching, Berglund shared a variety of woven patterns and in some instances highlighted the sources of these designs. The notes outlining her two-week course offered in 1943 indicate that among the twenty techniques made available to participants were a Swedish patterned rag rug, two "Crackle Weaves" (a renaming of the Swedish *jämlandsväv* pattern, one of which was "planned by Mr. Edward F. Worst of Chicago"), and a "Rosepath," which Berglund described as "a famous Swedish pattern and the basis of much European weaving."[35] Berglund may have known Worst personally and invited him to participate in the workshop; at the very least, she was familiar with his book and followed his published instructions for variations on woven patterns. Either way, her use of Worst's loom setup for a workshop hosted twenty-five years after *Foot-Power Loom Weaving* was first published demonstrates his ongoing role in promulgating knowledge and promoting weaving in America. In examining Berglund's explanations for the other sixteen loom setups at the workshop, none specify a national point of origin. Berglund would have been quite familiar with Swedish weaving as a result of her studies in Sweden, but her comment regarding "Rosepath" hints at the potential problems that attend national designations for patterns.

In 1967, an exhibition dedicated to Berglund's weaving underlined the continued and widespread impact that Scandinavian techniques and patterns had on her work. In the catalogue that accompanied the exhibition, a "Runner in Rosepath (Swedish, Rosengång)" is listed above a group of "Scandinavian Rug Patterns" that includes Swedish and Finnish types, and several other works in the exhibition specify Swedish, Finnish, Norwegian, or Danish sources of inspiration.[36] The catalogue's introduction further emphasizes the prominence of Scandinavian influences in Berglund's work: "The years of her artistic production, sound teaching, and active participation in the Scandinavian affairs of the community have contributed a major share to the continuity of Minnesota's artistic heritage."[37] Like Fjelde before her, Berglund's career emphasizes the impact that Scandinavian patterns and techniques have had on the discourse about weaving in America.

Roughly contemporaneous with Worst's weaving institute at Penland and Berglund's teaching at the University of Minnesota, Finnish immigrant Loja Saarinen was head of the textile department at Cranbrook Academy of Art from 1932 to 1942; she also ran Studio Loja Saarinen, a commercial weaving enterprise.[38] Saarinen trained as a sculptor rather than a weaver and studied weaving only briefly in Helsinki.[39] An intelligent and savvy artist, she understood the appeal of her Finnish and Scandinavian identity in America, an assertion supported by the possibly apocryphal story surrounding the establishment of Studio Loja Saarinen. Reportedly, George Booth, the founder of the Cranbrook Educational Community, asked her to make the textiles for the Cranbrook complex, inquiring, "Why don't you design some for us and let us send them to Finland where they do such beautiful weaving and have them woven on those looms." To which Saarinen responded, "Why not design them and weave them here?"[40] Booth thus understood the Finns to be accomplished weavers, and assumed that Saarinen, as a Finn—and a woman—would know how to have the requisite textiles produced in Finland. In

Interior view of Kingswood School dining hall, showing the *Festival of the May Queen* hanging, 1932

accepting his proposition and modifying it to her advantage, she capitalized on these notions.

Despite her limited experience as a weaver, Saarinen proved adept at managing the studio as well as the department of weaving and textile design, which she filled with Scandinavian artists. She hired Swedish artist Maja Andersson Wirde of the Handarbetets Vänner to teach at the academy; she also employed Wirde in her studio, along with several other weavers with Swedish training, including Lillian Holm.[41] Although Saarinen had a group of mainly Swedish weavers working for her, "Studio Loja Saarinen" remained the imprimatur of the works produced there.[42] Among these were textiles for the Saarinens' Cranbrook home as well as the Kingswood School for Girls, including the *Festival of the May Queen* hanging, an expansive weaving designed and woven for the school's dining hall (above). While the design may commemorate May Day celebrations at Cranbrook, the May Queen also was a popular subject among Arts and Crafts practitioners, a fact that hints at the potential medley of voices informing the work. The study for the hanging (p. 210) and a sample weaving (p. 211) provide insight into the operations of the studio. The sample features a single figure, identifiable as the attendant standing to the left of the queen in the hanging design. On the back, a label in Saarinen's handwriting notes, "This is a sample…. It was woven at Cranbrook Academy of Art in 1932. It was designed by Eliel and Loja Saarinen."[43] This label thus attributes the design to Loja and her husband specifically, but does not attribute the weaving. Surely Saarinen would have known who wove the sample, and yet did not choose to identify that individual. In an article on Saarinen's weavings from 1937, the full hanging is credited to "Studio of Loja Saarinen."[44] Some of the images that accompany the article have captions that attribute weavings to Cranbrook students, but Saarinen, like the figure of the May Queen herself, stands as the sole named representative of her studio's work. Although this choice reinforced the singularity of Saarinen's brand as a Finnish designer and weaver, it elides the labor involved in producing the hanging and in so doing contradicts a key imperative of the Arts and Crafts movement.

In the same article, the caption for the hanging describes it as a tapestry rather than a wall hanging, yet the author, art critic Florence Davies, notes the interchangeability of these terms, writing that the dining room wall "called for a wall hanging or tapestry."[45] Indeed, by this point in time, the word "tapestry" had come to encompass not just textiles woven in the tapestry technique, but any large decorative textile. Despite the somewhat confusing nomenclature, both the hanging and the sample were woven in the same technique, a plain weave with discontinuous wefts (also described as supplementary brocading wefts), rather than a tapestry weave. This technique, effectively employed, can produce a hanging that is large but, as Davies notes, remains "light and airy, even transparent in some areas."[46] The lightness is in part due to the fact that the structure is less dense compared to a tapestry weave, and so requires fewer materials (as well as less time) to produce. The transparency of this hanging's structure also suggests a familiarity with and understanding of the work of the Norwegian artist Frida Hansen (pp. 62–64).[47]

Studio Loja Saarinen produced a number of weavings in the discontinuous weft technique, noted as a specialty of the Handarbetets Vänner.[48] Among the studio's works executed in this manner is the "Cranbrook Map," with weaving attributed to Lillian Holm and Ruth Ingvarson (pp. 212–13).[49] Although Holm and Ingvarson, both Swedish, arrived at Cranbrook from the workshop of Märta Määs-Fjetterström, they both had experience with the discontinuous weft technique and eventually returned to Stockholm to study at the Handarbetets Vänner.[50] Holm would go on to use this technique in a number of works that she designed and wove herself, including her *First Sight of New York* hanging (p. 214). In addition to her weaving for Studio Loja Saarinen and her individual work, Holm taught at Cranbrook and the Flint Institute of Arts for decades.[51] Although the discontinuous weft technique was a specialty of the Studio and in part demonstrates the educational legacy of the Handarbetets Vänner in the United States, it cannot be designated as solely Swedish, or even solely Scandinavian. Much like Berglund's caveat about the rosepath pattern, the discontinuous weft technique has been and continues to be used widely in the production of woven textiles.

ELIEL SAARINEN
LOJA SAARINEN
Study for *Festival of the May Queen*
hanging, Kingswood School, 1932.
CAT. 137

ELIEL SAARINEN
LOJA SAARINEN
Studio Loja Saarinen
Sample weaving for *Festival*
of the May Queen **hanging,** Kingswood
School, 1932. CAT. 138

ELIEL SAARINEN
Studio Loja Saarinen
"Cranbrook Map" hanging, 1935.
CAT. 136

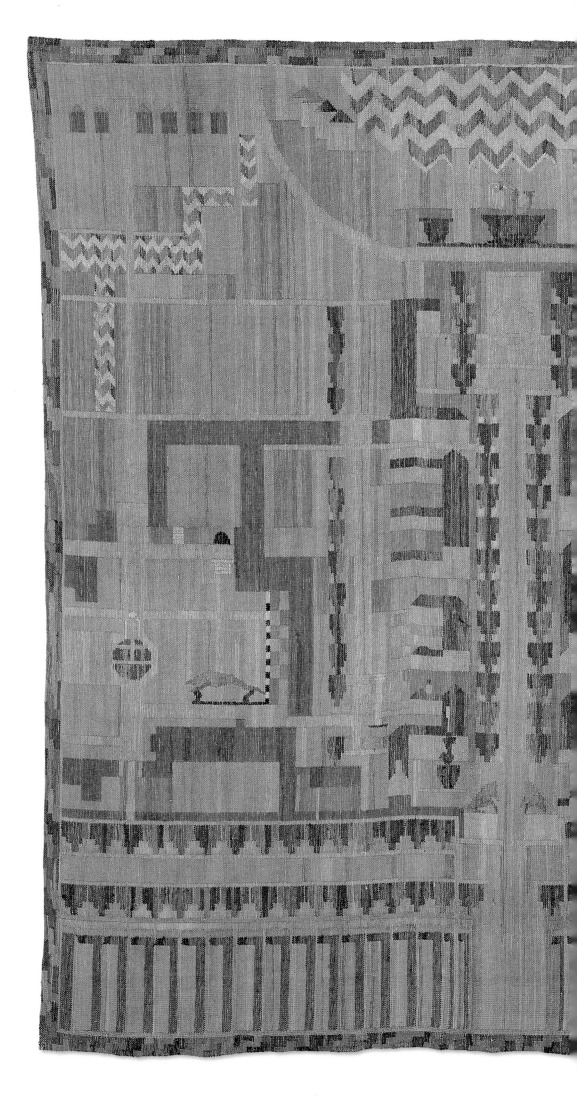

WARREN

Like Loja Saarinen, American textile designer, weaver, and entrepreneur Dorothy Liebes relied on the labors of in-house designers and weavers, yet remained the sole named designer associated with the textiles her studio produced.[52] Liebes studied weaving at the University of California, Berkeley with Anne Swainson, a Swedish immigrant who went on to head Montgomery Ward's Bureau of Design in Chicago.[53] Liebes's business, established in San Francisco in the 1930s, grew quickly and catered to dozens of clients across the country, including industrial manufacturers such as Goodall Fabrics and the Dobeckmun Company.[54] Although Liebes did not see herself as an interior designer,[55] she worked closely with such professionals and would supply them with art and furnishings that were not made in her studio. The handwoven tapestries of Finnish artist Martta Taipale were among these items, and Liebes served as Taipale's patron, mentor, and business partner. Close consideration of the professional relationship between Liebes and Taipale foregrounds additional questions regarding the particularly Scandinavian, or Finnish, character of materials and ideas. Their relationship was underway as early as November 1946, when the Dobeckmun Company wrote to Taipale: "At the suggestion of your good friend and admirer, Dorothy Liebes, we are sending you under separate cover a few sample spools of our non-tarnishing metallic yarns. Mrs. Liebes felt that you could make very effective use of these metallics in the lovely tapestries for which you are noted."[56] Dobeckmun had hired Liebes that year as a color stylist to promote Lurex, the "non-tarnishing metallic yarn" mentioned in the letter. In order to encourage textile designers, weavers, and manufacturers to employ this new material, Liebes used it in some of her own designs, including a striped furnishing fabric (p. 216).

In asking Dobeckmun to send yarns to Taipale, Liebes reinforced her importance to the company while supplying the artist with much-needed materials. Taipale and her sisters, who helped arrange the transport of the tapestries to America, corresponded frequently with Liebes from 1946 to 1952, and their letters convey the extreme austerity that Finland experienced in the postwar era. In 1946, in response to Liebes indicating that she had sent Lurex, Taipale's sister Hanna Kuusamo wrote with thanks, noting, "it would be a rescue for Martta to get any kind of yarn, because it is impossible here to get any yarn at all. I really do not know how our artists can create anything in this desparate [sic] situation."[57] Liebes also encouraged her studio staff to save scraps and sent them to Taipale in the hope that she would continue to weave her tapestries, which Liebes was busy marketing and selling.

In writing Taipale to tell her of another yarn shipment, Liebes also revealed her own approach to sales: "Everybody who comes in here asks about them and marvels that such beautiful tapestries are made in the world. I always tell them that no one but the Finnish people could create such a special kind of design and such really unique and beautiful textiles."[58] Liebes's statement seems surprising since Taipale's weavings, such as her tapestry (p. 196), feature the colorful yarns, including metallics, characteristic of Liebes's designs. Keenly aware of the appeal of Scandinavian design at the time, Liebes emphasized the Finnish character of the tapestries to her clients. To further this message, Liebes asked Taipale to give the tapestries titles "just the way paintings have names," and further specified the type of names Taipale should consider: "Do put some lovely Finnish names on them, even though we are unable to pronounce them."[59] Liebes expected that Finnish names would contribute to the authenticity and desirability of the tapestries as Scandinavian imports.

WARREN

Although Liebes was eager to capitalize on the popularity of Scandinavian design in marketing Taipale's work, the tapestries clearly incorporate the materials Liebes sent her, and their designs were informed by Liebes's clients' tastes. In 1952, in order to accommodate a particularly good client, Liebes wrote to Taipale asking her to make some larger tapestries "with a little more metal in them," and reassured the artist, "I'll be sure to send you more metal immediately."[60] Fortunately, by 1954, Taipale's material circumstances appear to have improved, and she wrote Liebes a happy letter from the Penland School of Crafts, where she had spent the summer and fall teaching tapestry weaving. Among her students was Lenore Tawney, who would credit Taipale for opening her eyes to the world of color.[61] Although Tawney remembers Taipale's poetics on color as a characteristic of her teaching, Liebes deserves some of the credit for originally sending the colorful scraps to Taipale, who ingeniously combined and incorporated these materials into her tapestries.

Beyond her clients' interest in Taipale's weavings as objects for their homes and art collections, Liebes understood that a wide swath of Americans had an appetite for handweaving. Following the publication of a profile on Liebes in *Collier's Magazine* in 1946, her studio received dozens of requests from across the United States for further information about where and how to learn to weave. In nearly all of the responses, Liebes (or her secretary) specified that the inquiring individuals should consult Worst's *Foot-Power Loom Weaving*. Liebes also recommended consulting relevant periodicals on weaving, and suggested enrolling in recreational classes at local colleges or universities.[62] Indeed, Liebes was not the only one to find Worst's foundational volume of continuing value, nor was Worst the only author to highlight and encourage individuals to pursue Scandinavian weaving. Several contributors to *The Weaver* (a popular magazine published by the yarn manufacturer Emile Bernat and Sons during the 1930s and into the 1940s) cover Scandinavian weaving and go into detail about methods, such as the discontinuous weft technique, and designs, including the rosepath.[63] Available across the United States, these publications, and numerous others of the same type, circulated among friends, weavers' guilds, and community organizations, and further embedded ideas about Scandinavian weaving in the narrative and practice of weaving in the United States.

Weavers and weavers' guilds continue to consult and promote these publications, and artists continue to immigrate to the United States. Helena Hernmarck, for example, was born and raised in Sweden and lived in Canada and England before settling in the United States in 1975. Although she is dedicated to the textile traditions of her native country, her weavings employ a variety of techniques.[64] While many of her Swedish American predecessors (including Wirde, Holm, and Ingvarson) chiefly employed the discontinuous weft technique to produce stylized designs for hangings with a delicate and light sensibility, Hernmarck's work embraces a pictorial photorealism that is rich and dense. Curator Sigrid Wortmann Weltge notes that Hernmarck does not rely on the Gobelin tapestry technique (also known as slit tapestry weave), as Fjelde did for her *Hiawatha* tapestry; rather, she charts her own path. In her early work she employed the familiar rosepath pattern, and now largely relies on a lush plain weave that incorporates supplementary brocading wefts, a structure that recalls the discontinuous weft technique promoted at the

Handarbetets Vänner.[65] Unsurprisingly, Hernmarck learned to weave there in 1958.[66] Her *Bay Street in Toronto* hanging, based on a photograph, exemplifies her approach and commemorates the time she spent living in the city (above). Moreover, the weaving represents her first attempt at producing an illusionistic sense of three-dimensional space; she depicted a scene with a distinct foreground and background, rather than treating the plane of the tapestry as a two-dimensional surface.[67] After architect Charles Bassett saw the weaving, he commissioned her to create the *Rainforest* tapestries for the Weyerhaeuser headquarters near Tacoma, Washington, which led to numerous further commissions.

Hernmarck's tapestries build on a strong foundation of weaving knowledge that includes technology, techniques, and styles. She has benefitted from the educational and professional networks that her predecessors established and the path they charted, which constitute a significant part of the framework for understanding weaving and textile design in the United States. Moreover, as a Swedish American weaver, Hernmarck participates in the long and distinguished history of immigration that is central to the history of American weaving, and indeed to the history of the nation. Ultimately, like Fjelde and so many others before her, she does not need to be ground in the "national hopper" (as per Boyesen's charge that opens this essay) or conform to an imagined homogeneous American identity; rather, she is free to pursue her goals with the tools that suit her vision.

HELENA HERNMARCK
Bay Street in Toronto hanging, 1970.
CAT. 59

1 Hjalmar Hjorth Boyesen, "The Scandinavian in the United States," *North American Review* 155, no. 432 (November 1892): 535. Boyesen was a Norwegian immigrant.

2 George Taylor Rygh, "The Scandinavian-Americans," *Literary Northwest* 2, no. 5 (February 1893): 271.

3 Marion Nelson, *Norway in America* (Decorah, IA: Vesterheim, 1989), inside front cover.

4 Gail Marie Aanenson, "The Life and Work of Miss Pauline Fjelde: Minnesota Weaver—Embroideress" (master of arts thesis, University of Minnesota, 1971), 7–8.

5 Aanenson, "Life and Work," 11–14.

6 "A Minneapolis Family of Artists," *Minneapolis: Metropolis of the Northwest* 2, no. 1 (August 1928): 33.

7 J. J. Skordalsvold, "The Gobelin Tapestry of Hiawatha and Minnehaha," *Jul i Vesterheimen* (1927), unpaginated [57–58].

8 "Famous Sculptor Discusses Fjelde's Hiawatha, Rejected by the Art Commission," *Minneapolis Journal*, January 24, 1903, 6.

9 "Gallant Hiawatha Honored by Minneapolis Children," *Star Tribune*, October 6, 1912. See also Nelson, *Norway in America*, 19–20; and Moira F. Harris, "Worthy of Their Own Aspiration: Minnesota's Literary Tradition in Sculpture," *Minnesota History* 55, no. 8 (Winter 1997–98): 366.

10 Skordalsvold, "The Gobelin Tapestry of Hiawatha and Minnehaha."

11 Mabel Tuke Priestman, "The Weaving of Norwegian Tapestry in America," *American Homes and Gardens* 5, no. 12 (December 1, 1908): 482; George Leland Hunter, "Tapestries in America," *International Studio* 47, no. 187 (September 1912): xxix–xxxv.

12 For the distinction between techniques, see Aanenson, "Life and Work," 63–64; and Irene Emery, *The Primary Structures of Fabrics* (Washington, DC: Textile Museum, 1966), 79–81. For the *Hiawatha* technique, see Aanenson, "Life and Work," 75. Fjelde discussed her study of tapestry in an article in a Norwegian American newspaper, noting that she worked with (among others) Augusta Christensen, head of the tapestry workshop at the Nordenfjeldske Museum of Applied Art from 1898 to 1900; "Kunstvaevning," *Kvindens Magasin*, no. 6 (March 1915). See also Jan-Lauritz Opstad, *The Nordenfjeldske Museum of Applied Art School and Studio of Art Weaving 1898–1909* (Trondheim, Norway: Nordenfjeldske Kunstindustrimuseum, 1983), 9.

13 For Brendekilde see Aanenson, "Life and Work," 17. Also see Lila Nelson, "A Forgotten Artist Remembered: The Tapestry Weaving of Pauline Fjelde," *Norwegian Textile Letter* 11, no. 1 (November 2004): 4, 6.

14 Olivia Mahoney, *Edward F. Worst: Craftsman and Educator* (Chicago: Chicago Historical Society, 1985), 10–12, 15.

15 Mahoney, *Edward F. Worst*, 15–16, 18.

16 Henry Goddard Leach, "Sweden—A Nation of Craftsmen," *The Craftsman* 23, no. 3 (December 1912): 296.

17 Leach, "Sweden," 296, 303.

18 Mahoney, *Edward F. Worst*, 25.

19 Mahoney, *Edward F. Worst*, 25.

20 Worst published two additional volumes, *Industrial Work for the Middle Grades* in 1919 and *How to Weave Linens* in 1926. See Mahoney, *Edward F. Worst*, 28–29.

21 Edward Worst, *Foot-Power Loom Weaving*, 2nd ed. (Milwaukee: Bruce Publishing, 1920), 4.

22 Worst, *Foot-Power Loom Weaving*, 121.

23 Beverly Gordon, "Spinning Wheels, Samplers, and the Modern Priscilla: The Images and Paradoxes of Colonial Revival Needlework," *Winterthur Portfolio* 33, no. 2/3 (Summer–Autumn 1998): 167–68.

24 Worst, *Foot-Power Loom Weaving*, 55.

25 Worst, *Foot-Power Loom Weaving*, 52.

26 Worst, *Foot-Power Loom Weaving*, 125.

27 Mahoney, *Edward F. Worst*, 25.

28 There also was a smaller version of the Lockport, named the "Rosemary loom"; Mahoney, *Edward F. Worst*, 28, 34.

29 Bonnie Willis Ford, *The Story of the Penland Weavers* (Penland, NC: Penland School of Handicrafts, 1941), 17. Additionally, in 1942, *Craft Horizons* called it "the standard—the indispensable—work on foot-power weaving"; Mrs. Harold Harper, "Books Both Old and New," *Craft Horizons* 2, no. 1 (November 1942): 27.

30 Ford, *The Story of the Penland Weavers*, 17–18.

31 Laurence Schmeckebier, *An Exhibition of Weaving by Hilma Berglund*, exh. cat. (St. Paul: Department of Fine Arts, University of Minnesota, 1967), 2.

32 See Marcia G. Anderson, "Art for Life's Sake: The Handicraft Guild of Minneapolis," in *Minnesota 1900: Art and Life on the Upper Mississippi 1890–1915*, ed. Michael Conforti (Newark: University of Delaware Press in association with the Minneapolis Institute of Arts, 1994), 180.

33 Marion T. Marzolf, "The Swedish Presence in 20th-Century American Weaving," in *Textile Narratives and Conversations: Proceedings of the 10th Biennial Symposium of the Textile Society of America, October 11–14, Toronto, Ontario* (Earleville, MD: Textile Society of America, 2006), 167; and Anderson, "Art for Life's Sake," 180.

34 Hilma Berglund, "The First Five Years of the Twin City Weavers' Guild," 1945, Weavers Guild of Minnesota, Minneapolis, 1–2, http://cdm16022.contentdm.oclc.org/cdm/ref/collection/p16022coll41/id/28.

35 Hilma Berglund, teaching notes, 1943, Twin Cities Weavers' Guild Institute, Weavers Guild of Minnesota, Minneapolis, 4–6, http://cdm16022.contentdm.oclc.org/cdm/compoundobject/collection/p16022coll41/id/349/rec/2.

36 Schmeckebier, *An Exhibition of Weaving*, 5–10.

37 Schmeckebier, *An Exhibition of Weaving*, 3.

38 Saarinen did not teach weaving courses at Cranbrook while heading the department, though she did hire instructors.

39 Leena Svinhufvud, "The *Cranbrook Map*: Locating Meanings in Textile Art," in *Imagining Spaces and Places*, ed. Saija Isomaa et al. (Newcastle upon Tyne, UK: Cambridge Scholars Publishing, 2013), 214.

40 Florence Davies, "The Weavings of Loja Saarinen," *The Weaver* 2, no. 1 (January 1937): 14. Also in this volume of *The Weaver* are articles dedicated to the *Rosengång*, or rosepath technique ("Interesting Developments on the 'Rosengang'") and an article titled "Scandinavian Art Weaving."

41 Christa C. Mayer Thurman, "Textiles," in *Design in America: The Cranbrook Vision 1925–1950*, exh. cat., ed. Robert Judson Clark and Andrea P. A. Belloli (New York: Detroit Institute of Arts and the Metropolitan Museum of Art, 1983), 180–81.

42 Svinhufvud, "The *Cranbrook Map*," 215.

43 Thurman, "Textiles," 183, 317.

44 Davies, "The Weavings of Loja Saarinen," 16.

45 Davies, "The Weavings of Loja Saarinen," 31.

46 Davies, "The Weavings of Loja Saarinen," 31.

47 See, for example, Priestman, "The Weaving of Norwegian Tapestry in America," 482; and "Tapestry Work Is a Revival of Norwegian Art," *Muncie Evening Press*, October 10, 1928, 8. For more on Hansen, see Hannah Pivo in this volume, 62–64.

48 Thurman, "Textiles," 177.

49 For more on the "Cranbrook Map," see Svinhufvud, "The *Cranbrook Map*."

50 Marzolf, "The Swedish Presence," 167–68.

51 Marzolf, "The Swedish Presence," 168.

52 Mary Schoeser and Whitney Blausen, "'Wellpaying Self Support': Women Textile Designers in the USA," in *Women Designers in the USA 1900–2000: Diversity and Difference*, ed. Pat Kirkham (New Haven and London: Yale University Press in association with the Bard Graduate Center for Studies in the Decorative Arts, 2000), 154–55; and Svinhufvud, "The *Cranbrook Map*," 215.

53 Dorothy Liebes, unpublished autobiography, Liebes papers, box 10, folder 1, Archives of American Art, Smithsonian Institution, 72–73. For more details on Swainson, see Carroll M. Gantz, *Design Chronicles: Significant Mass-Produced Designs of the 20th Century* (Atglen, PA: Schiffer, 2005), 79, 262; and Schoeser and Blausen, "Wellpaying Self Support," 152.

54 Joan Hess Michel, "Dorothy Liebes' Design and Weaving," *American Artist* 35, no. 4 (April 1971): 48; Nell Znamierowski, *Dorothy Liebes: Retrospective Exhibition*, exh. cat. (New York: Museum of Contemporary Crafts, 1970), 34. See also Regina Lee Blaszczyk, "Styling Synthetics: DuPont's Marketing of Fabrics and Fashions in Postwar America," *Business History Review* 80, no. 3 (Autumn 2006): 485–528.

55 Liebes to Mrs. Pihlajaman (Martta Taipale's sister), March 24, 1948, Liebes papers, box 10, folder 1.

56 Dobeckmun Company to Taipale, November 15, 1946, Liebes papers, box 10, folder 2.

57 Hanna Kuusamo to Liebes, November 18, 1946, Liebes papers, box 10, folder 1.

58 Liebes to Taipale, October 25, 1951, Liebes papers, box 10, folder 2.

59 Liebes to Taipale, December 15, 1947, Liebes papers, box 10, folder 2.

60 Liebes to Taipale, January 23, 1952, Liebes papers, box 10, folder 2.

61 Liebes to Taipale, November 5, 1954, and Taipale to Liebes, November 1954, Liebes papers, box 10, folder 3. For Tawney's sentiments regarding Taipale, see Margo Hoff, "Lenore Tawney: The Warp Is Her Canvas," *Craft Horizons* 17, no. 6 (November/December 1957): 16–17.

62 Liebes to Mrs. A. H. Webb, June 16, 1946; Dorothy Liebes Studio to Mrs. Marten Sutherland Estey, June 3, 1946; and Secretary to Mrs. Liebes to Mrs. Roy Wilkinson, June 4, 1946, Liebes papers, box 7, folder 1.

63 Nellie Sargent Johnson, "Interesting Ways to Use 'Laid-in' Technique," Esther Hoagland Gallup, "Interesting Developments on the 'Rosengang,'" and Elmer Wallace Hickman, "Scandinavian Art Weaving," *The Weaver* 2, no. 1 (January 1937): 4–7, 8–10, 20–24.

64 Sigrid Wortmann Weltge, "Helena Hernmarck," *American Craft* 59, no. 6 (December 1999–January 2000): 39; and Monica Boman, "Swedish Roots" and "Immigrant in Canada and England," in *Helena Hernmarck: Tapestry Artist*, trans. Robert Dunlap (Stockholm: Byggförlaget, 1999), 17–27, 53–54.

65 Weltge, "Helena Hernmarck," 9.

66 Monica Boman, "Swedish Roots" and "Helena Hernmarck—Biographical Sketch," in *Helena Hernmarck*, 17, 122.

67 Boman, *Helena Hernmarck*, 46.

THE KINGSWOOD SCHOOL FOR GIRLS AT CRANBROOK

BOBBYE TIGERMAN

The Kingswood School for Girls embodies a microcosm of several themes of *Scandinavian Design and the United States*, underlining Cranbrook's substantial contributions to American design. This lesser known Cranbrook institution, which opened in 1931, was conceived by Finnish immigrants, employed Finnish and Swedish immigrant labor, and represents a collaborative project of the entire Saarinen family.

Eliel Saarinen developed the architecture of the Kingswood campus, constructing a series of interconnected buildings along a natural lake. His unified decorative program used a telescoping column motif in architectural elements as well as ornamental details, such as stained glass and brickwork (right). Cranbrook's weaving studio, directed by his wife, Loja Saarinen, created all of the wall hangings and rugs for the buildings.[1] To complete this major commission, Loja recruited several formally trained Swedish weavers, including Maja Andersson Wirde, Lillian Holm, and Ruth Ingvarson.[2] Wirde returned to Sweden in 1933, but Holm and Ingvarson remained in Michigan, eventually becoming instructors at Cranbrook and nearby institutions such as the Flint Institute of Arts and Wayne State University.[3] Eliel and Loja's daughter, Pipsan Saarinen Swanson, created the delicate stencil decorations that adorn the auditorium and a ballroom, the latter of which was commonly referred to as "Heaven" (p. 222).[4]

Exterior view of Kingswood School, c. 1940

EERO SAARINEN
Stickley Brothers Furniture Company
Chair for Kingswood School dining hall, 1930–31. CAT. 132

CARL MALMSTEN
Firma David Blomberg
Chair from Carl Milles House at Cranbrook Academy of Art, designed 1926. CAT. 98

Interior view of Kingswood School ballroom (known as "Heaven"), with stencil decorations by Pipsan Saarinen Swanson, 1932

The Kingswood dining hall, which remains intact, represents the pinnacle of these collaborative efforts (p. 209). Eliel and Loja's son, Eero Saarinen, was responsible for the furnishings. His chair with vermilion painted decoration and upholstery closely resembles the chair from the Carl Milles House by Swedish furniture designer Carl Malmsten in its tablet-top form and color palette (p. 221). Malmsten was a highly esteemed Swedish craftsman, a modernist who did not eschew tradition.[5] Milles, Cranbrook's sculpture instructor, lived with a complete Malmsten dining set in his home, which Eero would have been familiar with, as Milles' house was located next door to Saarinen's parents' house on the Cranbrook campus. The younger Saarinen simplified the form of the Malmsten chair for heavy use in the dining hall while preserving the elegance of the overall shape and color combination. Lined with clear and stained glass windows on two sides, the airy Kingswood dining hall was also illuminated by standing lamps by Walter von Nessen and two aluminum torchères by Eliel Saarinen. The torchères flanked the massive *Festival of the May Queen* hanging. Eliel and Loja Saarinen worked together on the sketch for the hanging prior to Studio Loja Saarinen's execution of the woven study (pp. 210–11).[6]

Kingswood was a triumph of collaboration, a place that *Architectural Forum* enthused was "one of the most pointed lessons in cooperative designing which we have been fortunate enough to present in some time."[7] Built on immigrant contributions, the partnerships fostered both at Kingswood and in the broader Cranbrook community fundamentally shaped American design after World War II. Kingswood's collaborative origins and educational focus represent important elements of Cranbrook's legacy within American design.

1 See Erica Warren in this volume, 209–13.
2 Christa C. Mayer Thurman, "Textiles," in *Design in America: The Cranbrook Vision 1925–1950*, exh. cat., ed. Robert Judson Clark and Andrea P. A. Belloli (New York: Detroit Institute of Arts and the Metropolitan Museum of Art, 1983), 180–81.
3 Marion T. Marzolf, "The Swedish Presence in 20th-Century American Weaving," in *Textile Narratives and Conversations: Proceedings of the 10th Biennial Symposium of the Textile Society of America, October 11–14, 2006* (Earleville, MD: Textile Society of America, 2006).
4 Thurman, "Textiles," 188–89.
5 Edith Weigle, "Modern Design in Sweden: Another View of the Exposition of Decorative...," *Chicago Tribune*, August 24, 1930.
6 Gregory Wittkopp and Joe Houston, *Cranbrook Art Museum: 100 Treasures*, exh. cat. (Bloomfield Hills, MI: Cranbrook Art Museum, 2004), 102.
7 "The Kingswood School for Girls, Cranbrook, Michigan," *Architectural Forum* 56 (January 1932): 37.

MARIANNE STRENGELL

Designing for Automobiles

LESLIE S. EDWARDS

Finnish textile designer Marianne Strengell was widely known for her industrial designs that embodied "hand-made modernism"—textiles that appeared hand-loomed, but were produced by machine.[1] Strengell was educated in Helsinki, graduating from Taideteollisuuskeskuskoulu (Central School of Industrial Arts) in 1929. She then worked briefly at Svenska Slöjdföreningen (Swedish Arts and Crafts Society), assisting designer Elsa Gullberg with the Stockholm Exhibition of 1930. In Finland, designers pursued collaborations with industry while continuing to make handcrafted functional textiles well into the postwar period. Strengell brought this knowledge, as well as experience working with clients, with her to the United States in 1937, when she accepted Eliel Saarinen's offer to teach weaving at Cranbrook Academy of Art.

Strengell predicted that the shortage of materials during World War II would create "infinite opportunities in the synthetic field," and suggested that designers could collaborate with industry to develop new materials.[2] In her own work, she combined cotton, mohair, and wool with newly developed materials such as fiberglass yarns, Lurex, and even asbestos for architectural commissions.[3] At the annual meeting of the Society of Automotive Engineers in 1951,

Strengell stated that automotive upholstery was "impractical, impersonal and out of keeping with the new model cars."[4] Following this, brothers Ralph and Gordon Getsinger (alumni of Cranbook School for Boys) of Chatham Manufacturing in Elgin, North Carolina, visited her studio to discuss experimental upholstery fabrics for the company. Strengell subsequently collaborated with Chatham and wove hundreds of hand-made prototypes with yarns spun at the Chatham mill.

Strengell's inventive fiber combinations and weave structures set her apart as a designer-maker for industry. In 1954, Chrysler catered to women customers for the first time: their slogan for the November preview auto show was "never underestimate the power of a woman." The corporation introduced new textured upholstery fabrics of wool, cotton, and synthetic fibers featuring metallic threads and "the kind of colors seen in fashion magazines."[5]

Strengell wove the automotive upholstery for which she is most well-known primarily with the synthetic fibers nylon, viscose, Metlon, and Lurex. "It was piece dyed, colandered, and rubberized for production," resulting in a vibrant, glossy, and durable fabric.[6] The textile, later called "Taj Mahal," was manufactured by Chatham

MARIANNE STRENGELL
Chatham Manufacturing Company
"Taj Majal" upholstery fabric
for the 1959 Chrysler Imperial,
designed 1955. CAT. 149

for Chrysler Corporation's 1959 Imperial Crown Sedan, which featured four optional interior colorways—green, blue, tan, and silver (p. 224).[7] Chrysler presented four color variations of "Taj Mahal" to match the leather interior.[8] *Motor Trend* magazine wrote, "the feel of luxury in the Imperial is emphasized by the metallic threaded nylon upholstery; it looks and feels rich."[9] When it was included in a joint advertising campaign in *Vogue* geared at women consumers, the fashion-conscious aspect of the Imperial was emphasized—"glove-soft leathers, textured tweeds, custom-woven broadcloths in the shades you'll see again and again in the 1959 collections of every great couturier, here and abroad."[10] "Taj Mahal" epitomized Strengell's aspiration of designing for industry, which she had articulated over a decade before when she proclaimed that "I am very happy about the new relationship between manufacturer and designer.... Only by working smoothly and in close harmony can really good textiles be produced."[11]

1 Jennifer Scanlan, "Hand-made Modernism: Craft in Industry in the Postwar Period," in *Crafting Modernism: Midcentury American Art and Design*, exh. cat., ed. Jeannine Falino, History of Twentieth-Century American Craft 4 (New York: Abrams in association with the Museum of Arts and Design, 2011), 102.
2 Marianne Strengell Dusenbury, "Texture, Color and Quality," *California Arts and Architecture* 59 (November 1942): 32–33.
3 For Bittan Valberg, another textile designer who pursued this approach, see Monica Obniski in this volume, 267–69. Dorothy Liebes, Astrid Sampe, and Martta Taipale were also known for using synthetic materials.
4 Pauline Sterling, "Textile Designer Raps Poor Car Interiors," *Detroit Free Press*, January 13, 1951.
5 Ann Montgomery, "Chrysler Caters to Femmes with Rainbow-Hued Models," *Indianapolis News*, October 12, 1954.
6 Marianne Strengell, "A Personal Approach to Textile Design" (lecture, Cranbrook Academy of Art, Bloomfield Hills, MI, January 15, 1960), Marianne Strengell Papers, Cranbrook Center for Collections and Research, Bloomfield Hills, MI.
7 It is unclear when the textile was named "Taj Mahal." Whereas Chrysler's sales brochures referred to it strictly by number, the company's press release for the 1959 Auto Show referred to the fabric as "Crusader." The name "Taj Mahal" was likely attributed as late as 1980, when Strengell began offering her textile designs to museum curators across the country.
8 Bob Swartz (volunteer, Historical Services, Chrysler Group LLC), letter to author, January 30, 2013.
9 "Detroit's '59 Cars: Secrets from the Styling Studios," *Motor Trend*, September 1958, 31.
10 "The New Look of Beauty," advertisement, *Vogue*, January 1, 1959, 32–35. The advertisement also featured Elizabeth Arden cosmetics and Ben Zuckerman apparel.
11 Marianne Strengell, "Fabrics," *Arts and Architecture* (March 1948): 32.

"FELLOW CRAFTSMEN, TRY DENMARK SOMETIME"

Alma Eikerman in Scandinavia

MONICA OBNISKI

Metalsmithing educator Alma Eikerman found her calling as a female mentor in a field dominated by men. After earning a master's degree from Columbia University and teaching for a few years, Eikerman was recruited by Indiana University in 1947 to instruct design and metalsmithing and to build a jewelry program—a tall order, given that the field was in its infancy in the United States.[1] In 1948, Eikerman attended the Handy & Harman workshop in Providence, Rhode Island, where she learned to raise a bowl from a flat piece of silver under the instruction of Swedish court silversmith Baron Erik Fleming.[2] Eikerman subsequently took a leave of absence to study silversmithing in Denmark, Sweden, and France during the 1950–51 academic year. She planned to explore hollowware and bring "home some of the impulses" that she would learn in Scandinavia.[3]

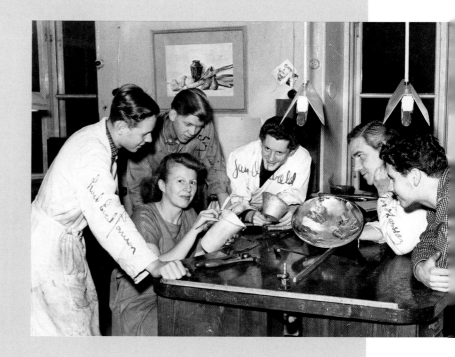

Alma Eikerman in Sweden, working
on a cocktail pitcher, 1950

ALMA EIKERMAN
Pendant, 1974. CAT. 31

ALMA EIKERMAN
Mocha pot, 1950. CAT. 30

She spent her first few days in Copenhagen examining silver in shops before asking Karl Gustav Hansen for instruction at his workshop in Kolding. She admired his craftsmanship, technical ability, and the simplicity of his designs.[4] Eikerman also sought advice from technical experts, receiving "short criticism and advice daily" from Hansen, talking with designers at the A. Michelsen and Georg Jensen silversmithies, and consulting other independent artists.[5] Eikerman continued to build her skills, such as crimping and raising silver in a straight line. She wrote to her friend about a hard day, during which she sustained two blisters and worked through two cracks, remarking, "You can know how awkward I am beside these highly skilled people."[6]

While in Denmark, Eikerman completed several projects, including a mocha pot (p. 227). When she finished the piece, she was given a locker at the workshop, a signal of achieving some level of proficiency. Eikerman also participated in "interesting design and aesthetic discussions,"[7] including a panel discussion with designers Karl Hansen and Børge Rasmussen, Henning Koppel from Georg Jensen, Asger Fischer of Den Permanente, and a representative from A. Michelsen that explored the topic of creative design instruction in Denmark and the United States.

Back at Indiana University, Eikerman developed a summer silversmithing workshop, first held in 1954. For the second workshop in 1955, Eikerman invited Hansen as a guest instructor. A contemporary article noted, "Mr. Hansen has developed from older forms a new pure contemporary design which still has qualities of traditional form."[8] This commentary underscores the elegant balance of new and old that Americans desired from Scandinavian designers in the postwar years.

Eikerman used the silversmithing skills she learned in Scandinavia throughout her life, but ultimately focused on jewelry, which she had not studied while abroad. She incorporated traditional techniques such as raising and forging, often crafting bulges that were counterbalanced by line, and she used gemstones prominently (p. 227). Her legacy includes the metalsmithing program at Indiana University as well as its many alumni who contributed to the American studio jewelry movement, such as Marjorie Schick and Helen Shirk (cat. 142), who also trained in Denmark. As a formative experience in her life, Eikerman wanted others to discover the treasures of Scandinavia, urging "fellow craftsmen, try Denmark sometime."[9]

1 *Reflections: A Tribute to Alma Eikerman, Master Craftsman*, exh. cat. (Bloomington: Indiana University Art Museum, 1985).
2 See Bobbye Tigerman in this volume, 191.
3 "Silver Design," *Tydske Tidende* (Kolding, Denmark), June 23, 1950, Alma Eikerman papers, Collection C621, Indiana University Archives, Bloomington.
4 Alma Eikerman, "As I See It," January 17, 1952, Report about Denmark/Sweden, Eikerman papers.
5 Eikerman, "As I See It."
6 Eikerman to Martha Brennan, June 15, 1950, Eikerman papers.
7 Notes (presumably for Paul Smith), Publications on Alma Eikerman, Eikerman papers.
8 Julianna Uphoff, "Jewelry 'Bests' on Display," Eikerman papers.
9 Eikerman, "As I See It."

REMEMBERING TAGE FRID

ROSANNE SOMERSON

I finished high school a year early and decided to pursue a summer course in rural Denmark. I had seen an advertisement for a class in creative writing and photography, two passions of mine at the time. The course was taught by experimental Danish and American artists in a thatched roof house in the middle of farmland in Jutland. I made some good photographs, learned rudimentary Danish, and fell in love with Denmark.

The next year I applied to Rhode Island School of Design (RISD) in Providence to study photography. In our first year, we were encouraged to take a course in a new field, and I had heard that there was a Danish man teaching in the woodshop. I went to check it out, wearing my custom-made wooden clogs from the local village shoemaker in my Danish town, and stumbled into a new world. The teacher was Hans Wolff; his colleague Tage Frid, also Danish, was away during that session, but upon his return I made an appointment with him to discuss taking more classes, as I had quickly become fascinated with the Danish influence in the RISD woodshop. I felt at home there, and I think Tage was surprised to meet a young woman interested in wood who also spoke Danish. And so began a lifelong interaction that would later lead to my assisting with his many articles for *Fine Woodworking* magazine, photographing and editing his first book for the same publisher, and eventually being asked to direct Tage's graduate program at RISD following his retirement.

Tage was like no one I had ever met. Having learned woodworking through the traditional apprenticeship system at a very young age, he possessed an awe-inspiring depth of woodworking knowledge. He understood the material in a way that seemed boundless, and his imagination and encouragement helped us to expand the design realm of its application. Ever practical, one of his many colorful catchphrases was "baby, it's cold outside," which spoke to his design philosophy of streamlined efficiency that would enable one to make a real living from a design studio. Yet he loved nothing more than seeing a young designer manipulate the material in a new, inventive way, or create an innovative furniture form that adopted his solid design principles and advanced them. Tage was a true master woodworker and teacher—irreverent, funny, challenging, and intensely supportive, even when he didn't personally love a design ("I'm not exactly dancing over it," he would say).

My table draws from a material reverence learned from Tage, but also pushes the notion of new form driven by the imagined emotive experience of the viewer (pp. 231–32). He frequently discussed the technique of laminating sandwiched wood to aluminum, which he used in liturgical work and that relied on new glue technologies. In homage, my table has a central "ribbon" of aluminum sandwiched between digitally printed wood that I created by using my own photography and converting an image into an applied pattern. I am thus translating his

SOMERSON

Remembering Tage Frid

aluminum sandwich idea into something that utilizes the technology of my time. Additionally, I was inspired by a detail from a Hans Wegner stool with open ends of wood, through which rattan was passed and pulled down. I used the same kind of form tension to create the space where the digitally printed wood/aluminum sandwich is pulled through the top and down to the base

pedestal. This approach of using personal interventions that added a sense of material ambiguity marked my work for decades. Tage both taunted and respected this approach. When visual ideas required too much verbal explanation, he called out "a big line of BS." His multifaceted critique and admiration summarize the dichotomous complexity of a true mentor.

TRAVEL ABROAD

KAJ FRANCK
Nuutajärvi Glassworks
Goblets, designed 1968, these
examples c. 1970–71. CAT. 40

These goblets, each made of four
different colors of glass blown in a mold
and fused together, were owned by
Marc Treib. Treib met and studied with
Franck while on a Fulbright fellowship
to Finland in 1966. Treib bought them
on a subsequent trip in 1970 or 1971.

BOBBYE
TIGERMAN

TRAVEL ABROAD Travel between the Nordic countries and the United States was a sustained form of cultural exchange that persisted over several decades, fostering enduring artistic bonds. International movement among designers was common in the early twentieth century—Nordic architects such as Alvar Aalto, Ferdinand Boberg, and Sven Markelius visited the national pavilions they designed for American world's fairs earlier in the century, and many Americans attended the landmark 1930 Stockholm Exhibition.[1] The frequency and duration of these transatlantic journeys increased after World War II with the advent of convenient jet travel, enabling younger designers to participate. American and Scandinavian cultural exchange was facilitated by formal academic programs, apprenticeships, travel fellowships, and independent projects. While American goods appealed to Nordic tastes, tariffs protecting local industries largely deterred American design imports. As such, one of the more effective avenues of American influence on Scandinavian design was interpersonal exchange—when Scandinavian

ERIK MAGNUSSEN
Gorham Manufacturing Company
Cubic **coffee service**, 1927. Silver
and ivory, 9 ½ × 21 ½ × 13 ⅜ in.
(24.1 × 54.6 × 34 cm). Rhode Island
School of Design, the Gorham
Collection, Gift of Textron, Inc.

INGRID DESSAU
Kristianstad County Handicraft Society
Manhattan **hanging**, 1953. CAT. 23

designers studied or worked in the United States, and when American designers traveled to Scandinavia to seek advanced training, teach, or collaborate with their Nordic counterparts. These transnational networks and the personal relationships that resulted were critical to the realization of many design developments.

For many Scandinavians, the vibrant New York City landscape was a source of abundant inspiration—Danish silversmith Erik Magnussen captured the city's explosive energy in his *Cubic* coffee service (p. 236) and Swedish textile designer Ingrid Dessau depicted the illuminated grids of New York skyscrapers in her *Manhattan* hanging (p. 237). While the prevailing immigration trend was for Scandinavians to settle permanently in the United States, Magnussen and Dessau are among the several Nordic designers who resided abroad temporarily.[2]

Among those who spent time in the U.S. before returning to Scandinavia was Josef Frank, a Jewish Austrian architect who sought to escape anti-Semitism in 1933 by moving with his Swedish wife to Stockholm, where he was hired as chief designer by Estrid Ericson, founder of the Swedish interior design shop Svenskt Tenn. Frank's furniture and textiles embodied a colorful and organic modernism rooted in the Viennese Secessionist aesthetic of his youth, which contrasted with the prevailing International Style. Following the Nazi invasions of Denmark and Norway, Frank and his wife fled to New York in late 1941.[3] He taught art history at the New School for Social Research for two years before focusing on what scholar Kristina Wängberg-Eriksson has described as "his most innovative and significant body of textile designs" for Svenskt Tenn in 1943–45.[4] Frank ultimately created fifty designs, many inspired by the American landscape (as he imagined it, as he did not travel), and a series of manuals of American flora and fauna. The *Manhattan* pattern featured rectangles and circles with color-coded maps of the city, each surrounded by gray ribbon-like borders that listed the principal attractions in each neighborhood (pp. 240–41). These textiles became Svenskt Tenn's most popular offerings, and some remain in production today. With the cessation of war, Frank returned to Stockholm in January 1946, resuming work for Svenskt Tenn and other Swedish design firms.

After World War II, both American and Scandinavian designers traveled back and forth frequently under the auspices of the U.S. government-sponsored Fulbright program, which was founded in 1946 to foster international educational exchange.[5] In 1949, architect Arne Korsmo and his wife, designer Grete Prytz Korsmo, were part of the first class of Norwegian Fulbright grant recipients to the United States. The Korsmos lived in Chicago, where Arne was a professor and Grete was a visiting student at the Institute of Design.[6] The Korsmos traveled extensively during their fellowship year and met many of the major figures in American architecture and design, including Charles and Ray Eames, Louis Kahn, Edgar Kaufmann, jr., James Prestini, Ludwig Mies van der Rohe, and Frank Lloyd Wright. Prytz Korsmo recalled that the exposure to American design approaches was especially formative—she learned about the professional practices of industrial designers (including the importance of research) and felt liberated to experiment with techniques, such as engraving on enamel. Most of all, the American preference for vividly colored tablewares emboldened her to introduce similar colors in her own enamel designs for Cathrineholm (cat. 79).[7] The Korsmos were close friends with Danish architect Jørn Utzon and his wife, Lis Utzon, who were also Fulbright fellows in the United States that year. The couples traveled to Mexico together to see the Maya ruins at Monte Albán (at the suggestion of Charles and Ray Eames), which so impacted Utzon that he attributed the platform substructure of the site as the inspiration for his most famous work, the Sydney Opera House.[8] In a reciprocal gesture, Arne Korsmo invited five Institute of Design professors to teach a summer course for Nordic students and designers at the Statens Håndverks-og Kunstindustriskole (National College of Art and Design) in Oslo in 1952 (below). The course followed the Institute of Design curriculum, focusing on basic principles such as drawing, modeling, construction, and materials knowledge. It exposed 120 Nordic students and designers to the Chicago school's approach, which itself was largely rooted in Bauhaus educational theories.[9]

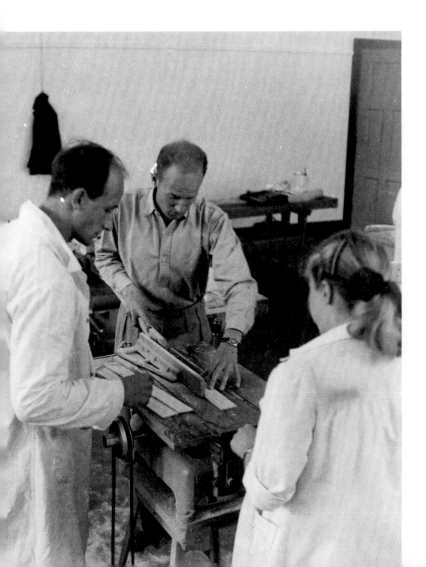

Industrial design professor Hugo Weber instructs Scandinavian students at the Institute of Design course in Oslo, 1952

JOSEF FRANK
Svenskt Tenn
Manhattan **textile**, designed 1943–44,
produced from 1947, this example 2018.
CAT. 42

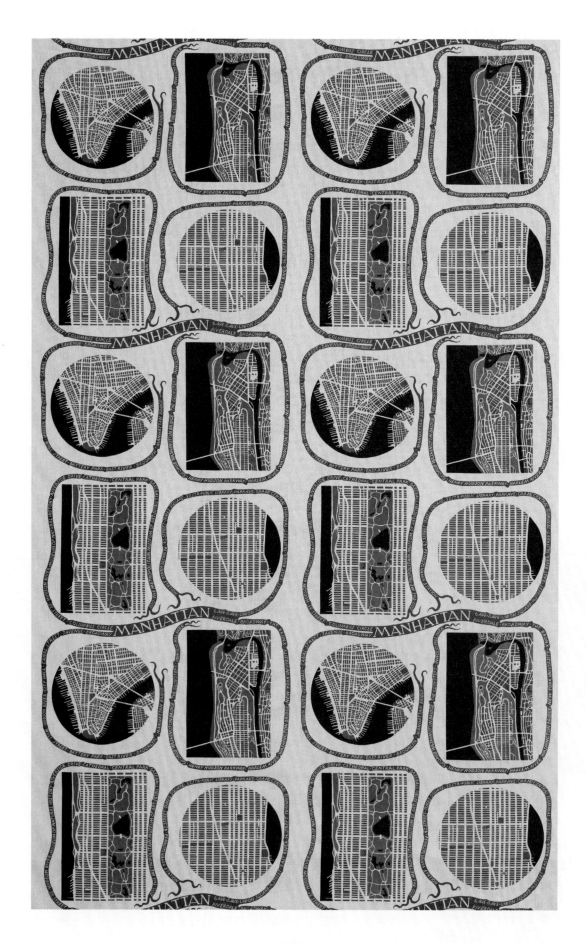

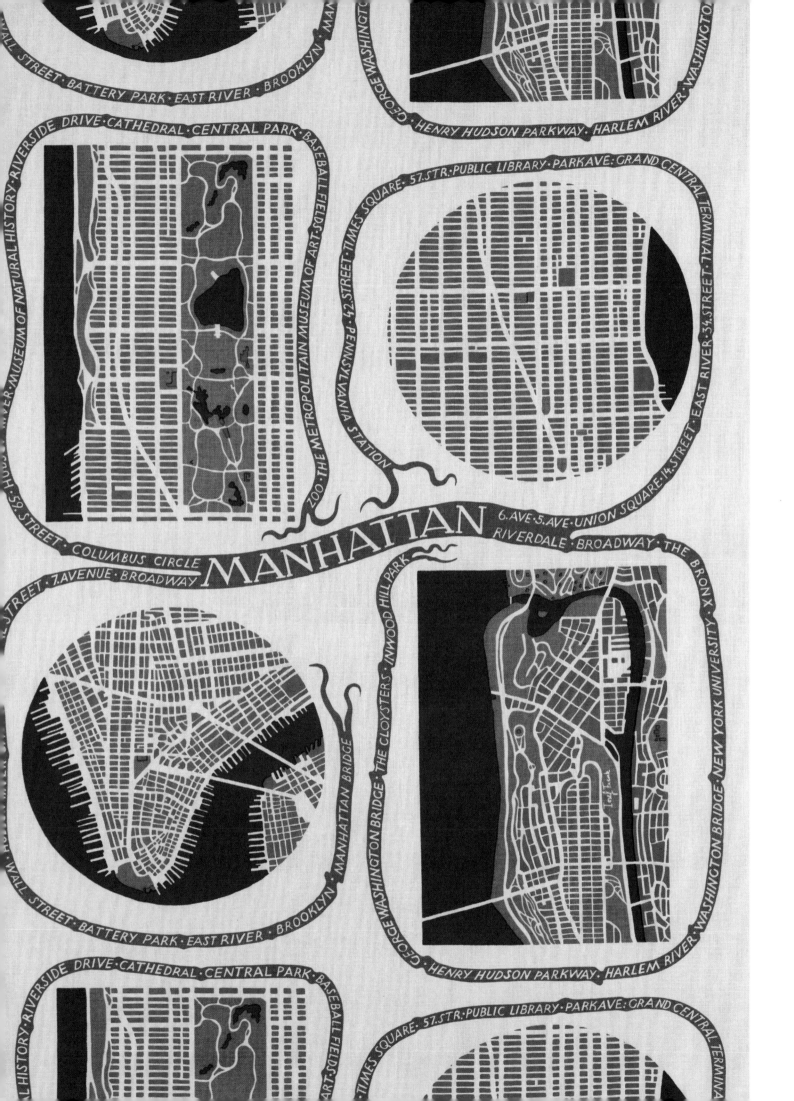

TIGERMAN

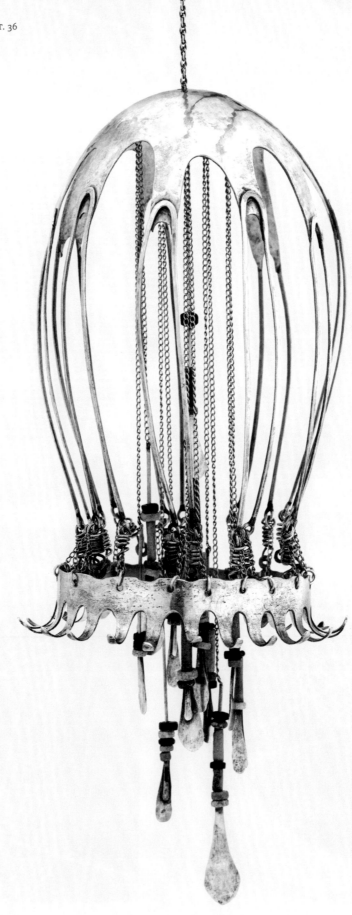

Another prominent Nordic designer to receive a Fulbright grant was Kaj Franck, who traveled to the United States in 1956. His first stop was Rhode Island School of Design, where he observed the industrial design curriculum and teaching methods.[10] He then made his way west on a lecture tour that ended in California, where he enrolled in ceramics classes at the University of California, Los Angeles.[11] Franck's lectures reviewed recent Finnish design developments, many of which he attributed to the country's harsh climate, specifically the vast differences between the short bitter days of winter and the long sun-drenched days of summer. This rhetoric linking nature and Finnish design would be employed often by Franck and others, especially in the *Design in Scandinavia* exhibition (which would open in Chicago two weeks after his talk there).[12] Throughout the year, Franck served as an emissary for Finnish design, heavily promoting the products of the Arabia factory (where he was artistic director) to American audiences. Franck must have run short of money, as John Junge, the U.S.-based sales manager of Wärtsilä Corporation, which owned Arabia, pleaded with his Helsinki counterpart Holger Carring to send financial assistance: "any amount which will be spent in this regard will come back twenty times!"[13]

Many American designers and craftspeople also received Fulbright fellowships, enabling them to acquire new skills while living abroad. Notable figures whose fellowship took them to Scandinavia included Glenda Arentzen (Denmark, 1965–66), Robert Ebendorf (Norway, 1963–64), Margaret and Robert Eskridge (Finland, 1957–58), Richard Fairbanks (Finland, 1959–60), Arline Fisch (Denmark, 1956–57 and 1966–68), James Hennessey (Sweden, 1969–70), Glen Kaufman (Denmark, 1959–60), Ronald Senungetuk (Norway, 1960–61), Helen Shirk (Denmark, 1963–64), and Nell Znamierowski (Finland, 1955–56). For jeweler Arline Fisch's second Fulbright fellowship to Denmark, she explained that she was "particularly interested in the idea of 'object jewels'—that is, jewels which have only a minor functional value but which are magnificent in their conception and elegant in the materials of which they are made."[14] While in Denmark, she became acquainted with a marine biologist who introduced her to the structures of jellyfish. She subsequently created *Hydra Medusa* (p. 242), in which she suggested in silver the sea creature's transparency and graceful movement.[15] Fisch, whose surname derives from the German word for "fish," has revisited aquatic forms several times in her career.[16]

The Scandinavian Seminar also afforded the opportunity for Americans to live and study in the Nordic countries. The program was founded in 1949 with a mission to provide educational opportunities and cultural immersion for American students by enrolling in a residential Scandinavian folk high school for a full academic year.[17] American furniture maker Jere Osgood attended in 1960–61 after studying with Danish American woodworker Tage Frid at the School for American Craftsmen (SAC). Osgood found that his American education provided him with technical knowledge, but not the sensitivity to materials that he learned at the Askov folk high school in Denmark. He recalled, "If I hadn't gone to Denmark I might not have been pushed over to a more personal kind of work."[18] Osgood learned about the Scandinavian Seminar through his SAC friend Daniel Jackson, who had completed the program in 1960, followed by a year in the studio of Danish cabinetmaker Peder Moos. Jackson's library ladder, made after returning to the United States, reflects the biomorphic curves also found in Moos' work (p. 246).[19]

In a few rare cases, Americans settled in Scandinavia for extended periods, establishing professional lives. Born in Russia and raised in Alaska and Seattle, craftsman James Krenov moved to Stockholm in 1947 and enrolled ten years later in the furniture school run by eminent Swedish cabinetmaker Carl Malmsten. After completing the course, he worked for decades as an independent craftsman in Bromma, a Stockholm suburb.[20] Krenov's work is renowned for its elegant simplicity and appreciation for the beauty of wood, as evident in his cabinet (p. 247; see also cat. 82). He specialized in the chest-on-stand form, characterized by the tall, narrow profile and attenuated legs found in Malmsten's work. In 1965–66, Craig McArt, an American Fulbright fellow studying furniture design at Konstfack (the University of Arts, Crafts, and Design) in Stockholm, met Krenov and interned with him in the summer of 1966. McArt was impressed by Krenov's genuine approach to materials and making, and recommended that Krenov teach a summer workshop at his alma mater, SAC.[21] Krenov proved to be a compelling teacher, and this workshop was the first of many that he taught at SAC and elsewhere in the United States and Europe. Several teaching engagements in the late 1970s at the Mendocino Woodworkers Association led to an invitation for Krenov to found the Fine Woodworking program at the College of the Redwoods in Fort Bragg, California. He moved there in 1981 and attracted dozens of students who appreciated his emphasis on basic cabinetmaking skills and his unabashed pleasure in working with wood.[22] Krenov reached many more woodworkers through his publications. His first book, *A Cabinetmaker's Notebook* (1976), is a soulful treatise on his woodworking philosophy that resulted from McArt's suggestion that Krenov document his ideas; this was followed by *The Joys of Cabinetmaking* (1979) and *James Krenov: Worker in Wood* (1981). By 1984, Krenov had sold more than 150,000 copies in all, a testament to his message's resonance.[23]

Such international exchanges continued to have meaningful consequences long after the initial contact. For example, Arline Fisch met the Danish jewelry instructor Ib Andersen on her second Fulbright to Denmark (1966–68); some years later, Andersen encouraged his student Hanne Behrens to study with Fisch at San Diego State University, where she was a professor. Fisch had just begun her exploration of knitting and weaving metallic threads, a direction that would occupy her for decades and become the subject of her influential 1975 book *Textile Techniques in Metal*. Behrens thrived in Fisch's class, making woven jewelry her own trademark—just one example that underscores the many ways in which postwar international travel and government support facilitated interpersonal exchange, allowing Nordic and American designers alike to extend their knowledge, personal networks, and influence.[24]

TIGERMAN

1 Leonard K. Eaton, "Richardson and Sullivan in Scandinavia," *Progressive Architecture* 47, no. 3 (March 1966): 168–71. The 1930 Stockholm Exhibition was extensively covered by American journalists; see, for example, Alma Luise Olson, "Sweden Will Reveal Its Art in Crafts," *New York Times*, March 16, 1930; Edith Weigle, "Modern Design in Sweden," *Chicago Tribune*, August 24, 1930; and Francis Keally, A.I.A., "My Impressions of the Stockholm Exhibition," *American Architect* 138 (December 1930): 34–43.

2 Jeannine J. Falino and Gerald W. R. Ward, *Silver of the Americas, 1600–2000: American Silver in the Museum of Fine Arts, Boston* (Boston: MFA Publications, 2008), 424; Helena Kåberg, "Ingrid Dessau Takes Manhattan: A Textile Pioneer Uniting Craft and Industry," *Journal of Modern Craft* 8, no. 2 (July 2015): 195–202.

3 Kristina Wängberg-Eriksson, "Life in Exile: Josef Frank in Sweden and the United States, 1933–1967," in *Josef Frank: Architect and Designer*, exh. cat., ed. Nina Stritzler-Levine (New Haven and London: Yale University Press, 1996), 62–77.

4 Kristina Wängberg-Eriksson, "Geometry in Disguise: A Modernist's Vision of Textile Design," in Stritzler-Levine, *Josef Frank: Architect and Designer*, 146.

5 Sam Lebovic, "From War Junk to Educational Exchange: The World War II Origins of the Fulbright Program and the Foundations of American Cultural Globalism, 1945–1950," *Diplomatic History* 37, no. 2 (2013): 280–312.

6 Karianne Bjellås Gilje, ed., *Grete Prytz Kittelsen: The Art of Enamel Design*, trans. Shari Gerber Nilsen (New York: W.W. Norton, 2012), 59–60, 77.

7 Gilje, *Grete Prytz Kittelsen*, 80, 82.

8 Richard Weston, "Platforms and Plateaux in Utzon's Architecture," in *Jørn Utzon: The Architect's Universe*, exh. cat., ed. Michael Juul Holm, Kjeld Kjeldsen, and Mette Marcus (Humlebæk, Denmark: Louisiana Museum of Modern Art, 2004), 28–35.

9 Kjetil Fallan, "Love and Hate in Industrial Design: Europe's Design Professionals and America in the 1950s," in *The Making of European Consumption: Facing the American Challenge*, ed. Per Lundin and Thomas Kaiserfeld (Basingstoke, UK: Palgrave Macmillan, 2015), 138; Gilje, *Grete Prytz Kittelsen*, 80.

10 Pekka Korvenmaa, *Finnish Design: A Concise History* (Helsinki: University of Art and Design, 2010), 178.

11 "Plan Design Lectures on Scandinavia," *Chicago Tribune*, April 8, 1956; "Visiting Finn Designer Sees Values of Folk Art to Modern Ceramics," *Los Angeles Times*, July 22, 1956. His correspondence with his family during this trip is partially published in *Kaj Franck: Universal Forms*, exh. cat., ed. Marianne Aav (Helsinki: Designmuseo, 2011).

12 Franck published an abridged version of his lecture in *Craft Horizons*; Kaj Franck, "Finland," *Craft Horizons* 16, no. 4 (July/August 1956): 24; a transcript of his May 1, 1956, lecture at the University of Chicago is preserved at the Designmuseo Helsinki. My thanks to Susanna Thiel for sharing this transcript.

13 John Junge to Holger Carring, April 16, 1956, Kaj Franck Archive, Designmuseo Helsinki.

14 Fulbright Proposal, 1966–67, Arline M. Fisch Papers, 1931–2015, Archives of American Art, Smithsonian Institution.

15 Fisch, conversation with author, October 31, 2018. While her Fulbright dates have been published as 1966–67 in the past, Fisch recalls that she remained in Denmark into 1968, when *Hydra Medusa* was made.

16 David Revere McFadden, ed., *Elegant Fantasy: The Jewelry of Arline Fisch* (San Diego and Stuttgart: San Diego Historical Society and Arnoldsche, 1999), 48.

17 See website for Scandinavian Seminar, www.scandinavianseminar.org; and "Study-Travel in Scandinavia," *Christian Science Monitor*, November 5, 1955, 18.

18 Rosanne Somerson, "Perfect Sweep," *American Craft* 45, no. 3 (June/July 1985): 30–34 at 34.

19 *Daniel Jackson: Dovetailing History*, exh. cat. (Philadelphia: University of the Arts, 2003).

20 Michael Stone, "The Quiet Object in Unquiet Times," *American Craft* 44, no. 1 (February/March 1984): 39–43.

21 McArt, correspondence with author, October 3, 2018.

22 On Krenov as a teacher, see James Krenov, *With Wakened Hands: Furniture by James Krenov and Students* (Bethel, CT: Cambium Press, 2000), and Ross Day, "A Krenov Student's Notebook," *Fine Woodworking*, Winter 2000–2001, 98–103.

23 Stone, "The Quiet Object."

24 Fisch, conversation with author, April 5, 2018.

American–Scandinavian Craft Exchange, 1945 to 1970

GLENN ADAMSON

Arline Fisch won a Fulbright to study craft in Denmark not once, but twice. The first time, in 1956, she was only twenty-five years old. Fresh from study at Skidmore College and a master's degree in art at the University of Illinois, she was enthusiastic but still relatively unskilled. To make matters worse, she didn't speak Danish, and after receiving the grant, encountered an unfriendly administrator at the Kunsthåndværkerskolen (School of Arts and Crafts) in Copenhagen. Suspicious that she planned to steal Danish ideas, he also found her interest in studying both ceramics and silversmithing perplexing. Perhaps it sounded like the plan of a dilettante. Yet Fisch persevered, first spending time at the school—not very satisfactorily—then at a privately owned manufactory, Bernhard Hertz Guldvaerefabrik, which took her on as an apprentice. She learned quickly, laying a foundation that would serve her well in her later work and teaching.

In 1966, Fisch—now an established figure in the American craft scene—returned to Denmark. She was treated with much greater respect this time, enjoying special access to museum collections, where she was deeply impressed by historical Mongolian jewelry, such as pectorals and ear ornaments. She also rented an independent shop space. Over the course of her second stay in Copenhagen, Fisch made an extraordinary group of large body ornaments similar to her *Front & Back* body ornament (p. 250), which was made upon her return to the U.S., as well as smaller objects inspired by sea life, such as jellyfish (p. 242). It was a great and productive time. Even so, she had reservations; Scandinavia seemed less intimidating than it had a decade earlier, but less exciting, too. "The change between the fifties and the sixties was astronomical," Fisch later recalled. "The craft world was very vibrant here [in the United States]. It didn't seem to be that vibrant in Denmark." She realized the country was "much too small and too traditional in its thinking to accept my work. They just thought it was odd."[1]

In the period between Fisch's two visits, much had indeed changed, in both the United States and the Nordic countries. So too had the relationship between the two regions, at least when it came to design: the international fashion for Scandinavian modern was past its peak. Fisch's experiences were so different, in part, because of her own changing perspective; but they were also

ARLINE FISCH
Front & Back body ornament, 1971.
CAT. 37

JOHN PRIP
Reed & Barton
Denmark tea and coffee service,
designed 1958. CAT. 116

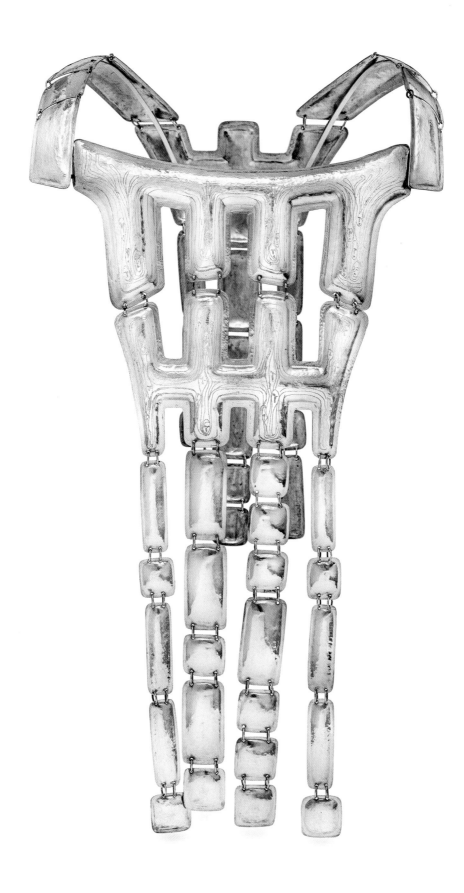

emblematic of these larger shifts. In the 1950s, Scandinavia seemed an ideal, even utopian, context for artisanal production. The region had perfected a symbiosis between the craftsperson and industry, precisely along the lines that many in the United States had sought to achieve. By the 1960s, though, the tables had turned. Americans, particularly those in Fisch's adopted state of California, were pioneering a new, experimental, and thoroughly individualistic approach to craft. The work being done in the Nordic countries seemed bland and outmoded in comparison. Indeed, younger Scandinavian makers now began looking to America for inspiration; some, such as Erik Gronborg, even moved there (p. 39). How did individual makers negotiate these developments, and what were the mechanisms of exchange? This essay will trace that story, attending to specific experiences like Fisch's, as well as the larger institutional framework that made them possible.

To understand why Scandinavian design seemed so powerfully attractive to Americans in the immediate postwar years, it is worth briefly sketching the state of affairs in the American craft

movement at the time.[2] A national council had been established, headquartered in New York City under the leadership of philanthropist Aileen Osborn Webb. During the war, she had successfully forged the disparate regional energies of American craft into a single organizational framework, complete with a shop, called America House, established in 1940 in Manhattan; a higher educational institute, the School for American Craftsmen (SAC), located in Rochester, New York, from 1950; an ambitiously edited and produced magazine, *Craft Horizons*; and as of 1956, the Museum of Contemporary Crafts (MCC), in a prestigious location on Fifty-Third Street in Manhattan, next to the Museum of Modern Art. The guiding ethos for all this activity was the designer-craftsman model, premised on the idea that industry would benefit from the contributions of artisans. The role of the craftsperson would be to prototype designs and consult on production, ensuring both quality and clarity of vision.

Unfortunately, American industry proved difficult to convince. Manufacturers aiming for the mass market tended to emphasize efficiency and

Toshiko Takaezu at work on her rug
Ao Ao at her home in Quakertown,
New Jersey, c. 1970

novelty, rather than integrity. There were a few success stories, most of which involved European émigrés who arrived with established track records of working in factory systems. Notably, several of these leading lights were from Scandinavia. The Finnish weaver Marianne Strengell taught textiles at Cranbrook Academy of Art according to the principle "first and always: research."[3] Dismissive of newness for its own sake, she received corporate commissions for automotive and architectural fabrics (pp. 223–25), and even worked with the Aluminum Company of America (Alcoa) to develop experimental textiles woven principally from aluminum thread.[4] The American-born but Danish-trained John Prip taught in the metals program at SAC, and was appointed "designer in residence" at silver manufacturer Reed & Barton in 1957, where he created the *Denmark* tea and coffee service (p. 251).[5] Tage Frid, also Danish, and a colleague of Prip's at SAC and later at Rhode Island School of Design (RISD), worked as a designer, too, even creating prototypes for the roadside restaurant chain Howard Johnson's.[6]

Other Scandinavians were active in the United States as teachers, including Finnish potter Maija Grotell at Cranbrook, Swedish weavers Ingeborg Longbers and Inge Werther Krok at the Penland School of Crafts in North Carolina, and Danish silversmith Hans Christensen, also at SAC. Danish silversmith Adda Husted-Andersen had come to New York City in 1930 and operated a retail shop there; she participated actively in Webb's nascent movement during and after the war, and helped train Glenda Arentzen, who became a silversmith herself.[7] Baron Erik Fleming, billed as "court silversmith to the king of Sweden," taught hollowware at the famed Handy & Harman workshops organized by Margret Craver immediately following the war, which were crucial in reviving metalworking techniques in the United States. Finnish weaver Martta Taipale's stint teaching at Penland in 1954 was decisive in opening up the field of tapestry to the great fiber artist Lenore Tawney at the beginning of her career.[8]

At Cranbrook, Strengell introduced students like Alice Kagawa Parrott and Toshiko Takaezu to the traditional Scandinavian *rya*, a long-pile rug typically made of wool.[9] Both intermittently wove carpets in the style over their careers. For Parrott, the *rya* appealed in part because it paired so well with her interest in natural vegetal pigments; the long

pile of the rugs made for an ideal textured receptor for dyes.[10] Despite training with Strengell, Parrott worked in many modes, and remarked that Lenore Tawney was the greatest influence on her career, which may be visible in her hangings of the late 1960s (p. 253).[11] For Takaezu, the *rya* was a means of achieving in textiles the same layered, veil-like compositions that she brought to her ceramic forms (below).[12] Another American, Nell Znamierowski, received instruction in Finland while on a 1955–56 Fulbright grant, learning to weave *rya* rugs at Taideteollinen oppilaitos (Institute of Industrial Arts) in Helsinki. Finding it a perfect medium in which to express the varied qualities of yarn, she promoted the technique upon her return to the United States.[13] Her *Icarus* rug demonstrates her painterly approach, featuring intensely colored yarns blended in subtle modulations (p. 254).

The reason that so many immigrant makers were comfortable as designers for industry and masters imparting skills to apprentices, despite (sometimes) limited English proficiency, is that they had experienced these roles firsthand in Scandinavia. Indeed, such arrangements were taken almost as a matter of course in the glassware, ceramics, furniture, and textile industries there. The logic behind this was not so much ideological as pragmatic. It was

ADAMSON

ROBERT EBENDORF
Coffeepot, 1963–64. CAT. 29

not about finding a viable role for the modern crafts-person, in other words, but rather an expectation that designers would necessarily have thorough technical grounding in the discipline. In the 1950s, mechanization was not widespread in Scandinavia. As was largely the case in Italy and Japan, the other two countries that exerted the strongest pull on the imagination of American craftspeople, fabrication was still done mainly by hand. Designers were able (even obliged) to work closely with skilled teams of artisans. The leading Scandinavian design schools, well aware of these dynamics, ensured that students were well trained in production techniques, or at least prepared to work with those who were. At the same time, the government sought to carefully plan the routes by which workers came into the work-shop or factory, either from apprenticeships or higher education.

This was the envy of those teaching in the more haphazard American system, which often lacked a firm vocational grounding, and offered few established pathways into the industrial workforce.[14] Many Americans who traveled to Scandinavia were amazed by the capabilities of makers there. Robert

Ebendorf recalled an experience at the Statens Håndverks-og Kunstindustriskole (National College of Art and Design) in Norway while on a Fulbright fellowship in 1963–64. A technician named Malum watched Ebendorf for a moment, as he tried to fit the hinges on a coffeepot (above), then wordlessly relieved him of the torch: "he stood there and soldered these hinges into place, and as he did this I stood there, and his hands and his knowledge of what was going on was like a surgeon doing open-heart surgery with one eye shut."[15] Similarly, both Jere Osgood and Daniel Jackson had their eyes opened to a whole realm of technique when they worked with Peder Moos in Copenhagen in the early 1960s, having already trained in the basics with Tage Frid at SAC. Both came back to America with vastly expanded skill sets, which they then taught to others. Osgood became well known for his use of jigs and steam-bending, including the challenging tapered lamination technique; Jackson went on to teach at Philadelphia College of Art (PCA), combining what he had learned of Danish cabinetmaking with Art Nouveau influences (p. 246).[16] Cranbrook gradu-ate Glen Kaufman traveled to Copenhagen on

ADAMSON

a Fulbright in 1959–60, and studied textile structure at the Kunsthaandværkerskolen. On his return, he taught textiles at the University of Georgia and parlayed his experiences into industry consultancy work, much on the European model.[17]

For most Americans, however, Scandinavian craft had to be appreciated at a distance. An exemplary case, which received much positive coverage in the American press, was that of the Finnish firm Wärtsilä, comprising the Arabia ceramic manufactory and the Nuutajärvi Glassworks. Among the many design luminaries who worked there were Kaj Franck, Saara Hopea, Kyllikki Salmenhaara, and two husband-and-wife teams, Tapio Wirkkala and Rut Bryk and Francesca and Richard Lindh. All maintained their own workshops within the factory, and produced what Americans called "studio" pieces alongside their designs for production. In a promotional piece written by Herman Olof (H. O.) Gummerus, managing director of Ornamo (Finnish Association of Designers), readers of *Craft Horizons* learned, "Here, overlooking the water and the wooded islands of the city, they work independently, supported by the company, yet entirely free to do anything they care to."[18] The magnetic power of that vision for Americans is suggested by personal connections that evolved in connection with Wärtsilä. Philadelphia jeweler Oppi Untracht, a specialist in South Asian jewelry, traveled to Finland in 1954, where he met Hopea; they married in 1960, initially living in New York and then returning for good to Finland in 1967. Potter Richard Fairbanks traveled to Finland in 1959 as a Fulbright scholar, and formed an artistic relationship with Salmenhaara during his time there; the two kept up a warm correspondence for years after and visited each other in their native countries (pp. 256–57).[19]

Firms such as Wärtsilä and Scandinavian government bodies alike used their reputation for fine craftsmanship strategically, realizing that there was much free promotional press to be had through this message. In 1957, for example, a special issue of *Design Quarterly* (published by the Walker Art Center in Minneapolis, a locus for Scandinavian immigration) claimed: "Industrial design in Finland is rooted even more firmly in the handicraft tradition than it is in the other Northern countries. The Finnish industrial designer is, almost without exception, a producing craftsman."[20] This idea was further substantiated by exhibitions, organized and funded either separately or jointly by the various Nordic countries. The most significant of these was *Design in Scandinavia*, which toured the United States from 1954 through 1957.[21] In the exhibition catalogue, Gotthard Johansson, president of the Svenska Slöjdföreningen (Swedish Arts and Crafts Society), stressed the legacy of folk crafts, the artisanal basis of contemporary manufactures, and the inherently democratic nature of Scandinavian societies. He explained that:

> It is no coincidence that we enjoy a reputation for a high standard in the design and quality of everyday objects, for our interest in these things is part of our makeup. In the old days, by producing a great many of the objects needed for everyday life, the Scandinavian took the responsibility for form and quality literally into his own hands. The modern counterpart to this is on the one hand the consistent policy of good design, which so many of the leading Scandinavian manufacturers follow and on the other hand the efforts of the growing consumer organisations to insist on quality and thus improve standards. Good everyday objects are largely the result of intimate relationship between producer and consumer.[22]

It was a subtle blend of messages, but all of them resonated with the aims of the American studio craft movement. For the general public, meanwhile, the dominant message of fine workmanship was probably what came through most strongly. Indeed, when the show arrived at the Brooklyn Museum, the *New York Times* described it straightforwardly as a "display of craft objects."[23]

In 1956, while *Design in Scandinavia* was still making its rounds in the United States, another exhibition of work from the region was mounted at the Museum of Contemporary Crafts in New York City. *Young Scandinavians* was displayed concurrently with the sixth installment of *Young Americans*, an annual exhibition that had originated at America House in 1950 and featured work exclusively by makers up to thirty years of age (p. 127).[24] With more than three hundred items across the two shows, the juxtaposition encouraged broad reflection on the differences between the two regions' craft cultures. The pair of exhibitions followed the new museum's inaugural exhibition, a general survey called *Craftsmanship in a Changing World*, suggesting just how important Scandinavian objects were as models to emulate. *Young Scandinavians*, like its larger predecessor *Design in Scandinavia*, was organized with financial and curatorial assistance from the various Nordic craft organizations (Landsforeningen Dansk Kunsthåndværk, Suomen Taideteollisuusyhdistys, Landsforbundet Norsk Brukskunst, and Svenska Slöjdföreningen). Given this, and the exhibition's focus on emerging talent, it is unsurprising that the theme of factory apprenticeship came through strongly. As the museum's press release put it: "The young Scandinavian receives an important part of his technical and design training and aesthetic experience within the framework of the factory where they are supplied with studios in which to design, create and experiment in their craft as a hand process—serving ultimately the needs of mass production."[25]

The following year, the American Craftsmen's Council held its first national conference in Asilomar, California. It was organized according to designer-craftsman principles, and addressed themes including socioeconomic outlooks and professional practices. Asger Fischer, the managing director of Den Permanente, a prominent design retailer in Copenhagen, delivered a keynote address.[26] Like H. O. Gummerus, Fischer constructed a narrative around Danish design that depicted an ideal harmony between business, design, and craftsmanship. In his remarks, Fischer presented Den Permanente as an aspirational model, glowingly describing the accomplishments of his organization in the hope of inspiring American emulations.[27] But ironically, it was the very success of Den Permanente (and Scandinavian design in general) that would soon destabilize its reception in America.[28]

Essentially, the problem was one of overproduction. Even by 1960, the *Metropolitan Museum of Art Bulletin* acidly noted that "a hundred shop windows in New York feature more or less debased versions of the best Danish furniture of today."[29] Demand for Scandinavian design was so high, particularly in the United States, that Nordic manufacturers were faced with a difficult choice: leave behind the artisanal mode of production that anchored the region's reputation, or refuse to mechanize and be priced out of the market. The dilemma exposed a weakness in the designer-craftsman logic: the quality of Scandinavian objects was not due only to the involvement of makers as designers, but also (and much more significantly) to the fact that skilled artisans had been responsible for *every* aspect of the production process. The experience at Johannes Hansen, the Copenhagen firm that manufactured Hans Wegner's furniture, was exemplary in this respect. As they expanded rapidly from a small urban workshop to a large suburban factory, they constantly had to negotiate a difficult question: how much automation was too much?[30]

In 1958, *Craft Horizons* published an extraordinary special issue that confronted this situation head-on (below). Conrad Brown, who had taken on the editorship of the magazine three years earlier, had just returned from a tour of the Nordic countries. His report amounted to a complete volte-face from the magazine's previous reporting. Boldly entitled "The Revolution in Scandinavian Design," it began with an editorial that sounded an alarm loud and clear: "This is the first report anywhere that a revolution is brewing in Scandinavian design…. This is not an organized revolt. It is simply that an extraordinary number of young designer-craftsmen for whom Scandinavian modern design has turned sour, have

gone to work in seclusion to do something positive about it."[31] The issue included full-page profiles of these young makers, whom Brown dubbed "Scandinavia's Young Dissenters," as well as a separate insert, a departure from the magazine's usual format. Brown described numerous encounters with emerging talents in Scandinavia who found the established modern styles to be increasingly "sterile," and who were suspicious of the motivations among their own prospective clientele: "a piece of contemporary art glass or ceramic of clean, classic form and exquisite finish had become 'the thing' to have, whether its new owner knew or cared anything about craft art or not."[32] Interestingly, he also claimed that this assessment was shared by the more established generation of designers at the leading firms: "The senior element who originated contemporary

CRAFT HORIZONS
Special issue: "The Revolution in
Scandinavian Design"
Magazine, March/April 1958. CAT. 179

Scandinavian design, instead of opposing an incipient design revolt, display today something akin to the nostalgia of the parent seeing a son off to war, bidding him luck while secretly wishing to be young enough to go along."[33]

Brown had doubtless noticed a genuine shift in the conversation among Scandinavian designers. But clearly, he was also strongly influenced by recent events in the United States and at his own publication. He and his colleague Rose Slivka, who would lead *Craft Horizons* through its greatest period after being named editor in 1959, shared a preference for progressive, even subversive reinventions of craft. They had already published profiles of Peter Voulkos and Lenore Tawney, the most innovative ceramist and weaver then active in America.[34] Brown explicitly framed his experiences in Scandinavia through this lens, identifying the twenty-six-year-old glass artist Erik Höglund as "clearly the most important figure in the coming revolution in Scandinavian design," and asking, "will Höglund turn out to be a Scandinavian Peter Voulkos?"[35]

Though the revolution that Brown predicted did not quite come to pass, his identification of a divergence within Scandinavian design was not entirely off the mark, and this debate was indeed carried out in full awareness of what was happening stateside. Over the course of the ensuing decade, Nordic makers started looking more and more to the individualistic and expressive American craft scene for inspiration; currents of influence were now running in both directions. In 1959, Thorvald Krohn-Hansen, director of the Nordenfjeldske Kunstindustrimuseum (National Museum of Decorative Arts and Design) in Trondheim, traveled in America for four months in conjunction with a touring exhibition of historical Norwegian tapestries, including to Santa Fe and San Francisco.[36] In what was likely the first instance of a Scandinavian institution acquiring contemporary craft from the United States, he returned with works for the collection by six artists that he had encountered on his travels, including paradigmatic "designer-craftsmen" such as Edith Heath (right) as well as more expressionist makers such as Alice Kagawa Parrott, Ed Rossbach, and Katherine Westphal.

Meanwhile, individual artists continued to travel back and forth. Sometimes their experiences followed the template that had been established in the 1950s, with Americans learning new skills in the Nordic countries, and Scandinavians dispensing

knowledge in the United States. Cranbrook metals graduate Michael Lacktman studied in Copenhagen in 1965–66, working with Henning Koppel and Nanna Ditzel of the silversmithing firm Georg Jensen. A bowl he made shortly after returning to the United States attests to the superlative hollowware forming techniques he absorbed (p. 262).

For others, though, new ideas rather than technical skills were the most valued currency of exchange. Marvin B. Lipofsky, an early participant in the studio glass movement, remembered the polite puzzlement that greeted his sculpturally adventurous work when he first began traveling to Scandinavia in the late 1960s.[37] By the end of the decade, he was creating ambitious handblown amoeboid sculptures at the Nuutajärvi Glassworks in Finland, finishing them with applied colors, flocking, mirroring and other effects back in his studio in Berkeley (p. 263).[38] Among those impacted by his visits was Heikki Kallio, who would go on to found a studio glass program in Helsinki along American lines. He later recalled his sense of discovery on meeting Lipofsky in 1970: "I had never seen it before. I found out this is a material you never learn perfectly, there is always something new, it's unlimited."[39]

Nordic artists visiting the United States were similarly inspired by the freedom they found there. Bertil Vallien, who graduated from Konstfack (the University of Arts, Crafts, and Design) in Stockholm in 1961, went to Los Angeles to take up a design position at a manufactory called HAL Fromholt Ceramics. This job afforded little room for experimentation, but he was surrounded by the vitality of the California craft movement. "I feel I really caught fire here," he remembers:

> Before coming here, I was one of those students who made nice teapots with fine glazes— all that. But seeing the attitude, the freedom of your craftsmen, particularly the potters— what life their work has!—I went back refreshed, my ideas completely changed. Now in Sweden we are trying to catch that way of working, to make very exciting things in the same approach as your young people here. This is really grafted from America. We are looking to the west now, to the leaders here— the real studio one-of-a-kind craftsman.[40]

Vallien's figural sculptures achieved immediate recognition in the United States; his work *The Bull Mountain* won a first place purchase prize in 1962 at the *Twenty-Second Ceramic National* at the Everson Museum of Art in Syracuse (p. 264).[41]

Bodil Manz, who had recently graduated from Denmark's Kunsthaandværkerskolen, had a similarly transformative experience in 1966 while visiting Peter Voulkos's program in Berkeley, together with her husband, Richard Manz, also a ceramist. She was captivated by the expressionist work being done there—"people were splashing things all over, it was fantastic"—and particularly impressed to see porcelain, a material she had associated exclusively with industrial manufacture, being mixed in huge machines and used for sculpture. Though the other students were initially dismissive of the Manzes' work, finding it too conservative, when they showed Voulkos their portfolios he was unexpectedly enthusiastic, characterizing their works as "*real* pots" and declaring, "it will be so good for my students to see them." Upon their return to Copenhagen, the couple established themselves as leading figures in the studio pottery community. Bodil Manz's distinctive idiom, with transfer-printed patterns on both the interior and exterior surfaces of thin-walled cast porcelain cylinders, could not be more different from Voulkos's work, but she views her time in Berkeley as important in steering her down a more experimental pathway.[42]

With figures such as Lipofsky, Vallien, and Manz, the American–Scandinavian craft exchange swung, pendulum-like, in another direction. What had begun as admiration for Nordic achievement

American–Scandinavian Craft Exchange, 1945 to 1970

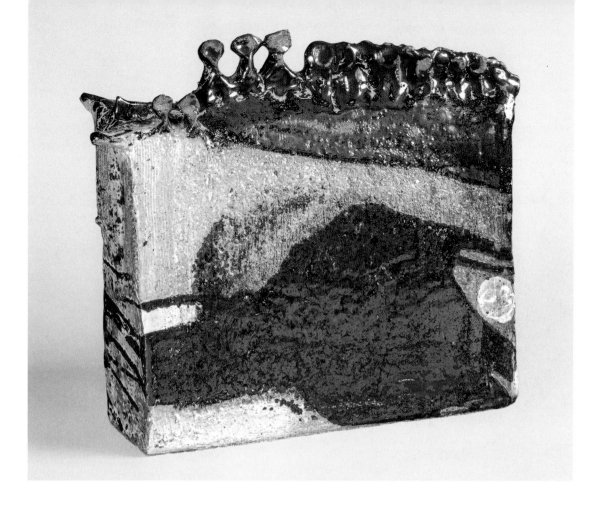

gradually became a more equal relationship, in which each culture found something to emulate in the other. There were other reasons, too, for the ending of Scandinavia's exalted position in the American craft firmament. First, the overall design climate had begun to shift away from the clean lines and organic materials that had prevailed in the postwar years, and toward styles such as Pop and postmodernism. In 1980, the influential *New York Times* architecture critic Ada Louise Huxtable wondered, "Whatever happened to Danish modern? Where has all the furniture gone that was such a tidal wave of good taste and good design in the 1950s?"[43] In fact, Nordic designers did contribute to the new styles (Denmark's Verner Panton being the most obvious example), but they lost ground to Italy, which became the preeminent influence internationally—a status signaled in the 1972 exhibition *Italy: The New Domestic Landscape*, at the Museum of Modern Art in New York. Tellingly, though artisans remained essential to Italian design in this period, their role was almost always unacknowledged and often actively disguised, in vivid contrast with Scandinavian modern.[44]

Another factor was the rapid development of the American craft scene itself. Following the triumph of the omnibus touring exhibition *Objects: USA*, beginning in 1969, it was clear that any sense of dependency on foreign models and instruction was over. According to Paul J. Smith, co-curator of that exhibition and director of the Museum of Contemporary Crafts from 1963: "There had been a lack of expertise to fill the needs, but then the rapid explosion of activity in America began to become universal. It didn't take long for places like Murano and Czechoslovakia to be overrun by Americans."[45] It was not so much that Scandinavian makers stopped coming to America, or that Americans stopped going there; rather, the region simply came to be considered as just one of many international areas of interest in a more globalized craft establishment.

Yet even as the overall picture transitioned to a more multilateral situation, the encounter between America and Scandinavia continued on in the works of many individual makers. In California's woodworking scene, for example, Danish influence persisted through the 1970s and beyond in the work of such figures as Arthur Espenet Carpenter, Sam

Maloof (below), John Kapel, and Bob Stocksdale, all of whom had originally learned their skills in the immediate postwar years. The so-called "California roundover," a simple technique used by Carpenter and Maloof that could be achieved either with a router or hand tools, had its ultimate source in the soft lines of Scandinavian design, in particular the work of Hans Wegner and Bruno Mathsson. Stocksdale's exquisitely turned bowls, meanwhile, were an individual development from wooden tablewares by the likes of Finn Juhl.[46] Similarly, though narratives of West Coast ceramics tend to focus primarily on radicals in the circles of Peter Voulkos and Robert Arneson, there were many other makers who continued to make "real pots" under the influence of Nordic models. Among these were Rupert Deese and Harrison McIntosh, both of whom designed for industry in the approved Scandinavian manner, and Laura Andreson, who exerted great influence through her teaching at the University of California, Los Angeles. Even today, Heath Ceramics (revived under new ownership in 2003) takes its cues not only from the firm's founder Edith Heath, but also the enlightened Scandinavian industrial model, in which artists work in factories making one-off pieces as well as designing for production.

Conversely, contemporary makers in the Nordic countries—among them, independent artists such as Zandra Ahl and Hanna Hansdotter, and collectives such as Uglycute and We Work In A Fragile Material—have rebelled openly against the tasteful inheritance of the postwar years. Characteristic of this revolution in Scandinavian design (to recall Conrad Brown's title from 1958) is the ongoing involvement of such insurrectionaries in the region's educational and industrial infrastructure. Governmental funding bodies, schools such as Konstfack, and companies such as Orrefors, Kosta Boda, and Gustavsberg all lend support to new talent at a level that is virtually unknown in the United States. For example, Ahl was hired as professor at Konstfack, having previously been one of its most outspoken critics, while emerging glass artist Hansdotter is a designer at Kosta Boda, Sweden's oldest glassworks.[47] And yet it would be difficult to imagine the current vibrant energy in the Scandinavian craft scene without the influence of Americans from the 1960s and later, and the continuing exchange of ideas since.

While the overall narrative of postwar influence of Scandinavia on American craft is one of rise and decline, the story also speaks to the inherent variability within the domain of craft, which at once encompasses folk practices, design prototypes, skilled fabrication, and artistic expression. In the 1950s and 1960s, these different currents were often in tension with one another, though in retrospect, they can be seen simply as facets of a complex whole. Unbreakable bonds of respect between the United States and the Nordic region were forged following World War II, and so too were deep currents of mutual influence. Today, at a time when postwar studio craft is being reappraised, the transformative encounter between America and Scandinavia must be seen as one of its greatest success stories.

SAM MALOOF
Chair, 1952. CAT. 99

1 Arline M. Fisch, oral history conducted July 29–30, 2001, by Sharon Church McNabb, Archives of American Art, Smithsonian Institution.

2 For an overview, see Glenn Adamson, "Gatherings: Creating the Studio Craft Movement," in *Crafting Modernism: Midcentury American Art and Design,* exh. cat., ed. Jeannine Falino, History of Twentieth-Century American Craft 4 (New York: Abrams in association with the Museum of Arts and Design, 2011), 32–48.

3 Alice Adams, "Marianne Strengell," *Craft Horizons* 23, no. 1 (January/February 1963): 36.

4 Barbara Paris Gifford and Leslie S. Edwards, "'Feminizing Alcoa Aluminum': Marianne Strengell and the *Forecast* Rug (1957)," *Journal of Modern Craft* 8, no. 2 (July 2015): 167–79. See also Leslie Edwards in this volume, 223–25.

5 "John Prip and Reed & Barton," *Craft Horizons* 24, no. 2 (March/April 1964): 39. An exhibition on his work for the company, titled *A Craftsman's Role in Modern Industry*, was held at the MCC in 1962. Also see Thomas S. Michie and Christopher Monkhouse, eds., *John Prip: Master Metalsmith*, exh. cat. (Providence and New York: Rhode Island School of Design and American Craft Museum, 1987).

6 Tage Frid, oral history conducted June 24, 1980–February 22, 1982, by Robert F. Brown, Archives of American Art, Smithsonian Institution. For more on Frid's influence, see Rosanne Somerson in this volume, 229–32.

7 Glenda Arentzen, oral history conducted November 12–13, 2012, by Jeannine Falino, Archives of American Art, Smithsonian Institution. The interview includes a detailed description of Husted-Andersen's shop, which was outfitted along traditional European lines.

8 See Bobbye Tigerman in this volume, 191–98.

9 Parrott remembered Strengell weaving *ryas* during her time at Cranbrook; see Alice Kagawa Parrott, oral history conducted July 10, 2005, by Paul J. Smith, Archives of American Art, Smithsonian Institution. See also Marianne Strengell, oral history conducted January 8–December 16, 1982, by Robert F. Brown, Archives of American Art, Smithsonian Institution.

10 Ann Marguerite Tartsinis, "The *Magic in the Dye Pot*: Mable Morrow, Alice Kagawa Parrott, and Sites of Exchange in Modern Weaving," *Journal of Modern Craft* 11, no. 1 (March 2018): 39–53.

11 "One Space—Three Visions, Interview with Alice Parrott, Santa Fe, New Mexico by Art Adair," Albuquerque Art Museum curatorial files.

12 On weavings by Takaezu, see Peter Held, *The Art of Toshiko Takaezu: In the Language of Silence* (Chapel Hill: University of North Carolina Press, 2011), 35–36.

13 C.V., Nell Znamierowski artist file, American Craft Council Library & Archives, Minneapolis, MN. Znamierowski published books such as *Step-by-Step Weaving* and *Step-by-Step Rugmaking* and taught at the Fashion Institute of Technology in New York and at workshops throughout the country.

14 Glenn Nelson, "Scandinavian Craft Schools, part one," *Craft Horizons* 21, no. 4 (July/August 1961): 38–39; Nelson, "Scandinavian Craft Schools, part two," *Craft Horizons* 21, no. 5 (September/October 1961): ix.

15 Robert Ebendorf, oral history conducted April 16–18, 2004, by Tacey Rosolowski, transcript, Archives of American Art, Smithsonian Institution, p. 29.

16 Edward S. Cooke Jr., *New American Furniture: The Second Generation of Studio Furnituremakers*, exh. cat. (Boston: Museum of Fine Arts, 1989).

17 Fred Schwartz, "Glen Kaufman," *Craft Horizons* 27, no. 1 (January/February 1967): 14–16 at 16.

18 H[erman] O[lof] Gummerus, "Wellspring of Scandinavian Design," *Craft Horizons* 16, no. 4 (July/August 1956): 30. Gummerus had previously worked as a press relations officer for Arabia. See Kevin Davies, "'A Geographical Notion Turned into an Artistic Reality': Promoting Finland and Selling Finnish Design in Post-War Britain c. 1953–1965," *Journal of Design History* 15, no. 2 (2002): 101–16.

19 *Essential Passions: Fairbanks/Salmenhaara Letters, 1959–1986*, ed. Dixie Parker-Fairbanks and Helen Abbott (Seattle: University of Washington Press, 1999); Matthew Kangas, *Richard Fairbanks, American Potter* (Seattle: University of Washington Press, 1993).

20 "15 Contemporary Finnish Designers," *Design Quarterly*, no. 37 (1957): 2.

21 Gotthard Johansson, "Design in Scandinavia," in *Design in Scandinavia: An Exhibition of Objects for the Home from Denmark, Finland, Norway, Sweden*, exh. cat., ed. Arne Remlov (Oslo: Kirstes Boktrykkeri, 1954), 15. See also Monica Penick and Monica Obniski in this volume, 93–97 and 129.

22 Johansson, "Design in Scandinavia," 15.

23 "Scandinavia Exhibit," *New York Times*, April 20, 1954.

24 Following the presentation at the MCC, *Young Americans and Young Scandinavians* traveled to the Washington County Museum of Fine Arts in Hagerstown, Maryland, and Rochester Memorial Art Gallery in New York State.

25 Museum of Contemporary Crafts, "Exhibition: Young Americans and Young Scandinavians," news release, 1956, Museum of Contemporary Crafts files, American Craft Council Library.

26 Jean A. Givens, "Craft, Commerce and Den Permanente," in "The Influence of Scandinavian Design," ed. Bobbye Tigerman, special issue, *Design and Culture* 7, no. 3 (2015): 335–56.

27 Asger Fischer, "The Position of the Craftsman in Denmark," *Asilomar: First Annual Conference of American Craftsmen* (New York: American Craftsmen's Council, 1957), 111.

28 "Asilomar: An On the Scene Report," *Craft Horizons* 17, no. 4 (July/August 1957): 30.

29 Rosine Raoul, "The Danish Tradition in Design," *Metropolitan Museum of Art Bulletin* 19, no. 4 (December 1960): 122. The article covered the 1960 exhibition *The Arts of Denmark*.

30 See Per H. Hansen, "Networks, Narratives, and New Markets: The Rise and Decline of Danish Modern Furniture Design, 1930–1970," *Business History Review* 80, no. 3 (Autumn 2006): 473.

31 Conrad Brown, "Coming: Revolution in Scandinavian Design," *Craft Horizons* 18, no. 2 (March/April 1958): 10.

32 Conrad Brown, "Scandinavia's Young Dissenters," *Craft Horizons* 18, no. 2 (March/April 1958): inserted pamphlet, p. 1.

33 Brown, "Coming: Revolution in Scandinavian Design," 10.

34 Conrad Brown, "Peter Voulkos," *Craft Horizons* 16, no. 5 (September/October 1956): 12–18; Margo Hoff, "Lenore Tawney: The Warp Is Her Canvas," *Craft Horizons* 17, no. 6 (November/December 1957): 14–19.

35 Brown, "Coming: Revolution in Scandinavian Design," 12. Höglund, a graduate of the Konstfack, went on to be a designer at Kosta Boda and a moderately successful sculptor.

36 Jan-Lauritz Opstad (former director, Nordenfjeldske Kunstindustrimuseum), email message to Bobbye Tigerman and Monica Obniski, February 5, 2018. The exhibition, and Krohn-Hansen's tour, were sponsored by the Smithsonian Institution in Washington, DC. See "Norwegian Tapestries," *Craft Horizons* 19, no. 6 (November/December 1959): 24 and *Norwegian Tapestries: An Exhibition Sponsored by the Government of Norway and Circulated by the Smithsonian Institution*, exh. cat. (Washington, DC: H.K. Press, 1959).

37 Cheryl White, "Marvin Lipofsky: Roving Ambassador of Glass," *American Craft* 51, no. 5 (October 1991): 47–51.

38 Suzanne Baizerman, ed., *Marvin Lipofsky: A Glass Odyssey* (Oakland: Oakland Museum of California, 2003), 123–24.

39 "Heikki Kallio," *Glass Art Society Journal*, no. 5 (1980): 72.

40 Dido Smith, "Bertil Vallien: 'Gentle Fantasies Done with Daring and Delight,'" *Craft Horizons* 27, no. 5 (September/October 1967): 9. Upon his return to Sweden in 1963, Vallien took up a studio design consultancy at Åfors Glasbruk and went on to be a leading exponent of sculptural glass.

41 "Show Time: The 22nd Ceramic National," *Ceramics Monthly* 10, no. 10 (December 1962): 22–25.

42 Bodil Manz, interview with author, August 6, 2018.

43 Ada Louise Huxtable, "The Melancholy Fate of Danish Modern Style," *New York Times*, August 21, 1980.

44 See Catharine Rossi, *Crafting Design in Italy: From Post-War to Postmodernism* (Manchester: Manchester University Press, 2015).

45 Paul J. Smith, interview with author, September 5, 2018.

46 See Edward S. Cooke Jr., "From Manual Training to Freewheeling Craft," in *Wood Turning in North America since 1930*, exh. cat. (Philadelphia and New Haven: Wood Turning Center and Yale University Art Gallery, 2003), 12–63.

47 For a helpful survey of this range of activity in Sweden, see *Gustavsbergs Konsthall Revisited*, exh. cat., ed. Maj Sandell, Lenny Leonardz, and Carin Kallenberg (Stockholm: Gustavsbergs Konsthall, 2017).

BITTAN VALBERG

Designing for the Fifth Wall

MONICA OBNISKI

When asked whether her designs had changed upon moving to the United States, Brit-Marie (known as Bittan) Bergh Valberg noted, "I am sure New York with its many influences has 'widened my view' much more than would have been possible in a small country like Sweden."[1] After graduating in 1948 from Konstfack (the University of Arts, Crafts, and Design) in Stockholm, Valberg began weaving rugs by hand for Swedish patrons.[2] She moved to the United States in 1956, and although she remained for only five years, her work was widely exhibited and published.[3]

Valberg initially worked in the New York studio of Dorothy Liebes, a textile pioneer who experimented with synthetic materials, which were appealing because they rendered textiles more durable.[4] One example was Chromspun, produced by Eastman Chemical Products Corporation. Eastman commissioned Valberg to fabricate hand-loomed *ryas* (a typically Scandinavian long knotted pile rug) using Chromspun, and one of these experimental rugs was shown in a 1958 exhibition at Georg Jensen, the New York luxury retailer.[5]

Valberg also used synthetic fibers in her line for Cabin Crafts, based in Dalton, Georgia.[6] The company's chairman, Fred Westcott, discovered Valberg's work at one of her New York exhibitions, and invited her to produce a line of rugs.[7] Valberg worked closely with the firm's staff through the entire production process.[8] She began with a watercolor or oil sketch, then wove a sample on a handloom with custom-dyed yarn before creating a worksheet for the weavers. The Cabin Crafts rugs used Acrilan, a synthetic fiber produced by the Chemstrand Corporation that Valberg hand-dyed to realize precise colors.[9] These rugs were hand-guided by an electric needle on a single-needle machine to achieve subtle textural and color effects within a realistic production time and at a reasonable cost.[10]

Her designs made waves—in fact, a "Blue Wave"—in the United States (p. 268). A handwoven version of this design was exhibited in *Wall Hangings and Rugs* (1957) at the Museum of Contemporary Crafts; Valberg was praised for her use of Swedish methods and acute awareness of color.[11] Her Cabin Crafts rugs—available in *rya* or *flossa* techniques at department stores across the country—had distinctive names like *Moon*

OBNISKI

Missile and *Circus Tent*, inspired by the American landscape she encountered while traveling. For Valberg, what she called "art rugs" were intended for the floor, which she considered a fifth wall—"an area to be decorated attractively, not just another area to cover up."[12] Valberg believed that these rugs were "a prime illustration of artistry walking hand-in-hand with modern technical progress. The brilliant color clarity, special textural effects and high level of quality and durability achieved with Acrilan enables us to take fine art rugs off the wall and walk on them with complete confidence."[13] In the United States, Valberg found the mechanized process provided her with more freedom, and the choice of materials—durable, synthetic fibers—tested her abilities. She returned to Sweden in 1961 with new knowledge that expanded her worldview.

1 Bittan Valberg, "Personal Thoughts behind My Designs," American Craft Council Artists' File Collection, Bittan Valberg file.

2 Lena Holger, *Bittan Bergh Valberg* (Stockholm: Raster Förlag, 2001).

3 Valberg's rugs were included in exhibitions at the Museum of Contemporary Crafts in 1956 and 1957, the Walker Art Center in 1958, and the High Museum of Art in 1960. Her work was also featured in *Vogue* (March 15, 1958), *Craft Horizons* (May/June 1957), and *House and Garden* (March 1958), among other publications.

4 For more on Liebes and synthetics, see Regina Lee Blaszczyk, "Designing Synthetics, Promoting Brands: Dorothy Liebes, DuPont Fibres and Post-war American Interiors," *Journal of Design History* 21, no. 1 (Spring 2008): 75–99.

5 "New Ways with Chromspun," *Interior Design* 28 (December 1957): 133, Valberg file; "Scandinavia Sends Rugs, Metal-Based Furniture," *New York Times*, January 15, 1958.

6 Anne Douglas, "More and More New Fibers," *Chicago Tribune*, January 9, 1959.

7 Edith Hills Coogler, "Rug Shows True Colors—Are You Fool or Angel?" *Atlanta Journal and Constitution*, September 11, 1960.

8 "Swedish Designs Created for Rugs," *New York Times*, November 19, 1958.

9 "Valberg—Artist in Yarns," *American Fabrics* 46 (Spring 1959): 70–71.

10 "Bittan Valberg Adapts the Handloomed Look to Less Costly Machine-Tufted Rugs," *Industrial Design* 7 (April 1960): 76–77.

11 Conrad Brown, "Valberg: A Swedish Weaver Comes Here to Study Trends in U.S. Textile Design and Adapt Them to Her Own Scandinavian Techniques," *Craft Horizons* 17, no. 3 (May/June 1957): 28–31.

12 Vivian Brown, "Scatter Rugs for Real Style," *Newark Advocate*, October 10, 1960.

13 "Drama Keys New Collection of Area Rugs," *Press and Sun-Bulletin* (Binghamton, NY), January 9, 1959.

Bittan Valberg

HOWARD SMITH

African American Artist in Finland

BOBBYE TIGERMAN

As an African American who settled permanently in Finland, Howard Smith represents a unique case in the history of U.S.–Nordic design exchange. In *South of Pico*, a history of Los Angeles' African American artistic community in the 1960s–70s, Kellie Jones observes that most of her subjects were migrants, having followed often-circuitous paths from the East and South to seek opportunity in California. Smith's trajectory, which included eight years in Los Angeles (from 1976 to 1984), reflects this pattern of movement typical of African American artists, which Jones calls "crisscrossing," though his path began by going East rather than West.[1]

Born in Philadelphia in 1928, Smith enrolled at the Pennsylvania Academy of the Fine Arts in 1960 following eight years in the army.[2] In 1962, a friend invited him to Helsinki to assist with Young America Presents, a U.S.-sponsored cultural festival.[3] Smith later explained that his eagerness to travel came from a desire to escape the systemic racism he had endured and the perceived lack of opportunities to work as an artist in his home country. "I didn't leave with any pleasant thought about the United States," he recalled, "I was at an impasse. There was nothing further to do, so I went."[4] While in Finland,

Smith met Matti Viherjuuri, director of the Markkinointi Viherjuuri advertising agency, which was responsible for the marketing of Young America Presents. Viherjuuri invited Smith to stay in Finland for a year following the festival, teaching English to ad agency employees and doing some design work, while also enjoying ample opportunity to work and travel.

Finland's small size (its population in 1962 was 4.5 million) meant that art and design circles were close-knit. Smith met many prominent figures, such as designers Antti Nurmesniemi and Vuokko Eskolin-Nurmesniemi, Marimekko founder Armi Ratia, and architect Juhani Pallasmaa, and began receiving commissions from architects and designers.[5] He worked extensively in a range of media, including drawing, painting, silkscreen, and textile and paper collage (later in his career, he also worked in ceramics and made steel sculptures). While the bulk of his artistic production was exhibited in gallery settings, he felt a strong impulse to make less expensive, more accessible work, especially for African Americans who generally had less money to spend on art.[6] Fortuitous in this respect was his 1967 meeting with Rudolf Berner, the owner of the Vallila silk company,

HOWARD SMITH
Vallila
Textile, designed c. 1978. CAT. 146

who invited Smith to create designs for printed textiles. Smith later recalled that "one surely interesting thing made possible by my being in Finland was the cooperation of industry, whereas in America we know that the Black artist has little, if any, possibility to work in a creative way with any industry. There, I was able to accomplish a good deal."[7]

The Vallila printed textiles were exceedingly popular as home decorations, with their cheerful images of flowers, birds, and landscapes in bold patterns and bright colors (p. 271). They were even exported internationally beginning in the 1970s, the first of Smith's works to be available in the United States since his departure for Finland. The Boston-based firm International Printworks framed them on stretchers and successfully promoted them as wall decorations.[8] Smith continues to live and work in Finland, where, in his estimation, he has enjoyed greater artistic success than would have been possible as an African American in his native country.

1 Kellie Jones, *South of Pico: African American Artists in Los Angeles in the 1960s and 1970s* (Durham, NC: Duke University Press, 2017), 4.
2 Most biographical information comes from Jussi Suomala, *Howard Smith* (Helsinki: Like Kustannus Oy, 2008). Additional information can be found in Elaine Levin, "Studio Ceramists in Finland," *Ceramics Monthly* 47, no. 5 (May 1999): 54–57.
3 Young America Presents was held as a counter-event to the Communist-backed 8th World Festival of Youth and Students, also in Helsinki. See Werner Wiskari, "American Backs Red Youth Fete; Another Sets Up Rival Exhibit," *New York Times*, July 27, 1962; and Henry Raymont, "A Frigid Finland Scorns a Festival," *Washington Post*, July 31, 1962.
4 "BAQ Interviews Howard Smith," *Black Art: An International Quarterly* 1, no. 2 (Winter 1976): 4.
5 Suomala, *Howard Smith*, 51.
6 "BAQ," 9.
7 "BAQ," 10. Smith was referring to his work for Vallila, but he would also have a productive relationship with the Arabia ceramics manufactory later in his career.
8 Maryann Ondovcsik, "Starting to Finn-ish," *Women's Wear Daily*, June 7, 1977, 28–29.

DESIGN FOR SOCIAL CHANGE

DESIGN FOR THE REAL WORLD: HUMAN ECOLOGY AND SOCIAL CHANGE
Victor Papanek, author
Book, 1971. CAT. 180

MONICA
OBNISKI

DESIGN FOR SOCIAL CHANGE   The turbulent social and political conditions of the late 1960s prompted some designers to think critically about their work and to envision a new role for design within society. American and Nordic designers were at the forefront of discourse on issues of sustainability, ergonomic design, and design for all abilities during this period and the decades that followed. A central figure of the 1960s design counterculture was the polemical Austrian American professor, activist, and writer Victor Papanek, whose book *Design for the Real World* (1971) lambasted consumption-driven design (p. 274).[1] He advocated for the industrial design field to abandon its previous objective of styling products that contributed to planned obsolescence, and instead to focus on environmental and social responsibility. Originally published in Sweden in 1970 as *Miljön och miljonerna: Design som tjänst eller förtjänst?* (The Environment and the Millions: Design as Service or Profit?) (p. 292), the book drew on his participation in the Scandinavian Design Students' Organization (SDO). Papanek's controversial lecture "Do-It-Yourself Murder: Social and Moral Responsibilities of Design," which became a chapter in *Design for the Real World,* was originally published in the 1968 SDO journal & (p. 276).

Papanek began traveling to Finland in 1966, the same year that the SDO was formed.[2] As an alliance of Nordic design students dissatisfied with contemporary education and practice, the SDO desired to create a new social agenda for design. The SDO organized seminars in the Nordic countries that included extensive American participation, with Papanek and inventor and architect R. Buckminster Fuller dominating much of the discourse.[3] The SDO held its first summer seminar in 1967 at Otaniemi, outside of Helsinki. Keynote speakers Kaj Franck, Papanek, and Fuller explicated the seminar's theme, "The Work Environment," and students realized such projects as a floating pavilion and a sauna. Subsequent seminars took on a similar rhythm. The first part of the 1968 seminar was held at Suomenlinna Island (near Helsinki) and featured the topic "Industry—Environment—Product Design," with Papanek, Fuller, architect-theorist Christopher Alexander, and Swedish environmentalist Hans Palmstierna (who was influenced by Rachel Carson's thesis in *Silent Spring* that pesticides have deleterious effects on nature) delivering lectures; it also hosted two hands-on projects: the design of a mobile reindeer slaughterhouse and playground equipment for children with cerebral palsy. Several days later, the group reconvened in Stockholm to discuss the topic "People and the Environment." The final seminar—held in Copenhagen during the summer of 1969—revisited the topic "People and the Environment II." The first iteration of what would become *Big Character Poster No. 1: Work Chart for Designers* emerged from this event (p. 277). Essentially, the poster was an organizational chart

&
Timo Aarniala, cover designer
Journal, no. 2, 1968. CAT. 178

VICTOR PAPANEK
Big Character Poster No. 1: Work Chart
for Designers, 1973 (conceived 1969).
CAT. 112

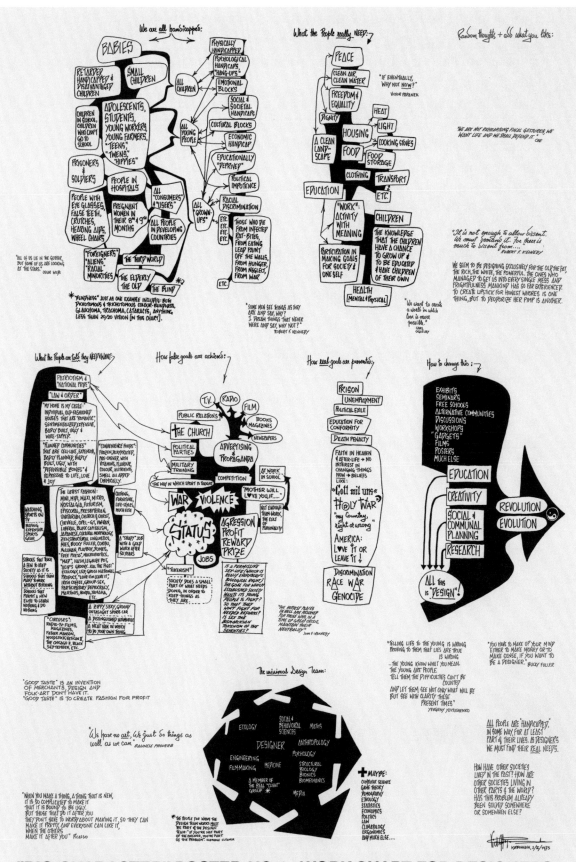

"BIG CHARACTER" POSTER NO. 1: WORK CHART FOR DESIGNERS.

outlining the moral and social duties of designers, and demonstrating how they could be empowered by working within multidisciplinary teams. A revised version of the hand-illustrated diagram, which appeared in *Design for the Real World*, was released in 1973 as a poster, "mark[ing] the beginning of [Papanek's] broader populist activism in the United States" and revealing the transnational exchanges occurring within the global design community.[4]

Through his lengthy lectures and design workshops, Papanek galvanized a generation of design students to apply theory to problems that, up to this point, were not seen as deserving of designers' time. At the first "People and the Environment" seminar, Papanek implored the students to focus on neglected fields of design, such as safety apparatuses and devices for underdeveloped populations, and urged them to employ theory to imagine real-world solutions.[5] One of these overlooked areas—the relationship between disability, safety, and accessibility—was examined at the 1968 Stockholm seminar. A clear manifestation of Papanek's teachings and ideas was the development of the International Symbol of Access (ISA) (below right).[6] The original symbol was developed by Danish student Susanne Koefoed during group work at the seminar (below left). Koefoed conceived the graphic while participating in a Papanek program that encouraged collaboration and design thinking. The symbol was eventually adopted by the nonprofit Rehabilitation International, who modified it to include a circle, turning the image into a person sitting in a wheelchair; this version is still widely used today.[7] Similarly, an interest in ergonomic and accessible design led Maria Benktzon, a student at Stockholm's Konstfack (the University of Arts, Crafts, and Design) during the 1968 summer seminar, to work with designer Sven-Eric Juhlin, beginning in the early 1970s. Together, they produced several products to help the disabled and elderly, with a broader goal of making better products for all users.

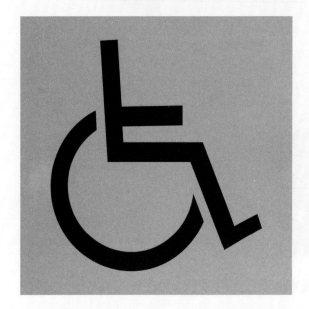

SUSANNE KOEFOED
Access symbol, 1968. CAT. 77

International Symbol of Access (ISA), 1969, designed by Karl Montan for Rehabilitation International.

In the United States, the field of ergonomics emerged from the work of the U.S. military during World War II and sought solutions to user-oriented design problems. Ergonomics found mainstream acceptance through the work of Henry Dreyfuss and his office.[8] Dreyfuss's books *Designing for People* (1955) and *The Measure of Man: Human Factors in Design* (1959) provided designers with information about international standard movements for able-bodied individuals.[9] Dreyfuss's efforts presaged the disability rights movement and related universal design movement that blossomed in the United States during the 1970s.[10] Together with Alvin R. Tilley, Joan Bardagjy, and David Harman, American industrial designer (and Cranbrook graduate) Niels Diffrient worked in Dreyfuss's office and co-authored a revised edition of *The Measure of Man*, called *Humanscale*, which featured a series of rotary selectors and guidebooks to help designers gauge dimensions for product design (pp. 280–81). Unlike earlier manuals that focused on averages in body size and abilities, this tool accommodated a range of bodies, including those in wheelchairs.

Research in disability during this period expanded the profile of some Nordic companies in the United States, including the Finnish firm Fiskars. Its U.S. presence was bolstered when designer Olof Bäckström developed the iconic orange plastic scissors grip in 1967, a breakthrough in ergonomic design (p. 281). In 1977, the company opened a manufacturing plant in Wisconsin to meet American demand for their products. Around this same time, Papanek and James Hennessey collaborated on the book *Nomadic Furniture* (1973), after they met while Hennessey was studying on a Fulbright fellowship to Sweden. Part of Papanek's critique of consumption, *Nomadic Furniture* was a resource for a peripatetic, contemporary lifestyle that embraced conservation of resources and a DIY spirit. This guide to building, adapting, or buying lightweight, portable, ecologically responsible furniture was followed by *Nomadic Furniture 2* a year later. Paramount for such an endeavor was an understanding of human measurement; while the authors suggested Dreyfuss's *The Measure of Man*, they acknowledged that information was lacking for "women, children, babies, the elderly, the obese, and the inhabitants of the so-called 'third world.'"[11] Although the focus of the hand-lettered book was to empower users to build their own furniture, it also suggested some readymade options for purchase, many of them Nordic. Dane Ole Gjerløv-Knudsen's roll-up bed was made of beech dowels and a linen canvas and could be broken down to a fraction of its size for easy transport, making it emblematic of the nomadic lifestyle (p. 291). In addition to noting retailing sources for the bed, the book featured

HUMANSCALE 1/2/3
Niels Diffrient, Alvin R. Tilley,
and Joan C. Bardagjy, authors
Henry Dreyfuss Associates, design firm
Manual and selector, 1974. CAT. 184

HUMANSCALE 4/5/6 and 7/8/9
Niels Diffrient, Alvin R. Tilley,
and David Harman, authors
Henry Dreyfuss Associates, design firm
Manuals and selectors, 1981. CAT. 184

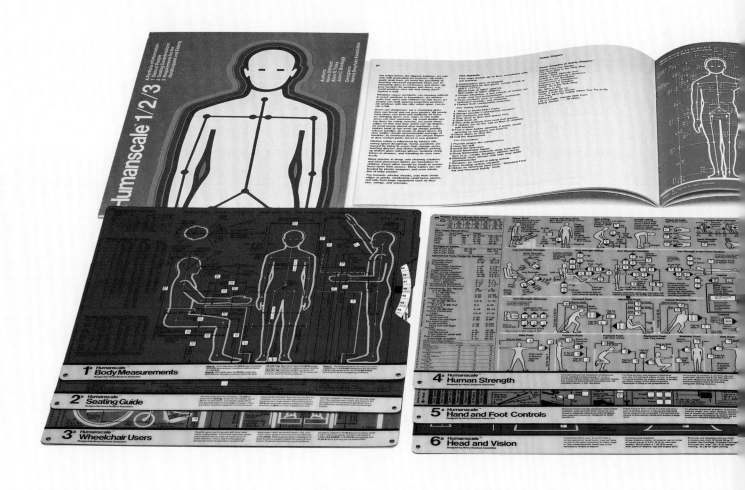

OLOF BÄCKSTRÖM
Fiskars
Scissors, first manufactured 1967.
CAT. 9

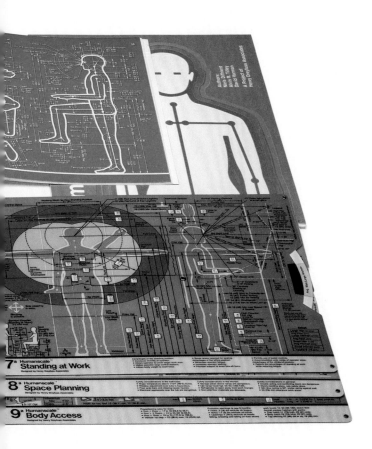

OBNISKI

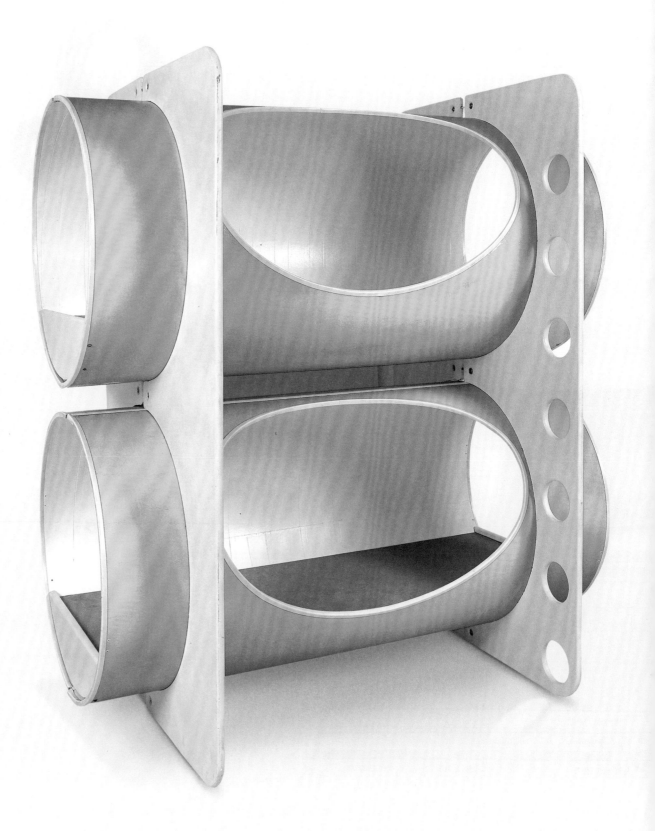

personal anecdotes: "Harlanne (Papanek's wife) & Vic have slept on beds like this in Sweden for four months → they are unbelievably comfortable."[12] They also recommended items by California designers Jim and Penny Hull, who developed a lightweight and inexpensive furnishings line using pre-fabricated fiberboard tubes, including the *BIG TOOBS* beds—a play and sleep environment for children that brought sustainability to the modern bedroom (p. 282).[13]

Mapping out the connections between *Design for the Real World*, *Nomadic Furniture*, and similar publications of the era suggests how concerns regarding topics such as pollution and the environment transcended national borders. For instance, the origins of Papanek's *Design for the Real World* are found in the design activism of late 1960s Scandinavia and Finland;[14] by contrast, in the introduction to *Nomadic Furniture*, Papanek and Hennessey inform readers that their publication aligns more closely with the *Whole Earth Catalog* than the glossy consumer-focused Scandinavian furniture magazine *Mobilia*.

Such progressive publications encouraged an ideology of self-reliance, allowing the individual to take control in environmentally friendly, anticonsumerist ways.[15] The *Whole Earth Catalog* was launched by Stewart Brand in 1968 as a challenge to mainstream society (p. 284). The catalog was published regularly until 1972 and intermittently after that. The *Whole Earth Catalog* embraced the cultures of communes, published essential writings by R. Buckminster Fuller, and suggested ways to save the planet by empowering the user—similar to the approach that Papanek and Hennessey had taken in *Nomadic Furniture*.[16] While the catalog was part of a broader critique of consumerism and late industrial capitalism during the period's social and political upheavals, it also became an American export, when, for example, a countercultural happening nicknamed "Woodstockholm" took place in Stockholm during the 1972 United Nations Conference on the Human Environment. Underscoring the ecological emergency that was engulfing the globe (prefiguring today's environmental and climate crises), the media-savvy Brand recognized the Stockholm conference as an opportunity to showcase the *Whole Earth Catalog*'s ideology to a new, global audience.[17]

Safety was also a concern of the period, and beginning in the postwar years, Swedish automobile manufacturer Volvo became synonymous with safety in the United States. The company's *122S*, first produced in 1956

in Sweden under the model name Amazon and introduced at the 1959 International Auto Show in New York, intentionally emulated American models through styling (p. 286, cat. 172).[18] The car was initially promoted as an elegant yet economical option, but in order to compete in a highly saturated market, Volvo relied on its safety innovations to define its brand identity. Volvo engineer Nils Bohlin designed the three-point seatbelt (a combination lap and chest belt), which became standard for front seats in Amazons for the Swedish market in 1959—a global first.[19] Following additional testing, the belts became standard in U.S. models in 1963.[20]

Given Volvo's reputation for safety innovation, it is unsurprising that the Museum of Modern Art invited the company to participate in a 1976 competition and exhibition called *The Taxi Project: Realistic Solutions for Today*. The museum asked manufacturers to design new prototypes of taxicabs for the American market that were economical, safe, accessible, and environmentally sustainable. The mandate required the participants to consider new standards of safety, comfort of the driver, ability to communicate, and ease of loading and unloading baggage and passengers, including those in wheelchairs.[21] Volvo, which had been committed to responsibly solving urban traffic problems since its involvement in the 1972 UN Conference on the Human Environment in Stockholm, created a prototype with a padded safety bar in lieu of seatbelts, bulletproof partitions, private compartment for the driver that included a refrigerator, and a low entrance allowing wheelchairs to enter the car without the use of ramps (p. 287).[22]

The late 1960s was a watershed moment for many aspects of society, and for some designers, it marked a significant shift for the discipline, as the aims of export and profit were replaced with activism and social change. The debates around consumer and environmental issues took place in the United States and Scandinavia, often collaboratively. While exchanges between these two regions continue to the present day, an accelerated pace of globalism emerged due to shifts in political borders and new technology after 1980, complicating the comparative model and introducing new issues for the design field. Contemporary designers' concern for solving systemic issues and addressing urgent global needs demonstrates the legacy of the late 1960s design critique activated in the United States and the Nordic countries.

OBNISKI

VOLVO
Poster, c. 1976. CAT. 163
This poster relates to Volvo's entry
in the Museum of Modern Art's
exhibition *The Taxi Project: Realistic
Solutions for Today.*

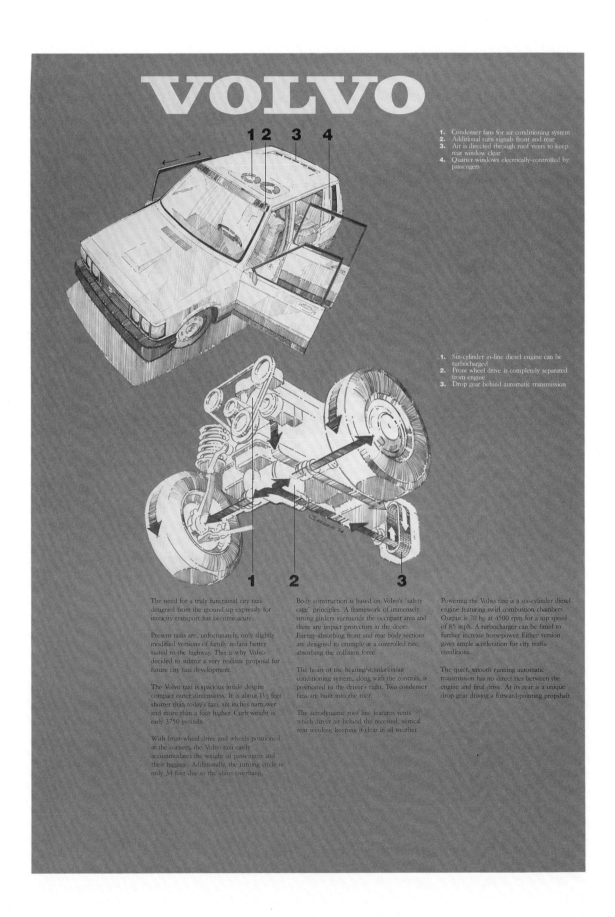

DESIGN FOR SOCIAL CHANGE

1 *Victor Papanek: The Politics of Design,* exh. cat., ed. Mateo Kries, Amelie Klein, and Alison J. Clarke (Weil am Rhein, Germany, and Vienna: Vitra Design Museum and University of Applied Arts Vienna, 2018).

2 Alison J. Clarke, "'Actions Speak Louder': Victor Papanek and the Legacy of Design Activism," *Design and Culture* 5, no. 2 (2013): 158.

3 Ida Kamilla Lie, "'Make Us More Useful to Society!': The Scandinavian Design Students' Organization (SDO) and Socially Responsible Design, 1967–1973," *Design and Culture* 8, no. 3 (2016): 327–61.

4 Clarke, "Actions Speak Louder," 164.

5 Victor Papanek, "Eyes for the Have-Nots," *Sweden Now* 2 (1968): 64.

6 Elizabeth Guffey, "The Scandinavian Roots of the International Symbol of Access," in "The Influence of Scandinavian Design," ed. Bobbye Tigerman, special issue, *Design and Culture* 7, no. 3 (2015): 357–76.

7 More recent developments in the field include the Accessible Icon Project: http://accessibleicon.org.

8 Jeffrey L. Meikle, "American Design History: A Bibliography of Sources and Interpretations," *American Studies International* 23, no. 1 (April 1985): 26.

9 Ellen Lupton, "Designing for People," in *Beautiful Users: Designing for People*, exh. cat. (New York: Cooper Hewitt, Smithsonian Design Museum in association with Princeton Architectural Press, 2014), 24.

10 Bess Williamson, "Getting a Grip: Disability in American Industrial Design of the Late Twentieth Century," *Winterthur Portfolio* 46, no. 4 (Winter 2012): 213–36.

11 James Hennessey and Victor Papanek, *Nomadic Furniture* (New York: Pantheon Books, 1973), 6.

12 Hennessey and Papanek, *Nomadic Furniture*, 101.

13 Alexandra Lange, "Toys as Furniture/Furniture as Toys," in *Serious Play: Design in Midcentury America*, exh. cat., ed. Monica Obniski and Darrin Alfred (New Haven and London: Yale University Press, 2018), 139.

14 Clarke, "Actions Speak Louder."

15 Hennessey and Papanek, *Nomadic Furniture*, 4.

16 For more on the *Whole Earth Catalog*, see *Whole Earth Field Guide*, ed. Caroline Maniaque-Benton with Meredith Gaglio (Cambridge, MA: MIT Press, 2016); Simon Sadler, "An Architecture of the Whole," *Journal of Architectural Education* 61, no. 4 (May 2008): 108–29; Andrew Kirk, *Counterculture Green: The Whole Earth Catalog and American Environmentalism* (Lawrence: University Press of Kansas, 2007); Fred Turner, *From Counterculture to Cyberculture: Stewart Brand, the Whole Earth Network, and the Rise of Digital Utopia* (Chicago: University of Chicago Press, 2006).

17 Felicity D. Scott, *Outlaw Territories: Environments of Insecurity/Architectures of Counterinsurgency* (New York: Zone Books, 2016), 132.

18 The first Volvo introduced to the United States was the *PV444* in 1955; Jeff Werner, "The Advantages of Being Swedish: Volvo in America," in *Scandinavian Design: Alternative Histories*, ed. Kjetil Fallan (Oxford: Berg, 2012), 209.

19 "Nils Bohlin, 82, Inventor of a Better Seat Belt," *New York Times*, September 26, 2002.

20 Richard Dredge, *Volvo Amazon: The Complete Story* (Ramsbury, UK: Crowood Press, 2016), 49.

21 *The Taxi Project: Realistic Solutions for Today*, exh. cat., ed. Emilio Ambasz (New York: Museum of Modern Art, 1976), 16.

22 Ambasz, *The Taxi Project*, 49.

Aspen Comes to Scandinavia

KJETIL FALLAN

Aspen came to Scandinavia in the final week of September 1979. In the history of design, the name of the Colorado town has come to stand for the series of conferences known as the International Design Conference in Aspen (IDCA), held from 1951 to 2004. Although the conference is closely associated with its venue, it traveled on two occasions—to London in 1978 and to Oslo in 1979. These two "Transatlantic Shop Talks," as they were called, were additions to (rather than in lieu of) the annual conferences in Aspen, and brought the IDCA establishment and its agenda in direct dialogue with local design cultures in the United Kingdom and Scandinavia.

Transatlantic exchanges in the realm of design were nothing new in the late 1970s, and a key characteristic of the history of these exchanges is their reciprocal nature. For instance, just as Scandinavian immigrants to the United States brought their visual and material culture along with them, returning migrants—especially those mid-twentieth-century transatlantic "commuters"—carried an impressive array of Americana with them back to their homelands.[1] Reciprocity can also be found in the genealogy of design idioms, such as Shaker furniture as one of the key influences on Danish modern design, the export success of which spawned a massive fashion for American-made, Danish- or Scandinavian-style furniture.[2] Similarly, U.S.–Scandinavian design diplomacy, reaching its zenith in the 1950s, was also a two-way street: while the Museum of Modern Art's *American Design for Home and Decorative Use* exhibition (funded by the United States Information Agency) toured Scandinavia, the equally ambitious and institutionally sanctioned *Design in Scandinavia* toured twenty-four museums across the U.S. and Canada.[3] At the heart of these exchanges were shifting understandings of design's social purpose, ranging from the *fin-de-siècle* notion of "beauty for all"[4] to the efforts toward using design as development aid in the 1960s and 1970s.[5]

Even as the social and environmental costs of consumer society (closely associated in Scandinavia with the United States) became increasingly apparent over the course of the 1960s, with major ramifications for designers' under-standing of their role in society, reciprocal U.S.–Scandinavian design relations flourished. In the realm of counterculture and design activism, Scandinavian design students and professionals found another America beyond both Coca-Cola consumerism and MoMA elitism. At the same time, their U.S. counterparts found another Scandinavia beyond refined teak furniture and supposedly democratic modernism.[6] James Hennessey, a student at the Illinois Institute of Technology in Chicago, traveled to Stockholm on a Fulbright scholarship in 1969, where he met Victor Papanek, beginning a fruitful collaboration that resulted in their two *Nomadic Furniture* books (p. 308), which discuss several

Scandinavian examples such as Ole Gjerløv-Knudsen's roll-up bed (p. 291).[7] At the United Nations Conference on the Human Environment held in Stockholm in June 1972, where Scandinavian designers lobbied inside and design students protested outside, Stewart Brand—editor of the legendary *Whole Earth Catalog*—turned the Swedish capital into "Woodstockholm" by setting up camp with his crew, in effect putting on a countercultural "sideshow" that at times distracted attention from the official conference, but never disrupted the proceedings.[8] The *Whole Earth Catalog* was also a source of inspiration for the landmark *ARARAT* (Alternative Research in Architecture, Resources, Art and Technology) exhibition at Stockholm's Moderna Museet in 1976.[9] But as the momentum of both the counterculture and political activism waned toward the end of the 1970s, the dynamics of U.S.–Scandinavian design relations shifted once again. When Aspen came to Scandinavia in 1979, it was part of an effort to realign interests along vectors of professionalism rather than activism, of problem-solving rather than revolution.

From its inception in 1951, the IDCA established a reputation as a hotspot for the principals of the design world. Backed by industrialist and philanthropist Walter Paepcke and his Aspen Institute (a nonprofit think tank founded in 1949), the IDCA was originally intended as a meeting ground for designers and business managers, but gradually evolved into an arena for exchanges internal to the design professions.[10] Still, this summer retreat for the well-groomed and well-heeled was not entirely cut off from the outside world. The twin forces of environmentalism and counterculture arrived at the IDCA simultaneously, and with considerable force, at the 1970 conference under the heading "Environment by Design." Sim Van der Ryn, the IDCA's countercultural liaison, invited groups such as Ecology Action, Environment Workshop, Farallones Institute, People's Architecture, and Ant Farm to attend the conference. Van der Ryn, a young architect and promoter of ecological design, was on the faculty at the College of Environmental Design at the University of California, Berkeley, and had acted as a liaison in the People's Park protests the preceding year. He succeeded in drumming up a radical attendance for the 1970 conference, where the IDCA got more than they had bargained for. To the organizers, the conference theme referred to the manmade environment as a site for, and product of, design intervention. The countercultural groups and environmental activists, on the other hand, were more concerned with the natural environment as threatened by human activity, including design. The result was a rather chaotic event where the invited groups boycotted the official program, staging instead a series of alternative happenings and performances.[11]

In addition, the specially invited French delegation also decided not to participate productively, restricting its contribution to a statement penned by Jean Baudrillard and read aloud by André Fischer during the closing session. The statement dismissed environmentalism wholesale as a political fad, an ideological smoke screen devised to divert people's attention away from the real problems of society, which, in Baudrillard's neo-Marxist analysis, were defined by capitalism and class conflict.[12] According to Gilles de Bure, another member of the rebellious French delegation, this sentiment resonated with parts of the IDCA establishment. Board member Saul Bass, for instance, "wasn't fooled" by the young environmentalists' insurrection, and declared that "the return to the land is a religious notion. The high priest tells us we are all bastards, but if we plant a tree, we will be pardoned."[13]

The turmoil at the 1970 conference resulted in some soul-searching by the IDCA board. Many felt disillusioned—so much so for Eliot Noyes that he resigned as president then and there—and there were discussions about whether the conference, at least in its current format, had run its course.[14] In the end, though, they decided to give it another chance. For the 1971 event, dubbed "Paradox," convener Richard Farson—founding dean of the newly established School of Design at the California Institute of the Arts (CalArts)—attempted to incorporate some of the radical thrust that had nearly toppled the previous meeting by addressing critical societal issues such as famine and feminism, as well as the (then-topical) quest for augmented consciousness. The choice of R. Buckminster Fuller and Victor Papanek as keynote speakers, as well as the inclusion of progressive feminist graphic designer Sheila Levrant de Bretteville, underlines Farson's effort to accommodate a younger and more radical audience. Papanek's appearance, in particular, speaks to an important Scandinavian influence. His recent, game-changing book, *Design for the Real World*, had largely been the product of his collaborations with Scandinavian design students, and was originally published in Swedish in 1970 under the far more polemical title *Miljön och miljonerna: Design som tjänst eller förtjänst?* (The Environment and the Millions: Design as Service or Profit?) (right).[15] Papanek thus brought a distinctly Scandinavian flavor to his campaign for socially and environmentally responsible design, both in his writings and his teaching, first at Purdue University and then at CalArts, where at the time of his Aspen keynote he had just replaced Farson as dean of the School of Design.[16] Ultimately, though, the aptly named "Paradox" conference exemplified the critique wielded by Jean Baudrillard at the previous event—that the establishment, here represented by the IDCA, will by any means necessary assimilate and incorporate dissenting forces to its own ends.[17] Thus, the institution's annual gathering returned to its former self: an arena for promotion of reformist rather than revolutionary change.[18]

Although the radical sentiment and countercultural activism that characterized the 1970 conference waned over subsequent meetings, the IDCA retained its allure for its primary audience—the international design establishment. Scandinavian delegates kept attending, sampling "this intensive way of meeting colleagues, exchanging ideas and experiences" at what one participant described as

Miljön och miljonerna: Design som tjänst eller förtjänst?, 1970. Victor Papanek, author

an "experiment in community."[19] When designer Hedvig Hedqvist of the Swedish Cooperative Union's textile studio and her husband, film producer Staffan Hedqvist of the Swedish Film Institute, attended the 1971 conference, they felt that the thin mountain air was thick with the aftermath of the previous edition. Although they appreciated Farson's efforts at harnessing some of the radical sentiment that had nearly torn the institution apart, the Swedish attendees were more alienated than impressed, explaining that, "For a European, the programme and the topics and the so-called progressive evaluations presented seemed somewhat naïve. Many of the issues—or, from an American point of view, 'problems'—under debate appear utterly obvious to us."[20] Not even Fuller's marathon lecture on the earth's resources won them over. Despite the revolutionary rhetoric, the Hedqvists concluded that "Revolution in the USA is not the same as in Europe; rather it can be equalled to liberalism."[21] With the political climate in Scandinavia perhaps more radical than ever, such an equation was the biggest paradox of all to the Swedish delegates.

Scandinavian delegates in Aspen lamented the apolitical nature of the discussions in subsequent years. Reflecting on his experiences at the 1973 conference, "Performance," designer and newly elected director of the Svenska Slöjdföreningen (Swedish Society of Crafts and Design) Lennart Lindkvist acknowledged the importance of discussing issues pertaining to "a new global consciousness: environmental destruction, energy crisis and consumption madness, the development of new public transport systems, of new modes of dwelling—of a new quality of life." But, he believed, with the political dimension ignored or suppressed, these debates tended to become toothless: "On these matters, everyone is touchingly in agreement and there are no noticeable conflicts of opinion—often due to a lack of political awareness."[22] The continuing depoliticization of design discourse at Aspen was epitomized by the title of the 1977 conference: "Shop Talk." With establishment figures such as Milton Glaser, George Nelson, and Saul Bass featured on the agenda, the IDCA was firmly back in the fold of corporate America and could focus on talking shop rather than saving the world. It was this iteration of the IDCA that came to Scandinavia two years later—not the countercultural/neo-Marxist rebellion of 1970.

The IDCA board convened in London in March 1978, meeting for the first time outside the United States. The objective was to strengthen ties with British colleagues, and to that end a joint symposium was organized for mutual exchange of ideas and experiences. Gathering three hundred design professionals, "Transatlantic Shop Talk—Aspen Comes to London" became the conceptual blueprint for a similarly motivated and structured event in Oslo the following year entitled "Transatlantic Shop Talk No. 2—Aspen Comes to Scandinavia" (pp. 294–95). Initiated, planned, and convened by the Norwegian Swedish couple Alf Bøe and Ulla Tarras-Wahlberg Bøe—partners both professionally and personally—this event provided the rare opportunity for Scandinavian design professionals to meet with some of their most prominent counterparts from the U.S. The American attendees included major figures like Saul Bass, Ivan Chermayeff, Milton Glaser, and George Nelson.[23] The symposium in Oslo was jointly sponsored by the IDCA and four of the national design organizations in Scandinavia—Dansk Designråd (Danish Design Council); Konstflitföreningen i Finland (Finnish Society of Crafts and Design); Landsforbundet Norsk Brukskunst (National Federation for Norwegian Applied Art); and Föreningen Svensk Form (Swedish Society of Crafts and Design).[24] Immediately following the London event, the Bøes contacted the IDCA with their proposal for a visit to Oslo, which was approved at the organization's board meeting in October 1978.[25]

Art historian Alf Bøe had attended the University of Oxford, where he specialized in the history of Victorian design theory, followed by postgraduate studies at the University of Oslo. Through subsequent appointments at Kunstindustrimuseet i Oslo (Oslo Museum of Decorative Arts), the Norwegian Design Centre, the University of Oslo, and, finally, as director of the City of Oslo Art Collections and the Munch Museum, Bøe was a key player in the organizational life of Norwegian art and design. His extensive professional network was strengthened through his marriage in 1972 to Ulla Tarras-Wahlberg, who was then director of the Svenska Slöjdföreningen. Joining forces, the Bøes were highly experienced and well connected, and few would be better

TST'2

Transatlantic shop Talk No. 2 - Aspen comes to Scandinavia

a two days' design symposium sponsored by
Dansk Designråd/Danish Design Council
Konstflitföreningen i Finland/Finnish Society of Crafts and
Design
Landsforbundet Norsk Brukskunst/Norwegian Society of
Arts and Crafts and Industrial Design
Föreningen Svensk Form/The Swedish Society for Industrial
Design
International Design Conference in Aspen/IDCA

Monday 24 September & Tuesday 25 September 1979
The Munch Museum, Tøyengaten 53, Oslo

Monday 24 September

morning

8.30	Registration of participants Main Hall, The Munch Museum
9.00	Welcome. Alf Bøe introduces today's chairman, the U.S. Ambassador to Norway, Mr. Louis A. Lerner
9.20	Introduction. Richard Farson, President, Board of Directors, International Design Conference in Aspen, IDCA
9.40	Illustrated History of the Aspen Conference Jack Roberts, Past President
10.00	Shop Talk Milton Glaser
11.15	The Swedish «10-gruppen» (Group of 10), designing for the textile industry. Inez Svensson, Stockholm
12.00	The Design Programme of the DSB, Danish State Railways. Jens Nielsen, Copenhagen
12.45	Film: «The Powers of Ten» by Charles & Ray Eames
13.00	Lunch in the museum's restaurant
14.00	Shop Talk Niels Diffrient
15.20	Factory and Office buildings in Finland Matti K. Mäkinen, Helsinki
16.00	Living quarters on off-shore platforms Njål R. Eide, Oslo
16.45	Films
17.00	End of day's programme

evening

19.30 (7.30 p. m.)	Supper, dancing, music etc. in the Munch Museum

Tuesday 25 September

morning

9.00	Wave Energy Projects; River & Harbour Laboratory Knut Bönke, Trondheim
9.45	Shop Talk Moshe Safdie
11.15	Study on the Ergonomics of the Hand Maria Benktzon, Stockholm
11.45	Establishing a glass work-shop in Kenya Mikko Merikallio, Helsinki
12.30	Films
13.00	Lunch in the museum's restaurant
14.00	Shop Talk Saul Bass
15.15	Discussion. Summing-up

During the symposium there will be four discussion facilitators,

Ralph Caplan, IDCA	George Nelson, IDCA
Per Mollerup, Denmark	Ulf Hård af Segerstad, Sweden

Biographies of all speakers will be available at the registration on Monday September 24

Please note the invitation for a reception given by the U. S. Ambassador and Mrs Louis A. Lerner at their residence Nobels gate 28, Oslo on Sunday September 23 at 7.30 p. m.

All participants are welcome

Aspen Comes to Scandinavia

placed to make Aspen come to Scandinavia. The Bøes had developed a close relationship to the IDCA. When they attended the 1978 Aspen conference, "Making Connections," it was on the invitation of board member and graphic designer Ivan Chermayeff.[26] Shortly afterward, in July 1978, Chermayeff and his wife, Jane Clark Chermayeff (director of education at the Cooper-Hewitt Museum in New York), visited the Bøes in Oslo.[27] The Scandinavian couple was subsequently appointed as international advisors to the IDCA Board of Directors.[28] Inspired by the "Japan in Aspen" topic of the 1979 conference, they harbored ambitions of "convincing the board of giving their 1982 conference a purely Scandinavian theme."[29]

Aspen's visit to Scandinavia, then, should be seen not as a singular episode, but as a key event that formed part of a more sustained, international exchange. This is also evident in the Bøes' desire to fund a scholarship allowing two young Norwegian industrial designers to attend the 1980 Aspen conference before assuming internships at New York design consultancies under the auspices of IDCA directors—a plan they proposed to their corporate sponsors following the Oslo symposium.[30] "Our people need to see professionalism on a high level, and in business," Alf Bøe explained.[31] Moreover, Bøe explicitly thought of the Oslo symposium as a way of "strengthening our network for the large Scandinavian design exhibition now being planned," alluding to the *Scandinavian Modern Design: 1880–1980* show opening at the Cooper-Hewitt Museum in New York in 1982.[32]

The symposium took place in Oslo on September 24 and 25, 1979, but the American delegation had arrived in Norway two days prior in Alf Bøe's hometown of Bergen for some acclimatization and sightseeing. Bøe had persuaded the director of the Norwegian State Railways (NSB) to lend them its special conference coach free of charge,[33] allowing the thirty-four American design dignitaries and their hosts to take the scenic route "across misty and snow-swept mountains to Oslo."[34] Aboard the train, Arild Johansen of NSB's design office presented the company's new and comprehensive design program developed under the leadership of industrial designer Odd Thorsen, defining the company's visual identity through logo, color, typography, signage, pictograms, and rolling stock.[35] The seven-hour journey, touted as one of the world's most scenic train rides, also included an IDCA board meeting. Arriving in Oslo the evening before the symposium, the American guests met up with the Scandinavian delegates at a reception hosted by U.S. Ambassador Louis A. Lerner, who also opened and chaired the proceedings the next morning, adding official luster to the event.[36]

The program followed the "shop talk" format of the 1977 conference in Aspen and the 1978 symposium in London. Alf Bøe, who was more interested in the business of culture and the culture of business than in radical politics and counterculture, favored a practice-centered outlook and its commercial context. To him, the "shop talk" entailed an emphasis on "factual information, reciprocal demonstration of work done, or projected. None or very little high-flying theoretical discussions."[37] Despite both his training and trade being steeped in the cultural realm, Bøe's emphasis on the practice- and business-end of design fits well with his longstanding efforts to shift the main thrust of both the professional practice and the public perception of Scandinavian design from the realm of art and culture to that of business and industry. There is thus a clear trajectory running from his legacy as curator at the Oslo Museum of Decorative Arts (where he organized the major 1963 exhibition *Norsk/Norwegian Industrial Design*, which showed the usual suspects—namely, furniture and domestic objects—alongside lawn mowers, echo sounders, chemical toilets, and motor torpedo boats) through his tenure as director of the Norwegian Design Centre (an institution firmly embedded in the political-industrial complex, founded by the Norwegian Export Council and the Federation of Norwegian Industries) to the "Transatlantic Shop Talk" in 1979.[38]

The program consisted of eleven designer presentations, four by American representatives of the IDCA and seven by Nordic designers (p. 295).[39] To avoid monotonous monologues and ensure a spirited exchange, there were four facilitators—two Americans and two Scandinavians: design critic Ralph Caplan and consultant designer George Nelson from the IDCA and Per Mollerup, editor of the Danish design magazine *Mobilia*, and Swedish art historian and design critic Ulf Hård af Segerstad from Scandinavia. They were chosen for their "quick-witted[ness]," and their brief was "to invigorate the discussion and keep it going."[40] In the program, the American presentations are unspecified, referred to only as "Shop Talk," suggesting that the lectures focused on the presenters' own recent projects. First was graphic designer Milton Glaser, followed by industrial designer Niels Diffrient, partner in Henry Dreyfuss Associates, and coauthor of the three-volume ergonomic design manual *Humanscale* (pp. 280–81). The IDCA presenters on day two were Israeli-Canadian architect and urban planner Moshe Safdie and graphic designer Saul Bass. Even if little is known about their lectures, this quartet representing the North American design establishment must have put on an impressive show for their Scandinavian colleagues.[41]

The Scandinavian projects presented between the American shop talks were a disparate assemblage, but in various ways all represented a kind of social responsibility—not the bourgeois "democratic modernism" emblematic of the brand of "Scandinavian Design" that was eagerly and successfully promoted in the United States in the 1950s and 1960s, but a new and more progressive approach to the social potentialities of design. The first presentation was by Inez Svensson of the Stockholm-based textile design collective 10-gruppen, which had been founded in 1970 in response to cutbacks in the traditionally strong and large Swedish textile industry. Svensson had served as chief designer for the Borås Wäfveri textile firm for twelve years following her return to Sweden in 1957 after studies at the School of the Art Institute of Chicago. 10-gruppen's bold, colorful patterns stimulated a new DIY/bricolage design culture, in stark contrast to the refined and harmonious aesthetics of the previous generation (p. 298). Creating their own workplace, the group also aimed to take greater control over all stages of the process from ideation to market, including opening their own retail outlet.[42] As such, 10-gruppen challenged design conventions in the spheres of both production and consumption. Still, they also collaborated with industry (including IKEA), and this was the topic of Svensson's talk in Oslo.

Next was Jens Nielsen, head of design and chief architect for the Danish State Railways (DSB), whose presentation of their design program echoed the more intimate presentation of the equivalent Norwegian scheme the IDCA delegation had heard on the train from Bergen. One of the first of its kind in Europe, the comprehensive and successful DSB design program introduced in 1971 included everything from typography, wayfinding, and color schemes for uniforms, rolling stock, and station buildings.[43] Of course, these programs are examples of corporate design—but the state-ownership and public-service orientation of these companies gave their design programs important civic and social functions. Adhering to the socially responsible corporate theme, Matti K.

TOM HEDQVIST
10-gruppen
The First Collection **poster**, 1972.
Silkscreen, 39 ½ × 28 ⅜ in.
(100.3 × 72.1 cm). Los Angeles County
Museum of Art, Marc Treib Collection,
M.2014.126.155

NJÅL R. EIDE
Drawing for offshore oil rig housing,
1977, from a brochure for the company
VIGORHUS. Courtesy of Norwegian
Petroleum Museum

Mäkinen, chief architect of the Finnish dairy cooperative Valio, talked about his experience designing factory and office buildings. Throughout the twentieth century, the cooperative movement developed as a distinct business model driven by ideological and social motivations, becoming a significant political, economic, and cultural force in Scandinavia—as well as a major player in design history.[44] In this way, co-ops such as Valio and state companies such as DSB are characteristic of the blurred lines and extensive collaborations between the private and public sectors that are central to the "Nordic model"—and presumably unfamiliar to the U.S. delegates in Oslo.

A context more familiar to the Americans was the petroleum industry—a newcomer to Norway following the discovery of vast quantities of oil on the Norwegian continental shelf in 1969. Architect Njål R. Eide presented his designs for living quarters on offshore platforms, a critical and challenging task with little precedent (p. 299). Eide was already firmly embedded in a transatlantic design culture, having worked on the interior design of the Norwegian–America Line's ocean liners *Sagafjord* (1965) and *Vistafjord* (1973). The affinities between luxury liners and utilitarian oil platform living quarters were probably limited, but the Norwegian–American connections were no less prominent in his more recent commission, as U.S. companies were heavily involved in the development of the Norwegian oil industry during the 1970s, providing both financial support and technical expertise. As a prepared response to Eide's presentation, Bøe invited the president of the National Association of Norwegian Architects, Ragnvald Bing Lorentzen, to suggest governmental aesthetic guidelines for offshore installations. According to Lorentzen, this suggestion did not go down well with the Americans: "This is politics," he recalls them shouting, "we do not involve ourselves in politics!"[45] Other Norwegian delegates recall that American participants were reluctant to discuss the environmental and political ramifications of the emerging Norwegian oil industry—and politics in general.[46] This aversion to engaging with the political dimensions of design reflects the experiences of Scandinavian delegates to the Aspen conferences discussed above, and points to a distinct difference between the two design cultures.

If Eide's presentation of design for offshore oil production represented what has since become the inescapable paradox of Norway's image as an environmentally progressive society, the other Norwegian project presented at the seminar showcased a different and much more ecologically sustainable energy technology: wave power. Physicist Knut Bønke of the Norwegian Institute of Technology's River and Harbour Laboratory presented their experiments with power-generating systems made up of numerous small interacting buoys anchored to the ocean floor. These systems were envisioned for operation along the western coast of Norway, where geographic and oceanographic conditions were favorable for this type of experimental energy technology.[47] Both the Norwegian projects presented were typologically far off the beaten track of Scandinavian–American design cultural exchanges. The organizers' highly unconventional choice of ambassadors for Norwegian design is reflected also in their successful recruitment of the Norwegian Ministry of Petroleum and Energy as one of the sponsors for the symposium—a body not typically associated with the design field.[48]

The final two Scandinavian projects presented at the event brought the discussions back onto dry land. Maria Benktzon, a founding partner of Ergonomi Design Gruppen, talked about its study of the ergonomics of the hand (p. 305). The Swedish consultancy, established in 1969, specialized in ergonomic design, and quickly became noted for its pioneering work on utensils for the physically impaired, including kitchen tools and cutlery manufactured by Gustavsberg.[49] With *Humanscale* author Niels Diffrient (who had given his shop talk the previous day) in attendance, it might have been expected that Benktzon's presentation would find a receptive audience—but her own recollection is that her distinctly user-centered approach did not resonate with the U.S. delegation, resulting in the rhetorical question of whether American users existed at all.[50] The final project shared Benktzon's concern for the underprivileged. Supported by the Finnish Society of Crafts and Design, glass artist and scientist Mikko Merikallio set up the Harambee Village Glass Industry in Kenya in 1976 to foster social and economic growth in the region.[51] Merikallio's project was a timely venture and part of a broader international effort to use design expertise as development aid.[52]

What, then, was the outcome of bringing Aspen to Scandinavia? Not surprisingly, the organizers' own official assessment of the symposium was positive: "While the Scandinavian participants were universally impressed by the extremely professional and competent, well-tailored presentations of our U.S. guests, they, on their side, appeared to be impressed by the sense of social responsibility pervading the presentations of many Scandinavian speakers."[53] Not everyone agreed with the Bøes' characterization, however. Interior architect and design critic Trinelise Dysthe's review of the event was also generally positive, but she felt that, measured against the colorful confidence and polished presentations of the American "big shots" (as she called them), the selected Scandinavian projects were too unconventional and thus did not resonate well with the audience.[54]

Architect Peter Butenschøn, who taught urban planning at Arkitekthøgskolen i Oslo (Oslo School of Architecture) and served as editor of *Byggekunst*, was not impressed by the symposium. Butenschøn had studied at Georgia Institute of Technology and Harvard University's Graduate School of Design in the late 1960s before joining the Boston architectural firm Kallmann & McKinnell, and thus had a better understanding of the American design world's elite professional culture than most Scandinavians.[55] He described the IDCA as an institution where "For a week every summer, the stars of the interdisciplinary American design heavens shine their light on visitors and on the grand theme of *design* in today's society."[56] This format did not travel well, at least not to Scandinavia, Butenschøn remarked: "There was jarring music arising in the meeting of the two cultures. In the summer breeze under lofty skies amongst the Aspen mountains, a guru show may provide a dose of enthusiastic inspiration for one's daily work. From the perspective of rigid rows of chairs in a sturdy Norwegian auditorium such a narcissistic elite seems less palatable."[57] To the repatriated Norwegian critic, the visiting American design dignitaries had no purchase on the social responsibility of their vocation. He continued:

The professional debate amongst the U.S design establishment is very different from the Norwegian one. There, one seems more concerned with parading Mies chairs into the boardrooms of banks than with the commodity aesthetics of the consumer society. What was marketed at the Munch Museum by Saul Bass, Moshe Safdie, and others were the familiar ingredients of an elitist commonness: An irreproachable radical rhetoric as wrapping paper for conventional formalistic exclusiveness. Interesting to behold, skillfully performed, but not particularly inspiring or applicable.[58]

But despite his aversion to the glossy, corporate professionalism of the American delegation, Butenschøn was not satisfied with the home team either. In his view, the unconventional choice of projects to represent Norwegian design at the symposium—Eide's oil platform living quarters and Bønke's wave energy research—were too far removed from the profession's mainstream and thus "not particularly reassuring and ingenious as a contrast."[59]

The social commitment characterizing the Scandinavian designers and projects presented to the IDCA community in Oslo may—albeit to varying degrees—have shared values with the student groups at the 1970 Aspen conference. Still, they also represented a type of professionally sanctioned design practice, and in no way resembled the rebellious, antiestablishment design activism imagined by the countercultural protests in Aspen nine years prior, which rallied against the detrimental social and environmental effects of mainstream commercial design. Even if the Aspen that came to Scandinavia in 1979 had by and large reverted to its pre-1970 self in terms of establishment rather than revolutionary values (with the aim of an amicable exchange of professional experience and future collaboration), the event revealed significant cultural discrepancies between American and Scandinavian design cultures. The polished, corporate professionalism displayed by the U.S. delegation provoked suspicion and criticism in their Scandinavian colleagues. Conversely, even if there is no record of the American viewpoint, the non-consumerist, socially responsible approach to design that characterized the bulk of the Scandinavian projects did not seem to resonate with IDCA representatives deeply connected to corporate America. As such, the "Aspen Comes to Scandinavia" symposium was a case of displaced dreams and misplaced means.

FALLAN

1 Jeff Werner, *Medelvägens estetik: Sverigebilder i USA* (Hedemora/Möklinta, Sweden: Gidlunds Förlag, 2008); Siv Ringdal, "110 Volts at Home: The American Lista," ed. and trans. Kjetil Fallan, *Journal of Design History* 27, no. 1 (2014): 79–96.
2 Maggie Taft, "Morphologies and Genealogies: Shaker Furniture and Danish Design," in "The Influence of Scandinavian Design," ed. Bobbye Tigerman, special issue, *Design and Culture* 7, no. 3 (2015): 313–34; Per H. Hansen, *Danish Modern Furniture 1930–2016: The Rise, Decline, and Re-emergence of a Cultural Market Category*, trans. Mark Mussari (Odense, Denmark: University Press of Southern Denmark, 2018), 249–57, 274–301.
3 Kjetil Fallan, "Love and Hate in Industrial Design: Europe's Design Professionals and America in the 1950s," in *The Making of European Consumption: Facing the American Challenge*, ed. Per Lundin and Thomas Kaiserfeld (Basingstoke, UK: Palgrave Macmillan, 2015), 134–56.
4 Ellen Key, *Skönhet för alla: Fyra uppsatser* (Stockholm, 1899). For an English translation, see Ellen Key, "Beauty for All," trans. Michelle Facos, *Art in Translation* 9, no. 4 (2017): 470–85.
5 Kjetil Fallan, "Design Culturing: Making Design History Matter," in *Design Culture: Objects and Approaches*, ed. Guy Julier et al. (London: Bloomsbury Academic, 2019), 19.
6 Ida Kamilla Lie, "'Make Us More Useful to Society!': The Scandinavian Design Students' Organization (SDO) and Socially Responsible Design, 1967–1973," *Design and Culture* 8, no. 3 (2016): 327–61; Elizabeth Guffey, "The Scandinavian Roots of the International Symbol of Access," *Design and Culture* 7, no. 3 (2015): 357–76.
7 James Hennessey and Victor Papanek, *Nomadic Furniture* (New York: Pantheon Books, 1973); James Hennessey and Victor Papanek, *Nomadic Furniture 2* (New York: Pantheon Books, 1974).
8 Felicity D. Scott, *Outlaw Territories: Environments of Insecurity/Architectures of Counterinsurgency* (New York: Zone Books, 2016), 115–66.
9 Christina Pech, *Arkitektur & motstånd: Om sökandet efter alternativ i svensk arkitektur 1970–1980* (Stockholm: Makadam, 2011), 98–131.
10 Alice Twemlow, "I Can't Talk to You If You Say That: An Ideological Collision at the International Design Conference at Aspen, 1970," *Design and Culture* 1, no. 1 (2009): 26–30.

11 Alice Twemlow, "'A Guaranteed Communications Failure': Consensus Meets Conflict at the International Design Conference in Aspen, 1970," in *The Aspen Complex*, ed. Martin Beck (Berlin: Sternberg Press, 2012), 110–35.

12 Felicity D. Scott, *Architecture or Techno-utopia: Politics after Modernism* (Cambridge, MA: MIT Press, 2007), 234–36; Caroline Maniaque-Benton, *French Encounters with the American Counterculture 1960–1980* (Farnham, UK: Ashgate, 2011), 19–20.

13 Gilles de Bure, "Les sommets d'Aspen," *CREE: Créations et Recherches Esthétiques Européennes*, no. 6 (November–December 1970), trans. Patricia Chen, http://www.rosab.net /en/the-aspen-design-conference-1970 /the-summits-of-aspen.html?lang=fr.

14 "Minutes of Meeting of the Board of Directors of the International Design Conference in Aspen, Saturday, June 20, 1970," in Beck, *The Aspen Complex*, 101–9.

15 Victor Papanek, *Miljön och miljonerna: Design som tjänst eller förtjänst?* (Stockholm: Bonniers, 1970); Kjetil Fallan, "'The "Designer"—The 11th Plague': Design Discourse from Consumer Activism to Environmentalism in 1960s Norway," *Design Issues* 27, no. 4 (2011): 41.

16 Alison J. Clarke, "Buckminster Fuller's Reindeer Abattoir and Other Designs for the Real World," in *Hippie Modernism: The Struggle for Utopia*, exh. cat., ed. Andrew Blauvelt (Minneapolis: Walker Art Center, 2015), 75.

17 Twemlow, "A Guaranteed Communications Failure," 126–31.

18 Alice Twemlow, *Sifting the Trash: A History of Design Criticism* (Cambridge, MA: MIT Press, 2017), 134.

19 Lennart Lindkvist, "Rapport utifrån 1," *Form*, no. 10 (1973): 386. All translations by the author unless otherwise specified.

20 Hedvig Hedqvist and Staffan Hedqvist, "Paradox i Aspen," *Form*, no. 7 (1971): 298.

21 Hedqvist and Hedqvist, "Paradox i Aspen," 298.

22 Lennart Lindkvist, "70-talets designideologi," *Form*, no. 1 (1974): 1.

23 "Transatlantic Shop Talk No. 2—Aspen Comes to Scandinavia. List of Participants," document from the private archive of Ulla Tarras-Wahlberg Bøe (hereafter Bøe archive), author's collection.

24 The Swedish organization was renamed from Svenska Slöjdföreningen to Föreningen Svensk Form in 1976. Although the name was translated as the Swedish Society for Industrial Design in the English-language symposium program, this is somewhat misleading, and I have for reasons of consistency chosen to use its current official English name, the Swedish Society of Crafts and Design, throughout.

25 "Amerikansk/skandinavisk designsymposium, Oslo September 1979," undated and unsigned draft by Ulla Tarras-Wahlberg Bøe and Alf Bøe, Bøe archive, author's collection.

26 Ivan Chermayeff to Alf Bøe and Ulla Tarras-Wahlberg Bøe, telegram, February 22, 1978, Bøe archive, author's collection.

27 Alf Bøe to Jane Clark Chermayeff and Ivan Chermayeff, June 3, 1978, Bøe archive, author's collection.

28 IDCA President Julian Breinart to Alf Bøe and Ulla Tarras-Wahlberg Bøe, August 25, 1982, Bøe archive, author's collection.

29 Alf Bøe to Byråsjef Chris Prebensen, Kulturkontoret, Det kgl, utenriksdepartement, August 29, 1979, Bøe archive, author's collection.

30 Template letter from Alf Bøe and Ulla Tarras-Wahlberg Bøe to various corporate sponsors, "Innbetaling av garantisum—Eventuelt bidrag til stipendier," November 12, 1979, Bøe archive, author's collection.

31 Alf Bøe to U.S. Ambassador Louis A. Lerner, October 16, 1979, Bøe archive, author's collection.

32 Alf Bøe to Grete Prytz Kittelsen, August 8, 1979, Bøe archive, author's collection.

33 Einar Schiong, Generaldirektørens kontor, Norges Statsbaner, to Alf Bøe, "Skandinavisk/amerikansk designkonferanse 1979—Bruk av NSB's konferansevogn Bergen–Oslo," January 17, 1979; Alf Bøe to Jernbanedirektør Knut Skuland, NSB, October 1, 1979, Bøe archive, author's collection.

34 Ulla Tarras-Wahlberg Bøe and Alf Bøe, "Report from Symposium 'Aspen comes to Scandinavia—Transatlantic Shop Talk II,'" draft report dated September 1979, Bøe archive, author's collection.

35 Odd Thorsen, "Design i NSB," *Byggekunst*, no. 5 (1979): 363–65.

36 Bøe and Bøe, "Report from Symposium."

37 Alf Bøe, "Aspen Comes to Oslo: An American/Scandinavian Design Conference," memorandum dated July 17, 1978, Bøe archive, author's collection.

38 Alf Bøe, ed., *Norsk/Norwegian Industrial Design* (Oslo: Kunstindustrimuseet i Oslo/Johan Grundt Tanum forlag, 1963); Alf Bøe, *The Norwegian Design Award: Its First Seven Years* (Oslo: Norwegian Design Centre, 1969); Kjetil Fallan, *Designing Modern Norway: A History of Design Discourse* (London: Routledge, 2017), 135–52.

39 Each Nordic country was represented by two designers, except Denmark, which had only one; "Transatlantic Shop Talk No. 2—Aspen comes to Scandinavia," seminar program, Bøe archive, author's collection.

40 Alf Bøe to Niels Diffrient, July 4, 1979, Bøe archive, author's collection.

41 Ulf Hård af Segerstad, "Telefon som äppelmunk," *Svenska Dagbladet*, October 2, 1979.

42 Lasse Brunnström, *Swedish Design: A History* (London: Bloomsbury, 2019), 164–65.

43 Lars Dybdahl, *Dansk Design 1945–1975: Produktdesign, Grafisk Design, Møbeldesign* (Copenhagen: Borgen, 2006), 312–15.

44 See, for example, Helena Mattsson, "Designing the 'Consumer in Infinity': The Swedish Cooperative Union's New Consumer Policy, c. 1970," in *Scandinavian Design: Alternative Histories*, ed. Kjetil Fallan (London: Berg, 2012), 65–82; and Per H. Hansen, *En lys og lykkelig fremtid: Historien om FDB-møbler* (Copenhagen: Strandberg, 2014).

45 Ragnvald Bing Lorentzen, communication with author, November 16, 2017.

46 Jan Jeppe Gauguin, communication with author, November 16, 2017; Benedicte Aars-Nicolaysen, communication with author, November 17, 2017.

47 See, for example, Charles Simeons, *Hydro-Power: The Use of Water as an Alternative Source of Energy* (Oxford: Pergamon Press, 1980), 68–70.

48 Alf Bøe to Minister of Petroleum and Energy Bjartmar Gjerde, August 30, 1979, Bøe archive, author's collection.

49 Lasse Brunnström, "Hjälpmedel för ett säkrare och jämlikare liv," in *Svensk industridesign: En 1900-talshistoria*, ed. Lasse Brunnström, 2nd ed. (Stockholm: Prisma, 2004), 317.

50 Maria Benktzon, communication with author, November 16, 2017.

51 Albert Lewis, "Harambee," *Glass Art* 4, no. 5 (1975): 16.

52 Merikallio's project was established the same year that the International Council of Societies of Industrial Design (ICSID) organized the symposium "Design for Need" in London, and was presented in Oslo the same year that ICSID teamed up with the United Nations Industrial Development Organization (UNIDO) for a congress in India on "Design for Development" and the ensuing Ahmedabad Declaration on Industrial Design for Development. See Julian Bicknell and Liz McQuiston, eds., *Design for Need: The Social Contribution of Design* (London: Pergamon, 1977); Singanapalli Balaram, "Design in India: The Importance of the Ahmedabad Declaration," *Design Issues* 25, no. 4 (2009): 54–79; and Alison J. Clarke, "Design for Development, ICSID and UNIDO: The Anthropological Turn in 1970s Design," *Journal of Design History* 29, no. 1 (2016): 43–57.

53 Bøe and Bøe, "Report from Symposium."

54 Trinelise Dysthe, "Design—en viktig del av miljøet," *Aftenposten*, October 30, 1979, 5.

55 *Norsk biografisk leksikon*, s.v. "Peter Butenschøn," by Ulf Grønvold, published September 29, 2014 , https: //nbl.snl.no/Peter_Butensch%C3%B8n.

56 Peter Butenschøn, "Amerikansk design på avveie," *Byggekunst*, no. 5 (1979): 369, italics in original.

57 Butenschøn, "Amerikansk design på avveie."

58 Butenschøn, "Amerikansk design på avveie."

59 Butenschøn, "Amerikansk design på avveie."

MARIA BENKTZON AND SVEN-ERIC JUHLIN

Designing for Independence

CARA MCCARTY

The pioneering work of Swedish industrial designers Maria Benktzon and Sven-Eric Juhlin was shaped by the activism and idealism that characterized socially responsible thinking in the 1960s. Most significantly, the new standards of function and aesthetics they developed for products made for people with disabilities and older adults helped shift the discourse from disability to ability. Juhlin's background was in industrial design, silver, and sculpture at Konstfack (the University of Arts, Crafts, and Design) in Stockholm, where he graduated in 1967. Benktzon studied at Konstfack from 1965 to 1969, initially focusing on textiles and fashion. But in 1968, she redirected her interests to designing for children with disabilities after participating in a Scandinavian Design Students' Organization (SDO) seminar.[1] She was especially inspired by design activist Victor Papanek,[2] whose advocacy for design as a force for social good "was an eye opener" that motivated her "to change the world, not just keep making things in the same way as previously."[3]

A formative influence on their work was Finnish industrial designer Henrik Wahlforss. Wahlforss laid much of the groundwork for Sweden's design innovations during the 1970s and 1980s, including work with occupational health and disability issues (with Per Uddén he designed the first electric wheelchairs for Permobil). Until the late 1960s, most assistive devices for people with disabilities were makeshift, one-of-a-kind items, created by occupational therapists or family members, and their clinical appearances often stigmatized their users. Benktzon and Juhlin recognized the lack of design in this area and saw the potential for creating aesthetically appealing, unobtrusive products.

MARIA BENKTZON
SVEN-ERIC JUHLIN
Ergonomi Design
Kitchen knife and cutting board,
designed 1973, produced 1974.
CAT. 10

For Benktzon, "aesthetics were the starting point, and then they became more involved in the physical aspects to make it function for diverse user needs."[4] According to Benktzon, this type of work was already being done in the United States and Great Britain, but conditions in Sweden had become ripe to support the effort. In 1972, Swedish distributor RFSU Rehab (now Etac) was founded to create new types of technical aids for older adults and people with disabilities, and the recently created Swedish Handicap Institute and the Swedish National Board for Technical Development were providing research development funds.[5]

Benktzon and Juhlin are perhaps best known for their series of eating and drinking implements for people with weakened hands (cat. 11). In 1971 they launched their career-long collaboration with a major grip and handle study, a project initiated by Wahlforss when Juhlin was working in the plastics department at AB Gustavsberg. Wahlforss and Juhlin had already designed the first advanced gripping tongs together in collaboration with male wheelchair users. Observing that the tongs' grip was too large for most women's smaller hands, Benktzon realized the importance of including the user throughout the entire process, designing *with* them, not just *for* them. This led to the subsequent study of grips and handles. Benktzon and Juhlin met with thirty individuals in their homes, where they conducted interviews and observed them engaging in their daily activities. They applied ergonomics research to create prototype products with wooden grips that directed the hand to grasp an object more effectively. One result was an entirely new kitchen knife and cutting board (p. 305). Used like a saw, the knife has an angled, vertical handle grip and large blade that is easily controlled. The accompanying cutting board is partitioned to safely guide the knife. Benktzon and Juhlin continued to study grip and movement patterns in their subsequent projects.[6]

The user-centered methodology that Benktzon and Juhlin practiced was the core philosophy of Ergonomi Design Gruppen, the collective where they worked for most of their careers.[7] In designing attractive, mass-produced useful objects for everyday life, their greatest impact has been to shift the emphasis on what people can do, rather than on what they cannot. Benktzon and Juhlin were early leaders of an inclusive design movement that has helped to give independence, dignity, and access to people whose needs were previously little understood and had been inadequately addressed.

1 Ida Kamilla Lie, "'Make Us More Useful to Society!': The Scandinavian Design Students' Organization (SDO) and Socially Responsible Design, 1967–1973," *Design and Culture* 8, no. 3 (2016): 327–61.
2 The first edition of Victor Papanek's provocative manifesto on socially responsible design, *Design for the Real World*, was published in Sweden in 1970 under the title *Miljön och miljonerna: Design som tjänst eller förtjänst?* (The Environment and the Millions: Design as Service or Profit?) (see p. 292).
3 Maria Benktzon, phone interview with author, February 11, 2019.
4 Benktzon interview.
5 Benktzon interview.
6 Maria Benktzon, "Designing for Our Future Selves: The Swedish Experience," *Applied Ergonomics* 24, no. 1 (February 1993): 19–27.
7 Henrik Wahlforss's company Ergonomi Design AB (founded 1970) moved in 1974 to Designgruppen's office (founded in 1969 by a group of designers that included Benktzon and Juhlin) and began collaborating. The two companies merged in 1979 to become Ergonomi Design Gruppen, a collective founded by the employees of both companies, including Maria Benktzon and Sven-Eric Juhlin. In 2001, it was renamed Ergonomidesign, and in 2012 it became Veryday; Maria Benktzon, email message to author, April 8, 2019.

JAMES HENNESSEY

To Sweden and Back

DANIELLE CHARLAP

U.S.–Scandinavian connections are sometimes a matter of chance—or so recalls designer James Hennessey. Hennessey was studying product design at the Illinois Institute of Technology in the late 1960s when he met visiting Swedish designer Krister Karlmark, who helped him apply for a Fulbright to attend Stockholm's Konstfack (the University of Arts, Crafts, and Design).[1] In the fall of 1969, Hennessey arrived in Sweden, a move that inspired a career-long interest in "products with minimal technology yet high functionality."[2] There, Hennessey also met Austrian American designer Victor Papanek.

By the time they crossed paths, Papanek had already developed a reputation as a polemical designer and critic. Papanek's visits to Scandinavia as a lecturer in the late 1960s and 1970s shaped his commitment to designing for need.[3] At the collaborative, socially minded Scandinavian Design Students' Organization (SDO) conferences (1967–69), his hands-on workshops emphasized interdisciplinary problem-solving and quick prototyping. Following his positive reception at the SDO conferences, Papanek was invited in January 1970 to Konstfack's metal department, where he oversaw a two-week workshop attended by Hennessey.[4] Hennessey's designs clearly impressed Papanek; tasked with creating a manual-powered transportation device, Hennessey and fellow visiting student Tillman

Fuchs designed a two-person, pedal-powered vehicle, which Papanek included in his book *Design for the Real World*.[5] Hennessey and Fuchs also won a Gustavsbergs Fabriker design challenge in 1970 with their *Fem Hörn* (five corner) vase created for hospitals, with a wavy-edged lip allowing for better drainage when turned upside down to dry.[6]

In the fall of 1970, Papanek and Hennessey independently moved to the California Institute of the Arts in Valencia. Papanek came as a professor (becoming dean in 1971), while Hennessey arrived as a graduate student, followed by appointments as assistant to the dean and assistant dean. Together they taught a summer course in 1972 that served as the impetus for their 1973 book, *Nomadic Furniture* (p. 308). Inspired by their students' often-changing living situations, and bolstered by the claim that Americans moved every two to three years on average, the book showcased lightweight furniture "that is easy to make, but… also folds, inflates, or knocks down or else is disposable while being ecologically responsible."[7] Papanek composed the handwritten text, while Hennessey drew and prototyped most of the designs, many of them based on their students' creations.[8]

A combination instruction manual and catalog showcasing items for purchase, *Nomadic Furniture* reflected broader counter-cultural impulses of the period. Its informal

NOMADIC FURNITURE
James Hennessey, author and illustrator
Victor Papanek, author and letterer
Book, 1973. CAT. 186

James Hennessey and his son Michael
sitting on "two-way chairs," based
on a design from *Nomadic Furniture 2*,
Saugus, California, 1974

CHARLAP

308

mixture of texts, drawings, and photos was similar to the watershed 1968 *Whole Earth Catalog* (p. 284). And while the title *Nomadic Furniture* romanticized a peripatetic life-style, the book's focus on the do-it-yourself ethos served as anticonsumerist critique.[9] Even when featuring commercially available products, the duo did not necessarily endorse buying them, instead sometimes offering Hennessey-designed adaptations to be repli-cated at home.[10] The book included several Scandinavian designs, such as Ole Gjerløv-Knudsen's roll-up bed (p. 291).

For Hennessey, the need for simple, easy-to-assemble, affordable furniture was not a theoretical one. By 1973, he and his wife, Sara, had moved five times in two years, followed by faculty appointments at the Rochester Institute of Technology, the University of Washington, and the Delft University of Technology in the Netherlands.[11] While in Delft, Hennessey directed research on user-interface design, with a focus on gestural control and screen manipulation, a substantial shift from his first time living abroad in Sweden.[12]

1 James Hennessey, conversation with author, November 6, 2018.
2 Hennessey, email message to author, December 16, 2018.
3 Alison J. Clarke, "'Actions Speak Louder': Victor Papanek and the Legacy of Design Activism," *Design and Culture* 5, no. 2 (2013): 151–68; Ida Kamilla Lie, "'Make Us More Useful to Society!': The Scandinavian Design Students' Organization (SDO) and Socially Responsible Design, 1967–1973," *Design and Culture* 8, no. 3 (2016): 327–61.
4 Lie, "Make Us More Useful," 351.
5 Victor Papanek, *Design for the Real World: Human Ecology and Social Change* (New York: Pantheon Books, 1971), 172.
6 Hennessey, conversation with author, November 6, 2018.
7 James Hennessey and Victor Papanek, *Nomadic Furniture* (New York: Pantheon Books, 1973), 1–2.
8 "Furniture on the Move: Martina Fineder Speaks with James Hennessey," *Mak/Zine* 1 (2013): 9–16.
9 Martina Fineder, Thomas Geisler, and Sebastian Hackenschmidt, "Nomadic Furniture—Does it Even Exist?," *Nomadic Furniture 3.0*, MAK Studies 23 (Zurich: Niggli, 2017), 22–45.
10 The popularity of *Nomadic Furniture* led to *Nomadic Furniture 2* (New York: Pantheon Books, 1974), and *How Things Don't Work* (New York: Pantheon Books, 1977), both coauthored by Papanek and Hennessey. Hennessey also published *The Nomadic Handbook* (New York: Pantheon Books, 1979), a how-to guide for packing, moving, and buying a home.
11 "Furniture on the Move," 10; Hennessey, email message to author, December 16, 2018.
12 Hennessey, email message to author, December 16, 2018.

JENS H. QUISTGAARD
Dansk Designs
Ice bucket, designed 1958. CAT. 119

CHECKLIST OF THE EXHIBITION

Danielle Charlap, Hannah Pivo, Monica Obniski, and Bobbye Tigerman

This checklist reflects the presentations at the Milwaukee Art Museum and the Los Angeles County Museum of Art. Unless otherwise noted, a name in uppercase letters indicates a designer, and any subsequent name indicates the maker or manufacturer of the object. Italicized titles indicate those originally conferred by the designer, while titles in quotation marks are later nicknames. Unless otherwise noted, the date is the date of design and fabrication. Height precedes width precedes depth. Dimensions for works on paper refer to the size of the sheet.

The checklist is accurate as of October 2019.

ALVAR AALTO (Finland, 1898–1976)
Huonekalu-ja Rakennustyötehdas (Finland)
1 | **Armchair,** model 41, designed 1931–32, this example 1930s
Birch
26 × 23¾ × 34½ in. (66 × 60.3 × 87.6 cm)
Los Angeles County Museum of Art, Gift of the 2015 Decorative Arts and Design Acquisition Committee (DA²), M.2015.93

Karhula-Iittala Glassworks (Finland)
2 | **"Savoy" vase,** designed 1936, this example late 1930s
Glass
5⅞ × 11⅛ × 9½ in. (14.9 × 28.3 × 24.1 cm)
Cooper Hewitt, Smithsonian Design Museum, Gift of Harmon Goldstone, 1990-61-2
P. 122

ANCHOR HOCKING GLASS CORPORATION (United States)
3 | *Swedish Modern* **mixing bowls,** designed c. 1957
Glass
Largest bowl: 4½ × 8¾ × 11 in. (11.4 × 22.2 × 27.9 cm)
Private collection
P. 79

JENS ANDREASEN (Denmark, 1924–1996)
4 | **Necklace,** 1960
Gold, turquoise
7¼ × 7¼ × ¼ in. (18.4 × 18.4 × 0.6 cm)
Exhibited in *The Arts of Denmark: Viking to Modern,* Metropolitan Museum of Art and other venues, 1960–61
The Metropolitan Museum of Art, Purchase Edward C. Moore, Jr. Gift, 1961 (61.7.7)
PP. 7 (detail), 158

IB ANTONI (Denmark, 1929–1973)
Vang Rasmussen (Denmark), client
5 | *Denmark: Famous for Fine Furniture* **poster,** designed 1964
Offset lithography
39½ × 24¾ in. (100.3 × 62.9 cm)
Same design exhibited at New York World's Fair, 1964
Milwaukee Public Library
P. 21

ARABIA (Finland)
6 | *Fennia* **vase,** designed c. 1902
Earthenware
13⅞ × 3⅞ × 3⅞ in. (35.2 × 9.8 × 9.8 cm)
Los Angeles County Museum of Art, Gift of Margaret and Joel F. Chen through the 2018 Decorative Arts and Design Acquisition Committee (DA²), M.2018.122
P. 23

ARNSTEIN ARNEBERG (Norway, 1882–1961)
7 | **Drawing of the United Nations Security Council Chamber,** c. 1949
Digital facsimile
18¹¹⁄₁₆ × 34¹⁵⁄₁₆ in. (47.5 × 88.7 cm)
National Museum of Art, Architecture and Design, Oslo, Norway
P. 131

8 | **Drawing of the United Nations Security Council Chamber,** c. 1949
Digital facsimile
18 × 34 in. (45.8 × 86.6 cm)
National Museum of Art, Architecture and Design, Oslo, Norway
P. 131

OLOF BÄCKSTRÖM (Finland, 1922–1998)
Fiskars (Finland)
9 | **Scissors,** first manufactured 1967
Plastic, stainless steel
8½ × 3 × 1 in. (21.6 × 7.6 × 2.5 cm)
Design Museum Helsinki
P. 281

MARIA BENKTZON (Sweden, born 1946)
SVEN-ERIC JUHLIN (Sweden, born 1940)
Ergonomi Design (Sweden), design firm
Gustavsberg (Sweden), manufacturer
10 | **Kitchen knife and cutting board,** designed 1973, produced 1974
Stainless steel, plastic
Knife: 4³⁄₁₆ × 13¹³⁄₃₂ in. (10.3 × 34 cm)
Nationalmuseum Sweden
P. 305

MARIA BENKTZON (Sweden, born 1946)
SVEN-ERIC JUHLIN (Sweden, born 1940)
Ergonomi Design (Sweden), design firm
RFSU Rehab (Sweden), manufacturer
11 | *Eat and Drink* **flatware, plate, mug, and goblet,** designed 1978
Stainless steel, plastic
Knife/fork: ¾ × 7¼ × 1¼ in. (1.9 × 18.4 × 3.2 cm)
Goblet: 6½ × 3⁵⁄₁₆ × 3⁵⁄₁₆ in. (16.7 × 8.4 × 8.4 cm)
Nationalmuseum Sweden

GERHARD BERG (Norway, born 1927)
12 | **Chair,** 1957–58
Fiberglass, metal, plastic
28¾ × 25⁹⁄₁₆ × 28¾ in. (73 × 65 × 73 cm)
National Museum of Art, Architecture and Design, Oslo, Norway

PETER BERG (born Norway, 1885–1959, active United States), designer (attributed)
YNGVE OLSSON (born Denmark, 1896–1970, active United States), chaser
Kalo Shop (United States)
13 | **Candelabra,** 1920–21
Silver
Each candelabrum: 15¾ × 10⅞ × 11 in. (38.1 × 25.4 × 27.9 cm)
The Art Institute of Chicago, Wesley M. Dixon, Jr. Endowment Fund, 1990.104.1–2
P. 50

SIGVARD BERNADOTTE
(Sweden, 1907–2002)
Georg Jensen Silversmithy (Denmark)
14 | **Urn,** 1939
Silver
12⅛ × 5 × 5 in. (30.8 × 12.7 × 12.7 cm)
Inscription: PRESIDENT FRANKLIN D ROOSEVELT AND MRS ROOSEVELT IN REMEMBRANCE OF OUR VISIT TO THE UNITED STATES • 1939 •
Gift of Crown Prince Frederik and Princess Ingrid of Denmark to President Franklin D. Roosevelt and Eleanor Roosevelt
Franklin D. Roosevelt Presidential Library and Museum, Hyde Park, NY

HARRY BERTOIA (born Italy, 1915–1978, active United States)
15 | **Necklace,** c. 1942–43
Brass
Choker circumference: 5¾ in. (14.6 cm)
Pendants, each approx.: 3½ × 2¼ × ⅛ in. (8.9 × 5.7 × 0.3 cm)
Cranbrook Art Museum

KAY BOJESEN (Denmark, 1886–1958)

16 | **Monkey toys**, designed 1951,
these examples 1955
Teak, limba, ebony
Height: 5½ in. (13 cm)
Purchased at Kay Bojesen's workshop,
Copenhagen, 1955
Collection of Forrest L. Merrill
P. 76

AMELIA HYDE CENTER

(United States, 1854–1918)
Pauline Fjelde (born Norway, 1861–1923, active
United States), seamstress and embroiderer
Thomane Fjelde Hansen (born Norway, 1871–1935,
active United States), seamstress
and embroiderer

17 | **Minnesota state flag**, 1893
Silk
Approx. 67 × 76 in. (170.2 × 193 cm)
Exhibited in the Women's Building,
World's Columbian Exposition,
Chicago, 1893
From the Collections of the Minnesota
Historical Society
P. 202

HANS CHRISTENSEN (born Denmark,
1924–1983, active United States)

18 | **Coffeepot**, designed c. 1956,
this example c. 1960
Silver, rosewood
9⅝ × 6⅝ × 5½ in. (24.5 × 16.8 × 14 cm)
Yale University Art Gallery, American Arts
Purchase Fund, 1978.90
P. 194

GODTFRED KIRK CHRISTIANSEN

(Denmark, 1920–1995)
LEGO (Denmark), design firm
Samsonite (United States), manufacturer

19 | **Town-Plan**, model 725, designed 1961
Cardboard, plastic
Box: 3¼ × 20¾ × 16½ in.
(8.3 × 52.7 × 41.9 cm)
Private collection
P. 109

VIOLET CHRISTOPHERSEN

(United States, 1900–1992)

20 | **Platter**, 1976
Wood, paint
14¼ ×16¾ × ¾ in. (36.2 × 42.6 × 1.9 cm)
Inscription: NORSE / Immigrant / 1825
Sesquecentennial 1975 / 1776 Bicentennial
1976 / USA
Vesterheim Norwegian-American Museum
P. 34

MARGRET CRAVER (United States, 1907–2010)

21 | **Bonbonnière**, 1938
Silver, enamel
2¾ × 5¼ × 5¼ in. (5.7 × 13.4 × 13.4 cm)
The Art Institute of Chicago, Americana
Endowment Fund, 1985.516a–b
P. 195

THOMAS DAM (Denmark, 1915–1989)
Dam Things Establishment (Denmark)

22 | **Dammit troll doll**, this example
manufactured c. 1963
Rubber, felt, wool
9½ × 8 × 4 in. (24.1 × 20.3 × 10.2 cm)
Patricia K. Jeys, Estate of Betty J. Miller
PP. 115, 336

INGRID DESSAU (Sweden, 1923–2000)
Kristianstad County Handicraft Society (Sweden)

23 | *Manhattan* hanging, 1953
Linen, wool
93¹¹⁄₁₆ × 59¹⁄₁₆ in. (238 × 150 cm)
Nationalmuseum Sweden
P. 237

CHARLES EAMES (United States, 1907–1978)
RAY EAMES (United States, 1912–1988)
Eames Office (United States), design firm
Molded Plywood Division, Evans Products
Company (United States), manufacturer
Herman Miller Furniture Company
(United States), distributor

24 | *DCW (Dining Chair Wood)*, designed 1946
Birch plywood, rubber, steel
29½ × 19¼ × 21½ in. (74.9 × 48.9 × 54.6 cm)
Milwaukee Art Museum, Gift of Kenneth
and James Kurtz, M1976.66
MAM only

Eames Office (United States), design firm
Molded Plywood Division, Evans Products
Company (United States), manufacturer
Herman Miller Furniture Company
(United States), distributor

25 | *DCW (Dining Chair Wood)*, designed 1946,
this example 1946–49
Rosewood, rubber, steel
29 × 19½ × 22 in. (73.7 × 49.5 × 55.9 cm)
Los Angeles County Museum of Art,
Decorative Arts and Design Council Fund,
M.2008.290.3
LACMA only

Eames Office (United States), design firm
Herman Miller Furniture Company
(United States), manufacturer

26 | *DAR (Dining Armchair Wire Base)*,
designed 1948–50
Fiberglass, steel, rubber
31⅛ × 24 × 18½ in. (79.1 × 61 × 47 cm)
Similar example exhibited in *American
Design for Home and Decorative Use*,
multiple Nordic venues, 1953–55
Milwaukee Art Museum, Gift of Mordecai
Kamesar Lee and Riva Lee Nolley from
the collection of their mother, Bernice
Kamesar Lee, M2013.68
MAM only

Eames Office (United States), design firm
Herman Miller Furniture Company
(United States), manufacturer

27 | *DAX (Dining Armchair X-base)*,
designed 1948–50, this example c. 1951–52
Fiberglass, steel, rubber
31½ × 25 × 23 in. (80 × 63.5 × 58.4 cm)
Similar example exhibited in *American
Design for Home and Decorative Use*,
multiple Nordic venues, 1953–55
Los Angeles County Museum of Art,
purchased with funds provided by Alice
and Nahum Lainer, M.2010.13
LACMA only
P. 188

CHARLES EAMES (United States, 1907–1978)
EERO SAARINEN (born Finland, 1910–1961,
active United States)
Marli Ehrman (born Germany, 1904–1982,
active United States), textile designer
Haskelite Manufacturing Corporation
(United States), manufacturer
Heywood-Wakefield Corporation
(United States), textile manufacturer

28 | **Chair**, 1940
Mahogany, wool (replaced)
32½ × 18 × 22 in. (82.6 × 45.7 × 55.9 cm)
Exhibited in *Organic Design in Home
Furnishings*, Museum of Modern Art,
New York, 1941
Los Angeles County Museum of Art,
Decorative Arts and Design Council Fund,
M.2008.290.1
P. 188

ROBERT EBENDORF (United States,
born 1938)

29 | **Coffeepot**, 1963–64
Silver, ebony
8 × 5 × 7⅝ in. (20.3 × 12.7 × 19.4 cm)
Yale University Art Gallery, American Arts
Purchase Fund, 1978.81
P. 255

ALMA EIKERMAN (United States, 1908–1995)

30 | **Mocha pot**, 1950
Silver, ivory
4¹³⁄₁₆ × 5⁵⁄₁₆ × 4⅛ in. (12.2 × 13.5 × 10.5 cm)
Gift in memory of Alma Eikerman, Eskenazi
Museum of Art, Indiana University
P. 227

31 | **Pendant**, 1974
Silver, chrysoprase
12½ × 6⅞ × 1 in. (31.8 × 17.5 × 2.5 cm)
David Owsley Museum of Art, Friends
of the Museum, 91.53
P. 227

GUÐMUNDUR EINARSSON

(Iceland, 1895–1963)
LYDIA PÁLSDÓTTIR (born Germany, 1911–2000,
active Iceland)
Listvinahús (Iceland)

32 | **Vase**, 1939
Stoneware
14¹⁵⁄₁₆ × 7½ × 7½ in. (38 × 19 × 19 cm)
Exhibited in the Iceland Pavilion,
New York World's Fair, 1939
Private collection
P. 161

RICHARD FAIRBANKS

(United States, 1929–1989)

33 | **Plate**, 1962
Stoneware
1⅝ × 11¾ × 11¾ in. (4.1 × 29.9 × 29.9 cm)
Smithsonian American Art Museum,
Gift of Mrs. Richard Fairbanks
P. 256

PAULDING FARNHAM (United States, 1859–1927)
Tiffany & Co. (United States)

34 ***Viking* punch bowl**, c. 1893
Iron, silver, gold, streaked ebony
Bowl: 11½ × 20¼ × 20¼ in.
(29.2 × 51.4 × 51.4 cm)
Exhibited in the Manufactures and Liberal Arts Building, World's Columbian Exposition, Chicago, 1893
The Metropolitan Museum of Art, Purchase, The Edgar J. Kaufmann Foundation Gift, 1969 (69.4)
P. 85

Tiffany & Co. (United States)

35 ***Viking* coffee set**, 1901
Silver, enamel, gemstones, ivory
Coffeepot: 9⅜ × 7¼ × 3½ in.
(23.8 × 18.4 × 8.9 cm)
Exhibited at the Pan-American Exposition, Buffalo, 1901
Newark Museum, Purchase, 1986 Members' Fund, 86.67a–d

ARLINE FISCH (United States, born 1931)

36 ***Hydra Medusa***, 1968
Silver, antique Egyptian faience beads
7 × 2½ × 2½ in. (17.8 × 6.4 × 6.4 cm)
Los Angeles County Museum of Art, Gift of the artist, M.2019.173
P. 242

37 ***Front & Back* body ornament**, 1971
Silver
Front panel: 17 × 8¾ × 1¼ in.
(43.2 × 22.2 × 3.2 cm)
Los Angeles County Museum of Art, Gift of Allison and Larry Berg through the 2014 Decorative Arts and Design Acquisitions Committee (DA²), M.2014.145a–b
P. 250

BARON ERIK FLEMING (Sweden, 1894–1954)
Atelier Borgila (Sweden)

38 **Dish**, 1932
Silver
3¾ × 9½ × 5 in. (9.5 × 24.1 × 12.7 cm)
The Metropolitan Museum of Art, Purchase, Edward C. Moore Jr. Gift, 1934 (34.101.1)

ANN-MARI FORSBERG (Sweden, 1916–1992)
Märta Måås-Fjetterström AB (Sweden)

39 ***Röd Krokus* (Red Crocus) hanging**, 1945
Linen, wool
84¼ × 55⅛ in. (214 × 140 cm)
Cooper Hewitt, Smithsonian Design Museum, Gift of Elizabeth Gordon, 1964-24-41
P. 12

KAJ FRANCK (Finland, 1911–1989)
Nuutajärvi Glassworks (Finland)

40 **Goblets**, model KF 486, designed 1968, these examples c. 1970–71
Glass
Largest goblet: 7⅝ × 3 × 3 in.
(19.4 × 7.6 × 7.6 cm)
Los Angeles County Museum of Art, Decorative Arts and Design Council Fund, and partial gift of Marc Treib, M.2019.160.1–.6
PP. 234–35

JOSEF FRANK (born Austria, 1885–1967, active Sweden)
Svenskt Tenn (Sweden)

41 ***Aralia* textile**, designed c. 1928, this example printed 2018
Linen
196⅞ × 51³⁄₁₆ in. (500 × 130 cm)
This pattern exhibited in the Swedish Pavilion, New York World's Fair, 1939
Los Angeles County Museum of Art, Gift of Svenskt Tenn, Stockholm, Sweden, M.2019.49.1

Milwaukee Art Museum, Gift of Svenskt Tenn, Stockholm, Sweden, M2019.7
P. 28 (detail)

Svenskt Tenn (Sweden)

42 ***Manhattan* textile**, designed 1943–44, produced from 1947, this example 2018
Linen
199¼ × 55 in. (506.1 × 139.7 cm)
Los Angeles County Museum of Art, Gift of Svenskt Tenn, Stockholm, Sweden, M.2019.49.2

Milwaukee Art Museum, Gift of Svenskt Tenn, Stockholm, Sweden, M2019.6
FRONT ENDPAPERS, PP. 240, 241 (detail)

TAGE FRID (born Denmark, 1915–2004, active United States)

43 **Stool**, 1979
Walnut
30⅛ × 19¾ × 15 in. (76.5 × 50.2 × 38.1 cm)
Yale University Art Gallery, Please Be Seated Collection, funded by Julian H. Fisher, B.A. 1969, in memory of Wilbur J. Fisher, B.A. 1926, and Janet H. Fisher, 2008.126.1
P. 230

GUTTORM GAGNES (Norway, 1906–1964)
David Andersen (Norway)

44 **Beverage set**, 1939
Enamel on gilded silver, wood
Teapot: 5¾ × 7 × 3 in. (14.6 × 17.8 × 7.6 cm)
Inscription: TO PRESIDENT/ FRANKLIN D. ROOSEVELT / AND MRS. ROOSEVELT / IN REMEMBRANCE OF OUR VISIT / TO HYDE PARK APRIL 1939 / FROM / OLAV MARTHA [facsimile signatures] / CROWN PRINCE AND CROWN PRINCESS / OF NORWAY
Gift of Crown Prince Olav and Princess Martha of Norway to President Franklin D. Roosevelt and Eleanor Roosevelt
Franklin D. Roosevelt Presidential Library and Museum, Hyde Park, NY
P. 128

SIMON GATE (Sweden, 1883–1945)
Orrefors (Sweden)

45 **Vase**, 1938
Glass
13¼ × 9¾ × 5½ in. (33.7 × 24.8 × 14 cm)
Inscription: PRESIDENT & MRS. FRANKLIN D. ROOSEVELT FROM GUSTAF ADOLF & LOUISE 1938
Gift of Crown Prince Gustaf Adolf and Princess Louise of Sweden to President Franklin D. Roosevelt and Eleanor Roosevelt
Franklin D. Roosevelt Presidential Library and Museum, Hyde Park, NY
P. 128

ALEXANDER GIRARD (United States, 1907–1993)
American Art Textile Printing Company (United States), manufacturer
Herman Miller Furniture Company (United States), distributor

46 ***Small Squares* textile**, designed 1952
Cotton
108 × 48 in. (274.3 × 121.9 cm)
This pattern exhibited in *American Design for Home and Decorative Use*, multiple Nordic venues, 1953–55
Milwaukee Art Museum, Purchase, with funds from Nici Teweles, M2018.26

OLE GJERLØV-KNUDSEN (Denmark, 1930–2009)

47 **Roll-up bed**, 1965
Beech, linen, rope
13¾ × 31⅕ × 78¾ in. (35 × 80 × 200 cm)
Designmuseum Danmark
P. 290–91

GORHAM MANUFACTURING COMPANY, DURGIN DIVISION (United States)

48 ***Viking Boat Centerpiece***, model D 900, designed c. 1905
Silver, brass
5½ × 13⅞ × 4⅞ in. (14 × 35.2 × 12.4 cm)
Collection of the Art Fund, Inc. at the Birmingham Museum of Art; Purchase with funds provided by Guy R. Kreusch
P. 87

GRANNAS A. OLSSONS HEMSLÖJD and NILS OLSSON HEMSLÖJD (Sweden)

49 **Dala horses**, these examples produced c. 1970s
Wood, paint
Large blue horse: 12½ × 12 × 3½ in.
(31.8 × 30.5 × 8.9 cm)
Collection of Todd Engdahl and Caroline Schomp
P. 34

VIOLA GRÅSTEN (born Finland, 1910–1994, active Sweden)
Nordiska Kompaniet's Textilkammare (Sweden), design firm

50 ***Masker* (Masks) textile**, c. 1950
Linen
86½ × 48 in. (219.7 × 121.9 cm)
Los Angeles County Museum of Art, Costume Council Fund and Decorative Arts and Design Council Fund, M.2017.170.2

VALBORG "MAMA" GRAVANDER
(born Sweden, 1888–1978, active United States)

51 **Rug**, 1949
Wool, linen
67 × 38 in. (170.2 × 96.5 cm)
Collection of Forrest L. Merrill
P. 47

CHARLES SUMNER GREENE
(United States, 1868–1957)
HENRY MATHER GREENE
(United States, 1870–1954)
Peter Hall Manufacturing Company
(United States)

52 **Armchair for the Robert R. Blacker
House**, 1907
Mahogany, ebony, oak, leather (replaced)
33⅜ × 24¼ × 21⅝ in. (84.8 × 61.6 × 54.9 cm)
Los Angeles County Museum of Art,
Gift of Max Palevsky and Jodie Evans,
M.89.151.4
P. 37

ERIK GRONBORG (Denmark, born 1931,
active United States)

53 **Bowl**, 1983
Stoneware
12½ × 10½ × 15⅜ in. (31.8 × 26.7 × 39.1 cm)
Los Angeles County Museum of Art,
Gift of Stanley and Betty Sheinbaum,
AC1998.244.6
P. 39

GRETA MAGNUSSON GROSSMAN
(born Sweden, 1906–1999, active United States)
Glenn of California (United States)

54 **Desk**, model 6200, designed 1952,
this example c. 1952–54
Walnut, iron, Formica
47⅝ × 23¾ × 40 in. (121 × 60.3 × 101.6 cm)
Los Angeles County Museum of Art,
Decorative Arts Deaccession Fund,
M.2007.37
P. 36

MAIJA GROTELL (born Finland, 1899–1973,
active United States)

55 **Vase**, c. 1950
Stoneware
11¾ × 13¾ × 13¾ in. (29.9 × 34.9 × 34.9 cm)
Milwaukee Art Museum, Purchase,
with funds from the Edward U. Demmer
Foundation, in memory of Cheryl
Robertson, Curator of Decorative Arts
at the Milwaukee Art Museum, 1979–81
and 1993–96, M2013.41
P. 184

EDWARD HALD (Sweden, 1883–1980)
Fritz Hickisch, engraver
Orrefors (Sweden), manufacturer

56 *Fyrverkeriskålen* (**Fireworks Bowl**),
designed 1921
Glass
8¾ × 11⅛ × 11⅛ in. (22.2 × 28.3 × 28.3 cm)
Exhibited in *Swedish Contemporary
Decorative Arts*, Metropolitan Museum
of Art and other venues, 1927
The Metropolitan Museum of Art,
Purchase, Edward C. Moore Jr. Gift, 1927
(27.96.5)
PP. 8–9

EDWARD HALD (Sweden, 1883–1980)
Orrefors (Sweden)

57 *Vindrosen* (**Wind Rose**) **plate**, designed
1925, this example 1957
Glass
2⁷⁄₁₆ × 15⅜ × 15⅜ in. (6.2 × 39.1 × 39.1 cm)
Similar example exhibited in *Swedish
Contemporary Decorative Arts*,
Metropolitan Museum of Art and
other venues, 1927
The Metropolitan Museum of Art,
Gift of A.B. Orrefors Glasbruk
and Johann Beyer, 1957 (57.107)
P. 125

FRIDA HANSEN (Norway, 1855–1931)

58 *Sommernattsdrøm* (**Summer Night's
Dream**) **portière**, 1914
Wool, silver thread
114³⁄₁₆ × 81⅛ in. (290 × 206 cm)
This design exhibited at the Carnegie
Institute, Pittsburgh, 1915
National Museum of Art, Architecture
and Design, Oslo, Norway
P. 63

HELENA HERNMARCK (Sweden, born 1941,
active United States)

59 *Bay Street in Toronto* **hanging**, 1970
Wool, linen, metallic thread
72 × 49 in. (182.9 × 124.5 cm)
Los Angeles County Museum of Art,
Gift of the artist, M.75.13
P. 218

LILLIAN HOLM (born Sweden, 1896–1979,
active United States)

60 *First Sight of New York* **hanging**, 1930s
Linen, cotton, wool, viscose rayon
82 × 64⅛ in. (208.3 × 162.9 cm)
Collection of the Flint Institute of Arts,
Flint, MI; Gift of Mrs. Lillian Holm in
memory of Ralph T. Sayles, FIA 1965.14
P. 214

JIM HULL (United States, born 1942)
PENNY HULL (United States, born 1943)
H.U.D.D.L.E. (United States)

61 *BIG TOOBS* **beds**, designed 1972
Fiber hardboard, wood, vinyl
84 × 77 × 48½ in. (213.4 × 195.6 × 123.2 cm)
Collection of Jordana Joseph
and Glen Saltzberg
P. 282

MAIJA ISOLA (Finland, 1927–2001)
Marimekko (Finland)

62 *Unikko* **textile**, designed 1964,
this example 1965
Cotton
119 × 54 in. (302.3 × 137.2 cm)
Cooper Hewitt, Smithsonian Design
Museum, Gift of Marimekko, Inc.,
1979-89-7
P. 71

DANIEL JACKSON (United States, 1938–1995)

63 **Library ladder**, 1965
Walnut, oak
78½ × 20½ × 25¾ in. (199.4 × 52.1 × 65.4 cm)
Smithsonian American Art Museum,
Gift of the James Renwick Alliance and
museum purchase made possible by
the Smithsonian Institution Collections
Acquisition Program
P. 246

ARNE JACOBSEN (Denmark, 1902–1971)
Fritz Hansen (Denmark)

64 **"Ant" chair**, model 3100, designed 1951
Plywood, chromium-plated steel
30½ × 16¼ × 18 in. (77.5 × 41.3 × 45.7 cm)
Los Angeles County Museum of Art,
gift of Norbert Schoenauer, courtesy
of The Montreal Museum of Decorative
Arts, AC1992.264.1
LACMA only

Fritz Hansen (Denmark)

65 *Egg* **chair**, designed 1958
Leather, chromed steel, aluminum,
fiberglass-reinforced polyurethane foam
41½ × 36 × 27½ in. (105.4 × 91.4 × 69.9 cm)
Milwaukee Art Museum, Gift from
the George R. Kravis II Collection,
M2018.180a,b
MAM only

BJÖRN JAKOBSON (Sweden, born 1934)
BabyBjörn (Sweden)

66 *Baby-Sitter* **bouncer chair**,
designed c. 1964
Cotton, steel
18½ × 20 × 26 in. (47 × 50.8 × 66 cm)
BabyBjörn

BJÖRN JAKOBSON (Sweden, born 1934)
LILLEMOR JAKOBSON (Sweden, born 1935)
BabyBjörn (Sweden)

67 *Hjärtenära* (**Close to the Heart**)
baby carrier, designed 1973
Cotton, steel, plastic
Main panel length: 17¾ in. (45 cm)
BabyBjörn

GEORG JENSEN (Denmark, 1866–1935)
Georg Jensen Silversmithy (Denmark)

68 **Necklace**, designed 1904
Silver, labradorite
Pendant: 3 × 1¾ in. (7.6 × 4.5 cm)
Newark Museum, 29.1361
P. 68

Georg Jensen Silversmithy (Denmark)

69 **"Grape" compote**, model 264A,
designed 1918
Silver
10½ × 10 × 10 in. (26.7 × 25.4 × 25.4 cm)
Collection of Jody and Dick Goisman
MAM only

Los Angeles County Museum of Art,
Gift of Miss Abigail von Schlegell, M.68.47
LACMA only
P. 334

KAREN MARIE JENSEN (born Denmark, 1878–1908, active United States)
LILLIAN POULSEN (United States, 1908–1991)

70 | **Doily**, started by Jensen c. 1908, finished later by Poulsen (Jensen's daughter)
Linen
19⅞ × 20½ in. (50.5 × 52.1 cm)
Museum of Danish America, Elk Horn, Iowa
P. 44

ERIK KRISTIAN JOHNSEN (born Norway, 1863–1923, active United States)

71 | **Chair**, 1900–1910
Wood
44 × 33½ × 28½ in. (111.8 × 85.1 × 72.4 cm)
Vesterheim Norwegian-American Museum

FINN JUHL (Denmark, 1912–1989)
Marianne Riis-Carstensen (China, born 1927, active Denmark), watercolorist

72 | **Design drawing for delegate's chair, United Nations Trusteeship Council Chamber**, 1950
Watercolor, pencil, ink on paper
16½ × 23½ in. (41.9 × 59.7 cm)
Designmuseum Danmark
P. 135

Baker Furniture, Inc. (United States)

73 | **Armchair**, model 400-½, designed 1951
Walnut, leather
32 × 28 × 24 in. (81.3 × 71.1 × 61 cm)
Milwaukee Art Museum, Bequest of Dr. Lucille Cohn, M2013.69
P. 78

WILHELM KÅGE (Sweden, 1889–1960)
Gustavsberg (Sweden)

74 | *Argenta* **platter**, model 1035, c. 1938
Stoneware, silver
2⅞ × 17 × 17 in. (7.3 × 43.2 × 43.2 cm)
Collection of Forrest L. Merrill
P. 16

ROBERT KING (United States, 1917–2014)
JOHN VAN KOERT (United States, 1912–1998)
Towle Silversmiths (United States)

75 | *Contour* **coffee service**, designed 1951–52
Silver, melamine
Coffeepot: 10 × 4⅜ × 7¼ in. (25.4 × 11.1 × 18.4 cm)
Collection of Jody and Dick Goisman

LARS KINSARVIK (Norway, 1846–1925)

76 | **Drinking horn**, 1890
Birch
13 × 18½ × 5½ in. (33 × 47 × 14 cm)
Exhibited in Norway's Court, Manufactures and Liberal Arts Building, World's Columbian Exposition, Chicago, 1893
Vesterheim Norwegian-American Museum
P. 120

SUSANNE KOEFOED (Denmark, born 1948)

77 | **Access symbol**, 1968
Contemporary vinyl reproduction of a design published in *Svensk Form* 10 (1968)
Variable dimensions
P. 278

GRETE PRYTZ KORSMO (Norway, 1917–2010)
J. Tostrup (Norway)

78 | **Bowl**, 1952
Silver, enamel
1¹⁵⁄₁₆ × 6⅝ × 6⅝ in. (5 × 16.9 × 16.9 cm)
Exhibited in *Design in Scandinavia*, multiple U.S. venues, 1954–57
Morten Zondag Kunstformidling AS, Oslo
P. 126

Cathrineholm (Norway)

79 | **Coffeepot**, designed 1965
Enameled cast iron, plastic
9 × 8¾ × 6 in. (22.9 × 22.2 × 15.2 cm)
Private collection
LACMA only

OLE H. J. KRAG (Norway, 1837–1916)
ERIK JØRGENSEN (Norway, 1848–1896)
Springfield Armory (United States)

80 | **Krag-Jørgensen rifle**, model 1892, designed 1892, produced from 1894, this example 1894
Steel, wood
6 × 49½ × 3½ in. (15.2 × 125.7 × 8.9 cm)
Similar model exhibited in U.S. Government Building, World's Columbian Exposition, Chicago, 1893
Smithsonian's National Museum of American History

HERBERT KRENCHEL (Denmark, 1922–2014)
Torben Ørskov & Co. (Denmark)

81 | *Krenit* **bowls**, designed 1953
Enameled steel
Largest bowl: 5⅜ × 9⅞ × 9⅞ in. (13.7 × 25.1 × 25.1 cm)
Milwaukee Art Museum, Gift from the George R. Kravis II Collection, M2018.128
P. 75

JAMES KRENOV (born Russia, 1920–2009, active United States and Sweden)

82 | **Cabinet**, 1991
Bird's-eye maple, doussie
58½ × 19½ × 12 in. (148.6 × 49.5 × 30.5 cm)
Los Angeles County Museum of Art, Gift of Michael Mills and Laureen Bedell, M.2019.258

ARNOLD KROG (Denmark, 1856–1931)
GERHARD HEILMANN (Denmark, 1859–1946)
Royal Copenhagen Porcelain Manufactory (Denmark)

83 | **Vase**, 1890
Porcelain
6⅞ × 3¾ × 3¾ in. (17.5 × 9.5 × 9.5 cm)
Exhibited in the Danish court, Manufactures and Liberal Arts Building, World's Columbian Exposition, Chicago, 1893
Collection of Elliot Ryser
P. 121

Royal Copenhagen Porcelain Manufactory (Denmark)

84 | **Vase**, 1892
Porcelain
7⁵⁄₁₆ × 8¹⁄₁₆ × 8¹⁄₁₆ in. (18.5 × 20.5 × 20.5 cm)
Exhibited in the Danish court, Manufactures and Liberal Arts Building, World's Columbian Exposition, Chicago, 1893
Collection of Elliot Ryser
P. 121

ARNOLD KROG (Denmark, 1856–1931)
OLUF JENSEN (Denmark, 1871–1934)
Royal Copenhagen Porcelain Manufactory (Denmark)

85 | **Ginger jar**, 1891
Porcelain
7⁵⁄₁₆ × 4¾ × 4¾ in. (18.5 × 12 × 12 cm)
Exhibited in the Danish court, Manufactures and Liberal Arts Building, World's Columbian Exposition, Chicago, 1893
Collection of Elliot Ryser
P. 121

MICHAEL LACKTMAN (United States, born 1938)

86 | **Bowl**, 1966
Silver
5⅜ × 10¾ × 10¾ in. (13.7 × 27.3 × 27.3 cm)
Los Angeles County Museum of Art, Gift of Michael Lacktman, M.2007.151
P. 262

JACK LENOR LARSEN (United States, born 1927)
WIN ANDERSON (United States, 1922–2009)
Jack Lenor Larsen, Inc. (United States), design firm
Aristocrat Embroidery Corporation (United States), manufacturer

87 | *Magnum* **textile**, designed 1970
Cotton, vinyl, nylon, polyester, Mylar
47⅜ × 47 in. (120.3 x 119.4 cm)
Los Angeles County Museum of Art, Decorative Arts and Design Council Fund M.2019.207
P. 187

OLGA LEE (United States, 1924–2015)
Ralph O. Smith Manufacturing Company (United States)

88 | **Lamp**, designed c. 1952, this example c. 1952–54
Aluminum, iron
27½ × 10 × 12 in. (69.9 × 25.4 × 30.5 cm)
Similar example exhibited in *American Design for Home and Decorative Use*, multiple Nordic venues, 1953–55
Los Angeles County Museum of Art, Decorative Arts and Design Council Fund, M.2007.186
P. 154

DOROTHY LIEBES (United States, 1897–1972)

89 | **Furnishing fabric**, 1948
Wool, cotton, rayon, silk, Lurex, metallic strip
114⅞ × 50½ in. (291.8 × 128.5 cm)
The Art Institute of Chicago, Gift of Dorothy Liebes Design, Inc., 1972.1142
P. 216

STIG LINDBERG (Sweden, 1916–1982)
Nordiska Kompaniet's Textilkammare (Sweden), design firm
Ljungbergs Textiltryck (Sweden), manufacturer
Knoll Associates, Inc. (United States), U.S. distributor
90 | *Fruktlåda* ("Apples") textile, 1947
Cotton
92½ × 50½ in. (235 × 128.3 cm)
Los Angeles County Museum of Art, Purchased with funds provided by Mrs. H. Grant Theis and Mrs. Vera Traub, M.2000.11
BACK ENDPAPERS

Gustavsberg (Sweden)
91 | "Pungo" (Pouch) vase, designed c. 1953
Stoneware
9½ × 5¼ × 4½ in. (24.1 × 13.3 × 11.4 cm)
Same model exhibited in *Design in Scandinavia*, multiple U.S. venues, 1954–57
Collection of Jody and Dick Goisman

TOM LINDHARDT WILS (Denmark, 1935–2007)
Multikunst Legepladser (now KOMPAN; Denmark)
92 | *Mudderkliren* (Sandpiper) springer,
designed 1971–72, this example 2017
EcoCore plastic, steel, polyamide
30 × 37 × 14 in. (76.2 × 94 × 35.6 cm)
KOMPAN, Inc.
P. 106

MARVIN B. LIPOFSKY (United States, 1938–2016)
Jaakko Niemi (Finland, 1926–2002), assistant
93 | *Suomi-Finland #4*, 1970
Glass
10 × 13 × 12 in. (25.4 × 33 × 30.5 cm)
Blown at Nuutajärvi Glassworks, Finland, finished by the artist in his studio in Berkeley, California
Estate of Marvin B. Lipofsky
P. 263

RALPH LYSELL (Sweden, 1907–1987)
KNUT HUGO BLOMBERG (Sweden, 1897–1994)
HANS GÖSTA THAMES (Sweden, 1916–2006)
North Electric Company (United States)
94 | *Ericofon* telephone, designed 1941,
this model designed c. 1961, this example 1962
ABS plastic, rubber, metal
8⅜ × 5 × 3⅞ in. (21.3 × 12.7 × 9.8 cm)
Similar design originally produced by Telefonaktiebolaget L. M. Ericsson, Sweden
Collection of Jody and Dick Goisman
P. 335

PER LYSNE (born Norway, 1880–1947, active United States)
John Lund (born Norway, 1884–1975, active United States), carpenter
95 | Chair, c. 1925
Wood, paint
30.5 × 30 × 20 in. (77.5 × 76.2 × 50.8 cm)
Vesterheim Norwegian-American Museum
P. 59

96 | Smorgasbord plate, c. 1940
Wood, paint
1 × 15¼ × 15¼ in. (2.5 × 38.7 × 38.7 cm)
Vesterheim Norwegian-American Museum
P. 60

ERIK MAGNUSSEN (born Denmark, 1884–1961, active United States)
Gorham Manufacturing Company (United States)
97 | *Modern American* cocktail set,
designed 1928, this example 1930
Silver, Bakelite
Tray: ⅞ × 15⅛ × 12¼ in. (2.2 × 38.4 × 31.1 cm)
Shaker: 12⅜ × 6�5/16 × 6�5/16 in. (31.4 × 16 × 16 cm)
Collection of Ravi R. Mathura and Danielle Klotzek
P. 53

CARL MALMSTEN (born Sweden, 1882–1972)
Firma David Blomberg (Sweden)
98 | Chair from Carl Milles House at Cranbrook Academy of Art, designed 1926
Wood, paint, rattan
34⅜ × 19¼ × 17½ in. (87.3 × 48.9 × 44.5 cm)
Millesgården Museum
P. 221

SAM MALOOF (United States, 1916–2009)
99 | Chair, 1952
Walnut, leather
30 × 21½ × 17 in. (76.2 × 54.6 × 43.2 cm)
Sam and Alfreda Maloof Foundation
P. 265

SVEN MARKELIUS (Sweden, 1889–1972)
Nordiska Kompaniet's Textilkammare (Sweden), design firm
Ljungsbergs Textiltryck (Sweden), manufacturer
Knoll Textiles, Inc. (United States), U.S. distributor
100 | *Pythagoras* textile, designed 1952
Cotton
67 × 51 in. (170.2 × 129.5 cm)
Los Angeles County Museum of Art, Costume Council Fund and Decorative Arts and Design Council Fund, M.2017.170.1
P. 66

STEINUNN MARTEINSDÓTTIR (Iceland, born 1936)
Glit (Iceland)
101 | Dish, 1961
Ceramic
3.1 × 13.8 × 13.8 in. (8 × 35 × 35 cm)
Collection of Anna Ólafía Guðnadóttir

BRUNO MATHSSON (Sweden, 1901–1988)
Firma Karl Mathsson (Sweden)
102 | Chair ("Easy Chair No. 1"), designed 1934
Maple, hemp
31 × 20 × 38 in. (78.7 × 50.8 × 96.5 cm)
Owned by Edgar Kaufmann, jr.
Fallingwater Collection, Western Pennsylvania Conservancy, 1985.338.2
LACMA only

Firma Karl Mathsson (Sweden)
103 | Work chair, model 41, designed 1934, this example c. 1940
Birch, hemp
32½ × 19 × 25½ in. (82.6 × 48.3 × 64.8 cm)
Likely purchased at Sweden House, New York, by architect Wallace Lee
Milwaukee Art Museum, Gift of Peter W. Lee, M2017.57
MAM only

HERBERT MATTER (born Switzerland, 1907–1984, active United States)
Knoll Associates, Inc. (United States), client
104 | *Single Pedestal Furniture Designed by Eero Saarinen* poster, c. 1957
Offset lithography
45 × 25⅞ in. (114.3 × 65.7 cm)
Los Angeles County Museum of Art, Decorative Arts and Design Council Fund

ROLF MIDDELBOE (Denmark, 1917–1995)
Landsforeningen Dansk Kunsthåndværk (Denmark), client
105 | *The Arts of Denmark: Viking to Modern* poster, 1960
Screenprint
16¼ × 21¾ in. (41.3 × 55.2 cm)
Used for *The Arts of Denmark* at the Metropolitan Museum of Art, 1960
Poster Collection, The Metropolitan Museum of Art Archives
P. 157

CARL MILLES (born Sweden, 1875–1955, active United States)
106 | Model for *Jonah and the Whale* fountain, 1932
Bronze
20⅟16 × 9⅟16 × 10¼ in. (51 × 23 × 26 cm)
Millesgården Museum
P. 182

IDA LAITURI NEVALA (born Finland, 1890–1977, active United States)
107 | Rag rug, c. 1916
Cotton
54½ × 26½ in. (138.4 × 67.3 cm)
Michigan State University Museum
P. 46

VUOKKO NURMESNIEMI (Finland, born 1930)
Marimekko (Finland)
108 | *Tyttö Rannalla* dress with *Pirput parput* pattern, pattern designed 1958, dress designed 1959
Cotton
Center back length: 28½ in. (72.4 cm)
Purchased by Jacqueline Kennedy at Design Research, Cambridge, Massachusetts, 1960
Design Museum Helsinki

Marimekko (Finland)
109 | *Heiluhelma* dress with *Nasti* pattern, pattern designed 1958, dress designed 1959
Cotton
Center back length: 37 in. (94 cm)
Purchased by Jacqueline Kennedy at Design Research, Cambridge, Massachusetts, 1960
Design Museum Helsinki

EDVIN ÖHRSTRÖM (Sweden, 1906–1994)
Orrefors (Sweden)
110 | Vase, 1939
Glass
8¼ × 7 × 7 in. (21 × 17.8 × 17.8 cm)
Exhibited in the Swedish Pavilion, New York World's Fair, 1939
The Metropolitan Museum of Art, Purchase, Edward C. Moore Jr. Gift, 1939 (39.154.5)

PETER OPSVIK (Norway, born 1939)
Stokke (Norway)

111 | *Tripp Trapp* chair, designed 1972
Beech, metal
30¹¹⁄₁₆ × 18⅛ × 19¹¹⁄₁₆ in. (78 × 46 × 50 cm)
National Museum of Art, Architecture
and Design, Oslo, Norway
P. 110

VICTOR PAPANEK (born Austria, 1923–1998,
active United States and Scandinavia)

112 | *Big Character Poster No. 1: Work Chart
for Designers*, 1973 (conceived 1969)
Reproduction print
47¼ × 32¼ in. (120 × 82 cm)
University of Applied Arts, Vienna,
Victor J. Papanek Foundation
P. 277

ALICE KAGAWA PARROTT
(United States, 1929–2009)

113 | *Bird Cage* hanging, c. 1968
Linen, wool, wood
70 × 36 × 1 in. (177.8 × 91.4 × 2.5 cm)
Collection of the Albuquerque Museum
P. 253

ELSE POULSSON (Norway, 1909–2002)
Joh. Petersen (Norway)

114 | **Textile from the United Nations Security
Council Chamber**, 1951
Rayon satin damask weave
9½ × 22 in. (24.1 × 55.9 cm)
Cooper Hewitt, Smithsonian Design
Museum, Gift of the Petersen Family
and Royal Norwegian Consulate General,
2015-12-1
PP. 6 (detail), 132–33

JAMES PRESTINI (United States, 1908–1993)

115 | Bowl, 1933–53
Walnut
4¼ × 12½ × 12½ in. (10.8 × 31.8 × 31.8 cm)
Milwaukee Art Museum, Gift of Ruth
and David Waterbury in honor of Glenn
Adamson, M2005.132
P. 155

JOHN PRIP (United States, 1922–2009,
active Denmark and United States)
Reed & Barton (United States)

116 | *Denmark* tea and coffee service,
designed 1958
Silverplate, plastic
Coffeepot: 9¾ × 7¾ × 4¾ in.
(24.8 × 19.7 × 12.1 cm)
Collection of Jody and Dick Goisman
P. 251

JENS H. QUISTGAARD (Denmark, 1919–2008)
Dansk Designs (United States), design firm

117 | *Kobenstyle* casseroles, designed 1955
Enameled steel
Red: 4¾ × 10¼ × 7¾ in. (12.1 × 26 × 19.7 cm)
Yellow: 5⅛ × 11½ × 9 in. (13 × 29.2 × 22.9 cm)
Private collection
OPPOSITE P. 1

JENS H. QUISTGAARD (Denmark, 1919–2008)
Dansk Designs (United States), design firm
Glud & Marstrand (Denmark), manufacturer

118 | *Kobenstyle* pitcher, designed 1955
Enameled steel, plastic
8 × 5¾ × 4 in. (20.3 × 14.6 × 10.2 cm)
Private collection
OPPOSITE P. 1

Dansk Designs (United States), design firm
Nissen (Denmark), manufacturer

119 | **Ice bucket**, designed 1958
Teak, metal
15¼ × 7⁹⁄₁₆ × 7⁹⁄₁₆ in. (38.7 × 19.2 × 19.2 cm)
Collection of Jody and Dick Goisman
MAM only

Los Angeles County Museum of Art,
Gift of Toru and Judy Nomura Iura,
M.91.120
LACMA only
P. 310

RALPH RAPSON (United States, 1914–2008)

120 | **Perspective drawing, United States
Embassy, Stockholm** (unbuilt proposal),
1951
Graphite on tracing paper
17⅝ × 25 in. (44.8 × 63.5 cm)
Cranbrook Art Museum
P. 172

121 | **Perspective drawing, United States
Embassy, Copenhagen**, c. 1951
Graphite on tracing paper
21 × 21 in. (53.3 × 53.3 cm)
Ralph Rapson Collection, Cranbrook
Archives, Cranbrook Center for Collections
and Research, Gift of Rip Rapson
P. 173

Knoll Associates, Inc. (United States), manufacturer
Marianne Strengell (born Finland, 1909–1998,
active United States), textile designer (attributed)

122 | **Rocker**, model 657W, with *Pebble Weave*
webbing, 1945–46
Birch, cotton canvas webbing (original)
28 × 27¾ × 32¼ in. (71.1 × 70.5 × 81.9 cm)
Minneapolis Institute of Art, Gift in
memory of Mary Rapson, to
commemorate her support of modern
design, by Kenneth and Judy Dayton,
Heino Engel (Germany), Dolly J. Fiterman,
William and Jane Hession, Philip W.
Pillsbury, Jr., John P. Sheehy, Philip and
Joanne Von Blon, and many other friends,
2000.164
P. 171

REIJMYRE GLASSWORKS (Sweden)

123 | **Goblet**, 1893
Glass
Height: 15¾ in. (40 cm)
Similar model exhibited in Swedish
Pavilion, World's Columbian Exposition,
Chicago, 1893
Nationalmuseum Sweden

MARIANNE RICHTER (Sweden, 1916–2010)

124 | **Sketch of tapestry for United Nations
Economic and Social Council Chamber**,
c. 1951
Watercolor on paper
5⅞ × 14⅝ in. (15 × 37.1 cm)
ArkDes, the Swedish Centre for
Architecture and Design
PP. 132–33

Märta Måås-Fjetterström AB (Sweden)

125 | **Curtain fragment from United Nations
Economic and Social Council Chamber**,
c. 1951–52
Wool, linen
48⁹⁄₁₆ × 42½ in. (123.3 × 108 cm)
Minneapolis Institute of Art,
Gift of Helena M. Hernmarck, 2008.57.9

ANNIKA RIMALA (Finland, 1936–2014)
Marimekko (Finland)

126 | **Girl's dress in *Petrooli* pattern**, pattern
designed 1963
Cotton
Center back length: 27 in. (68.6 cm)
Los Angeles County Museum of Art,
Gift of Mrs. Gerald Labiner, M.85.349.2a–b
P. 3

Marimekko (Finland)

127 | *Monrepos* dress in *Keidas* pattern,
dress and pattern designed 1967
Cotton
Center back length: 48½ in. (123.2 cm)
Los Angeles County Museum of Art,
Gift of Mrs. Gerald Labiner, M.85.349.3
P. 2

JENS RISOM (born Denmark, 1916–2016, active
United States)
Knoll Associates, Inc. (United States)

128 | **Chair**, model 650, designed 1941,
this example c. 1947
Maple, leather
29½ × 20⅛ × 28 in. (75 × 51.1 × 71.1 cm)
Inscription on metal tag: Central Post Fund
Property, Clarksville Base, Tennessee, 0299
Los Angeles County Museum of Art,
Gift of Mr. Oliver M. Furth and Mr. Sean
Yashar, M.2018.101
LACMA only
P. 118

Knoll Associates, Inc. (United States)

129 | **Chair**, model 650, designed 1941
Maple, jute
30¼ × 20½ × 24½ in. (76.8 × 52.1 × 62.2 cm)
Collection of Jody and Dick Goisman
MAM only

ED ROSSBACH (United States, 1914–2002)

130 | *Modular Construction* hanging, 1968
Cotton, linen, silk, raffia
65 × 50½ in. (165.1 × 128.3 cm)
Milwaukee Art Museum, Gift of Karen
Johnson Boyd, M1987.62
P. 186

KARL VON RYDINGSVÄRD (born Sweden, 1863–1941, active United States)

131 **Armchair**, c. 1905
White oak
34¾ × 25 × 32 in. (88.3 × 63.5 × 81.3 cm)
On loan from Kristina Dera, courtesy of the American Swedish Historical Museum, Philadelphia
P. 86

EERO SAARINEN (born Finland, 1910–1961, active United States)
Stickley Brothers Furniture Company (United States)

132 **Chair for Kingswood School dining hall**, 1930–31
Birch, paint, linen upholstery (replaced)
35½ × 17½ × 19⅜ in. (90.2 × 44.5 × 49.2 cm)
Cranbrook Art Museum
P. 221

Eszter Haraszty (born Hungary, 1920–1994, active United States), textile designer
Knoll Associates, Inc. (United States), manufacturer
Orinoka Mills (United States), textile manufacturer

133 ***Pedestal* ("Tulip") side chair,** model 151, with *Lana* ("Persimmon" colorway) upholstery, designed 1956, this example 1976
Fiberglass-reinforced polyester, aluminum, wool-nylon blend upholstery
31½ × 20 × 23½ in. (80 × 50.8 × 59.7 cm)
Milwaukee Art Museum, Gift of InterPlan O.P.I. and Knoll International, Inc., M1976.70
MAM only
P. 189

Knoll Associates, Inc. (United States)

134 ***Pedestal* ("Tulip") side chair**, model 151, designed 1956
Fiberglass-reinforced polyester, aluminum, wool-nylon blend upholstery
32 × 19½ × 21½ in. (81.3 × 49.5 × 54.6 cm)
Los Angeles County Museum of Art, Gift of Ted and Mary Kapenekas, M.2005.33.3
LACMA only

ELIEL SAARINEN (born Finland, 1873–1950, active United States)

135 **Drawing of the Chicago Tower, Lakefront Development Project**, 1923
Graphite on tracing paper
23½ × 17 in. (59.7 × 43.2 cm)
Cranbrook Art Museum
P. 180

Studio Loja Saarinen (United States), maker
Lillian Holm (born Sweden, 1896–1979, active United States), weaver (attributed)
Ruth Ingvarson (born Sweden, 1897–1969, active United States), weaver (attributed)

136 **"Cranbrook Map" hanging**, 1935
Linen, silk, wool
103½ × 123½ in. (262.9 × 313.7 cm)
Exhibited at the Golden Gate International Exposition, San Francisco, 1939
Cranbrook Art Museum
PP. 212–13

ELIEL SAARINEN (born Finland, 1873–1950, active United States)
LOJA SAARINEN (born Finland, 1879–1968, active United States)

137 **Study for *Festival of the May Queen* hanging**, Kingswood School, 1932
Watercolor, gouache, and pencil on tracing paper
28½ × 26½ in. (72.4 × 67.3 cm)
Cranbrook Art Museum
P. 210

Studio Loja Saarinen (United States)

138 **Sample weaving for *Festival of the May Queen* hanging**, Kingswood School, 1932
Linen, wool, rayon
86 × 45 in. (218.4 × 114.3 cm)
Cranbrook Art Museum
P. 211

KYLLIKKI SALMENHAARA (Finland, 1915–1981)

139 **Vase**, c. 1960
Stoneware
21⅝ × 9 × 9 in. (54.9 × 22.9 × 22.9 cm)
Collection of Forrest L. Merrill
P. 257

ASTRID SAMPE (Sweden, 1909–2002)
Kasthall (Sweden)

140 **Sample of *Pine* rug for Dag Hammarskjöld Library, United Nations**, 1961
Wool
59¹⁄₁₆ × 50³⁄₁₆ in. (150 × 127.5 cm)
Nationalmuseum Sweden
P. 167

TIMO SARPANEVA (Finland, 1926–2006)
Iittala Glassworks (Finland)

141 ***Orkidea* (Orchid) vase**, model 3868, designed 1953
Glass
10¼ × 3½ × 3½ in. (26 × 8.9 × 8.9 cm)
Milwaukee Art Museum, Gift of David and Anne Ryan, Minneapolis, M2019.8
P. 99

HELEN SHIRK (United States, born 1942)

142 ***Pendant with Phantom Quartz***, 1974
Silver, phantom quartz
14¼ × 9 × 1 in. (36.2 × 22.9 × 2.5 cm)
Los Angeles County Museum of Art, Gift of Lois and Bob Boardman, M.2013.221.33

OLAF SKOOGFORS (born Sweden, 1930–1975, active United States)

143 **Necklace**, 1974
Gilded silver, glass
10 × 5¼ × ½ in. (25.4 × 13.3 × 1.3 cm)
Los Angeles County Museum of Art, Gift of Lois and Bob Boardman, M.2016.21.49
P. 57

PEER SMED (born Denmark, 1878–1943, active United States)

144 **Cocktail shaker**, 1931
Silver
15 × 6¼ × 6¼ in. (38.1 × 15.9 × 15.9 cm)
The Art Institute of Chicago, restricted gift of Quinn E. Delaney; Wesley M. Dixon, Jr. Endowment Fund, 1990.179
P. 49

ELAINE SMEDAL (United States, 1922–2014)
ANNE TRESSLER (United States, 1910–1986, later Foote)
Memorial Union Workshop, University of Wisconsin, Madison (United States), printer
Campus Publishing Company (United States), publisher

145 ***Norwegian Design in Wisconsin* portfolio**, 1946
Serigraphy
14 × 11 in. (35.6 × 27.9 cm)
Milwaukee Art Museum Research Center
P. 30

HOWARD SMITH (United States, born 1928, active United States and Finland)
Vallila (Finland)

146 **Textile**, designed c. 1978
Linen
48 × 28 in. (121.9 × 71.1 cm)
Los Angeles County Museum of Art, Gift of Kenneth Erwin, M.2018.292
LACMA only
P. 271

Vallila (Finland)

147 **Textile**, designed c. 1978
Linen
50 × 28 in. (127 × 71.1 cm)
Private collection
MAM only

ROSANNE SOMERSON (United States, born 1954)

148 ***Water Ribbon Table***, 2019
Cherry, aluminum, digitally printed maple
35¹⁵⁄₁₆ × 48 × 30 in. (91.3 × 121.9 × 76.2 cm)
Collection of the artist
PP. 231, 232 (detail)

MARIANNE STRENGELL (born Finland, 1909–1998, active United States)
Chatham Manufacturing Company (United States), manufacturer
Chrysler Corporation (United States), client

149 **"Taj Majal" upholstery fabric for the 1959 Chrysler Imperial**, designed 1955
Viscose, Lurex, Metlon, cotton
115 × 62¾ in. (292.1 × 159.4 cm)
Cranbrook Art Museum
P. 224

150 **"Philippines" (also known as "Manila") textile**, designed 1951
Linen
94 × 50 in. (238.8 × 127 cm)
Cranbrook Art Museum

ELIAS SVEDBERG (Sweden, 1913–1987)
Nordiska Kompaniet (Sweden)

151 | *Triva* chair, designed 1954
Birch
29 11/16 × 16 1/8 × 19 5/16 in. (75.5 × 41 × 49 cm)
Nationalmuseum Sweden

EVA-LISA (PIPSAN) SAARINEN SWANSON (born Finland, 1905–1979, active United States)
Edwin Raphael Company, Inc. (United States)

152 | *Saratoga* textile (no. 6820),
designed 1952–62
Linen
113 3/4 × 46 1/2 in. (288.9 × 118.1 cm)
Cranbrook Art Museum
P. 178

EVA-LISA (PIPSAN) SAARINEN SWANSON (born Finland, 1905–1979, active United States)
J. ROBERT F. SWANSON (United States, 1900–1981)
ELIEL SAARINEN (born Finland, 1873–1950, active United States)
Johnson Furniture Company (United States)

153 | Nesting tables, designed 1939
Maple, stainless steel
Large table: 17 9/16 × 28 × 18 1/4 in.
(44.6 × 71.1 × 46.4 cm)
Milwaukee Art Museum, Purchase,
with funds from the Edward U. Demmer
Foundation, M2013.32a–c

J. ROBERT F. SWANSON (United States, 1900–1981)
Saarinen Swanson Group (United States),
design firm
Cray (United States), manufacturer

154 | Candelabrum, designed 1935,
manufactured 1947
Chromed brass
25 1/4 × 18 1/4 × 6 in. (64.1 × 46.4 × 15.2 cm)
Cranbrook Art Museum
P. 199

MARTTA TAIPALE (Finland, 1893–1966)

155 | Tapestry, c. 1954
Linen, wool, silk, rayon, cotton,
Lurex-wrapped cotton and rayon, Lurex,
metal foil-wrapped cotton
18 1/2 × 13 in. (47 × 33 cm)
Owned by Lenore Tawney
The Art Institute of Chicago,
Gift of Lenore Tawney, 1994.309
P. 196

TOSHIKO TAKAEZU (United States, 1922–2011)

156 | Vessel, 1960s
Stoneware
9 × 10 × 10 in. (22.9 × 25.4 × 25.4 cm)
Milwaukee Art Museum, Gift of the artist,
M2006.86
P. 185

ANNIKKI TAPIOVAARA (Finland, 1910–1972)
ILMARI TAPIOVAARA (Finland, 1914–1999)
Keravan Puuteollisuus (Finland)

157 | *Domus* armchair, designed 1946
Birch plywood, cotton (replaced)
33 1/2 × 23 1/8 × 25 in. (85.1 × 58.7 × 63.5 cm)
Owned by Ilmari Tapiovaara
Los Angeles County Museum of Art,
Gift of the 2017 Decorative Arts
and Design Acquisition Committee (DA²),
M.2017.232
P. 11

LENORE TAWNEY (United States, 1907–2007)

158 | *Reflections* hanging, 1959–60
Linen, cotton, wool, silk, viscose
55 7/8 × 29 1/2 in. (141.9 × 74.9 cm)
Owned by Elizabeth Gordon
Cooper Hewitt, Smithsonian Design
Museum, Gift of Elizabeth Gordon,
1964-24-66
P. 197

PAAVO TYNELL (Finland, 1890–1973)
Taito Oy (Finland)

159 | Chandelier, model 10106, designed 1948,
this example c. 1953
Brass
42 × 33 × 33 in. (106.7 × 83.8 × 83.8 cm)
Likely purchased at Finland House,
New York
The Montreal Museum of Fine Arts,
Liliane and David M. Stewart Collection
P. 70

BRIT-MARIE (BITTAN) VALBERG (Sweden, 1926–2003)
Cabin Crafts, Inc. (United States)

160 | "Blue Wave" rug, 1960
Acrylic fiber
48 × 72 in. (121.9 × 182.9 cm)
Private collection, relative of the artist
P. 268

KRISTIAN VEDEL (Denmark, 1923–2003)
Torben Ørskov & Co. (Denmark)

161 | Child's chair, designed 1957
Beech plywood
15 3/4 × 17 5/8 × 12 in. (40 × 44.8 × 30.5 cm)
Milwaukee Art Museum, Purchase,
with funds from the Demmer Charitable
Trust, M2018.23
P. 106

TONE VIGELAND (Norway, born 1938)
PLUS (Norway), distributor

162 | Neckpiece, 1965
Silver, amazonite
8 1/2 × 5 3/4 × 3/5 in. (21.7 × 14.6 × 1.5 cm)
National Museum of Art, Architecture
and Design, Oslo, Norway

VOLVO (Sweden), client
S. Edlund, draftsman

163 | Poster, c. 1976
Offset lithography
32 15/16 × 23 in. (83.7 × 58.4 cm)
Taxi prototype created for *The Taxi Project:
Realistic Solutions for Today*, Museum
of Modern Art, New York, 1976
Cooper Hewitt, Smithsonian Design
Museum, Gift of Ken Friedman, 1997-19-250
P. 287

GRETA VON NESSEN (born Sweden, 1898–1974, active United States)
Nessen Studio Inc. (United States)

164 | *SPH* (later known as "Anywhere") lamp,
model NS948, designed 1951
Enameled steel, aluminum, Bakelite, rubber
16 × 14 × 15 in. (40.6 × 35.6 × 38.1 cm)
Collection of Jody and Dick Goisman

KATSUJI WAKISAKA (Japan, born 1944, active Finland)
Marimekko (Finland), design firm
Dan River Inc. (United States), manufacturer

165 | *Bo-Boo* textile, designed 1975
Cotton, Fortrel polyester
95 3/4 × 66 3/4 in. (243.2 × 169.5 cm)
Los Angeles County Museum of Art,
Anonymous gift, M.2018.98.2
P. 111 (detail)

SIDNEY WAUGH (United States, 1904–1963)
Steuben Glass, division of Corning Glass Works
(United States)

166 | *Gazelle Bowl*, 1935
Glass
7 1/4 × 7 × 7 in. (18.4 × 17.8 × 17.8 cm)
The Metropolitan Museum of Art,
Purchase, Edward C. Moore Jr. Gift, 1935
(35.94.1ab)

Steuben Glass, division of Corning Glass Works
(United States)

167 | *Mariner's Bowl*, designed 1935,
this example 1939
Glass
15 1/2 × 15 1/2 × 2 1/4 in. (39.4 × 39.4 × 5.7 cm)
Milwaukee Art Museum, Purchase,
with funds from the Collectors' Corner,
M2018.275
P. 125

HANS WEGNER (Denmark, 1914–2007)
Fritz Hansen (Denmark)

168 | "China" chair, designed 1944,
this example 1976
American walnut
32 5/16 × 22 7/16 × 18 11/16 in. (82 × 57 × 47.5 cm)
Given by Queen Margrethe II on the
occasion of the United States Bicentennial,
1976
Cooper Hewitt, Smithsonian Design
Museum, Gift of the Danish Government,
1976-117-1-ab

Johannes Hansen A/S (Denmark)

169 | "The Chair," model JH501, designed 1949
Oak, cane
30 × 23 × 20 3/4 in. (76.2 × 58.4 × 52.7 cm)
Milwaukee Art Museum, Purchase, Erich C.
Stern Fund in memory of Lucia K. Stern,
M1991.199
MAM only

Johannes Hansen A/S (Denmark)

170 | "The Chair," model JH501, designed 1949,
this example c. 1965
Oak, leather
30 3/8 × 24 7/8 × 20 1/2 in. (77.2 × 63.2 × 52.1 cm)
Los Angeles County Museum of Art,
Museum Purchase, M.86.321.5
LACMA only
P. 310

BJØRN WIINBLAD (Denmark, 1918–2006)

171 | Punch bowl with lid, 1964
Faience
20½ × 14 × 14 in. (52.1 × 35.6 × 35.6 cm)
Frank Family Trust

JAN WILSGAARD (born United States, 1922–2016, active Sweden)
Volvo (Sweden)

172 | P122 ("Amazon") car, designed 1956, this example 1964
59¼ × 63½ × 175¼ in.
(150.5 × 161.3 × 445.1 cm)
Volvo Car USA

TAPIO WIRKKALA (Finland, 1915–1985)
Soinne et Kni (Finland)

173 | Leaf tray, 1951–54
Birch
1¾ × 13¾ × 7⅜ in. (4.5 × 34.9 × 18.7 cm)
Given by Tapio Wirkkala to Stanley Marcus of Neiman-Marcus department store
Milwaukee Art Museum, Purchase, with funds from the Demmer Charitable Trust, M2015.35
P. 94

EDWARD F. WORST (United States, 1866–1949)

174 | Table runner, c. 1920
Wool, cotton
84 × 34¾ in. (213.4 × 88.3 cm)
Collection of Edward F. Worst/Marc E. Worst
P. 206

RUSSEL WRIGHT (United States, 1904–1976)
Steubenville Pottery (United States)

175 | American Modern stack server and covered cup and saucer, designed c. 1937
Earthenware
Stack server: 6¾ × 7½ × 7½ in.
(17.2 × 19.1 × 19.1 cm)
Similar examples exhibited in American Design for Home and Decorative Use, multiple Nordic venues, 1953–55
Collection of Scott Vermillion

EVA ZEISEL (born Hungary, 1906–2011, active United States)
Castleton China Company (United States)

176 | Museum coffeepot, designed c. 1942–45
Porcelain
10⅛ × 7¾ × 5 in. (25.7 × 19.7 × 12.7 cm)
Same model exhibited in American Design for Home and Decorative Use, multiple Nordic venues, 1953–55
Los Angeles County Museum of Art, Decorative Arts and Design Council Acquisition Fund, M.2018.251a–b
LACMA only
P. 155

Milwaukee Art Museum, Gift of Historical Design, Inc., M2015.102a–b
MAM only

NELL ZNAMIEROWSKI (United States, born 1931)

177 | Icarus rug, 1969
Wool, linen
76 × 44⅛ in. (193 × 112.1 cm)
Smithsonian American Art Museum, Gift of S.C. Johnson & Son, Inc.
P. 254

BOOKS, MAGAZINES, AND EPHEMERA

&, no. 2, 1968
Timo Aarniala (Finland, 1945–2010), cover designer
Yrjö Sotamaa (Finland, born 1942), editor-in-chief
Scandinavian Design Students' Organization (SDO), publisher

178 | Journal
16½ × 11 in. (41.9 × 27.9 cm)
Design Museum Helsinki
P. 276

CRAFT HORIZONS (The Revolution in Scandinavian Design), March/April 1958
Conrad Brown (United States, 1922–2016), editor

179 | Magazine
11¾ × 8½ in. (29.8 × 21.6 cm)
Milwaukee Art Museum Research Center
P. 260

DESIGN FOR THE REAL WORLD: HUMAN ECOLOGY AND SOCIAL CHANGE, 1971
Victor Papanek (born Austria, 1923–1998, active United States and Scandinavia), author
Pantheon Books (United States), publisher

180 | Book
8¼ × 5¾ in. (21 × 14.6 cm)
Milwaukee Art Museum Research Center, Purchased with funds from the Alice and Lucia Stern Library Fund
P. 274

DESIGN IN SCANDINAVIA, 1954
Tapio Wirkkala (Finland, 1914–1985), layout and cover designer
Arne Remlov (Norway, 1914–1988), editor

181 | Exhibition catalogue
9 × 7½ in. (22.9 × 19.1 cm)
Milwaukee Art Museum Research Center, Gift of The Mae E. Demmer Charitable Trust
P. 95

ELEMENTARY SLOYD AND WHITTLING, 1906
Gustaf Larsson (born Sweden, 1861–1919, active United States), author
Silver, Burdett and Company (United States), publisher

182 | Book
7¾ × 6 in. (19.7 × 15.2 cm)
Private collection
OPPOSITE P. 336

HOUSE BEAUTIFUL (The Scandinavian Look in U.S. Homes), July 1959
Elizabeth Gordon (United States, 1906–2000), editor

183 | Magazine
12⅞ × 9¾ in. (32.7 × 24.8 cm)
Milwaukee Art Museum Research Center
P. 101

HUMANSCALE 1/2/3, 1974; **HUMANSCALE 4/5/6** and **7/8/9**, 1981
Niels Diffrient (United States, 1928–2013), author
Alvin R. Tilley (United States, 1914–1993), author
Joan C. Bardagjy (United States, born 1947), author of 1/2/3
David Harman (United States, born 1952), author of 4/5/6 and 7/8/9
Valerie Pettis (United States, born 1946), graphic designer
Henry Dreyfuss Associates (United States), design firm
The MIT Press (United States), publisher

184 | Manuals and selectors
1/2/3 set: 11⅞ × 9 × ⅜ in. (30.1 × 22.9 × 1 cm)
Milwaukee Art Museum Research Center, Purchased with funds from the Alice and Lucia Stern Library Fund
PP. 280–81

JUL I VESTERHEIMEN (Christmas in the Western Home), 1916
Anders M. Sundheim (born Norway, 1861–1945, active United States), editor and manager
Augsburg Publishing House (United States), publisher

185 | Annual
13⅝ × 10¼ in. (34.6 × 26 cm)
Vesterheim Norwegian-American Museum
P. 88

NOMADIC FURNITURE, 1973
NOMADIC FURNITURE 2, 1974
James Hennessey (United States, born 1945), author and illustrator
Victor Papanek (born Austria, 1923–1998, active United States and Scandinavia), author and letterer
Pantheon Books (United States), publisher

186 | Books
10⅞ × 8½ in. (27.6 × 21.6 cm)
Milwaukee Art Museum Research Center, Purchased with funds from the Alice and Lucia Stern Library Fund
P. 308

PRINT, December 1956–January 1957
Jorgen Hansen (Denmark, 1917–2009, active United States), cover designer
Lawrence A. Audrain (United States, 1910–1957), editor

187 | Magazine
11 × 8½ in. (27.9 × 21.6 cm)
Private collection

SCANDIA RESTAURANT, designed c. 1962
Bjørg Larsen (born Denmark, active United States), cover artist

188 | Menu
Offset lithography
16½ × 12⅞ in. (41.9 × 32.7 cm)
Private collection
P. 89

SPORTS ILLUSTRATED, December 26, 1960

189 | Magazine
11¼ × 8⅜ in. (28.6 × 21.3 cm)
Los Angeles County Museum of Art, Mr. and Mrs. Allan C. Balch Research Library
P. 18

CONTRIBUTORS

GLENN ADAMSON is Senior Scholar at the Yale Center for British Art and a curator, writer, and historian who works at the intersection of craft, design, and contemporary art. He was previously Director of the Museum of Arts and Design, New York.

ARNDÍS S. ÁRNADÓTTIR is an independent curator and design historian based in Reykjavík. She is a specialist in decorative arts and design of Iceland in relation to Scandinavia.

CHARLOTTE ASHBY lectures in art and design history at Birkbeck, University of London. Her research focuses on nationalism, internationalism, and modernity in the late nineteenth and early twentieth centuries.

GRAHAM C. BOETTCHER is the R. Hugh Daniel Director of the Birmingham Museum of Art in Alabama. He has published on an array of subjects in American fine and decorative arts, including the Viking Revival.

DANIELLE CHARLAP is a research assistant in the Department of Decorative Arts and Design at the Los Angeles County Museum of Art and a PhD candidate at the University of Southern California. She was formerly Associate Curator at the Museum of Jewish Heritage, New York.

LESLIE S. EDWARDS is an archivist at the Archives of Michigan in Lansing. She was previously Head Archivist at Cranbrook Archives, and has written numerous essays on textile designer Marianne Strengell.

KJETIL FALLAN is Professor of Design History at the University of Oslo. He is the editor of *The Culture of Nature in the History of Design* (Routledge, 2019) and the author of *Designing Modern Norway: A History of Design Discourse* (Routledge, 2017).

DIANA JOCELYN GREENWOLD is Associate Curator of American Art at the Portland Museum of Art. She recently co-curated and co-edited *In the Vanguard: Haystack Mountain School of Crafts, 1950–1969* (University of California, 2019).

DENISE HAGSTRÖMER is Senior Curator at the National Museum, Norway. Her PhD on design, architecture, and diplomacy was awarded jointly by the Victoria and Albert Museum and the Royal College of Art in London.

HELENA KÅBERG is an architectural and design historian with a focus on the late nineteenth and early twentieth centuries. She is Associate Professor of Art History at Uppsala University and Senior Curator at the Nationalmuseum Sweden.

ALEXANDRA LANGE is a design critic and author of *The Design of Childhood: How the Material World Shapes Independent Kids* (Bloomsbury, 2018). She has taught at New York University and the School of Visual Arts, New York.

CARA MCCARTY is Director of Curatorial at Cooper Hewitt, Smithsonian Design Museum. She has built collections and organized acclaimed exhibitions and publications, focusing primarily on modern and contemporary product design, textiles, and architecture.

MONICA OBNISKI is the Demmer Curator of 20th- and 21st-Century Design at the Milwaukee Art Museum. Her work explores modern and contemporary architecture, decorative arts, and design.

MONICA PENICK is an Associate Professor in the Department of Design in the School of Design and Creative Technologies at the University of Texas at Austin. Her expertise is in American architecture, design, and decorative arts.

HANNAH PIVO is a PhD student in the Department of Art History and Archaeology at Columbia University, New York. She was formerly a curatorial assistant at the Milwaukee Art Museum.

ROSANNE SOMERSON is a renowned woodworker, furniture designer, and teacher who has been advancing art and design for decades. She is President of Rhode Island School of Design.

BOBBYE TIGERMAN is the Marilyn B. and Calvin B. Gross Curator of Decorative Arts and Design at the Los Angeles County Museum of Art. Her previous exhibitions are *Beyond Bling: Jewelry from the Lois Boardman Collection* (2016) and *California Design 1930–1965: Living in a Modern Way* (2011).

ERICA WARREN is Assistant Curator in the Department of Textiles at the Art Institute of Chicago. She previously worked at the Philadelphia Museum of Art and the Minneapolis Institute of Art.

ACKNOWLEDGMENTS

In 2006, as we sat shoulder-to-shoulder in a small office within the Metropolitan Museum of Art's (MMA) American Wing, little did we know that several years later we would embark upon this international project together. Following a 2014 College Art Association call for papers, we realized that we had been thinking about Scandinavian design and its impact on the United States for many years—and thus our partnership began. We thank MMA curators Nonnie Frelinghuysen and Amelia Peck for their mentorship and friendship from the beginning.

A project of this scale has many dimensions, and we are extremely fortunate for the overwhelming support of so many individuals and institutions. The exceptional teams at the Los Angeles County Museum of Art (LACMA) and the Milwaukee Art Museum (MAM) were essential to realizing this complex undertaking. We are immensely grateful for the steadfast support of Michael Govan, CEO and Wallis Annenberg Director at LACMA, and Marcelle Polednik, Donna and Donald Baumgartner Director at MAM, who have encouraged us every step of the way. We would also like to thank deputy directors Zoë Kahr and Nancy Thomas (at LACMA) and Mark Zimmerman (at MAM) for their guidance in guaranteeing a successful exhibition.

At LACMA, we thank the extraordinary members of the Decorative Arts and Design department. Department head Wendy Kaplan was an unwavering source of encouragement and sage advice, and generously applied her editing prowess to several essays. Danielle Charlap was instrumental in many aspects of the exhibition's organization. With her keen analysis, extraordinary attention to detail, and industrious research skills, she uncovered much information about the designers and objects, led the drafting of the checklist, and wrote two essays. Minyoung Park managed all aspects of exhibition coordination with her customary grace and good spirit. Curators Rosie Mills and Staci Steinberger were generous colleagues, always willing to share knowledge and experience.

Exhibition designers Barbara Bestor, Andrea Dietz, Henry Cheung, and Brad Silling at Barbara Bestor Architecture, supported in their vision at LACMA by Victoria Turkel Behner, brought passion and inspired ideas to the project, realizing a stunning installation. Julia Latané and Matthew Driggs led the art preparation and installation team in handling each of the objects with consummate professionalism. David Karwan created the exhibitions graphics, using his deep knowledge of design to amplify the exhibition's themes. Patrick Heilman expertly managed the audiovisual elements, allowing us to bring the show to life with images and film.

Carolyn Oakes, Sabrina Lovett, Marciana Broiles, and Jessica Alonzo all managed the myriad logistical details of planning, budget, and installation. Brandy Wolfe wrote and managed the essential grants that allowed us to realize the show, and Rachel Zelaya, Lauren Bergman Siegel, Katie Kennedy, Brianne Bear, and Jennifer Snow also raised funds. Azzura Di Marcello skillfully handled the innumerable tasks related to borrowing and transporting objects. Alexis Curry, Douglas Cordell, Jessica Gambling, Tracy Kerr, and Kristi Yuzuki obtained the many library resources we requested. John Rice, Ashley Harris, and Jessica Youn oversaw the press and marketing campaign with the utmost professionalism. Tomas Garcia, Chi-Young Kim, Nandi Dill Jordan, and Agnes Stauber developed digital content, enabling us to reach the broadest possible audience. Chelo Montoya planned a compelling series of public programs.

The wide range of objects in the exhibition required the expertise of many labs in LACMA's Conservation Center, and we thank the center's director, Diana Magaloni, for her unstinting support. We especially acknowledge the expertise of object conservators John Hirx, Silviu Boariu, and Don Menveg, textile conservators Catherine McLean and Susan Schmalz and Andrew W. Mellon fellow Staphany Chang, and paper conservators Janice Schopfer and Erin Jue. We also thank Holly Rittenhouse for making mounts that showed each object to best advantage.

At the Milwaukee Art Museum, planning and execution of this complex exhibition was admirably undertaken by staff from many departments. Liz Flaig enthusiastically managed the contract negotiations, project timeline, and budget, with oversight by Margaret Andera; Lydelle Abbott Janes superbly oversaw the shipping, crating, and associated logistics for the exhibition and its two-venue Nordic tour; Rebekah Morin helped coordinate photography, which was shot by the talented John R. Glembin, for the catalogue; Heather Winter and Beret Balestrieri Kohn agreeably answered every conceivable library and archival request throughout the course of the project; Jim DeYoung with Terri White oversaw several conservation projects, alongside Richard Knight, Chris Niver, and Ryan Woolgar, who all helped objects look their best. The museum's preparator dream team, led by Arthur Mohagen III, confidently installed the exhibition. As always, a smart and stunning exhibition design by David Russick, ably assisted by Jessica Steeber and complemented by graphic design by Alison Kleiman, ensured that our ideas were thoughtfully manifested in a visually compelling manner. Ted Brusubardis and his team guaranteed that the audiovisual components seamlessly supported the exhibition. Sincerest appreciation is owed to Hannah Pivo, who demonstrated ingenuity, steadfast assistance, and an indefatigable spirit at every step of this intricate endeavor.

Fundraising for the exhibition was managed by the extraordinary development team of Therese Palazzari, Sara Tomilin, Kim Theno, and Kathy Emery, and overseen by Abby Ashley. Additional thanks are owed to Brigid Globensky and her devoted staff in the Education department for assisting with public programs, and to Amanda Peterson and her team—Christina Dittrich, Laura Simson, and Josh Depenbrok—who admirably handled publicity and communications.

We are indebted to the advisory committee that met in Los Angeles for three days in June 2018. This group of international scholars—Charlotte Ashby, Kjetil Fallan, Mirjam Gelfer-Jørgensen, Denise Hagströmer, Helena Kåberg, and Wendy Kaplan—examined the checklist and discussed the exhibition's themes at a critical juncture in the project. They provided essential feedback that helped shape the final outcome.

LACMA's publisher, Lisa Mark, championed this catalogue from the start, and we thank her for her constant support and guidance. We were fortunate to have the superlative talents of designers Lorraine Wild and Xiaoqing Wang of Green Dragon Office, who created a thoughtful visual identity for the book. Sara Cody edited the catalogue with aplomb, and Jean Patterson meticulously proofread this book. Piper Severance and Sarah Applegate skillfully coordinated image rights and photography requests. The beautiful photographs of LACMA objects are the expert work of Peter Brenner, Steve Oliver, and Jonathan Urban, ably supported by Laura Cherry. We also greatly appreciate the efforts of co-publisher Mary DelMonico at DelMonico Books • Prestel for ensuring the high quality and wide distribution of the publication.

We are deeply grateful to the book's contributing authors for their insightful scholarship: Glenn Adamson, Arndís S. Árnadóttir, Charlotte Ashby, Graham C. Boettcher, Danielle Charlap, Leslie S. Edwards, Kjetil Fallan, Diana Jocelyn Greenwold, Denise Hagströmer, Helena Kåberg, Alexandra Lange, Cara McCarty, Monica Penick, Hannah Pivo, Rosanne Somerson, and Erica Warren. Their outstanding new research has laid the foundation for future scholars to take up themes of transnational exchange.

This project would not have been possible without the sincere partnership of Helena Kåberg, Senior Curator at the Nationalmuseum, Sweden's museum of art and design, and Denise Hagströmer, Senior Curator at the Nasjonalmuseet in Oslo, who both understood the value of U.S. and Nordic collaboration when we first met in 2016. We also wish to thank their many colleagues, in particular the Nationalmuseum's Director General Susanna Pettersson and Director of Exhibitions Per Hedström and the Nasjonalmuseet's Director Karin Hindsbo, Program Coordinator Nina Frang Høyum, Deputy Director Stina Högkvist, and Project Manager Lita Ellingsen.

We would like to thank the many institutional, private, and corporate lenders for their assistance, generosity, and willingness to part with their objects for the duration of the exhibition: Andrew Connors and Josie Lopez (Albuquerque Museum); Kieran Long and Frida Melin (ArkDes); Sarah Kelly Oehler, Erica Warren, and Melinda Watt (Art Institute of Chicago); Maria Fagerström (BabyBjörn); Graham Boettcher (Birmingham Museum of Art); Susan Brown, Sarah Coffin, Caitlin Condell, Cara McCarty, Matilda McQuaid, Emily Orr, Kimberly Randall, and Yao-Fen You (Cooper Hewitt, Smithsonian Design Museum); Kevin Adkisson, Andrew Blauvelt, Steffi Duarte, and Corey Gross (Cranbrook Art Museum); Leslie Edwards, Gina Tecos, and Gregory M. Wittkopp (Cranbrook Center for Art Collections and Research); Robert La France and Denise Mahoney (David Owsley Museum of Art); Kristina Dera; Lars Dybdahl, Anja Lollesgaard, Christian Olesen, Christine Rosenlund, and Kirsten Toftegaard (Designmuseum Danmark); Harry Kivilinna, Jukka Savolainen, Leena Svinhufvud, Susanna Thiel, and Merja Vilhunen (Design Museum Helsinki); Todd Engdahl and Caroline Schomp; Anita Bracalente (Eskenazi Museum of Art, Indiana University); Justin Gunther, Rebecca Hagen, and Scott Perkins (Fallingwater Collection, Western Pennsylvania Conservancy); Tracee Glab and Heather Jackson (Flint Institute of Arts); Frank Family; Michelle Frauenberger (Franklin D. Roosevelt Presidential Library and Museum); Jody and Dick Goisman; Anna Ólafía Guðnadóttir; Patricia K. Jeys; Jordana Joseph and Glen Saltzberg; Katherine Ring (KOMPAN); Jeanette Bokhour (Estate of Marvin B. Lipofsky); Jim Rawitsch and Melanie Swezey-Cleaves (Sam and Alfreda Maloof Foundation); Ravi R. Mathura and Danielle Klotzek; Forrest L. Merrill; Medill Higgins Harvey, Cynthia Iavarone, Jim Moske, Rebecca Tilghman, Beth Wees, and Sylvia Yount (Metropolitan Museum of Art); Lynne Swanson (Michigan State University Museum); Evelina Berglund and Martin Liljekvist (Millesgården Museum); Paula Nameth (Milwaukee Public Library); Nicole LaBouff, Jennifer Komar Olivarez, and Ghenete Zelleke (Minneapolis Institute of Art); Sondra Reierson and Lori Williamson (Minnesota Historical Society); Diane Charbonneau and Jennifer Laurent (Montreal Museum of Fine Arts); Tova Brandt (Museum of Danish America); Knut Astrup Bull, Gudrun Eidsvik, Thomas Flor, Ole Høeg Gaudernack, Denise Hagströmer, Anne Kjellberg, Maren Mitdtal, and Birgitte Sauge (Nasjonalmuseet); Helena Kåberg (Nationalmuseum); Ulysses Dietz and Amy Hopwood (Newark Museum); Nora Atkinson, Jim Concha, Claire Denny, and Abraham Thomas (Renwick Gallery, Smithsonian American Art Museum); Elliot Ryser; Kristie DaFoe and David Miller (Smithsonian National Museum of American History); Rosanne Somerson; Scott Vermillion; Laurann Gilbertson (Vesterheim Norwegian-American Museum); Russell Datz (Volvo Car USA); Marc E. Worst; John Stuart Gordon (Yale University Art Gallery); and to the private collectors who wish to remain anonymous.

This exhibition drew upon the expertise of many archivists, scholars, designers, collectors, and curators in the United States and throughout the Nordic countries, including Svante Adde and Lena Holger; Thommy Bindefeld (Svenskt Tenn); Per and Runa Boman (Norway Designs); Ida Heiberg Bøttiger and Nicholas Manville (Georg Jensen); Tracey Beck and Trevor Brandt (American Swedish Historical Museum); David Conradsen and Genevieve Cortinovis (Saint Louis Art Museum); Kelly Conway and Alexandra Ruggiero (Corning Museum of Glass); Andrew Duncanson and Isaac Pineus; Kenneth Erwin; Peter Frid and Ann Randall; Valdemar Gerdin; Ingeborg Glambek; Beth Goodrich (American Craft Council); Rachel Gotlieb; Widar Halén (Nasjonalmuseet); Per H. Hansen; Helen Hustad; Paul Jackson; Björn and Josefin Jakobson; Bebe Pritam Johnson; Paul Kagawa; Bruce Karstadt, Curt Pedersen, and Inga Theissen (American Swedish Institute); Juulia Kauste (Museum of Finnish Architecture); Timo Keinanen; Kaisa Koivisto (Finnish Glass Museum); Pekka Korvenmaa; Alison Kowalski; Barbro Kulvik and Antti Siltavuori; Ida Kamilla Lie; Mats Linder; Tommi Lindh, Timo Riekko, and Mia Hipeli (Alvar Aalto Foundation and Museum); Kathleen Nugent Mangan (Lenore G. Tawney Foundation); Marion Marzolf; Craig McArt; Jean McElvain and Stephanie Zollinger (Goldstein Museum of Design); R. Craig Miller; Tina Froberg

Mortensen (LEGO); Anders Munch; Eric Nelson (Nordic Museum); Sanna-Kaisa Niikko (Marimekko); Jan-Lauritz Opstad and Karin Sinding (Nordenfjeldske Kunstindustrimuseum); Peter Opsvik and Anita Skogheim; Calle Østergaard (Dam Things); Juhani Pallasma; Birgit Lyngbye Pedersen; Maria Perers; Michael Prokopow; Rip Rapson; Minna Sarantola-Weiss (Helsinki City Museum); Molly Seegers (Brooklyn Museum); Claire Selkurt; Sigríður Sigurjónsdóttir and Þóra Sigurbjörnsdóttir (Hönnunarsafn Íslands, Museum of Design and Applied Arts); Yrjö Sotomaa; Elisabet Stavenow-Hidemark; Eve Strausmann-Pflanzer and Jill Shaw (Detroit Institute of Arts); Nina Stritzler-Levine (Bard Graduate Center); Adam Strohm and Ralph Pugh (Illinois Institute of Technology); Ulla Tarras-Wahlberg; Elisabet Tostrup; Destinee Udelhoven; Wendy VanDeusen (Longhouse Reserve); Michael von Essen; Eva Vincent; Tuija Wahlroos and Minna Turtiainen (Gallen-Kallela Museum); Pia Wirnfeldt and Allan Andersen (CLAY – Keramikmuseum Danmark); David Werner; Jeff Werner; Kerstin Wickman; Mats Widbom; Elizabeth Williams; Anna Womack (Nordiska Museet), and the many unnamed scholars whose work supported our own.

It has been an utmost privilege to get to know the designers whose work is included in the exhibition, including Maria Benktzon, Robert Ebendorf, Arline Fisch, Erik Gronborg, James Hennessey, Helena Hernmarck, Jim Hull, Björn and Lillemor Jakobson, Michael Lacktman, Jack Lenor Larsen, Peter Opsvik, Helen Shirk, Howard Smith, Rosanne Somerson, and Nell Znamierowski.

We wish to thank the many supporters for believing in the merit of this exhibition and publication. We are most indebted to the Terra Foundation for American Art for financial support throughout the course of the project—two U.S. curatorial travel grants to Scandinavia (2016), a convening grant to bring international scholars to Los Angeles (2018), and an exhibition grant to be able to present this show in the United States and in Sweden and Norway (2019). We are grateful to the Henry Luce Foundation's American Art Program for major support of the exhibition's presentation in Milwaukee and Los Angeles. Additional support was provided by Nordic Culture Point and the Barbro Osher Pro Suecia Foundation. We are also grateful to Dan Greenberg and Susan Steinhauser, the Nordic Culture Fund, and LACMA's Decorative Arts and Design Council for their support of the publication. Further research travel to the Nordic countries was made possible through additional assistance from OPSTART Nordic Culture Fund, the Royal Norwegian Embassy, the Royal Norwegian Consulate in San Francisco, the Swedish Council of America, and the Swedish Institute. The Milwaukee Art Museum is thankful to Ken, Andrew, and Margaret Krei, whose support in honor of Melinda is a lasting testament to her memory. MAM also acknowledges the Collectors' Corner and the Anders and Birgit Segerdahl family for their steadfast support.

Finally, we are incredibly grateful to our husbands, Michael Eisenstein and Jordan Diab, for enduring lengthy periods of absence while we researched the exhibition. Bobbye also thanks the village of grandparents and nannies who took care of Bella and Eva over these years. Without all of you, this project of a lifetime would not have been possible.

BOBBYE TIGERMAN
Marilyn B. and Calvin B. Gross Curator,
Decorative Arts and Design
Los Angeles County Museum of Art

MONICA OBNISKI
Demmer Curator of 20th- and 21st-Century Design
Milwaukee Art Museum

ILLUSTRATION CREDITS

Works and photographs are reproduced courtesy of the creators and lender of the materials depicted. The following images, keyed to page number, are those for which additional or separate credits are due.

back cover, 135: © 2020 House of Finn Juhl, photo: Designmuseum Danmark, by Pernille Klemp **front endpapers, 28, 240, 241:** designed by Josef Frank © 1943–45 Svenskt Tenn AB Stockholm, all rights reserved, photo © 2020 Museum Associates/LACMA **opp. 1, 75, 78, 79, 94, 106 top, 115, 121, 155 bottom, 184, 185, 199, 251, 335, 336:** photos © 2020 Milwaukee Art Museum, by John R. Glembin **2, 3:** © 2020 Marimekko, Inc., photos © 2020 Museum Associates/LACMA **6, 132–33 bottom:** © 2020 Else Poulsson, photo © 2020 Cooper Hewitt, Smithsonian Design Museum/Art Resource, NY **7, 157, 158:** © 2020 Artists Rights Society (ARS), New York/VISDA, image copyright © 2020 The Metropolitan Museum of Art, image source: Art Resource, NY **8–9, 125 top:** © 2020 Artists Rights Society (ARS), New York, image copyright © 2020 The Metropolitan Museum of Art, image source: Art Resource, NY **11, 23, 36, 37, 89, 118, 154, 155 top, 188, 234–35, 262, 294, 295, 310, opp. 336:** photos © 2020 Museum Associates/LACMA **12:** © 2020 Artists Rights Society (ARS), New York, photo © 2020 Cooper Hewitt, Smithsonian Design Museum/Art Resource, NY **15 top, 138:** photos courtesy Free Library of Philadelphia **15 bottom:** retrieved from the Library of Congress, https://www.loc.gov/item/2016804356 **16, 257:** photos © 2020 Museum Associates/LACMA, by M. Lee Fatherree **18:** David Drew Zingg (photo by SI Cover/Sports Illustrated via Getty Images/Getty Images) **21:** © 2020 Antoni Legacy, photo © 2020 Milwaukee Art Museum, by John R. Glembin **22:** © 2020 Artists Rights Society (ARS), New York, photo © 2020 Anna Danielsson/Nationalmuseum **24, 152:** digital images © 2020 The Museum of Modern Art/licensed by SCALA/Art Resource, NY **30:** © 2020 Elaine Smedal and Anne Tressler, photo © 2020 Milwaukee Art Museum, by John R. Glembin **33 top, 33 middle:** Eaton, Allen H. 1932. *Immigrant Gifts to American Life; Contributions of Our Foreign-Born Citizens to American Culture.* © 2020 Russell Sage Foundation, 112 East 64th Street, New York, NY 10065. Reprinted with permission, photos © 2020 Museum Associates/LACMA **33 bottom:** photo: ArkDes, the Swedish Centre for Architecture and Design **34 top:** © 2020 Violet Christophersen Estate, photo © 2020 Vesterheim Norwegian-American Museum **34 bottom:** photo © 2020 Museum Associates/LACMA, by Paul Salveson **39:** © 2020 Erik Gronborg, photo © 2020 Museum Associates/LACMA **41:** photo: Mark Proudfoot, used with permission from the Runestone Museum Foundation **44:** photo © 2020 Museum of Danish

America, Elk Horn, Iowa **46:** photo courtesy Michigan State University Museum **47:** © 2020 Valborg Gravander estate, photo © 2020 Museum Associates/LACMA, by M. Lee Fatherree **48:** © 2020 Estate of John Lagsdin, photo courtesy Anne T. Kent California Room, Marin County Free Library **49, 50, 195:** photos: The Art Institute of Chicago/Art Resource, NY **53:** photo © 2020 Museum Associates/LACMA, by Damon Adams **54 top:** photo courtesy the Gorham Company Archive, John Hay Library, Brown University **54 bottom:** photograph © 2020 Museum of Fine Arts, Boston **57:** © 2020 Estate of Olaf Skoogfors, photo © 2020 Museum Associates/LACMA **59, 60:** © 2020 Per Lysne Estate, photos © 2020 Vesterheim Norwegian-American Museum **61:** photo by Arthur M. Vinje. courtesy of Wisconsin Historical Society © 2020 Wisconsin State Journal **63:** photo by Dag Andre Ivarsøy/The National Museum of Art, Architecture and Design; Foundation for the Norwegian Museum of Decorative Arts and Design in Oslo **64, 88, 120:** photos © 2020 Vesterheim Norwegian-American Museum **66:** © 2020 Cora Ginsburg LLC, photo © 2020 Museum Associates/LACMA **68:** © 2020 Georg Jensen, photo © 2020 Newark Museum **70 left:** © 2020 DUX Interiors, Inc., photo © 2020 Milwaukee Art Museum, by John R. Glembin **70 right:** photo © 2020 Montreal Museum of Fine Arts **71:** © 2020 Maija Isola/Marimekko, Inc., photo © 2020 Cooper Hewitt, Smithsonian Design Museum/Art Resource, NY **73 top:** photo: unknown/The National Museum of Art, Architecture and Design **73 bottom:** photo: Svensk Form/The Swedish Society of Crafts and Design **76:** © 2020 Kay Bojesen Denmark, photo © 2020 Museum Associates/LACMA, by M. Lee Fatherree **77:** photo © 2020 Milwaukee Art Museum **81:** photo courtesy Boston Public Library **83:** photo by Museum of Science and Industry, Chicago/Getty Images **84:** photo © 2020 Leeds Art Foundation **85:** image copyright © 2020 The Metropolitan Museum of Art, image source: Art Resource, NY **86 top:** photograph by Hampus Öberg **86 bottom:** photo: Dale Quarterman/Maymont Mansion, Richmond, VA **87:** photo © 2020 Birmingham Museum of Art, by Sean Pathasema **93:** © 2020 House Beautiful, from Marion Gough's "Take a Trip to Scandinavia," (February 1951): 102; photo © 2020 Museum Associates/LACMA **95:** © 2020 Artists Rights Society (ARS), New York/KUVASTO, Helsinki, photo © 2020 Milwaukee Art Museum, by John R. Glembin **98:** photo by Maynard L. Parker, courtesy of The Huntington Library, San Marino, California. **99:** © 2020 Timo Sarpaneva, photo © 2020 Milwaukee Art Museum, by John R. Glembin **101:** © 2020 House Beautiful, photo © 2020 Milwaukee Art Museum, by John R. Glembin **104:** photo by Werner Wolff/The LIFE

Picture Collection via Getty Images **105:** 2020 © The LEGO Group, all rights reserved, photo courtesy The LEGO Group **106 bottom:** photo: Kompan, Inc. **107:** photo: K. Helmer-Petersen **109:** 2020 © The LEGO Group, all rights reserved, photo © 2020 Milwaukee Art Museum, by John R. Glembin **110:** photo: Annar Bjørgli/The National Museum of Art, Architecture and Design **111:** © 2020 Katsuji Wakisaka/Marimekko, Inc., photo © 2020 Museum Associates/LACMA **112:** BabyBjörn™, photo courtesy BABYBJÖRN® **114:** photo: Abbie Rowe, White House Photographs, John F. Kennedy Presidential Library and Museum, Boston **116:** photo by Ralph Morse/Life Magazine/The LIFE Picture Collection via Getty Images, digital image © 2020 Museum Associates/LACMA **122 top:** photo © 2020 Cooper Hewitt, Smithsonian Design Museum/Art Resource, NY, by John White **122 bottom, 290–91:** photo: Designmuseum Danmark, by Pernille Klemp **125 bottom:** © 2020 Sidney Biehler Waugh, photo © 2020 Milwaukee Art Museum, by John R. Glembin **126:** photo by Fotograf Morten Henden Aamot **127:** © 2020 American Craft Council Library & Archives, photo courtesy of American Craft Council Library & Archives **128 top:** image courtesy of the Franklin D. Roosevelt Presidential Library and Museum **128 bottom:** photo by On Location Studios **131 top:** © 2020 Arnstein Rynning Arneberg, photo: Annar Bjørgli/The National Museum of Art, Architecture and Design **131 bottom:** © 2020 Arnstein Rynning Arneberg, photo: Andreas Harvik/The National Museum of Art, Architecture and Design **132–33 top:** © 2020 Artists Rights Society (ARS), New York, photo courtesy ArkDes, the Swedish Centre for Architecture and Design collections (ARKM.1972-10-1713) **134:** photo © 1960 The Associated Press **140:** photo © 2020 Marcus Bornestav (CC BY-SA 4.0) **142 top:** photo: Axel Lindahl, Norsk Folkemuseum **142 bottom:** photo courtesy of the Smithsonian Libraries, https://library.si.edu/digital-library/book/picturesqueworloodavi **143:** Library of Congress, Prints & Photographs Division, photograph by Carol M. Highsmith (LC-DIG-highsm-12014) **147 top:** photo © 2020 Sundbyberg City Museum **147 bottom:** photo by Jordan McAlister **151:** photo by Paul Mayen, courtesy of the Western Pennsylvania Conservancy **159:** photo © 2020 Jari Jetsonen, courtesy of Alvar Aalto Museum **160:** photo: unknown/The National Museum of Iceland **161:** photo © 2020 Museum Associates/LACMA, by Ragnar Th. Sigurðsson/ARCTIC-IMAGES **164, 165:** photos: Nationalmuseum Archives **166:** photo: The United Nations Photo Library **167:** © 2020 Astrid Sampe, photo: Anna Danielsson/Nationalmuseum **171:** photo © 2020 Minneapolis Institute of Arts **172, 173 top:** © 2020 Ralph Rapson, photos © 2020 Cranbrook Center for Collections and Research, by PD Rearick **173 bottom:** © 2020

GEORG JENSEN
Georg Jensen Silversmithy
"Grape" compote, designed 1918. CAT. 69

RALPH LYSELL
KNUT HUGO BLOMBERG
HANS GÖSTA THAMES
North Electric Company
Ericofon **telephone**, designed 1941,
this model designed c. 1961, this example
1962. CAT. 94

Published in conjunction with
the exhibition *Scandinavian Design
and the United States, 1890–1980.*

This exhibition is co-organized by the Los Angeles
County Museum of Art and the Milwaukee Art
Museum.

The exhibition and international tour are made
possible through support from the Terra
Foundation for American Art. Major support
is provided by the Henry Luce Foundation.

Generous support is provided by Nordic Culture
Point. Additional support is provided by the
Barbro Osher Pro Suecia Foundation and the
Nordisk Kulturfond.

In Milwaukee, this exhibition is presented by the
Krei Family in memory of Melinda, with
generous support from the Milwaukee Art
Museum's Collectors' Corner and the Anders and
Birgit Segerdahl Family. Additional support is
provided by John Stewig and Dick Bradley in
memory of Dick's mother, Karine.

Generous support for the publication was
provided by Daniel Greenberg, Susan Steinhauser,
and The Greenberg Foundation. Additional
support for the publication was provided in part
by The Andrew W. Mellon Foundation.

Exhibition itinerary
Milwaukee Art Museum
May 15–September 7, 2020

Los Angeles County Museum of Art
October 18, 2020–February 15, 2021

Nationalmuseum Sweden
September 30, 2021–January 16, 2022

Nasjonalmuseet Oslo
March 17–July 31, 2022

Copublished in 2020 by Los Angeles County
Museum of Art and DelMonico Books • Prestel

Los Angeles County Museum of Art
5905 Wilshire Boulevard
Los Angeles, CA 90036
www.lacma.org

DelMonico Books, an imprint of Prestel,
a member of Verlagsgruppe Random House GmbH

Prestel Verlag
Neumarkter Strasse 28
81673 Munich

Prestel Publishing Ltd.
14–17 Wells Street
London W1T 3PD

Prestel Publishing
900 Broadway, Suite 603
New York, NY 10003
www.prestel.com

*Scandinavian Design and the United States,
1890–1980*
PUBLISHER Lisa Gabrielle Mark
EDITOR Sara Cody, with Jean Patterson
DESIGNERS Lorraine Wild and Xiaoqing Wang
for Green Dragon Office
PHOTO EDITOR Piper Severance,
with Sarah Applegate
INDEXER David Luljak
PRODUCTION MANAGER Karen Farquhar
for Prestel
COLOR SEPARATIONS Echelon Color,
Santa Monica

This book is typeset in Chaparral and Futura.

Library of Congress Cataloging-in-Publication Data

Names: Tigerman, Bobbye, 1978– | Obniski, Monica. |
    Los Angeles County Museum of Art, organizer, host
    institution. | Milwaukee Art Museum, organizer,
    host institution. | Nationalmuseum (Sweden), host
    institution. | Nasjonalmuseet (Norway), host institution.
Title: Scandinavian design and the United States, 1890–1980 /
    Bobbye Tigerman and Monica Obniski ; with
    contributions by Glenn Adamson, Arndís S. Árnadóttir,
    Charlotte Ashby, Graham C. Boettcher, Danielle Charlap,
    Leslie S. Edwards, Kjetil Fallan, Diana Jocelyn Greenwold,
    Denise Hagströmer, Helena Kåberg, Alexandra Lange,
    Cara McCarty, Monica Penick, Hannah Pivo, Rosanne
    Somerson, Erica Warren.
Description: Los Angeles, CA : Los Angeles County Museum
    of Art ; Munich ; New York : DelMonico Books · Prestel,
    2020. | Includes bibliographical references and index. |
    Summary: "Published in conjunction with the exhibition
    Scandinavian Design and the United States. This
    exhibition was organized by the Los Angeles County
    Museum of Art and the Milwaukee Art Museum.
    Exhibition itinerary: Milwaukee Art Museum: May 15–
    September 7, 2020; Los Angeles County Museum of Art:
    October 18, 2020–February 15, 2021; Nationalmuseum
    Sweden: September 30, 2021–January 16, 2022;
    Nasjonalmuseet Oslo: March 17–July 31, 2022"
    — Provided by publisher.
Identifiers: LCCN 2019037419 | ISBN 9783791359168
    (hardcover)
Subjects: LCSH: Design—Scandinavia—Exhibitions. | Art
    and society—United States—Exhibitions. | Scandinavia—
    Foreign relations—United States—Exhibitions. | United
    States—Foreign relations—Scandinavia—Exhibitions.
Classification: LCC NK979 .S33 2020 | DDC 745.0948—dc23
LC record available at https://lccn.loc.gov/2019037419

ISBN: 978-3-7913-5916-8

Printed and bound in China

ELEMENTARY SLOYD AND WHITTLING

LARSSON

SILVER, BURDETT & COMPANY